Powering e-Collaboration Through AI, Machine Learning, and Internet of Things

Jingyuan Zhao
University of Toronto, Canada

IGI Global
Scientific Publishing
Publishing Tomorrow's Research Today

Vice President of Editorial	Melissa Wagner
Director of Acquisitions	Mikaela Felty
Director of Book Development	Jocelynn Hessler
Production Manager	Mike Brehm
Cover Design	Jose Rosado

Published in the United States of America by
IGI Global Scientific Publishing
701 East Chocolate Avenue
Hershey, PA, 17033, USA
Tel: 717-533-8845 | Fax: 717-533-7115
Website: https://www.igi-global.com E-mail: cust@igi-global.com

Library of Congress Cataloging-in-Publication Data

Names: Zhao, Jingyuan, 1968- editor.
Title: Powering e-collaboration through AI, machine learning, and Internet of things / edited by Jingyuan Zhao.
Description: Hershey, PA : Engineering Science Reference, [2026] | Includes bibliographical references and index. | Summary: "This book is a collection of recent advancements in the collaboration technologies and tools of AI, machine learning, and IoT, uncovering the potential AI, machine learning, and IoT hold for organizations and the future of work itself, with a focus on state-of-the-art approaches, methodologies, and systems for the design, development, deployment, and innovative use of those technologies and applications to advance organizations"-- Provided by publisher.
Identifiers: LCCN 2025005804 (print) | LCCN 2025005805 (ebook) | ISBN 9798337323725 (hardcover) | ISBN 9798337323732 (paperback) | ISBN 9798337323749 (ebook)
Subjects: LCSH: Artificial intelligence--Industrial applications. | Artificial intelligence--Medical applications. | Internet of things--Industrial applications. | Internet of things--Medical applications.
Classification: LCC TA347.A78 P69 2026 (print) | LCC TA347.A78 (ebook) | DDC 670.285/63--dc23/eng/20250513
LC record available at https://lccn.loc.gov/2025005804
LC ebook record available at https://lccn.loc.gov/2025005805

British Cataloguing in Publication Data
A Cataloguing in Publication record for this book is available from the British Library.

Table of Contents

Detailed Table of Contents

Chapter 1

Priyadharsini Rathinavel, University of Strathclyde, Glasgow, UK
R. N. Ravikumar, Marwadi University, Rajkot, India
S. Aarthi, Marwadi University, Rajkot, India
Masruk Habib, Marwadi University, Rajkot, India
Navbakhor Salaeva, Urgench State University, Urgench, Uzbekistan
Jamshid Pardaev, Termez University of Economics and Service, Termez,
*   Uzbekistan*

Modern workplaces are increasingly blending artificial intelligence (AI) with human teams to boost efficiency and decision-making. Through AI, machine learning, and Internet of Things (IoT) technologies, businesses streamline operations, enhance communication, and improve task execution. AI systems automate routine tasks, offer real-time data sharing via e-collaboration tools, and support remote work and virtual team management through predictive analytics. AI assistants and chatbots further aid in project management, service delivery, and data flow. These innovations foster productivity and collaboration but also raise concerns about security and ethics. This research explores AI-human coordination with a focus on voice-command interfaces, personalized learning, and AI-powered creative support, offering strategies to integrate AI into operations and strengthen the human-machine partnership.

Chapter 2

Hitesh Mohapatra, School of Computer Engineering, Kalinga Institute
*   of Industrial Technology, Bhubaneswar, India*
Abhishek Guru, Department of Computer Science and Engineering,
*   Mats School of Engineering and Technology, MATS University,*
*   Raipur, India*
Ashwini Kumar Pradhan, School of Computer Science and Engineering,
*   Galgotias University, Greater Noida, India*

The integration of Artificial Intelligence (AI) and the Internet of Things (IoT), known as AIoT, is driving significant advancements in smart collaboration across industries. By combining IoT's data-gathering capabilities with AI's analytical power, AIoT systems enable real-time decision-making, automation, and optimization in areas like manufacturing, healthcare, and smart cities. This chapter examines how AI interprets IoT-generated data to enhance efficiency, sustainability, and productivity. Key use cases are highlighted, demonstrating the synergy between AI and IoT in improving processes, reducing energy consumption, and bolstering safety measures. Challenges such as data security, latency, and device compatibility are addressed, with potential solutions like edge computing and secure frameworks proposed. The chapter concludes with a forward-looking perspective on how AIoT can transform industries and reshape human-machine collaboration, paving the way for smarter, more connected environments.

Chapter 3
    Muhammad Usman Tariq, Abu Dhabi University, UAE & University
      College Cork, Ireland

Improving organizational cooperation through AI-controlled decision-making systems changes team functioning, communication, and innovation. By integrating artificial intelligence into collaborative processes, companies can analyze huge data records, predict results, and automate everyday technology. It means that teams can focus on creative and strategic tasks. AI tools support clearer communication, faster consensus formation, and more intelligent resource allocation, reducing traditional obstacles across departments and regions. However, for successful integration, attention must be paid to transparency, ethical considerations, and human supervision to ensure trust and equity. Challenges such as algorithm bias and cybersecurity risks exist. However, the possibilities for more agile, more resistant, and innovative teamwork are immeasurable. Because of AI-controlled decision-making systems, businesses can be more efficient and create more sustainable and collaborative environments for the future.

Chapter 4
    Mustafa Kayyali, Maaref University of Applied Sciences, Syria

As AI-driven platforms reshape how scholars collaborate, new ethical, security, and privacy concerns have come to the forefront. This chapter explores the complex terrain of AI-powered academic collaboration, where the promise of efficiency and connectivity often coexists with heightened risks of data misuse, surveillance, and opaque decision-making. Drawing from current case studies and theoretical frameworks, we examine how personal data, intellectual property, and academic freedom are being redefined in this new landscape. Particular attention is given to how algorithmic bias and ethical blind spots may undermine equity and trust within global academic networks. We also explore institutional responsibilities and the emerging frameworks guiding the responsible use of AI in higher education. Ultimately, this chapter advocates for a careful, values-driven approach to technological integration—one that champions transparency, inclusivity, and the safeguarding of academic integrity in an era of unprecedented digital interdependence.

The intersection of Artificial Intelligence, Machine Learning, and the Internet of Things is reshaping the contours of higher education. This chapter explores how these technologies are not merely enhancing but fundamentally transforming teaching, learning, and research practices. From AI-powered personalized learning systems to IoT-connected classrooms that sense and respond to student needs, the academic landscape is being redefined. Machine learning opens doors to predictive insights in both pedagogy and research, helping educators and scholars make data-informed decisions. Yet, amid the innovation, questions around equity, ethics, and institutional readiness remain. This chapter critically examines both the potential and the pitfalls, offering a grounded perspective on how AI, ML, and IoT are enabling a new era of collaborative, intelligent education.

The integration of AI-powered chatbots and virtual assistants in higher education is rapidly reshaping how institutions communicate, teach, and support their learners. These tools go beyond automation—they personalize learning experiences, offer real-time academic guidance, and help bridge the gap between students and institutional services. This chapter explores how these technologies are being embedded within universities to enhance student engagement, streamline administrative processes, and support mental wellness. Drawing on case studies and current applications, it also examines the nuanced challenges of maintaining ethical AI use, preserving data privacy, and fostering genuine connection in digital interactions. As educational institutions increasingly embrace e-collaboration, this chapter argues that the future of academic success will hinge on a thoughtful balance between technological efficiency and human-centered design. In doing so, it offers a roadmap for educators, technologists, and policymakers navigating the evolving landscape of AI in education.

Chapter 7
Practical Implication of Generative AI in the Science and Art Imaging
Process: Generative AI Is for Poets.. 165
Jean Constant, Hermay.org, USA

Generative art using autonomous systems like algorithms and mathematical rules offers unique visual experiences, often associated with aesthetic statements. A constructive dialogue is emerging around the legitimacy of this form of artistic representation, the AI's role in the creative process, and its ability to convey visual information of aesthetic value. This paper aims to contribute to this discussion by reviewing extensive literature on the topic and testing AI systems specifically designed to generate images with prompts or directives. Using traditional art evaluation criteria such as composition, originality, and technical skill, this research's findings provide valuable insights and encourage thoughtful reflection on the societal, legal, and educational implications of AI integration in art programs. Further, this experiment raises important questions about the definitions of creativity and authenticity. Such considerations are crucial for preparing students and future generations of professionals to express themselves both visually and creatively.

Chapter 8
Plant Disease Identification and Pesticides Suggestion Using Deep Learning . 193
B. Swapna, Dr. MGR Educational and Research Institute, India
G. Chaitanya Gowd, Dr. MGR Educational and Research Institute,
India
G. Chiranjeevi, Dr. MGR Educational and Research Institute, India
S. Deepa, Velammal Engineering College, India
D. Senthil Kumar, RMK College of Engineering and Technology, India
S. Anandhi, Dr. MGR Educational and Research Institute, India

Plant health management is vital for maximizing crop yields. However, traditional methods of identifying plant diseases and suggesting appropriate Pesticides are often labour-intensive, time-consuming, and prone to human error. It proposes an automated system that utilizes drones equipped with advanced imaging sensors and recommend suitable Pesticides based on real-time data. The drone captures high-resolution images of crops and analyses them using image processing techniques to identify symptoms of various plant diseases. By employing deep learning models trained on large datasets of diseased and healthy plant images, the system can classify the type and severity of the disease. Simultaneously, soil health data and environmental conditions are considered to suggest an optimal fertilizer plan for the affected area. This system provides several benefits, including faster disease detection, precise identification, reduced labor costs, and increased efficiency in Pesticides usage. It enables farmers to take timely and accurate actions, resulting in improved crop health and productivity

India is emerging as one of the major players in global economy. To keep in pace with the global scenario there is a requirement of implementation of AI in Indian economy. AI has helped in transformation by increasing productivity and reducing inefficiency. In India AI implementation is still a challenge. Lack of proper infrastructure and financial literacy has impacted the AI implementation. Banks, Financial Institutions, and MSMEs have benefitted from AI disruption. AI has helped MSMEs in saving cost by enhancing productivity and reducing operational risk. AI can also help SMEs in inventory control, production management. To make AI a success greater efforts are needed from all the segments of society. AI has contributed to financial inclusion by bringing underserved sections of society to main stream banking. AI has also helped in providing cost effective and affordable banking services world wide.

This chapter explores the evolving role of Artificial Intelligence (AI) in driving sustainable development. It begins by defining AI as per the 2024 EU AI Act and assessing current global advancements. The discussion focuses on AI's contributions to the Sustainable Development Goals (SDGs), with examples in healthcare, education, climate action, and urban planning. It also raises critical concerns, including algorithmic bias, privacy risks, environmental impact, and exclusion of marginalized communities. Key regulatory frameworks from the EU, USA, China, and India are examined to highlight governance gaps and opportunities. The chapter asks whether AI can be a reliable force for equity and sustainability and proposes solutions like ethical-by-design systems, global cooperation, and participatory policymaking. It concludes that AI, if responsibly governed, can significantly accelerate sustainable outcomes while upholding human dignity and environmental balance.

Preface

Artificial intelligence (AI), Machine Learning and Internet of Things (IoT) have revolutionized numerous industries and organizations. In an era characterized by hybrid work models and global collaboration, it's imperative to recognize the indispensable role of collaboration technologies. Collaboration technologies offer many significant benefits that can greatly improve how an organization works. Whether you are a researcher, a developer, a manager, or a learner, you need effective tools to collaborate and communicate with your peers, mentors, clients, or users. These advanced tools are the linchpin that bridges geographical gaps, ignites creativity and empowers real-time decision-making in the modern organizational landscape.

The concept of electronic collaboration (e-collaboration) is first put forwarded by Dr. Ned Kock in early 2000s (Kock & D'Arcy, 2002; Kock, Davidson, Ocker, & Wazlawick, 2001; Kock, 2004, 2005). As the evolution of industrial revolution from 3.0 to 4.0, emerging technologies have been transforming the e-collaboration. In the past, people have had to adapt to collaborative tools, but emerging technologies makes it possible for technology to adapt to people. There is growing importance being placed on collaboration workflows to improve collaborative experiences. E-collaboration opens new opportunities where systems can collaborate without any human intervention and solve engineering problems efficiently and effectively.

Internet of Things provides a network of objects that are embedded with sensors, software, and other technologies with a purpose of connecting and exchanging data with other devices and systems. Meanwhile, one of the main ingredients of e-collaboration is machine learning (Centenaro et al., 2021; Motlagh et al., 2020; Ho, 2023). The use of Machine Learning techniques in the context of human-AI collaboration was presented by Semeraro and his team (Misbahuddin et al., 2023). They reviewed over 45 papers to perform clustering of works based on the type of collaborative tasks, evaluation metrics and cognitive variables modelled are proposed; it outlined the importance of Machine Learning algorithms to incorporate time dependencies and collaborative effectiveness (Semeraro et al., 2023). More recently AI is transforming the way we work, learn, and communicate, taking a leading role in collaboration technologies. From virtual assistants to innovative video conferencing, the use of AI is driving greater levels of efficiency and collaboration in organizations around the world. As AI becomes more embedded in organization-level applications, AI is revolutionizing organizational communication and collaboration. Therefore, integrating AI into advanced collaborative tools is a rapidly evolving field. Furthermore, AI's impact on organizations is highlighted through examples like Microsoft's Copilot for IT, which utilizes organizational data and real-time user context to deliver customized, AI-driven solutions.

This integration allows for seamless content creation, collaboration, and task automation tailored to specific business needs. In the context of hybrid work challenges and global collaboration, AI-powered e-collaboration plays a crucial role. AI is changing how we collaborate and redefining success in today's world. AI is changing the landscape of modern organizations rapidly and reshaping organizational operations and fundamentally alters how we connect, learn, and innovate at work. Meanwhile, Machine Learning based methods and technologies have emerged in AI and the convergence of Machine Learning and Internet of Things will complement each other to produce a greater impact and availability of e-collaboration in difference services including healthcare, education, supply chain, transportation, and power sectors.

In this book, we will explore the most effective e-collaboration through AI, Machine Learning and Internet of Things. As beneficial as collaboration technologies can be, we should not overlook potential drawbacks, e.g., security issues and the likelihood of miscommunication. Future research must address these issues with interdisciplinary collaboration between computer science and psychology and advance robust theoretical frameworks to realize the full potential of technologies driven collaboration. To drive meaningful innovation and efficiency, organizations need to establish effective strategies to enhance intra- and inter-organizational collaboration, ensuring that the integration of AI, Machine Learning and Internet of Things meets organizational goals without disruption.

This book is a collection of recent advancements in powering e-collaboration through technologies and tools such as AI, Machine Learning and Intent of Things, uncovering the potential AI, Machine Learning and Intent of Things holds for organizations and the future of work itself, with a focus on state-of-the-art approaches, methodologies, and systems for the design, development, deployment, and innovative use of those technologies and applications to advance organizations. This book will comprehensively power e-collaboration, not only studying applications, types, benefits, functions, concerns and trends of e- collaboration, but also bringing together AI, Machine Learning and Intent of Things and e-collaboration to drive powerful tech tools that simulate human intelligence (Wilson, 2018a, 2018b). The book is organized into 10 chapters. A synopsis of each chapter is given below.

CHAPTER OVERVIEW

Chapter 1 (*Augmenting Human Capabilities AI's Impact on Collaborative Workflows*) discusses AI assistants and chatbots further aid in project management, service delivery, and data flow, but also raise concerns about security and ethics. This chapter explores AI-human coordination with a focus on voice-command interfaces, personalized learning, and AI-powered creative support, offering strategies to integrate AI into operations and strengthen the human-machine partnership.

Chapter 2 (*Integrating Artificial Intelligence and IoT for Smarter Collaboration*) examines how AI interprets IoT-generated data to enhance efficiency, sustainability, and productivity. Key use cases are highlighted, demonstrating the synergy between AI and IoT in improving processes, reducing energy consumption, and bolstering safety measures. The chapter concludes with a forward-looking perspective on how AIoT can transform industries and reshape human-machine collaboration, paving the way for smarter, more connected environments.

Chapter 3 (*Enhancing Organizational Collaboration Through AI-Driven Decision-Making Systems*) proposes that, for successful integration, attention must be paid to transparency, ethical considerations, and human supervision to ensure trust and equity. Challenges such as algorithm bias and cybersecurity risks exist. However, the possibilities for more agile, more resistant, and innovative teamwork are immeasurable. Because of AI-controlled decision-making systems, businesses can be more efficient and create more sustainable and collaborative environments for the future.

Chapter 4 (*Security, Privacy, and Ethical Considerations in AI-Powered Academic Collaboration*) explores the complex terrain of AI-powered academic collaboration, where the promise of efficiency and connectivity often coexists with heightened risks of data misuse, surveillance, and opaque decision-making. This chapter advocates for a careful, values-driven approach to technological integration—one that champions transparency, inclusivity, and the safeguarding of academic integrity in an era of unprecedented digital interdependence.

Chapter 5 (*AI, Machine Learning, and IoT in Higher Education*) explores how these technologies are not merely enhancing but fundamentally transforming teaching, learning, and research practices. From AI-powered personalized learning systems to IoT-connected classrooms that sense and respond to student needs, the academic landscape is being redefined. This chapter critically examines both the potential and the pitfalls, offering a grounded perspective on how AI, ML, and IoT are enabling a new era of collaborative, intelligent education.

Chapter 6 (*The Role of AI-Powered Chatbots and Virtual Assistants in Higher Education*) explores how these technologies are being embedded within universities to enhance student engagement, streamline administrative processes, and support mental wellness. This chapter argues that the future of academic success will hinge on a thoughtful balance between technological efficiency and human-centered design. In doing so, it offers a roadmap for educators, technologists, and policymakers navigating the evolving landscape of AI in education.

Chapter 7 (*Practical Implication of Generative AI in the Science and Art Imaging Process*) provides valuable insights and encourage thoughtful reflection on the societal, legal, and educational implications of AI integration in art programs. Further, this experiment raises important questions about the definitions of creativity and authenticity. Such considerations are crucial for preparing students and future generations of professionals to express themselves both visually and creatively.

Chapter 8 (*Plant Disease Identification and Pesticides Suggestion Using Deep Learning*) claims that, by employing deep learning models trained on large datasets of diseased and healthy plant images, the system can classify the type and severity of the disease. This system provides several benefits, including faster disease detection, precise identification, reduced labor costs, and increased efficiency in Pesticides usage. It enables farmers to take timely and accurate actions, resulting in improved crop health and productivity.

Chapter 9 (*AI and Digital Transformation Changing Landscapes of Emerging Economies in Asian Sub-Continent*) presents that AI implementation in India is still a challenge. Lack of proper infrastructure and financial literacy has impacted the AI implementation. To make AI a success greater efforts are needed from all the segments of society. AI has contributed to financial inclusion by bringing underserved sections of society to mainstream banking. AI has also helped in providing cost effective and affordable banking services worldwide.

Chapter 10 (*Holistic Study of the Role of AI in Sustainable Development- Study of the Jurisdictions of the United States of America, the European Union, and India*) asks whether AI can be a reliable force for equity and sustainability and proposes solutions like ethical-by-design systems, global cooperation, and participatory policymaking. It concludes that AI, if responsibly governed, can significantly accelerate sustainable outcomes while upholding human dignity and environmental balance.

Jingyuan Zhao
University of Toronto, Canada

REFERENCES

Centenaro, M., Costa, C. E., Granelli, F., Sacchi, C., & Vangelista, L. (2021). A Survey on Technologies, Standards and Open Challenges in Satellite IoT. *IEEE Communications Surveys and Tutorials*, *23*, 1693–1720.

Ho, C. M. (2023). Research on Interaction of Innovation Spillovers in the AI, Fin-Tech, and IoT Industries: Considering Structural Changes Accelerated by COVID-19. *Financial Innovation*, *9*, 7.

Kock, N. (2005). *Business process improvement through e-collaboration: Knowledge sharing through the use of virtual groups*. Idea Group.

Kock, N. (2008). Designing e-collaboration technologies to facilitate compensatory adaptation designing e-collaboration technologies. *Information Systems Management*, *25*(1), 14–19.

Kock, N., & D'Arcy, J. (2002). Resolving the e-collaboration paradox: The competing influences of media naturalness and compensatory adaptation [Special issue on electronic collaboration]. *Information Management and Consulting*, *17*(4), 72–78.

Kock, N., Davison, R., Ocker, R., & Wazlawick, R. (2001). E-collaboration: A look at past research and future challenges [Special Issue on E-Collaboration]. *Journal of Systems and Information Technology*, *5*(1), 1–9.

Misbahuddin, M., Azad, A. K. M., & Demir, V. (2023). Machine-to-Machine Collaboration Utilizing Internet of Things and Machine Learning. *Advances in Internet of Things*, *13*, 144–169.

Motlagh, N. H., Mohammadrezaei, M., Hunt, J., & Zakeri, B. (2020). Internet of Things (IoT) and the Energy Sector. *Energies*, *13*, 494.

Semeraro, F., Griffiths, A., & Cangelosi, A. (2023). Human-Robot Collaboration and Machine Learning: A Systematic Review of Recent Research. *Robotics and Computer-integrated Manufacturing*, *79*, 102432.

Wilson, H. J., & Daugherty, P. R. (2018a). Collaborative intelligence: Humans and ai are joining forces. *Harvard Business Review*, *96*(4), 114–123.

Wilson, H. J., & Daugherty, P. R. (2018b). *Human + Machine: Reimagining Work in the Age of AI*. Harvard Business Review Press.

Chapter 1
Augmenting Human Capabilities:
AI's Impact on Collaborative Workflows

Priyadharsini Rathinavel

University of Strathclyde, Glasgow, UK

R. N. Ravikumar

https://orcid.org/0009-0009-3705-1681

Marwadi University, Rajkot, India

S. Aarthi

https://orcid.org/0009-0006-9064-2091

Marwadi University, Rajkot, India

Masruk Habib

https://orcid.org/0009-0006-2231-8839

Marwadi University, Rajkot, India

Navbakhor Salaeva

Urgench State University, Urgench, Uzbekistan

Jamshid Pardaev

Termez University of Economics and Service, Termez, Uzbekistan

ABSTRACT

Modern workplaces are increasingly blending artificial intelligence (AI) with human teams to boost efficiency and decision-making. Through AI, machine learning, and Internet of Things (IoT) technologies, businesses streamline operations, enhance communication, and improve task execution. AI systems automate routine tasks, offer real-time data sharing via e-collaboration tools, and support remote work and virtual team management through predictive analytics. AI assistants and chatbots further aid in project management, service delivery, and data flow. These innovations foster productivity and collaboration but also raise concerns about security and ethics. This research explores AI-human coordination with a focus on voice-command interfaces, personalized learning, and AI-powered creative support, offering strategies to integrate AI into operations and strengthen the human-machine partnership.

DOI: 10.4018/979-8-3373-2372-5.ch001

1. INTRODUCTION

The amazing changes occurring in the movement of corporate functions, together with AI and human resources, are being prompted by the flurry of activity in contemporary workplaces, which are accompanied by surprises at every turn. AI, Machine Learning, and the Internet of Things being drawn together with the natural human resources scenarios greatly enhance productivity and help better partnerships in labour. These technologies are no longer simply tools but organs in the modern organizational nucleus that will synergize with it all the while augmenting human ability thereby multiplying productivity and efficiencies. The future possibilities thrown open by the AI are upon the imbalances ever imposed upon mankind during challenges, and today, with the help of AI interaction innovation, one can see major automation of critical business processes, transparency in decision processes and interface for cracking through team barriers (Al-Nabet, 2021). Therefore, it works in an opposite direction to optimize its own operations, enhance mutual communication and receiving data, something that up until now seemed almost impossible.

AI-based predictive analytics and machine learning algorithms have greatly supported improved performances in remote operation and virtual team management. The different AI framework serving as chatbots and voice technicians is reshaping project management and service delivery; at the same time, IoT integration helps accelerate data flow and provides real-time operational monitoring. Still, even amid their limitless advantages, greater potentials also entail the imminent threats of cybersecurity issues and rising ethical questions. This chapter highlights not just the ways AI-injected workplaces fit into the AI-human collaboration paradigm, but also how in so many other ways such technologies have been fashioned into reforms on workflow processes, maximize productivity, and engender a closely knit workforce while juggling with the huge challenges and concerns arising along its way (Aviyanti et al., 2022).

1.1 Overview of AI Integration in the Workplace

AI itself, rather, is one that modifies the established mode of working in an organization by which it interacts generally with either internal teams or external stakeholders. Development of specialized technologies based on AI, formerly relegated to specialized industries or research laboratories, has made organizations put AI technologies at the core of most daily operations, allowing a streamlining process, improving decision-making, and boosting productivity as a whole. By automating boring tasks, and giving "intelligent" insights into resolving complicated issues,

AI systems are quickly becoming the best friends in organizations (Côrte-Real et al., 2020).

All channels of work, communication, processing, and decisions supporting each field incorporate AI. AI tools such as chatbots, virtual agents, and automated workflow lessen time wasted on doing things, such that there are restrictions on the amount of employee time invested in error-prone data entry and unimportant work. Finally, it has also changed the view on things organizations consider significant, from those related to customer service to supply chain activities, by using the capacity of massively sophisticated AI tools to analyze disparate data sets and obliquely derive predictive insights.

1.2 Importance of AI, Machine Learning (ML), and IoT in Enhancing Operational Superiority

Advancements in AI, ML and IoT converge to enable very high levels of operational efficiency and innovation. Artificial intelligence has intelligent systems for processing large quantities of data, automatically carrying out complex processes and creating real-time actionable insights. It has predictive analytical capabilities, improved decision-making processes, and the facilitation of collaborative workflows for solving problems (Dwivedi et al., 2021). Machine Learning (ML) is an aspect of AI that focuses on writing algorithms allowing systems to learn from and adapt to their own experiences, good and bad, without being explicitly programmed. Thus, in a work environment, ML algorithms are capable of pattern recognition, prediction, and process improvement through constant learning via data.

The Internet of Things (IoT) is the bridge between the physical objects and the internet where real-time information either circulates among devices, sensors, and systems. IoT helps in timely decision-making associated with the current condition of the machines, staff, inventory, and external environment. Of all these, the interlinkage of systems, intelligence, and speed enhances innovation in operations, through AI, ML, and IoT. Such operational excellence is achieved through optimal resource use, effective communication, automation of decision-making processes, and predictive capabilities for real-time action (Howard & Schulte, 2024).

Table 1. AI, ML, and IoT Functional Contributions to Operational Efficiency

Technology	Core Functionality	Operational Benefit
AI	Intelligent processing of data, automation	Real-time insights, enhanced decision-making
ML	Self-learning algorithms from data	Continuous process improvement, pattern recognition
IoT	Device connectivity and real-time data sharing	Equipment monitoring, real-time feedback

The table 1 summarizes how AI, Machine Learning, and IoT each contribute uniquely to operational excellence. It highlights their functions in data processing, learning from experience, and device interconnectivity. Together, they drive innovation, automation, and real-time responsiveness.

1.3 Overview of the Collaborative Impact of AI on Workflows

Figure 1. Collaborative Impact of AI on Workflows

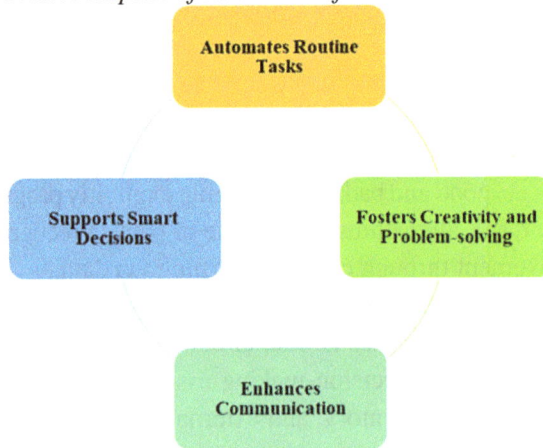

The Fig.1 highlights the important reasons why AI helps in team collaboration and makes the process permanent. AI starts by managing repetitive activities such as schedule making, data inputting and documenting which frees people to focus on more important tasks. At this point, Business Intelligence helps teams work creatively and find ways to solve problems by brainstorming based on data. Besides, communication is eased by AI with virtual assistants and chatbots which lead to quick updates, effective coordination and proper information exchange. In addition, AI supplies quick and valuable information to help teams decide smarter and quicker. When all these elements are joined, team productivity, collaboration and innovation improve a lot. By using AI, teams can work together more effectively by making different aspects of teamwork and communication smoother. Through automation, it helps with scheduling meetings, handling data and managing documents, so employees are able to focus on higher priority and meaningful work. Thanks to AI, people in different professions can now join forces and use instant data analysis to help them make confident and quick decisions. AI also allows for better communication through virtual assistants and chatbots which are responsible for managing queries, sending updates and booking meetings so information is shared in a smooth manner. AI contributes to creativity and building good solutions by helping in brainstorming meetings and providing smart insights, allowing people to come up with new ideas in any situation (Pishgar et al., 2021). These elements mean AI will definitely drive human collaboration by increasing productivity, improving decision making, and allowing teams to work regardless of geographical or physical barriers. It is safe to say that once organizations adopt it, the contribution to transformative collaborative work will only augment in time, making the workplace even more dynamic, effective, and adaptive.

AI is playing a big role in changing how teams at work collaborate by overseeing routine technological work like arranging meetings, reviewing expenses, etc. Having automation in place allows workers to move their attention from doing routine admin work to working on tasks that add value and require collaboration. Besides, AI speeds up and improves team choices by always offering quick analysis and forecasts. A wide range of options is considered by collecting feedback from many stakeholders in the company which further strengthens the decision process. By using AI, teams can easily exchange information and coordinate their work, especially when managing big and complicated projects involving many areas of work.

Moreover, AI makes team collaboration happen on the spot, so team members can work with each other regardless of their schedules. When individual contributors use virtual assistants and chatbots, they can communicate, update each other and organize meetings more effectively. AI helps people be more creative and solve tough problems since it supports brainstorming, links people's ideas and produces new and knowledge-based solutions. All in all, AI makes teamwork easier by helping complete tasks faster, choosing the best solutions and supporting teams at any location (Ramesh, 2021). As adoption of AI in organizations grows, its effect on teamwork activities is set to rise, resulting in more lively, flexible and productive places of work.

2. AI AND HUMAN PERSONNEL SYNERGY

The AI and human personnel synergy means a fundamental change in the work environment, meaning AI is augmenting rather than replacing the worker. This represents a shift to a collaborative setting where one learns from the other. Artificial intelligence does not eliminate human capabilities; it enhances them. If there is an aspect of a job that is repetitive, data-driven, or laborious, AI can handle that allowing humans to shift gears and concentrate on the strategic aspects of their jobs, focusing on critical thinking, creativity, and decision-making requiring emotional intelligence, ethical and moral standards, and adaptability.

By coupling the cognitive power of AI with humanistic insight and experience, there are solutions to problems that neither could solve independently. An example is that AI can process large data sets in seconds, while humans can interpret the analysis in light of organization's goals or social action. In a creative domain, AI tools can offer ideas on creative or design process automation, but there would still be a need for human to shape, refine and align positive outcomes with brand values or user expectations. It fosters efficiency, innovation, and flexibility in the 21st century workplace and enables the development of new roles that could emerge as a result of this new integration with artificial intelligence, such as AI trainers and data ethicists (Sallam et al., 2023). Ultimately, taking us to a future where a complementary relationship develops that AI enhances and saving human workers does not replace us to a more cogs in the machine, mechanistic, assembly line, easy-to-replace at-will workplace.

2.1 Complementary Strengths

Artificial Intelligence (AI) is able to handle great amounts of data, reveal difficult patterns and complete tasks in a very short time. It is strong because it analyzes multiple kinds of data and provides helpful future forecasts for decision makers. Meanwhile, humans have special characteristics such as being creative, having emotions, understanding ethics and seeing situations from different angles. Certain jobs require these features most of all since they involve empathy, keen judgment and inventive thinking. Working together, the abilities of AI and human intelligence produce effective and complete results. Together, using AI for analysis and humans for intuition and creative thought will deliver enhanced organizational performance over and above either can do alone(Sodiya et al., 2024).

2.2 Enhancing Productivity and Innovation

Efficiency is boosted as AI takes over time-consuming tasks leaving the human race with the valuable time they need to think strategically or creatively. Human beings applying contextual understanding apply data-driven insights on the other end from AI to make the critical decisions that have to be made. They also receive an open atmosphere in which the creativity of both sides can thrive, thereby developing innovative solutions and even business opportunities.

2.2.1 Real-world Examples

- **Marketing:** AI study produced better ad copy and images indicating AI-human collaboration success in creativity.
- **Customer service:** The easy routine inquiries will be handled by the AI chatbots while the human agents help toward growth of customer happiness by handling complex inquiries.
- **Healthcare:** AI will provide help in diagnosing diseases based on the analysis of medical data, for which the healthcare professional will care for the patient taking care of the results.

2.2.2 Challenges and Needs

Despite all these advantages from the human-machine combination, there are still specifications that need to be addressed such as data privacy and ethics, together with lifelong learning and training. It should also budget for the transparency and fairness of AI systems against the values of humans to retain the trust and usability of the systems.

2.3 Role of AI in Augmenting Human Mental Competencies

AI applications are meant to take on the following functions: complex analyses of data; finding patterns; doing tedious works; and providing time for human beings to engage more in higher-order cognitive functions, such as creativity, strategic thinking, and emotional intelligence. By referring repetitive and data-intensive tasks to AI, this allows employees to focus more on innovative problem-solving (Song et al., 2022).

2.4 Examples of AI Collaboration Tools and Communication Systems

Modern AI-powered tools simply facilitate all forms of work and relationship collaboration and communication within organizations having AI in collaboration tools helps teams to improve both their communication and the management of projects. Integrating AI with Slack makes communication among team members simpler by including functions like auto-summary, a smart search system and auto replies. Because of real-time translations, transcription and meeting highlights, teams in different countries can now participate in common activities. With Notion AI, people can simplify project management and documentation by asking for help with writing, translation, sorting tasks and developing suitable workflows for them. As for Asana, its AI functions allow projects to be launched automatically, progress to be monitored and status information to be sent straight away which gives it more power for data sharing and teamwork in resolving challenges.

Table 2. Examples of AI Collaboration and Communication Tools

Tool/Platform	AI Features	Organizational Function
Slack + AI	Summarization, auto-replies	Internal communication
Microsoft Teams	Real-time translation, meeting summaries	Cross-border collaboration
Notion AI	Writing, translation, task workflows	Project management and knowledge work
Asana (AI version)	Project auto-setup, tracking	Workflow automation

The table 2 outlines key AI-powered tools that enhance communication and workflow efficiency in organizations. It lists platforms like Slack, Teams, and Notion with their intelligent features. These tools improve internal coordination and task management.

2.5 Impact on Organizational Decision-Making and Operational Functions

Using AI models, one can inform from distant data sources to develop an automated model to extract wisdom and provide suggestions from interpreting such data. It is bringing revolution, and indeed the revolution in the making, as far as its applications are concerned all through the life span. AI-based agents like ChatGPT use different areas such as human resource management, finance, planning, etc. and automated current solution work into tasks like payroll processing or policy enforcement while allowing professionals to focus on strategic decisions.

For example, even Workday is able to enhance streamlining internal operations through via its Illuminate AI Agents that automate queries and work into internal operation of the organization while increasing performance and cutting down overhead costs. Similarly, AI-or operational power can analyze huge quantities of data for identification and blanket market gating, e.g., predicting next-failure equipment and market contract-flow, and thus attain higher operational efficiencies (Sunday & Vera, 2018).

3. AI-DRIVEN E-COLLABORATION TOOLS

The modern workplace of blended work and AI-integrated tools use e-collaboration tools to communicate, interacting and manage workflows. e-collaboration tools are prospective collaboration applications that use AI-created a connective layer which transformed collaboration engagement whether real-time or asynchronously. These tools provide an innovation environment which enables collaboration, improves productivity and efficiencies when working through workflows. By automating repetitive tasks, enabling communication in real-time, and offering intelligent suggestions which provide low friction collaboration experiences in group/task interactions further builds a collective science and experience of productive efforts in teamwork. Intelligent collaboration features such as smart meeting creation, meeting-at-a-glance summaries, real-time language translation in meetings, and automated sentiment analysis provided coordination of group collaboration with diverse and remote teams.

Typically, collaborative working environments or platforms offer various intelligent capabilities while using AI to support intelligent assistance task or activity prioritize, resource allocation, and awareness of progress, and limits time to concentrate on strategic and creativity related activities (De Vass et al., 2018). Hybrid and remote measures are important and using intelligent collaboration will be a necessity for hybrid and remote organizations to keep performance high and engaged. The following section summarizes current capabilities and status of leading AI-powered collaboration tools in the evolving digital workspace.

Figure 2. AI-Driven E-Collaboration Tools

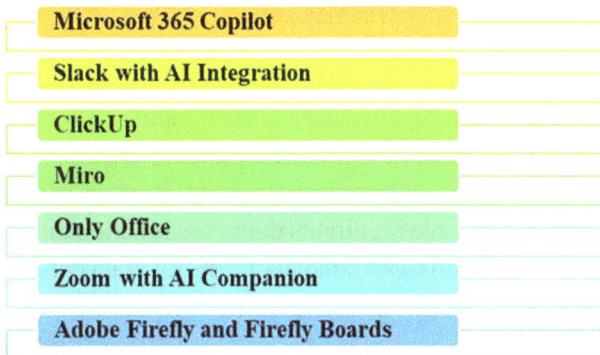

Microsoft 365 Copilot

Slack with AI Integration

ClickUp

Miro

Only Office

Zoom with AI Companion

Adobe Firefly and Firefly Boards

The Fig.2 presents a visual list of popular AI-integrated collaboration tools used in modern workplaces. It highlights platforms like Microsoft 365 Copilot, Slack,

ClickUp, Miro, and others that enhance productivity, communication, and creativity through artificial intelligence.

Table 3. Overview of AI-Driven E-Collaboration Tools

Tool	Description	Key AI Features
Microsoft 365 Copilot	Integrated into Word, Excel, PowerPoint, and Outlook to assist users in drafting, analyzing, summarizing, and minimizing repetitive tasks.	AI-powered search across platforms, multimedia-to-document generation, "Notebooks" and "Pages" for collaboration.
Slack with AI Integration	Enhances team communication and workflow efficiency through intelligent automation.	Voice notes and conversation summaries, auto-replies, integration with Google Drive, GitHub, and AI chatbots.
ClickUp	A project management platform that enhances productivity and communication.	Task reminders, document processing, ClickUp Brain for task insights, and intelligent time management.
Miro	A collaborative whiteboard tool for idea generation and workshops.	Miro Assist for content creation, idea organization, and AI-generated presentations from notes.
OnlyOffice	Collaborative suite for document editing and project tracking.	ChatGPT plugin for summarization, translation, text generation, and customizable AI assistant integration.
Zoom with AI Companion	Video conferencing platform enhanced with intelligent meeting tools.	AI Companion to summarize meetings, draft documents from transcripts, and automate workflows.
Adobe Firefly & Firefly Boards	Creative tools integrated with generative AI for design collaboration.	Text-to-image/video generation, Firefly Boards for brainstorming and visual collaboration, integration with Creative Cloud apps.
Glean	Enterprise search tool that improves information access across workplace tools.	Role-based personalized search, task prioritization, email drafting using generative AI.

The table 3 presents a comparative overview of popular AI-enhanced electronic collaboration tools used in modern digital workplaces. Each tool leverages artificial intelligence to automate tasks, enhance productivity, improve communication, and streamline workflows. The table highlights their core functionalities and unique AI features, aiding users in selecting suitable platforms for team collaboration, project management, and creative work.

3.1 AI-Enabled Tools for Data Collection and Exchange

AI-based platforms refine data-gathering and information-sharing processes among teams:

Figure 3. AI Tools for Data Collection & Exchange

The Fig.3 shows the AI-powered tools like Glean and Survey Tools. Glean facilitates intelligent enterprise search across platforms, while Survey Tools like Qualtrics or Typeform automate data collection and analysis. Together, they represent a seamless flow of information combining data retrieval with user feedback to support informed decision-making.

Table 4. Smart Tools for AI-Driven Data Collection and Sharing

Tool	Description	Key AI Features / Benefits
Glean	An enterprise search tool that centralizes information from platforms like Slack, Confluence, and Google Drive.	Role-based personalized search, secure access control, saved 1,500+ hours/month, accelerated onboarding by 20%.
Survey Tools	Platforms like Survey Sparrow, Typeform, and Qualtrics automate data collection and analysis.	AI-driven response analysis, real-time insight generation, enhanced decision-making.

The Table 4 presents a comparison of AI-enabled tools designed to streamline data collection and exchange within organizations. It highlights how platforms like Glean and various AI-powered survey tools enhance information retrieval and automate data analysis. These tools contribute to improved efficiency, faster onboarding, and more informed decision-making by leveraging role-based personalization and intelligent insight generation.

3.2 Optimizing Team Interactions and Operational Performance

AI introduces the following avenues for enhancing team synergy and operational efficiency:

Figure 4. Enhancing Teamwork & Efficiency

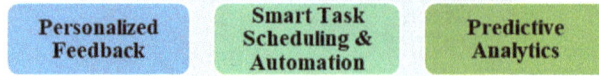

| Personalized Feedback | Smart Task Scheduling & Automation | Predictive Analytics |

AI enhances teamwork, efficiency, and ultimately performance across multiple operational areas. AI can leverage automated monitoring and feedback through tools like TAIFA that provide contextualized feedback about the organization as a team; analyzing the dynamics of interaction can indicate strengths and weaknesses of individual members, leading to motivated engagement, and possible stronger team dynamics. AI platforms can also reduce meeting time with analytics that create engagement, and tasking, as well as babysit the boundary of a hybrid work situation, which keeps teams aligned to work toward the organization's goals at their own pace. AI applies predictive analytics on large data sets and considers the grouping and patterns of trends comparing and differentiating them into simple a demand forecast, including patterns (in supply chain) to understand when action should be taken and which is also a component of performance overall. (Adeleye et al., 2024).

Table 5. Enhancing Team Interactions and Operational Performance through AI

AI Functionality	Outcome for Teams	Operational Benefit
Personalized Feedback	Performance insights	Team cohesion
Intelligent Scheduling	Time management	Productivity boost
Predictive Analytics	Forecasting demand	Efficient resource allocation

The table 5 details AI applications that support team collaboration and optimize operations. It includes AI-driven feedback, scheduling, and predictive analytics. These technologies foster synergy, performance tracking, and efficient resource use.

3.3 Boosting Productivity Through AI Technologies in Collaborative Work Environments

AI is not only can dramatically enhance team productivity when you work together, making it easier for your teammates to focus on strategic and creative problem solving without these repetitive tasks and move towards more profitable productivity. Also, AI can continually assess large amounts of data for your crucial real time decision making that is fast moving and critical pace in and of itself legitimate decisions to maintain momentum while prioritizing timely decisions. AI can assess how to improve how we work together, e.g. how we communicate either in response to trends, patterns, g. recommend improving communication creating more collaboration, better dynamic teams, more efficiencies, better innovations, better performance (Atolagbe-Olaoye, 2025).

4. AI AND REMOTE WORK: TRANSFORMING COLLABORATION AND PRODUCTIVITY

Remote work is being transformed by AI which allows team members to collaborate more, exchange messages with ease and stay productive. As teams gradually work together over the internet, virtual assistants, chatbots and smart scheduling solutions are helping to automate tedious jobs and make the workflow better. Tools such as Microsoft Teams and Slack include AI features to make it easy to keep conversations up-to-date, record meetings and offer immediate translation for everyone, no matter where they are. With AI, teams can review predictions and insights from data and decide quickly using facts. In addition, ClickUp and Notion AI are useful because they arrange tasks and update information automatically. The use of brainstorming and generative tools helps teams to develop new ideas even if they work from different places. Because of the progress in remote work, AI continues to support workers by bridging differences in time zones, automating tasks and making collaboration efficient, diverse and successful.

4.1 AI Collaboration Tools

With the help of AI, teams now work more efficiently by automating tasks, improving how they communicate and assisting in making choices. They use artificial intelligence to help make workflows faster, manage information and increase team productivity in any work scenario. Microsoft 365 Copilot helps users by summarizing papers, writing emails and examining statistics on spreadsheets. Thanks to AI, Slack makes it possible to quickly review talks, get auto-replies and search messages more productively. Tasks are organized and projects can be tracked with the help of AI by using ClickUp and Notion AI which reduces the need for human planning. Miro enables people to share ideas visually and its AI aids in making presentations, while Adobe Firefly helps develop visual content because of its AI-based tools for images and videos (Chan et al., 2024). As a result, Zoom and other video conferencing software now give live summaries, allow automatic note-taking and produce documents during the meeting. The use of technology also makes sure that teams save time and properly understand what is being discussed. With Google Drive and GitHub, AI collaboration tools help teams work on data and tasks without any problems. As businesses keep developing, these tools will encourage teams to be more efficient, creative and effective even when working across different places.

4.2 Optimize Your Remote Work Operations

To have effective remote work, you should mix technology, ways to communicate and boost productivity tools, with AI as a key component. Because AI can schedule meetings, handle emails and sort papers, employees do not have to worry about time-consuming tasks, giving them more time for important jobs. Applications like Microsoft Teams, Slack and Zoom have AI features that capture meetings through transcription, translate messages instantly and notify people in real time. Such platforms like ClickUp, Asana and Notion AI make it easier for teams to communicate and monitor their work. In addition, AI chatbots and virtual assistants are useful during daily work by answering questions, providing notifications and ensuring the work goes on as planned.

Organizations should not forget to ensure that sharing data is secure and their systems are strongly linked to the cloud for better optimization. Thanks to Glean and Only Office, data can be put in one place and the right controls can be set for easier information gathering. With the use of AI-based tools, businesses can engage their workers better, cut down on workflow delays and keep up productivity even when teams are far from each other. The use of these tools makes working remotely easier and encourages people to team up, be adaptable and prepare for the future.

Table 6. AI Optimizations in Remote Work Operations

AI Function	Purpose	Benefit in Remote Work
Predictive Analytics	Identify bottlenecks	Improved efficiency
Task Automation	Eliminate repetitive tasks	Focus on high-value work
Smart Scheduling	Cross-timezone coordination	Optimized time usage

The table 6 presents AI functions that enhance remote work, such as automation, smart scheduling, and predictive analytics. These tools address challenges of distributed teams. The result is increased productivity and better workflow coordination across time zones.

4.3 Increasing Productivity Using AI Technologies

Artificial Intelligence serves to support remote work by improving real-time decision making through ongoing analysis of data to allow informed decisions by distributed teams effectively and efficiently. AI can augment project management, with AI-assisted models, such as Asana. Project management models anticipate project scheduling and task dependencies by accelerating workflows associated with coordinating input between tasks. AI applications address troubleshooting and often determine fault and remedy issues with speed, significantly reducing downtime, and therefore, productivity related to remote working environments (Pishgar et al., 2021).

5. SECURITY AND ETHICAL CONCERNS

More and more, AI plays an important role in teamwork, so securing and adhering to ethics is very important now. Data privacy is a main issue since AI handles a huge amount of personal and business information. It means that unauthorized access to the system can result in possible abuses or exposures of protected data. Moreover, these tools may also suffer from different cyber-attacks such as prompt injection and approaches that attempting to alter their responses or disrupt the overall system. A further serious issue that comes up is Identity and Access Management (IAM). When AI agents operate together, it is important to have powerful identity management systems in place to stop unauthorized access and keep people accountable. Lacking proper defense, AI systems can turn into targets for exploitation in digital environments. In addition, making sure that AI is used ethically encourages transparency, fairness and safe use (Hossain et al., 2025). It is necessary for organizations to put tough data governance rules in place and frequently observe interactions involving AI to address risks. As AI develops, the chances of its misuse go up, making it necessary to put in place strong security and watch over its ethical use. Dealing with these issues is necessary for guarding information as well as encouraging trust in AI for remote and hybrid work.

5.1 Ethical Matters

Artificial intelligence technology presents ethics challenges that must be addressed if one wishes to see its responsible use. The presence of biases in Artificial Intelligence algorithms is thus an issue that is significantly troubling. Whenever these systems entrenched to some extent prejudices within the training set, eventually, a disproportionate decision gets passed down. Another major concern from the standpoint of competition arises as AI automation might simply displace jobs, thus aggravating problems of economic inequality and workforce security (Kedar, 2023). Another great concern is the lack of transparency in artificial intelligence operations. Numerous systems work as "black boxes," making it impossible to understand the decision-making process, hence undermining confidence and accountability. Moreover, the prospect for the misuse of artificial intelligence, e.g., for mass surveillance or autonomous weapons, raises serious ethical questions with profound consequences for society.

5.2 Mitigation Strategies

Companies need to be provided with comprehensive governance frameworks with explicit rules and procedures tied to ethical norms to ensure that AI technology is utilized ethically and responsibly. Audit programs and assessments should be conducted regularly to uphold these frameworks. These programs ought to be designed primarily to keep a continuous analysis of AI systems and in the process mitigate biases, security weaknesses, and ethical dilemmas. Transparency is yet another necessary thing: AI models should be developed to provide simple explanations that are easy to understand for their decisions (Lai et al., 2021). Such a transparent approach will strengthen the faith of the users in the models as well as their sense of responsibility.

Still, continued education and training are needed for all the stakeholders to equip them with the knowledge and skills required to understand, govern, and use AI technology responsibly. A holistic approach in this aspect ensures that any possible hazards are minimized and helps to build a culture that nurtures ethical consciousness and proactive engagement with AI at every level of an organization. In the longer term, this paves the way for AI systems that contribute positively yet always safeguard fundamental human rights, justice, and privacy. Addressing security, and ethical issues can help organizations realize the full potential of AI while minimizing the associated risks, thus forming collaborative environments based on responsible and trustworthy AI technologies (Liang et al., 2024).

5.3 Barriers to Successful AI-Human Collaboration: Security and Ethics

In order to ensure that the use of AI systems in workplaces is ethical and equitable, addressing a number of fundamental problems raised by those AI systems is vital. When AI is deployed, it is frequently accompanied by large amount of personal, organizational and contextual data. Warranting permission, data security, abuse of surveillance capabilities are all concerns that arise. Data privacy and data surveillance are front and center in concerns being raised. Solely providing and accounting for bias and discrimination is another major concern as AI algorithms can reinforce and amplify existing biases based on the data on which they were trained. In practice this leads to unfair outcomes in hiring, performance management matters, and talent management processes. The larger problem is that when AI systems are employed, they are metaphorically and literally "black boxes" where transparency and ethical accountability are lacking. These decisions made by AI are hard to understand or argue with it breaks down trust. Finally, there is the ethical and economic implications of job losses caused by automation. The comments have to do with income and jobs; we should be taking to take stock of what productivity means, and then find ways to support the people who are affected (Pikas et al., 2022).

Table 7. Security and Ethical Barriers in AI-Human Collaboration

Concern	Description	Implication
Data Privacy & Surveillance	Excessive data collection	Risk of misuse and breaches
Bias in Algorithms	Prejudiced training data	Discrimination in decision-making
Lack of Transparency	"Black box" AI systems	Low trust and accountability
Job Displacement	Automation of roles	Economic inequality

The table 7 identifies major risks and ethical concerns in AI deployment, including privacy, bias, and job displacement. It explains their implications on trust, fairness, and workplace stability. Addressing these barriers is essential for responsible AI integration.

5.4 Addressing Concerns in Interaction Between Humans and Automated Machines

In order to ensure the responsible and ethical use of artificial intelligence (AI) technology, it is crucial for organizations to have a solid governance framework that includes clear rules and processes that are consistent with ethical standards and align with organizational strategies. Transparency and explainability are also very important for AI systems. AI systems should be constructed to produce intelligible reasoning for their decisions, thereby fostering trust and making it easier to detect and correct potential errors and biases. Encouragement of inclusion in AI oversight through the input of diverse teams helps make errors less likely and better helps fulfil the needs of all stakeholders in the systems (Saklamaeva & Pavlič, 2023). Additionally, it is important for the staff to have on-going education and training to acquire the competencies to understand, manage, and use AI technology ethically. Establishing an ethos of educated, thoughtful engagement with AI technology, not only increases the chance of responsible use but reduces potential hesitancy to adopt.

5.5 Ethical Implications of AI in Workplace Settings

The use of artificial intelligence in the workplace can have a large impact on employee autonomy - especially when it is used in performance management and decision-making while disregarding employee rights and freedoms and this can lead to an erosion of autonomy and (as the complexity of AI driven decisions raises questions of accountability) even disempowerment. This complexity of AI decision-making can raise issues about accountability regarding decisions that may have negative or unintended consequences, and it is important that we develop transparent accounts of accountability when it comes to managing such consequences effectively. Using artificial intelligence also has demographic implications for society in the long term; while there are operational advantages to delicate on the ground aspect, there are also impacts on labour markets, changes in skills required, and, if not carefully managed, the potential to exacerbate societal inequalities. These wider implications highlight the need for planning that incorporates not just the efficacy of a business, but also the ethical and social responsibilities of the organisation (Seyi-Lande & Onaolapo, 2024).

6. AI AND NATURAL VOICE COMMAND

AI and natural voice command systems are changing the way people and machines work together by making it possible to talk to each other without using your hands. These systems use artificial intelligence and natural language processing (NLP) to understand and react to spoken instructions correctly, which makes processes go more smoothly and efficiently. Voice-enabled AI boosts productivity by reducing the need for manual input, especially in places where multitasking is necessary or physical interfaces are not possible. Employees may use voice commands to plan meetings, get information, handle projects, or operate equipment. This makes things run more smoothly and cuts down on the time spent on ordinary chores. These systems also become better over time via machine learning, which makes them more customized and aware of their surroundings. This makes the user experience better and the system runs more smoothly. As speech technology becomes better, it will be added to collaboration tools and business platforms, which will make workplaces even more automated. This will create smarter, more responsive settings that enable dynamic, real-time decision-making and better employee engagement.

6.1 Enhanced Human-Machine Interaction through AI Processing of Voice Commands

Siri, Alexa, and Google Assistant are examples of artificial intelligence voice assistants that are able to transform spoken words into actions via the use of strong algorithms. Acoustic and linguistic models are used in order to comprehend patterns of speech and the complexities of language. This allows the user to engage in interactions that are more aware of the environment in which they are operating. By enabling workers to handle the communication devices in an organization using voice commands, voice recognition allows employees to communicate without using their hands and provides improved access (Sowa & Przegalinska, 2020).

6.2 Teaching AI Learning Systems to Being Human-Centric at Work

Instruction of artificial intelligence learning systems in the workplace to be human-centric is causing a transformation in the method in which individuals grow and develop professionally. The ability of artificial intelligence to personalize learning by adapting material to the specific requirements, capabilities, and preferences of an individual may result in increased engagement and efficiency. Through the analysis of data on performance, behavior, and learning styles, artificial intelligence is able to provide recommendations for training programs that are in line with the objectives and learning speed of an employee. Through the use of this focused method, training is not only guaranteed to be relevant but also to have an effect. Human resource solutions that are powered by artificial intelligence also improve the employee experience by providing chances for AI-guided mentoring, personalized career pathways, and predictive insights into workforce trends. By using these tools, firms are able to proactively promote the growth of their employees, boost employee retention, and produce future leaders. Companies are able to cultivate a culture of continual development, inclusiveness, and empowerment by putting human needs at the core of AI-driven learning. This helps to ensure that technical innovation is aligned with individual objectives and the success of the business.

6.3 Creative Support Systems Powered by AI

The concept of creativity in the workplace has been rethought as a result of the automation of monotonous jobs and the enhancement of innovation. The concept of using tools that are powered by generative artificial intelligences in the process of developing content designs and solutions and applying them for the most effective strategic goals is undergoing a radical transformation. Zaha Hadid Architects is a good example of a company that has increased its creativity and efficiency by using AI technologies in the creation of breakthroughs in design processes (Tortorella et al., 2021).

7. INTEGRATED AI AND IoT

Artificial Intelligence (AI) and the Internet of Things (IoT) are now combined into something called AIoT. This has changed how businesses work in a big way by letting smart systems do real-time data processing, predictive analytics, and making decisions on their own. This tremendous convergence lets connected devices and sensors gather huge volumes of data. AI systems then look at this data to find useful information and automate tasks. Because of this, businesses gain from better safety measures, faster innovation, and more efficient operations. AIoT makes predictive maintenance possible by finding problems with equipment before they cause it to break, optimizing energy use, and making workflows easier via process automation. AIoT systems may also adjust to new situations and make judgments on their own, which means that people don't have to be involved in routine or high-risk operations as much (Ajirotutu et al., 2024). This change makes industrial settings smarter and more responsive, which is what contemporary businesses need to be able to adapt, be sustainable, and be productive. It also supports scalable and future-ready infrastructure across all industries.

7.1 Create Connected IoT Systems to Deliver Improved Outcomes

Bringing together IoT systems is necessary for corporations, since it ensures smooth data exchange, continuous observation and smart automation. These systems make use of sensors, devices and cloud platforms for the constant exchange of data. Organizations achieve a better picture of what is going on if they bridge the connection between assets, environments and people. In healthcare, the use of connected IoT helps with managing patients remotely and giving them customized care. They allow manufacturing companies to conduct predictive maintenance, lessen periods of downtime and save money. In smart cities, linked infrastructure improves how road traffic works, conserves energy and safeguards the public. AI and machine learning are used to study the collected data and make recommendations that save resources, offer better experiences and help optimize the use of data (Lyons et al., 2023). It is important to consider scalability, security and interoperability when designing for long-term results. All things considered, when IoT devices are linked, organizations are equipped to move fast, save resources and respond well to changes.

7.2 Collaborative AI and IoT Systems in Modern Industrial Settings

The combination of AI and IoT is making a big impact on industries today by allowing robots to act on their own, quick decisions and more efficient operations. Integrated systems depend on IoT sensors to regularly gather information from machines, products and processes. With all this data in hand, AI algorithms help detect possible problems, see what needs maintenance, plan resources better and support better safety measures. Smart factories use AI with IoT to maintain their equipment efficiently and lower their downtime as well as costs. Through AI, robots and people can team up to perform different duties, boosting both accuracy and productivity. Also, by using data from IoT, AI makes supply chains faster and more able to adjust when needed. Such technologies boost productivity and also make it possible for industry to grow and adapt to changes (Roldán Martinez, 2023). Even so, before using collaborative AI-IoT systems, it is necessary to deal with issues like data privacy, making different systems work together and protecting them from cyber-attacks. If handled properly such practices become the base for Industry 4.0, helping traditional industries become smarter and more connected.

8. PRACTICAL APPLICATIONS AND CASE STUDIES: AI-HUMAN COLLABORATION IN THE WORKPLACE

AI, short for Artificial Intelligence, is getting applied in workplace environments, making employees much better and transforming operations in the workplaces. Such teamwork brings about improved performance, greater efficiency, and stronger innovation within and across industries.

8.1 Honeywell and Google Partnership

Honeywell has made the announcement that it has entered into a strategic relationship with Google in order to combine artificial intelligence (AI) and industrial data. The goal of this cooperation is to completely automate processes and increase efficiency across all activities. The purpose of this partnership is to bring together Honeywell's experience in industrial automation with Google's sophisticated artificial intelligence and cloud computing capabilities (Meek et al., 2016). This will pave the way for manufacturing and supply chain solutions that are more intelligent and efficient.

Honeywell intends to enhance decision-making via real-time data analysis, optimize industrial processes, and minimize downtime by using the artificial intelligence and machine learning capabilities that are available on Google Cloud. Facilitating the shift of industries toward autonomous operations will be the primary emphasis of the alliance, which will concentrate on predictive maintenance, energy saving, and process automation.

When combined with Google's artificial intelligence-driven analytics, Honeywell's significant expertise in industrial control systems will make it possible for enterprises to achieve previously unattainable levels of efficiency (Mahmoudi et al., 2023). It is anticipated that the connection would enable processes to be streamlined, reduce the amount of human interaction, and improve safety in high-risk areas.

In light of the fact that businesses are increasingly adopting digital transformation strategies, this collaboration highlights the rising significance that artificial intelligence plays in Industry 4.0. Together, Honeywell and Google want to establish new standards for operational excellence by using insights driven by artificial intelligence. They intend to provide scalable solutions for industries such as manufacturing, logistics, and energy. The alliance shows a common vision for a future in which artificial intelligence-driven automation will change industrial productivity by making operations quicker, safer, and more cost-effective. This relationship places both organizations at the forefront of smart manufacturing innovation, which is becoming more important as industries continue to grow (Munz et al., 2023).

8.2 Artificial Intelligence Cities

Melbourne is at the forefront of smart urban innovation, making it a leader among AI-Cities. In order to demonstrate the revolutionary potential of smart technologies in urban management, cities such as Melbourne are leading the way in the integration of artificial intelligence, the internet of things, and fifth-generation wireless networks. The city of Melbourne is becoming more efficient in terms of traffic flow, energy consumption, trash management, and emergency response systems by integrating artificial intelligence into its infrastructure and public services. It is possible for the city to anticipate and alleviate congestion by using sensors driven by artificial intelligence and real-time data analytics (Sahoo et al., 2024). Additionally, the city may minimize energy consumption in public buildings and improve public safety by implementing intelligent surveillance.

Additionally, 5G connection assures that Internet of Things devices may communicate with one another without any interruptions, which enables speedier decision-making and automation. The purpose of this program is to demonstrate how artificial intelligence-driven smart cities may enhance the quality of life for citizens, as well as efficiency and sustainability. The method that Melbourne has taken may serve as an example for other cities who are interested in using AI and IoT for more intelligent urban planning. The future of urban life will be characterized by infrastructure that is data-driven, automated, and highly responsive. This will be the case as more municipalities embrace these technologies.

8.2.1 Ethical Issues

The quick introduction of AI and related technologies into organizations raise many ethical and social issues that need to be tackled. It is becoming more important to address privacy and data ownership. The large amount of private information managed by AI systems has raised doubts about who controls the data and how privacy if protected. When there are no clear rules and everything is not open, the danger of data being used incorrectly or accessing it without authority increases. Another problem is that robots may replace workers (Tabassi, 2023). Because AI and IoT are automating many activities in manufacturing, administration and customer service, job loss could happen on a large scale. For this reason, companies should offer their workers programs to help them gain the skills needed for their new roles and compete in the job market.

Lastly, it is necessary to ensure that AI systems are just and impartial. These algorithms may end up with biased results because of the data they have been given or because of problems in their design. To address discrimination, developers have to pay special attention to ethical AI design and constantly track and correct the system's errors. Taking care of these problems is essential for right and fair AI use. Integrating AI and IoT into industries is not merely a technological upgrade but also a fundamental strategic move toward the development intelligent, responsive and efficient industrial ecosystems (Kim, 2021). To reap the maximum benefits of AIoT innovation for sustainable growth, organizations must address the relevant challenges and ethical concerns.

8.3 Real Life Examples of AI and Humans Working Together

Artificial intelligence shows its greatest value when it helps people instead of taking over what they do. AI finds use in different industries to boost human talents, help with better decisions and raise efficiency. Artificial intelligence excels at carrying out the same tasks, but people bring in their creative and thinking abilities to form the final outcome. You will find below some real applications that demonstrate the working synergy of AI and human specialists.

8.3.1 Healthcare: Radiologists and AI Imaging Systems

In healthcare, radiologists work together with AI imaging systems in detection of cancers with great accuracy. AI quickly analyzes medical scans and flags potential problems, the experience and judgment of the human doctor being necessary for the conclusion of the diagnoses made. In this manner, it is achieved by better accuracy than either of them independently.

8.3.2 Finance: Financial Analysts and Machine Learning Algorithms

These analysts depend on algorithms to spot market trends-not easy, often impossible, or difficult things to find by careful observation alone. Such AI systems can be fed with massive amounts of data until it finds some pattern or anomaly that will serve as an insight for the analyst to come up with investment strategies or risk management.

8.3.3 Customer Service: AI Chatbots and Human Agents

Companies like Telstra and Bunnings would use AI chatbots to process customer requests or inquiries that require repetitive data such as product information or account management. These types of inquiries bring the customer service efficiency level up to another level, leaving more challenging inquiries for the human agents.

8.3.4 Insurance: AI Enhanced Business Process Automation

In insurance, AI helps automate claim part identification that earlier used to be done manually. The automation indicated improvements both in operational capacity and scalability, therefore attesting the real applicability of AI for business process optimization.

Table 8. Real-Life AI-Human Collaboration Examples

Industry	AI Role	Human Role	Benefit
Healthcare	Analyze scans, flag anomalies	Final diagnosis, patient care	Accuracy & efficiency
Finance	Spot trends, analyze big data	Interpret patterns, make decisions	Insightful strategies
Customer Service	Handle FAQs, simple queries	Manage complex interactions	Scalability
Insurance	Process automation	Oversight and escalation	Faster claims & consistency

The table 8 showcases real-world cases of AI supporting humans in various sectors like healthcare, finance, and customer service. It illustrates complementary roles of AI and humans. These collaborations lead to improved accuracy, productivity, and user satisfaction.

8.4 AI-Driven Transformation of Operations and Performance

AI is greatly influencing the way organizations work by introducing automation, better decision-making processes and flexible structures. Automating routine jobs is one of the greatest achievements. Currently, AI makes it possible for automated systems to take care of routines such as data entry, meeting scheduling and client service. As a result, people working in the organization can focus on important strategy and creativity which leads to better productivity and cost savings (Jha, 2019). Also, AI makes decision-making more efficient by examining a lot of data and presenting useful insights instantly. It helps everyone understand their tasks better which leads to better results for the organization.

AI is also leading to the formation of flexible and decentralized ways organizations are structured. With these systems in place, organizations can react faster to market changes and changing customer needs which improves both their efficiency and teamwork. AI has helped business processes in automation to significantly improve by recognizing and optimizing those activities with no real value to the business (Jones et al., 2021). In the insurance sector, AI is being used to make processes more efficient by picking out problems and managing tasks that don't need human attention. All in all, AI gives businesses the power to be more intelligent, flexible and efficient as competition rises. The real-world cases and examples bring forward the AI-human collaboration that is causing a change in workplace dynamics for enhanced performance, efficiency, and innovation in multiple industries.

9. CONCLUSION

AI, ML, and IoT are being integrated into workplace environments to mark the onset of a new transformation in organizational operations. These entities look at enhancing human capabilities for reshaping collaborative workflows, driving efficiency, and fostering innovation across industries. AI is a very powerful tool to augment human mental capabilities. Using data analytics and predictive modelling, an AI system brings actionable insights to employees, who can then make informed decisions. For instance, with AI-enabled e-collaboration tools, team members can communicate and share data seamlessly, regardless of geographical locations. The outcome is that while humans are focused on strategic tasks, AI takes care of data-heavy tasks. Accordingly, this synergy leads to optimization in performance and productivity.

The convergence of AI and IoT has birthed smart systems for real-time collection and analysis of data. In industries, connected IoT devices monitor equipment health while AI algorithms predict maintenance needs to reduce downtime and enhance operational efficiencies. The manufacturing process, resource management, and integration with IoT for smart factories have become quite effective with an AI-based solution that is employed by one of the companies, ASUS. In this style, AI-AI truly started changing how work from an environment where virtual teams can work collaboratively with one another. Predictive analytics and machine learning algorithms are mainly used for operational planning so that all resources can be made available just in time.

Project management tasks are streamlined with AI assistants and chatbots, relieving stress from everyone while ensuring the service quality and communication among distributed teams. The gains brought into play by AI-augmented teamwork are flaunted; however, barriers still need to be worked through: security issues and ethical matters. To gain acceptance and protect, the key items to guarantee will be data privacy, algorithmic bias prevention, and transparent pathways for AI decision-making. Companies should draft extensive cybersecurity policies and ethical principles that recognize and diminish AI integration-related risks. In an optimistic approach, it fits slowly into the ongoing changed paradigms of functioning: where AI would aid human activities. In the process of improvement, AIs would be becoming more subtle about human emotions, likes and dislikes, and behaviours, which will aid collaboration.

The other side, which enhances the personalization and dynamic aspects of workflows, is where developments of AI will cater to human feedback. In conclusion, AI-ML-IoT integrated strategically into workplace environments can hugely extend human capabilities. Organizations using these technologies will further enable innovative, effective, and responsive collaborative workflows to meet the dynamically changing needs of the contemporary workplace. Of course, one ought to consider any barriers to the realization of such progressions for individuals and organizations.

REFERENCES

Adeleye, O. O., Eden, C. A., & Adeniyi, I. S. (2024). Innovative teaching methodologies in the era of artificial intelligence: A review of inclusive educational practices. *World J. Adv. Eng. Technol. Sci.*, *11*(2), 69–79.

Ajirotutu, R. O., Garba, B. M. P., & Johnson, S. O. (2024). AI-driven risk mitigation: Transforming project management in construction and infrastructure development. *World J. Adv. Eng. Technol. Sci.*, *13*(2), 611–623.

Al-Nabet, N. (2021). A case study of the benefits of the IoT in the Qatari retail industry. *Studies in Business and Economics*, *24*(1), 86–107.

Atolagbe-Olaoye, A. (2025). Collaborative information behavior and human-AI context in group work. *International Journal of Library and Information Services*, *13*(1), 1–16.

Aviyanti, R. D., Widiasmara, A., Devi, H. P., Nurhayati, P., Chairunnisa, D. M., & Zami, M. T. A. (2022). Digital Entrepreneurship Assistance for Handicraft SMEs in Cileng Village. *Int. J. Comm. Serv. Learn.*, *6*(2), 221–230.

Chan, T. A. C. H., Ho, J. M.-B., & Tom, M. (2024). Miro: Promoting collaboration through online whiteboard interaction. *RELC Journal*, *55*(3), 871–875.

Côrte-Real, N., Ruivo, P., & Oliveira, T. (2020). Leveraging internet of things and big data analytics initiatives in European and American firms: Is data quality a way to extract business value? *Information & Management*, *57*(1), 103141.

De Vass, T., Shee, H., & Miah, S. J. (2018). The effect of "Internet of Things" on supply chain integration and performance: An organisational capability perspective. *AJIS. Australian Journal of Information Systems*, ●●●, 22.

Dwivedi, Y. K., Hughes, L., Ismagilova, E., Aarts, G., Coombs, C., Crick, T., Duan, Yanqing, Dwivedi, R., Edwards, J., Eirug, A., Galanos, V., Ilavarasan, P. V., Janssen, M., Jones, P., & Kar, A. K., Kizgin Hatice and Kronemann, B., Lal, B., Lucini, B., Medaglia, R., Le Meunier-FitzHugh, K., … Williams, M. D. (2021). Artificial Intelligence (AI): Multidisciplinary perspectives on emerging challenges, opportunities, and agenda for research, practice and policy. *International Journal of Information Management*, *57*(101994), 101994.

Hossain, S., Fernando, M., & Akter, S. (2025). Digital leadership: Towards a dynamic managerial capability perspective of artificial intelligence-driven leader capabilities. *Journal of Leadership & Organizational Studies*, *32*(2), 189–208.

Howard, J., & Schulte, P. (2024). Managing workplace AI risks and the future of work. *American Journal of Industrial Medicine*, *67*(11), 980–993.

Jha, N. (2019). AI voice assistant implementation for enhanced user experience and efficiency. *The Pharma Innovation*, *8*(1), 725–728.

Jones, V. K., Hanus, M., Yan, C., Shade, M. Y., Blaskewicz Boron, J., & Maschieri Bicudo, R. (2021). Reducing loneliness among aging adults: The roles of personal voice assistants and anthropomorphic interactions. *Frontiers in Public Health*, *9*, 750736.

Kedar, M. M. (2023). How effective is AI in whiteboard? *INTERANTIONAL JOURNAL OF SCIENTIFIC RESEARCH IN ENGINEERING AND*, *07*(12), 1–6.

Kim, S. (2021). Exploring how older adults use a smart speaker-based voice assistant in their first interactions: Qualitative study. *JMIR mHealth and uHealth*, *9*(1), e20427.

Lai, Y., Kankanhalli, A., & Ong, D. (2021). Human-AI Collaboration in Healthcare: A Review and Research Agenda. *Proceedings of the 54th Hawaii International Conference on System Sciences*.

Liang, Q., Gou, J., Wang, Z., & Dabić, M. (2024). Affordances and constraints of automation and augmentation. *Journal of Global Information Management*, *32*(1), 1–27.

Lyons, J. B., Hobbs, K., Rogers, S., & Clouse, S. H. (2023). Responsible (use of) AI. *Frontiers in Neuroergonomics*, *4*, 1201777.

Mahmoudi, H., Camboim, S., & Brovelli, M. A. (2023). Development of a voice virtual assistant for the geospatial data visualization application on the web. *ISPRS International Journal of Geo-Information*, *12*(11), 441.

Meek, T., Barham, H., Beltaif, N., Kaadoor, A., & Akhter, T. (2016, September). Managing the ethical and risk implications of rapid advances in artificial intelligence: A literature review. *2016 Portland International Conference on Management of Engineering and Technology (PICMET)*.

Munz, P., Hennick, M., & Stewart, J. (2023). Maximizing AI reliability through anticipatory thinking and model risk audits. *AI Magazine*, *44*(2), 173–184.

Pikas, E., Pedó, B., Tezel, A., Koskela, L., & Veersoo, M. (2022). Digital Last Planner System whiteboard for enabling remote collaborative design process planning and control. *Sustainability*, *14*(19), 12030.

Pishgar, M., Issa, S. F., Sietsema, M., Pratap, P., & Darabi, H. (2021). REDECA: A novel framework to review artificial intelligence and its applications in occupational safety and health. *International Journal of Environmental Research and Public Health, 18*(13), 6705.

Ramesh, S. (2021). Leveraging the Internet of Things in commerce: A transformational frontier. *International Journal of Information Technology and Computer, 12*, 26–30.

Roldán Martinez, D. (2023). SymbIAG: A collaborative approach to AI governance. In 4th International Conference on AI ML, Data Science and Robotics. United Research Forum.

Sahoo, D. K., Hung, T. H., Kumar, A., & Kanwal, P. (2024). Ethical AI in entrepreneurship. In *Advances in Business Strategy and Competitive Advantage* (pp. 137–164). IGI Global.

Saklamaeva, V., & Pavlič, L. (2023). The potential of AI-driven assistants in scaled agile software development. *Applied Sciences (Basel, Switzerland), 14*(1), 319.

Sallam, K., Mohamed, M., & Wagdy Mohamed, A. (2023). Internet of Things (IoT) in supply chain management: Challenges, opportunities, and best practices. Sustain. Mach. Intell. J., 2.

Seyi-Lande, O., & Onaolapo, C. (2024). Elevating business analysis with AI: Strategies for analysts. *International Journal of Management Research and Economics, 4*(2), 1–7.

Sodiya, E. O., Umoga, U. J., Amoo, O. O., & Atadoga, A. (2024). AI-driven warehouse automation: A comprehensive review of systems. *GSC Adv. Res. Rev., 18*(2), 272–282.

Song, R., Cui, W., Vanthienen, J., Huang, L., & Wang, Y. (2022). Business process redesign towards IoT-enabled context-awareness: The case of a Chinese bulk port. *Business Process Management Journal, 28*(3), 656–683.

Sowa, K., & Przegalinska, A. (2020). Digital coworker: Human-AI collaboration in work environment, on the example of virtual assistants for management professions. In *Digital Transformation of Collaboration* (pp. 179–201). Springer International Publishing.

Sunday, C. E., & Vera, C. C.-E. (2018). Examining information and communication technology (ICT) adoption in SMEs. *Journal of Enterprise Information Management, 31*(2), 338–356.

Tabassi, E. (2023). *Artificial intelligence risk management Framework (AI RMF 1.0)*. National Institute of Standards and Technology.

Tortorella, G. L., Narayanamurthy, G., Sunder, M. V., & Cauchick-Miguel, P. A. (2021). Operations Management teaching practices and information technologies adoption in emerging economies during COVID-19 outbreak. *Technological Forecasting and Social Change, 171*(120996), 120996.

Chapter 2
Integrating Artificial Intelligence and IoT for Smarter Collaboration

Hitesh Mohapatra
https://orcid.org/0000-0001-8100-4860

School of Computer Engineering, Kalinga Institute of Industrial Technology, Bhubaneswar, India

Abhishek Guru
https://orcid.org/0000-0002-2479-6424

Department of Computer Science and Engineering, Mats School of Engineering and Technology, MATS University, Raipur, India

Ashwini Kumar Pradhan
https://orcid.org/0000-0002-1822-4235

School of Computer Science and Engineering, Galgotias University, Greater Noida, India

ABSTRACT

The integration of Artificial Intelligence (AI) and the Internet of Things (IoT), known as AIoT, is driving significant advancements in smart collaboration across industries. By combining IoT's data-gathering capabilities with AI's analytical power, AIoT systems enable real-time decision-making, automation, and optimization in areas like manufacturing, healthcare, and smart cities. This chapter examines how AI interprets IoT-generated data to enhance efficiency, sustainability, and productivity. Key use cases are highlighted, demonstrating the synergy between AI and IoT in improving processes, reducing energy consumption, and bolstering safety measures. Challenges such as data security, latency, and device compatibility are addressed, with potential solutions like edge computing and secure frameworks proposed. The

DOI: 10.4018/979-8-3373-2372-5.ch002

chapter concludes with a forward-looking perspective on how AIoT can transform industries and reshape human-machine collaboration, paving the way for smarter, more connected environments.

1. INTRODUCTION

1.1. Overview of AI and IoT

Artificial Intelligence (AI) and the Internet of Things (IoT) are two of the most transformative technologies of the 21st century, reshaping industries, businesses, and everyday life. Artificial Intelligence (AI) refers to the capability of machines and computer systems to mimic human intelligence, including learning, reasoning, problem-solving, perception, and decision-making. AI technologies range from simple rule-based systems to advanced machine learning algorithms that can predict outcomes, recognize patterns, and make decisions with minimal human intervention. Internet of Things (IoT) is the interconnected network of physical devices embedded with sensors, software, and other technologies to collect and exchange data with other systems over the internet. These devices can range from simple sensors monitoring environmental conditions to complex systems like smart refrigerators, autonomous vehicles, and industrial machinery (Alhilali & Montazerolghaem, 2023). The power of IoT lies in the ability of these devices to communicate, share data, and function in a coordinated manner.

1.2. Evolution of AI and IoT Technologies

Both AI and IoT have evolved significantly over the years, shaped by technological advances and market needs. AI's evolution began in the mid-20th century with early attempts to create machines capable of performing tasks that require human-like intelligence. Over time, the development of machine learning, natural language processing, computer vision, and deep learning has pushed AI into the mainstream (Al-Turjman et al., 2024). AI is now capable of performing complex tasks such as self-driving cars, image recognition, and real-time speech translation. IoT's evolution can be traced back to the idea of connected devices in the early 1980s. However, IoT truly took off in the late 2000s when advances in wireless technology, cloud computing, and affordable sensors made it possible to connect billions of devices globally. Today, IoT has applications across sectors including healthcare, smart homes, cities, and industries.

1.3. The Convergence of AI and IoT: AIoT

The integration of AI with IoT, commonly referred to as Artificial Intelligence of Things (AIoT), marks a significant leap in technological innovation. AIoT brings together AI's ability to analyze vast amounts of data and make intelligent decisions with IoT's real-time data collection and device connectivity. This convergence allows for more efficient, intelligent systems that can not only monitor and collect data but also make autonomous decisions and optimize processes based on that data (Anwar et al., 2024). Benefits of AIoT include enhanced efficiency, automation, predictive maintenance, and personalization. In a factory, for instance, IoT sensors can monitor equipment performance in real-time, while AI algorithms can predict failures and suggest preventive actions. In smart homes, AIoT enables devices to learn users' preferences and automate tasks such as adjusting the thermostat or controlling lighting based on their routines. The synergy between AI and IoT opens the door to smarter, more connected systems that are capable of driving innovation and transformation across various sectors (Apat et al., 2022).

2. KEY TECHNOLOGIES IN AIoT

The convergence of Artificial Intelligence (AI) and the Internet of Things (IoT) relies on a blend of advanced technologies that support intelligent, interconnected systems. These technologies enable the collection, analysis, and automation of vast amounts of data, unlocking new possibilities for smart, efficient systems. Below are the key technologies driving AIoT (Awaisi et al., 2024).

2.1. Artificial Intelligence: Core Concepts and Techniques

AI technologies form the backbone of AIoT by allowing machines to process, analyze, and make decisions based on data gathered by IoT devices. There are several core concepts that define AI in AIoT such as Machine learning is a subset of AI that focuses on the ability of machines to learn from data without being explicitly programmed. In the AIoT context, ML enables systems to analyze large datasets collected from IoT devices, identify patterns, and make real-time decisions or predictions. For example, in smart manufacturing, ML algorithms can predict equipment failures by analyzing sensor data over time. Deep learning, a more advanced subset of machine learning, involves artificial neural networks with multiple layers, mimicking the human brain's neural connections. Deep learning algorithms are particularly effective in tasks such as image recognition and natural language processing. In AIoT, DL plays a significant role in applications like smart surveillance systems that can recognize faces or detect unusual activities from video feeds collected by IoT cameras. NLP enables machines to understand, interpret, and respond to human language. In AIoT applications like smart assistants or smart home systems, NLP allows users to interact with devices using voice commands (Baker & Xiang, 2023). The AI engine can process these commands and activate IoT devices accordingly, such as adjusting the thermostat or controlling home security systems. Computer vision is an AI technology that allows machines to "see" and interpret visual data. With the use of cameras and sensors, IoT systems can gather real-time visual information, and AI algorithms can process this data for various applications, such as object detection, facial recognition, or anomaly detection in manufacturing. Reinforcement learning (RL) is another branch of AI where systems learn through trial and error. RL models can be used in AIoT systems to enable autonomous decision-making. For example, in industrial robots, RL algorithms can optimize task performance by continuously improving from past experiences (Balas et al., 2019).

2.2. Internet of Things: Enabling Technologies

IoT is built upon a combination of hardware and software components that enable the seamless collection and transmission of data between devices. Here are some of the core technologies that can be integrated with AI such as Sensors are devices that detect and respond to changes in an environment, such as temperature, motion, or pressure. Actuators, on the other hand, perform actions based on signals received from sensors or AI-driven instructions. In AIoT systems, sensors gather data that is processed by AI algorithms, and actuators can carry out intelligent actions, such as adjusting equipment settings or alerting operators to potential issues. The success of IoT depends on reliable connectivity for data transmission between devices (Chang et al., 2021). Various communication protocols, including Wi-Fi, Bluetooth, Zigbee, and 5G, enable devices to connect and exchange information in real-time. 5G technology, in particular, is a game-changer for AIoT because it offers ultra-low latency, higher bandwidth, and more reliable connections, making it ideal for real-time applications like autonomous vehicles or smart factories. Edge computing brings data processing closer to the source of data generation, reducing the reliance on cloud-based servers. This technology is crucial for AIoT applications that require real-time analysis and decision-making. For example, in a smart manufacturing plant, edge devices can analyze data from IoT sensors locally and make immediate decisions to optimize processes, without the need for cloud communication.

Despite the rise of edge computing, cloud computing still plays a vital role in AIoT. The cloud provides scalable storage and computing power to process large volumes of data generated by IoT devices. AI models can be trained in the cloud using vast datasets and then deployed to edge devices for real-time operation. Additionally, cloud platforms allow AIoT systems to integrate with broader services, including data analytics and monitoring tools. As IoT systems generate and transmit large amounts of sensitive data, ensuring security is a priority (Cheng et al., 2024). Blockchain technology is increasingly being integrated into AIoT systems to provide secure, decentralized data exchange. By encrypting and verifying each transaction or data exchange, blockchain enhances the security and transparency of AIoT networks, particularly in supply chain and logistics applications.

2.3. AIoT Architecture

AIoT systems are built on a complex architecture that combines AI technologies with IoT infrastructure, resulting in an intelligent, real-time decision-making system. The following components make up a typical AIoT architecture:

- Data Collection Layer: This layer consists of IoT sensors, devices, and gateways that gather data from the physical environment. Data can range from temperature readings in a smart home to complex operational data from industrial machinery. These devices collect real-time information continuously and send it to the next layer for processing (Dankan Gowda et al., 2024).
- Data Processing and AI Layer: In this layer, the data collected from IoT devices is processed and analyzed using AI models. Depending on the application, data processing can occur either on edge devices (edge computing) or in the cloud. AI algorithms, such as machine learning models, analyze the data, identify patterns, and generate insights or decisions. This layer is responsible for transforming raw data into actionable intelligence (Era et al., 2024).
- Action Layer: Once AI algorithms have analyzed the data, the action layer triggers responses or actions based on the insights gained. For instance, in a smart home system, AI might decide to adjust the thermostat based on temperature sensor data or turn off lights when no motion is detected. In industrial settings, AIoT systems can instruct machines to adjust operating conditions for optimal efficiency (Garg & Singh, 2021).
- Communication and Control Layer: This layer manages the communication between various IoT devices and ensures that control commands from AI systems are delivered accurately and securely. It involves protocols for data exchange, security mechanisms, and device synchronization.
- Edge AI: Edge AI refers to the process of deploying AI models directly on IoT devices or at the network's edge, rather than relying solely on cloud-based AI processing. This setup brings intelligence closer to the data source, allowing for faster decision-making and reducing latency. For instance, in au-

tonomous vehicles, edge AI is critical for processing sensor data in real-time to make driving decisions (Haroun et al., 2021).

Figure 1. Architecture of AIoT functioning

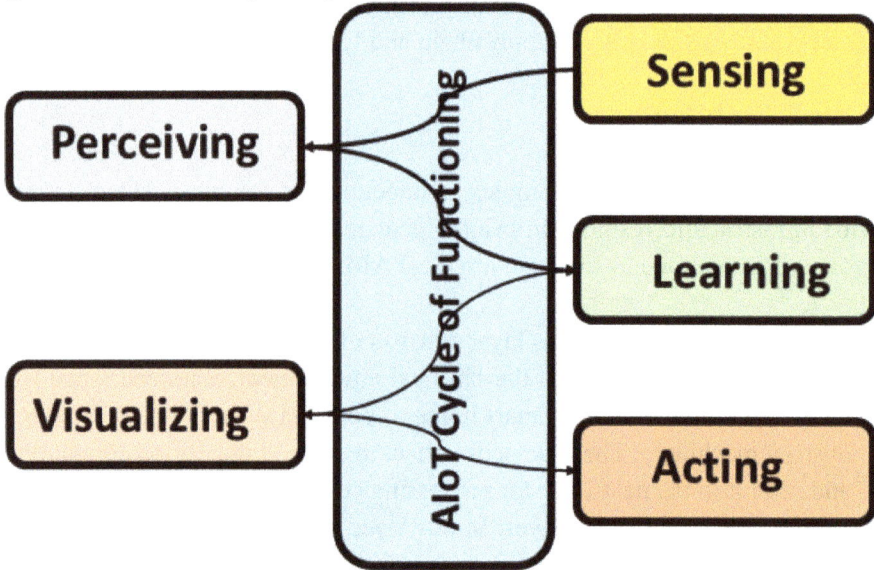

By integrating these technologies, AIoT systems become intelligent, responsive, and adaptive, with the ability to analyze data in real-time and make decisions that improve efficiency, safety, and user experiences. The AIoT Cycle of Functioning, as depicted in the diagram, illustrates the interconnected processes that enable AIoT systems to operate effectively. It begins with perceiving, where IoT devices sense their environment through various sensors, capturing data such as temperature, motion, or visual input. This sensed data is then fed into AI systems that engage in learning, processing patterns and insights from the information gathered. Once learning occurs, the system moves to acting, where decisions are made, and actions are executed automatically or with minimal human intervention. Finally, the visualizing component ensures that the outcomes, patterns, and system behaviors are presented in an understandable form, allowing stakeholders to monitor, interpret, and refine system performance. Together, these stages create a continuous loop of sensing, learning, acting, and visualizing, which forms the foundation of intelligent, adaptive AIoT systems.

3. APPLICATIONS OF AIoT

The integration of Artificial Intelligence (AI) and the Internet of Things (IoT) has led to the development of AIoT systems that offer transformative applications across various industries. By combining the real-time data collection of IoT with AI's data analysis and decision-making capabilities, AIoT enables smarter, more autonomous systems. This section explores key applications of AIoT in areas such as smart homes, cities, healthcare, industrial automation, and transportation (Hou et al., 2023).

3.1. AIoT in Smart Homes

AIoT plays a pivotal role in making homes smarter, more energy-efficient, and user-friendly.

- Home Automation: AIoT-enabled smart homes are equipped with interconnected devices such as smart thermostats, lights, and appliances that can be controlled remotely or autonomously. AI algorithms analyze users' habits and preferences to optimize home environments. For instance, a smart thermostat can learn the homeowner's routine and adjust the temperature automatically, reducing energy consumption.
- Energy Efficiency: AIoT systems can help reduce energy usage by intelligently managing devices. Sensors in a smart home can detect whether a room is occupied and adjust lighting or heating accordingly. AIoT-powered energy management systems can also predict peak energy usage and schedule the operation of high-consumption devices during off-peak hours.
- Home Security: AIoT enhances home security through smart surveillance systems, doorbell cameras, and motion detectors. These systems not only monitor the home in real-time but also use AI to detect unusual activity or identify known individuals. If suspicious activity is detected, the system can alert homeowners and law enforcement.

Figure 2. Popular papers in AIoT

3.2. AIoT in Smart Cities

The adoption of AIoT in smart cities aims to improve urban living by making cities more efficient, sustainable, and safer. AIoT applications in smart cities include traffic management, public safety, and infrastructure monitoring.

- Traffic Management: AIoT systems can optimize traffic flow by monitoring traffic conditions in real-time using IoT sensors and cameras. AI algorithms can analyze this data to adjust traffic signals dynamically, reduce congestion, and reroute traffic in case of accidents. AIoT also plays a role in optimizing public transportation schedules, ensuring that buses and trains operate efficiently (Iqubal et al., 2025).
- Public Safety: AIoT enhances public safety through smart surveillance and monitoring systems. AI-powered cameras can analyze live video feeds from city streets to detect criminal activities, accidents, or unusual behavior. AIoT systems can automatically alert law enforcement or emergency services, allowing for a quicker response.
- Waste Management: IoT sensors installed in waste bins can monitor their fill levels and notify waste management services when bins are full. AI can optimize waste collection routes, reducing fuel consumption and operational costs. This results in more efficient waste management and cleaner cities.

3.3. AIoT in Healthcare

AIoT is revolutionizing healthcare by enabling more personalized, data-driven care and improving patient outcomes. Applications of AIoT in healthcare include remote patient monitoring, predictive diagnostics, and AI-powered medical devices.

- Remote Patient Monitoring: AIoT-enabled wearable devices and sensors can continuously monitor patients' vital signs such as heart rate, blood pressure, and glucose levels. These devices transmit real-time data to healthcare providers, allowing them to track patients' health remotely. AI algorithms can analyze this data to detect abnormalities or potential health issues early, enabling preventive care and reducing hospital visits (Liu et al., 2024).
- Predictive Diagnostics: AIoT systems can analyze large volumes of patient data to predict potential health problems before they occur. For instance, AI can identify patterns in a patient's medical history and current health data, allowing for early diagnosis of chronic conditions such as diabetes or cardiovascular diseases. This leads to more proactive and personalized treatment plans.
- AI-Powered Medical Devices: Medical devices powered by AIoT, such as smart infusion pumps or AI-assisted surgical tools, offer greater precision and automation in healthcare delivery. For example, AIoT-enabled insulin pumps can automatically adjust insulin levels based on real-time glucose data, ensuring optimal patient care without the need for manual intervention.

The evolution of AIoT in healthcare has transformed the industry from basic remote monitoring to advanced, intelligent care delivery. Initially, AIoT-enabled wearable devices and sensors allowed continuous tracking of vital signs like heart rate, blood pressure, and glucose levels, providing real-time data to healthcare providers and enabling early detection of health issues. As AI algorithms advanced, the focus expanded to predictive diagnostics, where large datasets were analyzed to anticipate potential health risks and support proactive, personalized treatment plans for conditions such as diabetes and cardiovascular disease. Today, AIoT powers sophisticated medical devices that deliver precise, automated care, such as smart infusion pumps and AI-assisted surgical tools, reducing human error and enhancing patient outcomes. Together, these developments have shifted healthcare toward a more connected, data-driven, and patient-centered model.

3.4. AIoT in Industrial Automation

In industrial automation, AIoT is driving the next wave of efficiency and productivity by enabling smarter factories, predictive maintenance, and optimized operations. AIoT in Industry 4.0 integrates AI with industrial IoT (IIoT) to create highly automated and data-driven production environments.

- Predictive Maintenance: AIoT systems can continuously monitor the condition of machinery and equipment in industrial settings. IoT sensors collect data on parameters such as temperature, vibration, and pressure, while AI algorithms analyze this data to predict when a machine is likely to fail. By identifying potential issues before they cause downtime, AIoT enables predictive maintenance, reducing operational disruptions and repair costs (Matin et al., 2023).
- Operational Efficiency: AIoT enables factories to optimize production processes in real-time. For example, IoT sensors can monitor energy usage, machine performance, and environmental conditions on the production floor, while AI systems use this data to adjust processes for maximum efficiency. AIoT can also automate quality control by using computer vision to inspect products for defects.
- AIoT in Industry 4.0: Industry 4.0 refers to the fourth industrial revolution, characterized by the integration of digital technologies into manufacturing. AIoT plays a crucial role in this transformation by enabling smart factories where machines, systems, and humans work together seamlessly. AI-driven analytics can optimize supply chains, improve inventory management, and enhance overall productivity.

The evolution of AIoT in industrial automation is transforming factories into highly efficient, data-driven ecosystems as part of the industry 4.0 revolution. Initially, AIoT advanced predictive maintenance by using IoT sensors to monitor machinery conditions and AI algorithms to forecast potential failures, reducing downtime and repair costs. As the technology matured, AIoT expanded its role in optimizing operational efficiency by analyzing real-time data on energy consumption, machine performance, and environmental factors, allowing factories to fine-tune production processes and automate quality control. Today, AIoT is a cornerstone of smart factories, where interconnected machines, systems, and humans collaborate seamlessly, leveraging AI-driven analytics to optimize supply chains, enhance inventory management, and boost overall productivity, marking a major leap forward in industrial automation and competitiveness.

3.5. AIoT in Transportation and Logistics

AIoT has transformative potential in transportation and logistics, leading to safer, more efficient, and cost-effective operations. From autonomous vehicles to real-time tracking systems, AIoT is reshaping how goods and people move.

- Autonomous Vehicles: AIoT is the driving force behind autonomous vehicles (self-driving cars), which rely on IoT sensors such as cameras, radar, and LiDAR to gather data about their surroundings. AI processes this data in real-time to make driving decisions, such as steering, braking, and acceleration. Autonomous vehicles have the potential to reduce accidents, improve traffic flow, and transform urban mobility.
- Fleet Management: AIoT solutions can optimize fleet operations by tracking vehicle performance, fuel consumption, and driver behavior. AI algorithms can analyze this data to optimize routes, reduce fuel usage, and predict vehicle maintenance needs. This results in cost savings, improved safety, and more efficient delivery times.
- Real-Time Tracking: In logistics, AIoT enables real-time tracking of goods throughout the supply chain. IoT sensors attached to shipments can monitor factors like location, temperature, and humidity. AI algorithms analyze this data to provide insights on delivery status, potential delays, and product conditions. AIoT systems can also automate warehouse operations, optimizing inventory management and reducing human error (Mohapatra, 2021).

AIoT is revolutionizing transportation and logistics by creating safer, more efficient, and cost-effective systems that reshape how goods and people move. At the forefront are autonomous vehicles, which combine IoT sensors like cameras, radar, and LiDAR with real-time AI processing to make driving decisions, promising reduced accidents and smoother urban mobility. In fleet management, AIoT enhances operational efficiency by tracking vehicle performance, fuel usage, and driver behavior, allowing AI algorithms to optimize routes, cut fuel costs, and predict maintenance needs. Additionally, AIoT transforms logistics through real-time tracking, where IoT sensors monitor shipment location and conditions while AI provides insights into delivery status, potential delays, and inventory management, ultimately streamlining supply chains and reducing human error.

4. CHALLENGES AND LIMITATIONS OF AIoT INTEGRATION

Despite the transformative potential of AIoT, its implementation comes with several challenges and limitations. These challenges range from technical complexities to security concerns, ethical dilemmas, and regulatory issues. This section explores the key barriers that organizations face when integrating AI and IoT systems to create smarter, more efficient solutions.

4.1. Technical Challenges

The integration of AI and IoT into cohesive AIoT systems is a complex technical process. Several challenges arise during the deployment and scaling of AIoT solutions:

- Data Interoperability and Integration: AIoT systems rely on data collected from a wide range of IoT devices, often using different protocols and standards. Integrating data from heterogeneous devices and ensuring that it is compatible with AI models can be a significant challenge. The lack of standardized data formats and communication protocols across industries makes it difficult to achieve seamless interoperability between devices from different manufacturers (Mohapatra, 2024).
- Scalability of AIoT Systems: As the number of connected devices in an AIoT system increases, so does the volume of data that needs to be processed and analyzed. Ensuring that AIoT systems can scale to handle large amounts of data in real-time is a significant technical challenge. This requires robust infrastructure, high-performance computing capabilities, and efficient algorithms to process and analyze data at scale without latency issues.
- Complexity of AI Models: While AI models are powerful, they often require a high level of expertise to design, train, and deploy. Many AIoT applications require custom AI models tailored to specific tasks, which adds to the complexity of deployment. Additionally, real-time AI processing in AIoT systems demands computational power, often requiring edge computing solutions to reduce the latency associated with cloud-based AI analysis.
- Energy Consumption: The energy consumption of AIoT systems, especially in resource-constrained environments like remote sensors or mobile devices, can pose a challenge. AI algorithms, especially deep learning models, can be resource-intensive. Developing energy-efficient AI algorithms and optimizing IoT devices to work in low-power conditions is critical to the success of AIoT, particularly in applications like smart cities and agriculture.

4.2. Data Privacy and Security Concerns

AIoT systems generate and transmit massive amounts of data, raising concerns about privacy, security, and data protection. These concerns are heightened by the sensitive nature of the data collected, such as personal health information or real-time location tracking.

- Data Privacy Risks: AIoT systems collect vast amounts of data from IoT devices, including sensitive personal data. This raises concerns about the privacy of individuals and the potential misuse of data. For example, in smart homes, data about the occupants' routines, habits, and preferences can be collected and potentially exploited if not properly protected. Organizations must implement strong data protection mechanisms, including encryption, anonymization, and compliance with data privacy regulations like the GDPR (General Data Protection Regulation).
- Cybersecurity Threats: IoT devices are often the target of cyberattacks due to their relatively weak security measures. AIoT systems, being interconnected networks, are highly vulnerable to hacking, data breaches, and other cyberattacks. Cybercriminals can exploit vulnerabilities in IoT devices to gain unauthorized access to the entire AIoT network. Securing AIoT systems requires robust encryption protocols, regular software updates, and the implementation of secure authentication and access control mechanisms (Muhammed et al., 2024).
- Data Integrity and Accuracy: AI models rely on accurate and reliable data to make informed decisions. However, if IoT devices transmit inaccurate or corrupted data, the AI model may make flawed decisions, leading to negative consequences. Ensuring the integrity of data at every stage, from collection to transmission and analysis, is crucial for the reliability of AIoT systems.

4.3. Ethical and Social Challenges

AIoT systems raise a host of ethical and social concerns, especially when it comes to AI's role in decision-making and its impact on the workforce.

- Ethical Implications of AI Decision-Making: As AI becomes more integrated into IoT systems, it is increasingly responsible for making autonomous decisions. This raises ethical concerns, especially when these decisions impact human lives. For example, in healthcare, AIoT systems may make decisions about a patient's treatment based on real-time data. If AI models are biased or flawed, these decisions could have serious consequences. Ensuring transparency and fairness in AI algorithms is essential to mitigate ethical risks (Parihar et al., 2023).

- Job Displacement and Workforce Transformation: The widespread adoption of AIoT systems in industries such as manufacturing, transportation, and logistics has the potential to displace jobs traditionally held by humans. As AIoT systems automate tasks that were once manual, many workers may find their skills outdated. While AIoT can create new job opportunities in areas such as data analysis and system maintenance, organizations must invest in upskilling and retraining their workforce to mitigate the negative impact on employment.

- Bias and Fairness in AI Algorithms: AI models are only as good as the data they are trained on. If the data used to train AI models in AIoT systems is biased, the models will produce biased outcomes. For instance, AIoT systems in smart cities could unintentionally prioritize services in affluent areas while neglecting underprivileged communities. Ensuring that AI models are trained on diverse and representative datasets is critical to promoting fairness and avoiding unintended biases.

Figure 3. Overall impact of AIoT on various factors

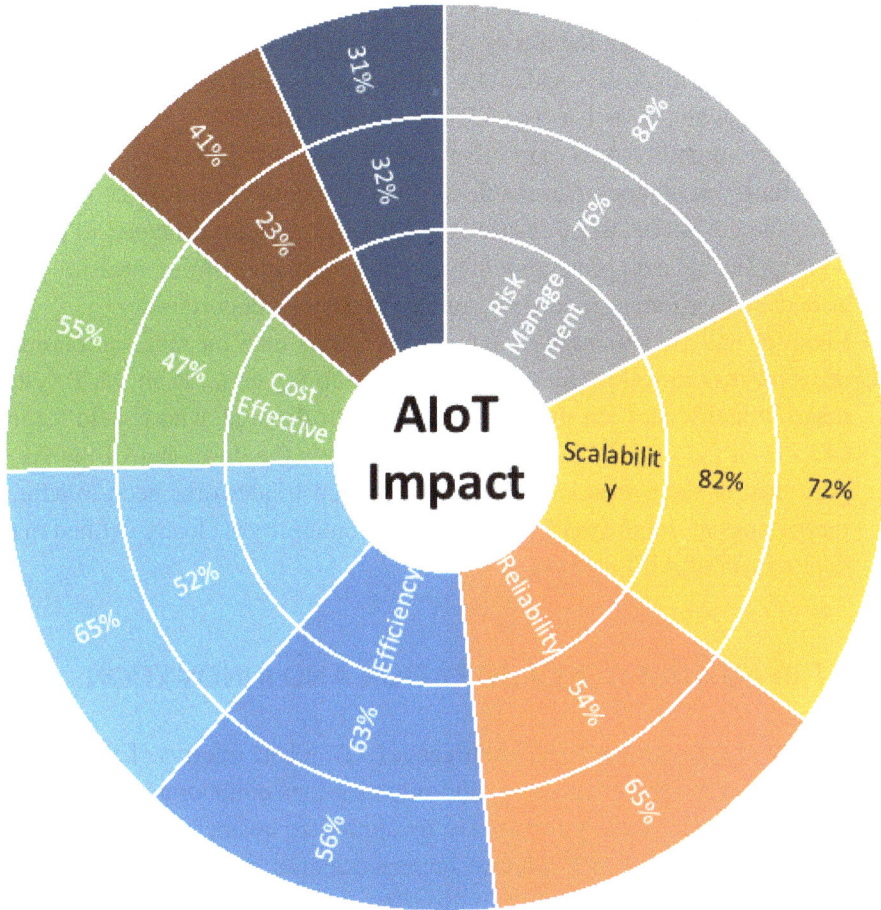

4.4. Regulatory and Legal Issues

As AIoT systems proliferate across industries, governments and regulatory bodies are grappling with the need for new laws and regulations to address the challenges posed by these technologies.

- Lack of Clear Regulatory Frameworks: AIoT is a rapidly evolving field, and regulatory frameworks have struggled to keep pace with the advancements in technology. In many industries, there are no clear guidelines on the use of AIoT systems, especially regarding data privacy, security, and liability. For example, in the case of autonomous vehicles, questions arise about who is responsible in the event of an accident caused by an AIoT-powered system. Governments and regulatory bodies must develop comprehensive legal frameworks to govern the use of AIoT technologies (Prabha et al., 2022).

- Compliance with Data Regulations: AIoT systems must comply with data protection regulations such as the GDPR, HIPAA (Health Insurance Portability and Accountability Act), and other industry-specific laws. Non-compliance with these regulations can result in severe penalties and loss of consumer trust. Organizations must ensure that AIoT systems are designed to comply with applicable data protection laws, including implementing measures such as data encryption, user consent, and the right to data portability.
- Liability and Accountability: As AIoT systems take on more autonomous decision-making roles, questions of accountability arise. If an AIoT system makes a faulty decision that results in harm or damage, who is held responsible? Is it the manufacturer of the IoT devices, the developer of the AI algorithms, or the operator of the system? Legal frameworks need to address these issues of liability and ensure that accountability is clearly defined in the deployment of AIoT systems.

5. AIoT IN FUTURE COLLABORATION AND INNOVATION

The synergy between Artificial Intelligence (AI) and the Internet of Things (IoT) is reshaping how humans, machines, and organizations collaborate and innovate. As AIoT systems evolve, they promise to revolutionize business models, promote sustainable development, and enhance human-machine interaction. This section explores the future potential of AIoT in fostering smarter collaboration and driving innovation across industries.

5.1. AIoT and Human-Machine Collaboration

One of the most promising aspects of AIoT is its potential to enhance collaboration between humans and machines. As AIoT systems become more sophisticated, they will work alongside humans in various industries, improving efficiency, decision-making, and overall productivity.

- Enhancing Human Decision-Making: AIoT systems can process large amounts of data in real-time and provide actionable insights to human operators. In healthcare, for instance, AIoT devices can monitor patients' vital signs and provide doctors with real-time recommendations for treatment. This human-machine collaboration allows for faster, more accurate decision-making, reducing the margin of error and improving patient outcomes (Salama & Abdellatif, 2022).

- Collaborative Robotics (Cobots): In industrial settings, AIoT enables the use of collaborative robots or Cobots—robots designed to work alongside humans. Cobots equipped with AIoT systems can assist human workers in tasks such as assembling products, handling materials, or performing quality control. These robots learn from human operators and continuously optimize their performance, resulting in more efficient production processes.

- Remote Collaboration: AIoT is enabling new forms of remote collaboration, where teams across the globe can work together in real-time using smart connected devices. For example, AIoT-powered collaboration platforms allow architects and engineers to work on building designs simultaneously, while AI assists with data analysis and optimization. In industries such as oil and gas, remote AIoT systems monitor equipment in offshore facilities and allow technicians to collaborate with AI-powered systems to diagnose and solve problems remotely (Shah et al., 2022).

5.2. AIoT and Business Innovation

AIoT is driving innovation across industries by enabling new business models and transforming existing ones. The integration of AI and IoT opens up opportunities for more intelligent and automated systems, creating value in unprecedented ways.

- Business Models Driven by AIoT: AIoT enables the rise of new business models such as "product-as-a-service" (PaaS), where businesses offer smart products with ongoing AI-driven services. For example, in the manufacturing industry, companies can provide equipment with AIoT-enabled predictive maintenance services, where customers pay based on usage or uptime rather than purchasing the equipment outright. This model reduces the total cost of ownership and ensures that equipment is always optimized for performance (Swain et al., 2025).

- Transforming Industries with AIoT: AIoT is transforming industries such as agriculture, energy, and retail by enabling smarter, data-driven decision-making. In agriculture, AIoT systems analyze data from soil sensors, weather forecasts, and crop health monitors to help farmers make informed decisions about planting, irrigation, and harvesting. In retail, AIoT-powered smart shelves and personalized shopping experiences are driving innovation by delivering tailored recommendations to customers based on real-time data.

- AIoT-Enabled Services: AIoT is also creating opportunities for businesses to offer new services. For example, in transportation and logistics, AIoT enables real-time tracking of goods, predictive maintenance of fleets, and dynamic route optimization. This not only improves operational efficiency but also enhances customer satisfaction through faster, more reliable service delivery.

5.3. AIoT in Sustainable Development

AIoT has the potential to play a critical role in addressing global challenges related to sustainability and environmental conservation. By leveraging AI and IoT technologies, industries can adopt more sustainable practices, reduce resource consumption, and mitigate the effects of climate change.

- AIoT Applications for Energy Conservation: AIoT systems are being deployed to optimize energy consumption in smart buildings, factories, and cities. By monitoring and analyzing real-time data from sensors, AIoT systems can identify areas where energy is being wasted and automatically adjust energy usage (Thakur et al., 2023). For example, smart grids use AIoT to balance energy demand and supply in real-time, ensuring that energy is distributed efficiently and minimizing waste. AIoT-powered energy management systems can also predict peak usage times and shift non-essential energy consumption to off-peak hours, reducing overall energy demand.
- AIoT in Smart Agriculture: In agriculture, AIoT systems are being used to promote more sustainable farming practices. AIoT solutions can monitor soil health, water levels, and crop growth, allowing farmers to optimize resource usage and reduce water and fertilizer waste. Precision agriculture, enabled by AIoT, ensures that resources are applied exactly where and when they are needed, improving crop yields while minimizing environmental impact. Additionally, AIoT systems can predict weather patterns and soil conditions, allowing farmers to take proactive steps to mitigate the effects of climate change.
- AIoT for Environmental Monitoring: AIoT can also be deployed to monitor environmental conditions and assess the health of ecosystems. IoT sensors can track air and water quality, while AI algorithms analyze this data to detect pollution, identify trends, and predict future environmental risks. In smart cities, AIoT systems can monitor pollution levels in real-time and provide insights that help authorities implement measures to reduce emissions and protect public health.

5.4. The Future of AIoT: Predictions and Trends

As AIoT continues to evolve, several key trends are emerging that will shape the future of this technology. These trends highlight the potential of AIoT to drive further innovation, collaboration, and transformation across industries.

- Edge AIoT: The rise of edge AIoT—AI processing at the edge of the network, closer to where data is generated—will be a major trend in the coming years. Edge AIoT reduces latency and enables real-time decision-making in applications such as autonomous vehicles, industrial automation, and healthcare. As edge computing technology matures, AIoT systems will become faster, more reliable, and more capable of handling large volumes of data in real-time.
- 5G-Enabled AIoT: The widespread adoption of 5G technology will be a game-changer for AIoT, enabling faster data transmission, higher bandwidth, and lower latency. 5G will unlock new possibilities for AIoT applications in areas such as smart cities, transportation, and telemedicine, where real-time connectivity is essential. AIoT systems will benefit from the enhanced performance of 5G networks, allowing for more seamless collaboration between devices and AI systems (Wang et al., 2023).
- AIoT for Personalized Experiences: AIoT systems will increasingly focus on creating personalized experiences for users by analyzing data in real-time and adapting to individual preferences. In industries such as retail, hospitality, and healthcare, AIoT systems will offer tailored recommendations, products, and services based on users' behavior and needs. This trend toward personalization will drive customer satisfaction and improve business outcomes.
- AIoT for Autonomous Systems: The future of AIoT will see the rise of fully autonomous systems, where AIoT devices make decisions and take actions without human intervention. Autonomous vehicles, drones, and robots powered by AIoT will revolutionize industries such as transportation, logistics, and defense. These systems will rely on AIoT to process data in real-time, navigate complex environments, and make intelligent decisions on the fly.
- AIoT in the Circular Economy: AIoT will play a critical role in supporting the circular economy, where resources are reused and recycled to minimize waste. AIoT systems can monitor product life cycles, track materials, and optimize resource usage to ensure that products are used efficiently and recycled when no longer needed. This trend will help industries reduce their environmental footprint and move toward more sustainable business practices.

6. CASE STUDIES OF AIoT IMPLEMENTATIONS

Real-world applications of AIoT have demonstrated the transformative potential of integrating Artificial Intelligence and the Internet of Things across various industries. These case studies highlight how companies are leveraging AIoT to drive innovation, improve efficiency, and address industry-specific challenges. In this section, we explore notable examples of AIoT implementations in manufacturing, healthcare, smart cities, and transportation.

6.1. AIoT in Manufacturing: Siemens and Predictive Maintenance

Company: Siemens
Application: Predictive Maintenance

Siemens, a global leader in industrial automation, has successfully integrated AIoT into its manufacturing processes through predictive maintenance. Siemens uses AIoT to monitor and maintain industrial equipment, ensuring that machinery operates efficiently with minimal downtime.

- IoT Sensors for Data Collection: Siemens installs IoT sensors on critical machinery to continuously monitor parameters such as vibration, temperature, and pressure. These sensors collect real-time data and transmit it to an AI system for analysis (Yan, 2024).
- AI-Powered Predictive Maintenance: The AI system analyzes the data using machine learning algorithms to identify patterns and detect early signs of equipment failure. By predicting when a machine is likely to break down, Siemens can schedule maintenance proactively, preventing costly downtime and reducing repair expenses.
- Impact: Siemens' AIoT-powered predictive maintenance has led to significant improvements in equipment uptime, operational efficiency, and cost savings. The implementation has also minimized unplanned breakdowns and extended the lifespan of machinery.

This case study highlights how AIoT is revolutionizing the manufacturing industry by enabling more efficient and intelligent maintenance practices, ultimately boosting productivity and reducing costs.

6.2. AIoT in Healthcare: IBM Watson Health

Company: IBM Watson Health
Application: Personalized Healthcare and Predictive Diagnostics

IBM Watson Health leverages AIoT to transform healthcare by combining AI-driven data analysis with IoT-enabled medical devices. This synergy enables real-time patient monitoring and personalized treatment plans based on individual health data.

- IoT Devices for Remote Monitoring: IBM Watson Health uses wearable devices and IoT sensors to continuously monitor patients' vital signs, including heart rate, blood pressure, and glucose levels. These devices collect real-time data from patients and transmit it to Watson's AI-powered analytics platform.
- AI-Driven Insights and Personalized Care: Watson's AI system analyzes patient data in real-time, providing healthcare professionals with actionable insights. By detecting early warning signs of health conditions, such as irregular heartbeats or fluctuations in glucose levels, the AI system enables doctors to intervene before a patient's condition worsens. Additionally, Watson can recommend personalized treatment plans based on the patient's medical history and current health data (Zhang & Tao, 2021).
- Impact: AIoT-powered remote monitoring has improved patient outcomes by enabling early diagnosis, reducing hospital readmissions, and ensuring continuous care. The combination of AI-driven insights and IoT-based monitoring has made healthcare more data-driven, precise, and patient-centric.

This case study illustrates how AIoT is enhancing personalized healthcare, making it possible for doctors to provide proactive and customized care for patients while improving efficiency in healthcare delivery.

6.3. AIoT in Smart Cities: Barcelona's Smart City Project

City: Barcelona
Application: Smart City Infrastructure and Public Services

Barcelona is a leading example of how AIoT can be used to build smarter, more efficient cities. The city has implemented a wide range of AIoT solutions to improve urban living, enhance public services, and promote sustainability.

- Smart Sensors for Urban Monitoring: Barcelona has deployed IoT sensors across the city to monitor everything from air quality and noise levels to traffic flow and waste collection. These sensors gather real-time data on environmental conditions and city infrastructure.

- AI for Data Analysis and Decision-Making: AI algorithms analyze the data collected by IoT sensors to optimize urban services. For example, the city uses AIoT to manage traffic lights dynamically, adjusting them in real-time to reduce congestion and improve traffic flow. Similarly, AIoT-powered waste collection systems notify sanitation services when bins are full, allowing for more efficient waste management.

- Sustainability and Energy Efficiency: Barcelona's AIoT systems help optimize energy consumption in public buildings and street lighting. IoT sensors monitor energy usage, and AI algorithms adjust lighting and heating systems based on real-time needs, reducing energy consumption and carbon emissions.

- Impact: Barcelona's smart city initiatives have resulted in improved quality of life for residents, reduced environmental impact, and more efficient public services. AIoT has made the city more responsive to the needs of its inhabitants and more sustainable in its resource management.

This case study demonstrates how AIoT is enabling cities to become more intelligent and efficient, with real-time data-driven decision-making enhancing both public services and environmental sustainability.

6.4. AIoT in Transportation: Tesla's Autonomous Driving Technology

Company: Tesla
Application: Autonomous Vehicles and Smart Transportation

Tesla is at the forefront of AIoT-powered transportation with its autonomous driving technology. Tesla's self-driving cars combine IoT sensors with AI algorithms to navigate roads, monitor traffic, and make real-time driving decisions.

- IoT Sensors for Real-Time Data Collection: Tesla's autonomous vehicles are equipped with a suite of IoT sensors, including cameras, radar, and LiDAR, to collect data on the car's surroundings. These sensors continuously monitor road conditions, other vehicles, pedestrians, and traffic signals, providing real-time data to the car's AI system.

- AI for Autonomous Driving: Tesla's AI system processes the data from IoT sensors in real-time, allowing the car to make driving decisions autonomously. The AI system uses machine learning algorithms to recognize objects, predict traffic patterns, and navigate complex driving environments. Tesla's AIoT-powered cars can accelerate, brake, steer, and change lanes without human intervention.

- Impact: Tesla's AIoT-powered autonomous driving technology has revolutionized the automotive industry, paving the way for safer, more efficient transportation. The real-time analysis of road conditions and predictive driving decisions has reduced the risk of accidents and improved traffic flow. Tesla's AIoT system also continuously learns and improves based on data collected from the entire fleet of Tesla vehicles, making the technology more robust over time.

This case study highlights how AIoT is transforming transportation by enabling fully autonomous vehicles that can operate safely and efficiently in complex environments.

7. CONCLUSION AND FUTURE DIRECTIONS

7.1. Recap of AIoT's Impact on Industry and Society

The convergence of Artificial Intelligence (AI) and the Internet of Things (IoT), known as AIoT (Artificial Intelligence of Things), is reshaping industries, transforming businesses, and enhancing the way we live and work. Throughout this chapter, we have explored the vast potential of AIoT across sectors such as manufacturing, healthcare, smart cities, and transportation. By merging AI's ability to process and analyze data with IoT's capacity to collect and communicate real-time information, AIoT creates smarter, more responsive systems.

- AIoT's Key Contributions: AIoT has driven efficiency, automation, and cost savings across industries, enabling predictive maintenance in manufacturing, personalized healthcare solutions, and intelligent city infrastructures. In addition, AIoT has allowed for real-time decision-making, reducing the need for human intervention in complex environments like autonomous vehicles and smart factories.
- Societal Impact: AIoT has enhanced quality of life by making homes smarter, cities more sustainable, and healthcare more accessible. By leveraging real-time data, AIoT enables businesses and governments to respond more effectively to the needs of individuals and communities, contributing to smarter, more efficient public services and improving daily life.

7.2. Future Research and Development in AIoT

As AIoT continues to evolve, there are several key areas where research and development will play a crucial role in realizing its full potential. These future directions will help address existing challenges and open up new opportunities for innovation.

- Scalability and Energy Efficiency: One of the key challenges facing AIoT systems is the ability to scale effectively as the number of connected devices grows. Future research must focus on developing more efficient algorithms and energy-efficient hardware that can handle the processing and transmission of large amounts of data in real time. Edge AIoT, which enables AI processing closer to the source of data, will play a critical role in overcoming this challenge.
- AI Model Optimization: The development of AI models tailored for specific AIoT applications is another area that requires attention. Future research will need to focus on optimizing AI models for real-time applications, ensuring they are lightweight, efficient, and capable of running on resource-constrained devices. Advances in machine learning, deep learning, and reinforcement learning will drive improvements in AIoT systems' decision-making capabilities.
- Data Privacy and Security: As AIoT systems handle increasingly sensitive data, ensuring privacy and security will remain a priority. Future research will need to explore advanced encryption techniques, secure communication protocols, and privacy-preserving AI models. Blockchain technology and decentralized security frameworks may offer solutions to enhance the security and transparency of AIoT systems.
- Human-AIoT Collaboration: The integration of AIoT into everyday life raises questions about the nature of human-machine collaboration. Research into collaborative robotics (cobots), intuitive user interfaces, and ethical AI decision-making will be essential for ensuring that AIoT systems work effectively alongside humans while respecting human values and autonomy.

7.3. Final Thoughts on AIoT's Potential for Smart Collaboration

AIoT represents the next frontier in smart collaboration, with the potential to revolutionize industries and societies alike. By creating systems that can analyze vast amounts of real-time data and make intelligent decisions, AIoT enables seamless collaboration between machines, devices, and humans. From improving operational efficiency in industries to enhancing personal convenience in smart homes, AIoT is unlocking new possibilities for smarter, more connected systems.

- **AIoT's Role in Innovation:** AIoT will continue to be a driving force behind business innovation. Companies that leverage AIoT's capabilities will be able to create more responsive, data-driven products and services. AIoT has the power to redefine business models, allowing for new approaches like product-as-a-service and personalized customer experiences.
- **AIoT and Sustainable Development:** As the world faces increasing environmental challenges, AIoT will play a critical role in promoting sustainability. By optimizing energy usage, improving resource management, and enabling smarter agriculture, AIoT will contribute to sustainable development goals and help industries reduce their environmental footprint.
- **AIoT's Long-Term Vision:** In the long term, the integration of AI and IoT will lead to fully autonomous systems capable of operating with minimal human intervention. Autonomous vehicles, smart cities, and self-regulating industrial systems will become more commonplace, creating a future where AIoT-powered systems improve the efficiency, safety, and sustainability of both industries and societies.

As AIoT continues to evolve, it will shape the future of smart collaboration across sectors, unlocking new possibilities for innovation, sustainability, and human-machine interaction. By addressing the challenges of scalability, security, and ethical decision-making, AIoT will drive the next wave of technological transformation, leading to a smarter, more connected world.

REFERENCES

Al-Turjman, F., Altinay, F., & Gazi, Z. A. (2024). *Artificial intelligence of things (AIoT): Current and future trends*. Elsevier.

Alhilali, A. H., & Montazerolghaem, A. (2023). Artificial intelligence based load balancing in SDN: A comprehensive survey. *Internet of Things : Engineering Cyber Physical Human Systems*, 22, 100814. DOI: 10.1016/j.iot.2023.100814

Anwar, R. W., Ismael, A., & Qureshi, K. N. (2024). Advanced AIoT applications and services. *Artificial Intelligence of Things (AIoT)*, 21-33. https://doi.org/DOI: 10.1201/9781003430018-3

Apat, H. K., Sahoo, B., Mohanty, S., & Sahoo, K. S. (2022). A scalable software-defined edge computing model for sustainable smart city Internet of things (IoT) application. *SDN-Supported Edge-Cloud Interplay for Next Generation Internet of Things*, 125-148. https://doi.org/DOI: 10.1201/9781003213871-7

Awaisi, K. S., Ye, Q., & Sampalli, S. (2024). A survey of industrial AIoT: Opportunities, challenges, and directions. *IEEE Access : Practical Innovations, Open Solutions*, 12, 96946–96996. DOI: 10.1109/access.2024.3426279

Baker, S., & Xiang, W. (2023). Artificial intelligence of things for smarter healthcare: A survey of advancements, challenges, and opportunities. *IEEE Communications Surveys and Tutorials*, 25(2), 1261–1293. DOI: 10.1109/comst.2023.3256323

Balas, V. E., Kumar, R., & Srivastava, R. (2019). *Recent trends and advances in artificial intelligence and Internet of things*. Springer Nature.

Chang, Z., Liu, S., Xiong, X., Cai, Z., & Tu, G. (2021). A survey of recent advances in edge-computing-Powered artificial intelligence of things. *IEEE Internet of Things Journal*, 8(18), 13849–13875. DOI: 10.1109/jiot.2021.3088875

Cheng, L., Gu, Y., Liu, Q., Yang, L., Liu, C., & Wang, Y. (2024). Advancements in accelerating deep neural network inference on AIoT devices: A survey. *IEEE Transactions on Sustainable Computing*, 9(6), 830–847. DOI: 10.1109/tsusc.2024.3353176

Dankan Gowda, V., Kaur, M., Srinivas, D., Prasad, K. D., & Shekhar, R. (2024). AIoT integration advancements and challenges in smart sensing technologies for smart devices. *Advances in Computational Intelligence and Robotics*, ●●●, 42–65. DOI: 10.4018/979-8-3693-0786-1.ch003

Era, C. A., Rahman, M., & Alvi, S. T. (2024). Artificial intelligence of things (AIoT) technologies, benefits and applications. *2024 4th International Conference on Emerging Smart Technologies and Applications (eSmarTA)*, 1-6. https://doi.org/ DOI: 10.1109/esmarta62850.2024.10638992

Garg, A., & Singh, A. K. (2021). Applications of Internet of things (IoT) in green computing. *Intelligence of Things: AI-IoT Based Critical-Applications and Innovations*, 1-34. https://doi.org/DOI: 10.1007/978-3-030-82800-4_1

Haroun, A., Le, X., Gao, S., Dong, B., He, T., Zhang, Z., Wen, F., Xu, S., & Lee, C. (2021). Progress in micro/nano sensors and nanoenergy for future aiot-based smart home applications. *Nano Express*, 2(2), 022005. DOI: 10.1088/2632-959x/abf3d4

Hou, K. M., Diao, X., Shi, H., Ding, H., Zhou, H., & De Vaulx, C. (2023). Trends and challenges in AIoT/IIoT/IoT implementation. *Sensors (Basel)*, *23*(11), 5074. DOI: 10.3390/s23115074 PMID: 37299800

Iqubal, S., Khan, S., Pant, N., Sarkar, S., Rey, T., & Mohapatra, H. (2025). A study on IoT-enabled smart bed with brain-computer interface for elderly and paralyzed individuals. *Advances in Medical Technologies and Clinical Practice*, ●●●, 61–88. DOI: 10.4018/979-8-3693-7703-1.ch004

Liu, S., Guo, B., Fang, C., Wang, Z., Luo, S., Zhou, Z., & Yu, Z. (2024). Enabling resource-efficient AIoT system with cross-level optimization: A survey. *IEEE Communications Surveys and Tutorials*, *26*(1), 389–427. DOI: 10.1109/comst.2023.3319952

Matin, A., Islam, M. R., Wang, X., Huo, H., & Xu, G. (2023). AIoT for sustainable manufacturing: Overview, challenges, and opportunities. *Internet of Things : Engineering Cyber Physical Human Systems*, *24*, 100901. DOI: 10.1016/j.iot.2023.100901

Mohapatra, H. (2021). Socio-technical challenges in the implementation of smart city. *2021 International Conference on Innovation and Intelligence for Informatics, Computing, and Technologies (3ICT)*, 57-62. https://doi.org/DOI: 10.1109/3ict53449.2021.9581905

Mohapatra, H. (2024). The role of 6G in empowering smart cities enabling ubiquitous connectivity and intelligent infrastructure. *Advances in Civil and Industrial Engineering*, ●●●, 237–264. DOI: 10.4018/979-8-3693-8029-1.ch009

Muhammed, D., Ahvar, E., Ahvar, S., Trocan, M., Montpetit, M., & Ehsani, R. (2024). Artificial intelligence of things (AIoT) for smart agriculture: A review of architectures, technologies and solutions. *Journal of Network and Computer Applications*, *228*, 103905. DOI: 10.1016/j.jnca.2024.103905

Parihar, V., Malik, A., Bhawna, Bhushan, B., & Chaganti, R. (2023). From smart devices to smarter systems: The evolution of artificial intelligence of things (AIoT) with characteristics, architecture, use cases and challenges. *Engineering Cyber-Physical Systems and Critical Infrastructures*, 1-28. https://doi.org/DOI: 10.1007/978-3-031-31952-5_1

Prabha, C., Singh, J., & Rasool, R. (2022). Applications-oriented smart cities based on AIoT emerging technologies. *AIoT Technologies and Applications for Smart Environments*, 37-56. https://doi.org/DOI: 10.1049/pbpc057e_ch3

Salama, A. K., & Abdellatif, M. M. (2022). Aiot-based smart home energy management system. *2022 IEEE Global Conference on Artificial Intelligence and Internet of Things (GCAIoT)*, 177-181. https://doi.org/DOI: 10.1109/gcaiot57150.2022.10019091

Shah, R. U., Verma, J. P., Jain, R., & Garg, S. (2022). AIoT technologies and applications for smart environments. *AIoT Technologies and Applications for Smart Environments*, 199-214. https://doi.org/DOI: 10.1049/pbpc057e_ch11

Swain, B., Raj, P., Singh, K., Singh, Y., Singh, S., & Mohapatra, H. (2025). Ethical implications and mitigation strategies for public safety and security in smart cities for securing tomorrow. *Advances in Information Security, Privacy, and Ethics*, ●●●, 419–436. DOI: 10.4018/979-8-3693-6859-6.ch019

Thakur, R., Panse, P., Bhanarkar, P., & Borkar, P. (2023). AIoT: Role of AI in IoT, applications and future trends. *Research Trends in Artificial Intelligence: Internet of Things*, 42-53. https://doi.org/DOI: 10.2174/9789815136449123010006

Wang, Y., Zhang, B., Ma, J., & Jin, Q. (2023). Artificial intelligence of things (AIoT) data acquisition based on graph neural networks: A systematical review. *Concurrency and Computation*, *35*(23). Advance online publication. DOI: 10.1002/cpe.7827

Yan, J. (2024). AIoT in smart homes: Challenges, strategic solutions, and future directions. *Highlights in Science. Engineering and Technology*, *87*, 59–65. DOI: 10.54097/8hzgaf51

Zhang, J., & Tao, D. (2021). Empowering things with intelligence: A survey of the progress, challenges, and opportunities in artificial intelligence of things. *IEEE Internet of Things Journal*, *8*(10), 7789–7817. DOI: 10.1109/jiot.2020.3039359

Chapter 3
Enhancing Organizational Collaboration Through AI–Driven Decision– Making Systems

Muhammad Usman Tariq
https://orcid.org/0000-0002-7605-3040
Abu Dhabi University, UAE & University College Cork, Ireland

ABSTRACT

Improving organizational cooperation through AI-controlled decision-making systems changes team functioning, communication, and innovation. By integrating artificial intelligence into collaborative processes, companies can analyze huge data records, predict results, and automate everyday technology. It means that teams can focus on creative and strategic tasks. AI tools support clearer communication, faster consensus formation, and more intelligent resource allocation, reducing traditional obstacles across departments and regions. However, for successful integration, attention must be paid to transparency, ethical considerations, and human supervision to ensure trust and equity. Challenges such as algorithm bias and cybersecurity risks exist. However, the possibilities for more agile, more resistant, and innovative teamwork are immeasurable. Because of AI-controlled decision-making systems, businesses can be more efficient and create more sustainable and collaborative environments for the future.

DOI: 10.4018/979-8-3373-2372-5.ch003

INTRODUCTION

AI-controlled decision-making has shifted from the exciting possibilities of a key part of today's e-collaboration. Whether teams are distributed across several cities or continents, AI acts as a quiet and powerful partner, analyzing the vast amount of information, predicting possible outcomes, and supporting human judgment with data-controlled knowledge. Instead of replacing human decisions, AI improves her, offering smarter, faster, and sometimes even more ethical methods than the team can devise. In addition to relying on intuition and scattered data, teams have AI tools that can synthesize complex information in real-time, propose best practices, flag potential risks, and recommend the next best step. This type of expanded decision-making makes today's remote and hybrid teams more efficient than ever. It's about deeper understanding. AI tools can record subtle patterns in which communication styles lead to better project outcomes, what meetings are needed, what time we waste, and which teams work together. Learn and develop a collaboration platform with users through algorithms for machine learning. These systems don't just store information (Chourasia et al., 2024). They interpret it. Imagine a platform where a particular project team will thrive under a particular structure and automatically learn to propose similar structures for future projects. AI is increasingly embedded in project management systems, customer relationship management platforms, and team collaboration apps. It creates passive tools and active participants in the work process. It creates reactive decisions and dynamics that allow forecasting teams to respond to topics and take advantage of opportunities before launching as soon as data trends are displayed. Machine learning provides the ability to "think" beyond what AI explicitly programmed. Through analysis of previous projects, communication flows, market conditions, or internal workflows, machine learning models can recognize inefficiencies and predict and propose improvements that even experienced managers may miss. For example, ML recognizes that the product development cycle is consistent during the testing phase and recommends strategies based on previous successful interventions. It's not just about following deadlines. It learns the nuances of human work (Hamadaqa et al., 2024). This type of learning changes the way an organization configures a team, assigns tasks, and prioritizes projects. IoT devices continuously supply real data streams in AI systems, enriching decision-making.

Think of a multinational company managing field processes in which sensor-equipped machines report real-time performance. Or adapt intelligent meeting rooms that adapt lighting, sound, and air quality to maximize team focus during meetings. These are not futuristic ideas. You'll pass now. AI, ML, and IoT form a symbiotic ecosystem in which real actions provide data in AI systems and interpret this data to inform human teams of better, faster, and more accurate decisions. This feedback loop for learning, adaptation, and optimization has fundamentally changed collaboration in the modern business world. Traditionally, teams were strongly based on hierarchical structures, on which decisions flowed from top to bottom, often limited by the perceptions and experiences of some people. AI-controlled collaboration tools allow everyone on your team to access real-time insights and make decisions more democratic and integrated (Ali et al., 2024). AI will showcase the field by providing each team member with the same high-quality data for their work. Instead of discussing time, teams can focus on interpreting data support recommendations and strategies for the next step. This joint access to knowledge promotes transparency, reduces false communication, and creates more trust within the team. People feel safer knowing decisions are based on rich, carefully analyzed information rather than intestinal emotions. Teams meet frequently because members have different interpretations of success. AI Control Project Management Tools can clearly map goals, pursue progress in real-time, and automatically update all changes or risks. This constant feedback loop helps to coordinate and focus everyone and reduces unnecessary effort and misunderstanding.

Additionally, AI can analyze team and individual performance against organizational goals, giving managers implementationable insights into where necessary support can be improved efficiency and where risks arise (Sabah et al., 2024). This type of visibility is a player for organizational efficiency. Instead of responding to problems, organizations can deal with them with the oldest signs after they become critical, making the entire structure very resilient and more responsive. However, integration of AI into collaboration does not occur without challenges. One of the biggest hurdles is the structure of trust in how it is used, not just in the technology itself. People must trust that AI systems make a fair and impartial recommendation that data protection is protected and autonomy is not compromised (Rezaei et al., 2024). The transparency of the capabilities of the AI model, how decisions are made, and the data used are essential. Organizations seeking to impose AI solutions without clear communication or user buy-in are often resolved or worse. Change management and ongoing education are essential. Not only will teams need to understand how these tools can be used, but they should also understand how to question AI recommendations when necessary and how to maintain critical thinking and technical support. AI systems are as good as FED data. If there is distortion in historical data, AI can accidentally immortalize or even enhance it. Organizations are responsible for examining data, monitoring AI results for fairness, and proactively correcting systematic bias corrections. Emotional AI allows the system to understand human emotions more accurately, providing sensitive and efficient support. Edge AI, which processes data locally instead of sending it to a central server, is faster, safer, and more secure for teams using sensitive data. Blockchain technology can bring unprecedented transparency and trust to multi-party cooperation, allowing participants to pursue data integrity, pursue project contributions, and automate contracts with intelligent contracts without the need for intermediaries. Teams aren't the only tools for collaboration. You become your active team member, provide timely knowledge, label it, and help harmonize your workflow without being asked. AI does not reduce human creativity, innovation, or empathy (Ronak, 2024). Instead, they enhance them by reducing noise, repetitive tasks, and information overload. Virtual design teams use AI to simulate and test product ideas in real-time. Medical research teams share results across the continent in ways that would have been impossible a decade ago. Nonprofit organizations coordinate disaster support efforts to predict care needs requirements and optimize delivery routes. Startups use AI to find global partners, investors, and markets at lightning speeds.

UNDERSTANDING AI-DRIVEN DECISION-MAKING IN COLLABORATION

Artificial Intelligence - Supported decisions quickly become one of the foundations of modern organizational life. People who talk about AI today often imagine self-driving cars and intelligent robots. However, AI's deepest and most immediate effects may occur quietly in meeting rooms, laptops, and virtual collaboration platforms (Alabi et al., 2024). AI-supported decision-making processes use artificial intelligence systems to improve, notify, and sometimes automate decision-making processes. It is important to understand that AI is not a substitute for human decisions in most contexts. It's a partnership with you. Instead of exchanging it, it is to expand human intelligence. An important principle regulates how this cooperation between humans and machines develops. An important principle is that AI should enhance human skills rather than reduce them. Transparency is another important principle. Users need to know when and how AI will affect decisions, which data will be used, and which distortions are available. Accountability remains firmly rooted in the human hands. AI can provide knowledge and recommendations, but ultimately, it must be responsible for decision-making. The third important principle involves continuous learning. AI systems must not be static. You need to learn from feedback, develop based on changes in data patterns, and adapt to new challenges and environments. After all, ethics must lead every step and ensure that AI-supported decisions are fair and integrated, respecting privacy and dignity. Native AI makes DSS systems much more dynamic and capable. One type is the data control DSS. AI can analyze huge data records to reveal patterns and generate knowledge influencing strategic or operational decisions (Ali et al., 2024). For example, in retail, AI-driven DSS can track customer behavior at several touchpoints and recommend marketing strategies and inventory adjustments. Another type is communication-driven DSS. It often focuses on enabling collaboration and information exchange in real-time.

AI can help filter and complete messages, summarise discussions, or recommend follow-up campaigns based on conversations. Model-oriented DSS uses AI to run simulation and predictive models, helping companies test different scenarios and results before performing procedures. These are often used in finance, healthcare, or urban planning. This urban planning is expensive and, of course, uncertain. Knowledge-driven DSS, sometimes called expert systems, uses AI to mimic the decision skills of human experts and provide recommendations based on structured rules or experience. Finally, the Document Control DSS system uses AI to access much-unstructured information, categorizing and analyzing what makes decision-makers easily accessible to important insights hidden in reports, e-mails, contracts, or investigations. All types of DSS uniquely use AI. However, they all aim to adjust the strategic goals of intelligent, faster, and more harmonious organizations. Predictive analytics uses historical data, machine learning, and statistical algorithms to predict future outcomes. In business collaboration, predictive analytics can predict project schedules and determine which customer segments are most likely to respond to campaigns or which supply chain compounds are most susceptible to obstacles (Alabi et al., 2024). This foresight allows teams to actively reactively, plan for unforeseen events, optimize resources, and use opportunities before competitors discover them. In a collaborative environment, secular tasks can be generated, such as sorting e, updating project management boards, generating reports, and planning meetings without human intervention. It encourages human employees to focus on high-quality tasks such as strategic thinking, creative problem-solving, and relationship structures. By spending half the time hunting data, clarifying misconceptions, and firing crises at the last minute, the forecasting system expects needs and potential obstacles, and the automated system runs workflows proactively and smoothly. For example, in marketing teams, predictive analytics shows that certain demographics are increasingly interested in product lines, and intelligent automation tools quickly create targeted social media content creation, allocate ad spend, and plan campaigns without managers being able to monitor every step manually. Similarly, a predictive model for supply chain management may predict an increase in demand for a particular component. However, an automated system automatically adapts and updates logistics partners. It changes the work type and human efforts from tasks to strategic supervision (Artene et al., 2024).

However, companies need to rethink their tools and thinking to integrate these technologies into the decision-making process. Trust is essential. Team members should trust that the predictive model is robust, that automation does not introduce more errors than deletion, and that its role is not diminished but increases. It is where training becomes an essential factor. Not only do employees need to understand how to use AI tools, but they also need to understand how the findings of AI-generated knowledge critically interpret the correct questions and know when to override automated decisions. Otherwise, there is a risk of falling into what some scientists call "auto-strip." The structure of AI alphabetization within the team ensures that the human element remains strong and that people view AI as a partner rather than a black box dictator. When AI systems predict people about employee performance, customer behavior, or health risks, they have a moral responsibility to ensure that they are not used to discriminate or contaminate individuals (Narne et al., 2024). Teams need to develop ethical framework conditions for using knowledge of AI-generated findings in decision-making, particularly in sensitive areas such as settings, advertising campaigns, and customer profiles. Transparency, explanation, and fairness must be incorporated into the DNA of AI-powered collaboration systems. Otherwise, you can compensate for the efficiency and foresight benefits of losses associated with trust, morality, and calling. Context is essential. However, the creative sparks of humans remain irreplaceable. Understanding AI tools' domain-specific strengths and limitations allows businesses to use them carefully and more effectively. Hybrid models, where people are checked and refined by people, are often the best balance of speed, accuracy, and creativity. AI systems better understand not just content but in context. By understanding natural language, AI can interpret more subtle forms of communication, such as irony, humor, and tensionless tension in a collaborative environment. Predictive analysis goes beyond simple outcome predictions for modeling complex and dynamic systems with multiple interaction variables. Intelligent automation once expanded into the realm of subtle or judges (Elhaddad & Hamam, 2024). Customer service, negotiation, and human resource management were considered customer service. Like AI tools, it uses human values, creativity, empathy, and judgment, and how they are used. Successful organizations in this new landscape treat AI as a powerful ally. However, they must clearly understand its limitations and constantly commit to ethical, human-centered decisions. It builds a culture where data and predictions provide information. However, it does not dictate where automation supports but is not marginalized and where collaboration remains a deeply human work. It's about how companies integrate this technology into the culture, workflow, and ethical frameworks. It's about designing a transparent, integrated, and resilient system. It's about making your teams faster and having more foresight, empathy, and creativity to make them better. AI can be incredible partners on this trip, but they are still people who have to decide what future they want to build (Badmus et al., 2024).

AI TECHNOLOGIES ENABLING SMARTER COLLABORATION

Machine learning has become one of the most powerful tools for analyzing and interpreting collaborative organizational data. This is because teams generate much information from e-mail, chat messages, video conferencing, project tactics, and workflow protocols. It is where machine learning shows true strength. In contrast to traditional data analysis methods, machine learning algorithms can learn patterns and relationships within data without being explicitly programmed for every possible scenario. It can reveal hidden trends, recognize anomalies, predict outcomes, and recommend actions based on previous behavior (Bagheri et al., 2024). When applied to data collaboratively, machine learning can demonstrate knowledge about how teams work, where bottlenecks arise, which communication styles are most effective, and how different collaboration tools are used. By analyzing project management software, for example, it is possible to determine that certain types of tasks are typically delayed when, for example, certain types of tasks are held between specific departments and provide managers with opportunities and process efficiency to smooth out early. It can also highlight which team members are central communication centers, helping organizations better understand information flow. For mood analysis, machine learning can assess the emotional tone of team communication and even provide signs of deposition, conflict, and burnout before these issues become visible to human managers (Nguyen & Vo, 2024). Whether this analyzes the productivity of five startups or pursues global intra-company interactions with thousands of employees, machine learning systems can scale accordingly. Continuously learn from new data and improve predictions and interpretations over time. This dynamic capability allows businesses to transition from reactive management relationships to active management bonds. Managers can recognize early indicators and implement data-driven interventions instead of immortality. However, effective use of machine learning requires careful consideration of privacy and ethical issues. Cooperative data often includes sensitive or personal data. Organizations should ensure that data is anonymized when possible and that knowledge is used to strengthen their teams rather than monitoring them improperly or improperly. Transparency in how data is used and the algorithm's capabilities are essential to employee trust employees. When thoughtfully implemented, machine learning can help powerful allies create healthier, more effective, and integrated collaborative environments. Communication has always lived a life of collaboration. From a practical standpoint, this means that AI systems summarise meetings, extract important action elements from e-mails and chat messages, translate conversations in real-time across languages, and recognize the emotional tone and implicit meaning behind words. For example, an NLP-enabled assistant can listen to brainstorming sessions, automatically generate a list of suggested ideas, group them into topics, and send a summary of your design before the meeting ends (Biswas et al., 2024). When someone says, "I'll take care of it until Friday," it recognizes it. It automatically creates task assignments on the due date in the project management system. NLP systems can trigger actions with other software tools by interpreting natural language input. Team members can say or tap. "We plan a follow-up meeting with our design team next week." The NLP system will also take over the preparation of calendar invitations, confirming the availability of participants' proposals for the era, and even creating an agenda based on previous meeting features (Kulkov et al., 2024). This level of seamless interaction dramatically reduces friction between communication and action, allowing teams to move faster and focus more on the work entity than logistics.

Additionally, NLP tools can provide real-time language support for multilingual teams, ensuring that language barriers do not hinder cooperation. Automatic translation, understanding of context-related phrases and cultural references, and adaptation of audience (formal pairs) adaptation are increasingly within reach. However, just like machine learning, you need to work closely together to treat NLP delivery (Elkahlout et al., 2024). The feigning of medical by AI, data protection concerns, and the possibility of distortion of voice models are real challenges. Companies must ensure that NLP tools are continuously refined to maintain human oversight for critical communication and that the system is learned from revisions and feedback. Well done, NLP doesn't just make cooperation easier. It makes technology more integrated, dynamic, and human, allowing people to adapt to how they naturally express themselves rather than adapting to rigid systems. In the meantime, the Internet of Things (IoT) adds a decision process in a collaborative environment, adding another layer of refinement. In a joint context, IoT extends the types and data sources used to discuss decisions. Imagine an intelligent office where sensors monitor meeting room occupancy, temperature, noise levels, and air quality. You can also supply this data to a collaboration platform to optimize meeting planning, suggest the best environment for different tasks, or recommend remote working days if office conditions are not ideal (Ekundayo, 2024). Wearables that pursue health metrics can provide anonymized data to enable businesses to identify patterns related to employee wellness, stress, and productivity, allowing better support systems and interventions. In manufacturing or logistics, IoT devices for devices and programs can be delivered with real-time status updates. It allows teams to work together more effectively by knowing exactly where they are and what conditions they have arrived in. Decisions previously based on incomplete, outdated, or used data are now based on in-depth, real-time knowledge. Teams no longer have to guess whether there is a delay in the remote site. Check live data and adjust your plans immediately (Chenna, 2024).

Project managers don't have to ask how team members use common workspaces. IoT data provides objective insights. Safety decisions can also be improved. For example, a connected helmet or Western could portray a supervisory authority when an employee enters a dangerous area or when the device works outside of a safe parameter. However, IoT integration in joint decisions also leads to new challenges (Michael et al., 2024). Data security is critical, especially concerning sensitive operational or personal information. Organizations must ensure that IoT devices are adequately protected, data flows are encrypted, and access is strictly controlled. The availability of information also poses a risk of data overload. You may not always be useful. Companies often need intelligent systems operated by machine learning and NLP to filter, interpret, and present IoT data in a way that supports decision-makers rather than overwhelming. Employees need to understand the value of networked systems, ensure these technologies support them, and don't ask.

Transparency is essential regarding what data is collected, how it is used, and the benefits it brings to individuals and teams. If IoT-enabled cooperation is done correctly, cooperation can lead to smarter, faster, and more humane decisions (Biswas et al., 2024). Not only will teams be more efficient, but they will also be more recoiling and able to tailor the actual conditions under which the work is being done, such as being more recoil (through better use of resources). Machine learning is a sense of patterns and predicts future outcomes. NLP closes the gap between human language and machine campaigns and supplies more fluids. IoT justifies real-time decision-making processes and concrete data from the physical world. These technologies allow for a new type of organizational intelligence distributed by networks of people, devices, and algorithms, although not limited to personal thoughts and report pages. However, knowledge of the possibilities of these technologies requires more than just providing. It requires intentional design, ethical reflection, interdisciplinary cooperation, and continued dialogue between engineers, managers, front workers, and clients. You build work that will improve human creativity and judgment with the intelligent tools around you and will not reduce. It creates decision processes that are more transparent, more integrated, and responsive to the complexities of the modern world. When agility, empathy, and innovation are more important than ever, NLP and IoT, in a thoughtful integration of machine learning, collaborative environments not only provide better ways to achieve business outcomes but also become a future of richer and more humane work (Chourasia et al., 2024).

AI-Powered Collaboration Platforms

In all industries, real-world case studies show how AI-controlled enterprise CO collaboration systems can change how teams interact, solve problems, and drive innovation. Watson Workspace was developed as an innovative digital workspace and used cognitive computing to help teams work more efficiently. You can prioritize tasks, summarise conversations, suggest the following action, and even recognize the emotions behind team communication. The team discovered that Watson could provide a snapshot of critical updates, significant tasks, and areas that require attention instead of manually creating endless chat protocols or e-mails to understand the project's status. In software development, where projects are highly iterative and involve multiple stakeholders, this ability to determine the most important information in real-time helped teams focus and reduce decision-making (Bagheri et al., 2024). Similarly, Salesforce's Einstein AI offers another case study in which AI is built directly into sales and marketing teams for collaboration. Einstein analyzes customer interactions, suggests next steps, characterizes potential issues, and recommends content that can be used by a particular customer based on historical patterns. In reality, this means that teams can automatically adjust their strategies and spend more time gathering more than basic information without spending time in meetings to pursue their strategies. In Microsoft - Teams, AI automatically generates transcripts, highlighting key moments and filling records by creating action elements (Chenna, 2024). Large global organizations such as multinational banks and consulting companies rely on these characteristics to maintain seamless communication across different times and languages. Although it's a pandemic, these AI traits were useless when remote cooperation became the norm. They have become essential lifelines. They allowed the team to maintain a common understanding of the project, even if the meeting was missing or asynchronous.

In another industry, healthcare collaboration platforms such as Nuances Dragon Medical One use AI to transcribe and understand conversations between physician patients. Physicians can quickly and accurately share notes, knowledge, and patient history across all departments, improving interdisciplinary collaboration and patient outcomes (Samara et al., 2024). These case studies show that AI-controlled collaboration systems are not only faster communication but fundamentally changing the quality, depth, and intelligence of cooperation itself to achieve a degree of cohesion and responsiveness that teams can't do. Tools like Zoom, Slack, Trello, and Asana are integrating AI to support distributed cooperation in increasingly demanding ways. For example, Zoom integrates AI control features such as virtual summary summary, automatic highlight roll, background noise reduction, and real-time language translation. These tools fill essential gaps in remote environments, such as the difficulty of keeping long meetings in mind, managing intercultural communication, and maintaining commitment to virtual meetings. AI-reinforced Slack has helped you prioritize messages, suggest answers, and place users when they haven't answered essential threads. It is essential in remote configurations where communication overload is a real problem. Instead of hoping employees are ultra-high sexological across dozens of channels and notifications, AI acts as an intelligent filter, ensuring that no vital information is lost due to noise.

Similarly, project management tools like Asana and Trello AI are embracing better tasks and project forecasting. Now, you can predict potential project delays based on team activity, tasks, and historical final rates (Ekundayo, 2024). For example, suppose a critical path task remains incomplete for several days. In that case, the system can proactively suggest that it is possible to communicate resources and adapt appointments. Remote teams are very beneficial as they don't always naturally have luxurious informal checks done in physical offices. AI-based assistants maintain a pulse for the project's health, allowing managers and teams to intervene early. Tools like the digital whiteboard platform Milo also include AI-recommending templates for group ideas during brainstorming sessions. These characteristics are particularly valuable in hybrid conferences, with some participants being personal and others being personal. AI ensures that television tasks are not enthusiastic from the discussion and that their contributions are recorded and evaluated simultaneously. The best AI control tools for remote and hybrid teams must not be noticeable. They improve cooperation without taking over the acquisition and provide support in the background rather than forcing users into a strict workflow (Tariq, 2025).

Early tools for cooperation are treated more or less the same, providing a uniform interface, functionality, and workflow. However, AI allows systems to get to know each other over time through individual preferences, work habits, learning styles, and team dynamics, allowing for a documented experience of many tailors of co-operation. For example, AI can observe that certain users prefer to receive project activities through accurate dashboards rather than long reports or that another team member responds better to visual task boards than lists (Gupta & Jaiswal, 2025). Over time, the system subtly adapts how information is presented and alerted to optimize all users' productivity and cognitive style. This personalization will also be extended to a collaborative learning environment. Platforms like Coursera for business and LinkedIn learning are increasingly used for professional development in collaborative environments, using AI to personalize learning paths. Team members working on a collaborative project can recommend courses or microloans that correspond to the immediate skills observed in interaction, such as conflict solution techniques, when discussion tensions are rising or when teams adapt to changes in priorities. It also means adapting to the needs of the team or department. AI can recognize when teams' collaboration styles will shift. It could change from exploring and brainstorming a project to strictly adjusting the execution as deadlines approach and adapting accordingly. For example, the system could suggest opening early-stage ice-breaking exercises and discussion requirements but then prioritize checklist tools, deadline reminders, and optimized approval workflows. AI staff will also improve inclusiveness (Huang & Niyomsilp, 2025). By analyzing patterns, AI can help determine when a particular voice controls the debate but others fail. The system then, to ensure a more balanced cooperation, B. You can suggest interventions such as anonymized ideas and round-robin interview requests. Similarly, AI-powered collaboration technology can adapt to accessibility requirements and provide tailored traits for other people with disabilities, including real-time lessons, screen reader compatibility, voice control, and other disabilities, allowing everyone on the team to contribute perfectly. How much should an AI system show users' preferences and needs without explicit permission? How can an organization ensure that personalization does not increase bias or exclude alternative work methods incorrectly? Future developers and organizations will address these issues by increasing transparency, allowing users to control their data, and allowing individuals to choose adaptive characteristics. When personalization is treated thoughtfully, it does not imply a beneficial fit. It means enhancing diversity and allowing people to work together naturally and effectively. We respect that two users or teams are not the same and that collaborations are recognized and supported in total and not smoothly. They allow us to collaborate in a way that was unimaginable ten years ago, to the limits of time, space, culture, language, and even skills. They create a space where creativity, empathy, and strategic thinking can be improved through intelligent systems that deal with everyday life tailored to meaningful human needs. However, knowing this possibility does not only mean buying the latest tools. It requires cultural change, openness, continuous learning, ethical responsibility, and a deep commitment to human-centered design. Organizations that embrace these principles not only record profits in terms of efficiency and innovation. Cooperation is not a struggle. It is a joy. It builds work that not only acts as a barrier but as a bridge between people's best ideas, skills, and efforts.

INTEGRATING GENERATIVE AI FOR DECISION-MAKING

AI supports brainstorming, and content generation fundamentally alters the dynamics of organizational cooperation, leading to new modes of collective creativity. Traditionally, brainstorming sessions were put together, teams were put together in a common physical space, and ideas were captured based on free verbal exchanges and handwritten notes or whiteboards. Now, AI offers a whole new layer of support. Tools like Chatt, Jasper, and other AI content generators can be integrated into a collaborative platform and act as invisible team members. These systems can quickly create ideas lists based on input requests, propose alternative perspectives, and identify gaps in thought that could lead to human participants missing. For example, suppose your marketing team is trying to develop a slogan for a new campaign. In that case, AI can quickly create hundreds of potential options based on brand values, target demographics, and emotional tone (Hao et al., 2024). Human employees can then search for these options and search in ways that remix and refine them to accelerate the creative process dramatically. Besides volume alone, AI can bring unexpected angles to brainstorming surfaces, such as metaphors, cultural references, or knowledge of niche markets that may not spontaneously produce human teams limited by their own experiences or biases. This dynamic leads to a richer and vaster session of generating ideas that teams don't have to start from the empty side, and they can skip faster and higher. In collaboration with co-authoring projects, the creation of reports, marketing materials, technical documentation, or academic AI tools can act as co-authors, provide designs, and clarify passage descriptions, adaptations of tones for different target groups, and even cited sources. Instead of replacing human creativity, these tools often enhance them. For example, product development teams can perform product descriptions in brainstorming, improve AI for various customers, and summarise the results (Neiroukh et al., 2024). The editorial team generates several versions of the article. It allows you to select the structure or language best suits your goal. The net effect is the democratization of content creation. Those who may not consider themselves "good writers" can be proactive because they know that there are intelligent systems that turn ideas into consistent, professional expressions (Tariq, 2025).

For multilingual teams, AI-generated translations remove barriers to communication and make content easier to create across the region. It significantly impacts global organizations that harmonize brand voices and enable local coordination simultaneously (Neiroukh et al., 2024). With all these types, AI changes from passive tools to active employees, not just what the team creates but how they create. Generation AI can simulate several scenarios, propose models, predict results, propose strategies, and provide experimental sandboxes without the high cost or time investments traditionally required. Take Product Design: Teams can enter parameters and propose hundreds of design retellings that allow human experts to evaluate feasibility, aesthetics, and market adjustments. In business strategies, the AI competitive landscape can analyze market entries, simulate market entries, and propose alternative business models based on developing consumer behavior. You must not get bored of AI, be emotionally tied to ideas, or suffer from groupthink (Elhaddah and Hamam, 2024). Even if human energy and creativity decrease, they propose new angles and require assumptions. It makes AI a powerful partner in combating complex, multidimensional problems that traditional brainstorming is fast but can lead to tough solutions (Kumar, 2024). Generation AI can propose new research paths in scientific discovery, provide new coding solutions for software development, and consider alternative strategies for commitment in the community of social enterprises. For example, the health innovation team can be used to acquire interventions for inactive population groups as dozens of service models are rapidly generated based on demographic, geographical, and economic data. Instead of working one after another and testing ideas, teams can look into large solutions simultaneously (Artene et al., 2024). It is not only because it accelerates decision-making but also because it accelerates learning and because teams can quickly see what works and what doesn't. In this context, the isolated moments of genius are less than the structure of rich, repetitive dialogue between human intuition and mechanical exploration.

In organizations with evil problems, poorly defined, unstable, and interconnected organizations provide a scaffolding where human teams can maintain their flexibility and imagination without being overwhelmed (Revathy et al., 2024). Generation AI can propose new research paths in scientific discovery, provide new coding solutions for software development, and consider alternative strategies for commitment in the community of social enterprises. For example, the health innovation team can be used to acquire interventions for inactive population groups as dozens of service models are rapidly generated based on demographic, geographical, and economic data. Instead of working one after another and testing ideas, teams can look into large solutions simultaneously. It is not only because it accelerates decision-making learning, and teams can quickly see what works and what doesn't. In this context, creativity is not about the isolated moments of genius but about creating rich, repetitive dialogues between human intuition and mechanical quests. The main issue is distortions that AI can embed in recommendations for generated configurations. AI models learn from huge data records from the Internet and other sources of human knowledge. These sources include implicit bias such as gender, breed, culture, socioeconomic status, or other dimensions (Soori et al., 2024). If AI proposes ideas, content, or solutions, this could incorrectly increase stereotypes or alienate certain votes. For example, if the AI -BrainStorming -Tool marketing campaign generates ideas, this indicates disproportionate imagery and the dominant culture of messaging while simultaneously overlooking the prospects of minorities. If these biases are not controlled, the organization can perform its operations, leading to ethical mistakes, reputational risks, and market marginalization. Organizations may rely on AI editions if machine recommendations must be objective or correct (Badmus et al., 2024). AI costs only as good as the data and models behind it. Without critical human evaluations, teams, strategies, or stories risk being false, exclusive, or ineffective. It is especially dangerous in sensitive areas such as healthcare, education, and public order. Biased or contextualized recommendations can cause actual damage. Together, the ethical use of AI requires organizations to maintain a strong human supervision mechanism and ensure that AI proposals are interrogated and supplemented by various human perspectives.

Clarity is another essential ethics column. Teams need to know how humans interact with AI-generated content compared to human-generated ideas. Hidden AI support can undermine trust, mainly if stakeholders later determine that a key strategic decision, creative work, or initiative for commitment in the community is influenced by machines rather than humans (Kaggwa et al., 2024). Clear labeling, open discussion about how AI tools are used, and inclusion of AI ethics training in organizational learning programs are all steps to foster transparency. Additionally, teams must be allowed to challenge or reject AI recommendations without stigma, reinforcing that AI is an employee, not a dictator, and is an employee in a creative process. If AI generates content or ideas, who belongs? Do team members contribute to the AI that is valued? Should intellectual property guidelines be updated to reflect the mixing nature of human and machine cooperation? These questions are not only academic but have a significant impact on employee morality, legal compliance, and the integrity of the creative industry. Some organizations either experiment with great AI systems as co-creators or recognize their role in project documentation. Others access IP frameworks to ensure that human employees retain the ultimate wealth and control their work, even if AI plays a key role in the creation process. If the machine can create poetry, create logos for designs, propose business models, and create new brainstorming products, what remains about creativity? The powerful answer is that human creativity isn't merely creating output. It concerns meaning, emotional responses, ethical judgments, and cultural management (Joseph et al., 2024). AI helps to create opportunities, but the people interpret them, choose, give them intentionally, and bring them back to life in a way. Therefore, collaboration with AI can expand human creative potential, rather than reduce it, if implemented ethically and thoughtfully. It frees you from repeating tasks, inciting new connections, challenging blind spots, or imagining that you didn't present yourself. To maximize AI's potential, companies excited and paying attention must contact opportunities to improve cooperation and remain vigilant to remain at the bias, transparency, property, and irreplaceable value of human insight. AI is a powerful partner but must lead to human values, critical thinking, commitment to inclusion, and responsibility (Frimpong & Wolfs, 2024). If an organization manages this balance well, it can create a collaborative environment in which the human imagination and the finest mechanical intelligence are not in competition but harmoniously to solve today's problems and invent the possibilities of tomorrow.

AI And IoT IN SMART WORKPLACE COLLABORATION

The Internet of Things (IoT) has become a transformative force that enables real-time collaboration across industries, employment, and even remote teams in various world regions. Traditional collaboration ideas were once intended to meet faces, rely on planned calls, or often sway e-mails with delayed or fragmented communication. Thanks to IoT, collaboration is no longer limited by geography or time. With millions of connected, seamlessly communicating devices, teams can quickly access collaborative information, monitor project progress in real-time, and interact with digital systems that continuously provide the latest data. For example, sensors embedded in the manufacturing floor can provide live production updates to teams beyond their capabilities. Engineers, operating managers, and sales teams can adjust direct measurements when production issues arise. Intelligent badges and wearables can indicate employee location or security status. It can be essential in dangerous environments when managing team tasks under urgent conditions. A collaboration platform powered by IoT technology allows for integrated environmental management, including language, video and document approval, live analytics, environmental management, and even room temperature adaptation (Yi & Ayangbah, 2024). environments are equipped with many IoT devices and sensors sent directly to the AI platform to optimize the meeting experience physically or effectively before, during, and after participants. For example, intelligent cameras in these rooms can automatically focus on the person who speaks, ensuring that the TV channel feels more committed and involved. The cleverly embedded microphone captures crystal clear audio on the table and ceiling so that AI's real-time transcription service can easily document discussions. Often integrated into these intelligent meeting setups, virtual assistants have the best time for meeting planning based on participant availability, memory, a summary of action points after the meeting, and even the best time for follow-up based on participant work patterns.

Additionally, AI Systems can analyze participants' previous meetings and calendars to predict agenda articles and ensure that meetings are concentrated and productive. Automating these daily yet essential aspects of meetings involves an AI-controlled, intelligent environment focusing on strategy, creativity, and problem-solving rather than problem-solving tasks. This integration of IoT and AI creates connected spaces that continually optimize the environment to predict human needs, learn from behavior, and support deeper and more meaningful collaboration (Frimpong and Wolf, 2024). IoT-enabled workflow automation means that processes can be automatically triggered and managed based on data collected by interconnected devices. In an office environment, this is as simple as determining the occupancy sensor that the meeting room is empty, automatically updating the availability status of the room, saving time for employees looking for available rooms. IoT sensors monitor inventory in real-time in more complex scenarios such as supply chain management, automatically reorganize supply when thresholds are reached, and procurement teams provide information about status updates without manual intervention. In the healthcare sector, medical devices in the IOT network can continuously monitor the key functions of patients and draw attention to care teams as soon as deviations from a safe community are determined, leading to faster interventions and more coordinated answers between doctors, nurses, and professionals. For example, in large corporate offices, AI can monitor anonymized drawing data by employees switching between different floors and common areas and propose opportunities for reorganizing rooms to improve cooperation and reduce congestion. Bonded to the occupancy sensor, the innovative HLK system can automatically set up heating, cooling, and lighting, reducing energy costs and improving comfort when needed. When workflows are optimized by these intelligent, fast-responsive, fast-speed systems, employee productivity is not only because tasks are automated but because employees can focus their energy on higher quality, creative, and strategic activities than secular management (Tariq, 2025).

IoT plays an even more critical role in distant and hybrid work environments where cooperation can be introduced across distances across friction. On devices connected to IoT, distributed teams remain synchronized with joint access to real-time data. In a global project management scenario, teams from different time zones can interact with live dashboards that update as soon as the task is completed. Milestones are achieved or identified. IoT-connected whiteboards allow brainstorming sessions in various countries with drawings, notes, and mental cards that occur in all participants (Gupta and Jaiswal, 2025). The intelligent conferencing system can automatically adjust audio settings to ensure optimal communication quality for all, based on the number of participants registered in the meeting. For example, AI systems that analyze IoT-collected data can also recognize collaboration trends to determine whether a particular team is overloaded. However, other teams are insufficient, and they recommend exposing management strategies. An intelligent desk and chair with IoT sensors can monitor attitudes and suggest adjustments to avoid repeated voltage damage. Environmental sensors can monitor air quality, noise levels, and lighting conditions and automatically optimize them for maximum concentration and comfort. Portable devices can promote movement disruptions to pursue employee physical activity and avoid sedentary work patterns. AI systems that analyze these wellness data can identify trends that affect productivity, such as B. It suggests a correlation between low focus levels and low focus levels and interventions at the tissue level. By integrating wellness data into key figures, businesses can create a humanitarian and supportive environment that improves performance and long-term commitment and satisfaction of their employees (Hai et al., 2024). Apart from the sole calendar memory and management setting, the Advanced Virtual Assistant can act as a knowledge repository and quickly raise relevant documents, previous meeting notes, or project stories during discussion. It can recommend collaborators based on skills and availability, enable real language translation at multinational conferences, and suggest workflows for complex projects based on best practices. Over time, some virtual assistants can now learn about team preferences. For example, specific teams prefer shorter discussions, or certain people are remarkably productive at certain times of the day and adapt to planning and communication accordingly. This personalization leads to a more fluid and intrusive collaboration experience where logistics friction is minimized, and teams can function more naturally than forcedly. For example, the expected expectations of office devices mean that, for example, a printer, copier, or network server could potentially cause a collaborative project to derail. Virtual replicas of digital twins across physical assets or workplaces are always common in production and urban planning industries, allowing teams to simulate changes, optimize layouts, or test strategies together in a virtual environment before implementation (Huang and Niyimsilp, 2025).

Security, Privacy, and Trust in AI Collaboration Systems

Beçause AI-controlled collaboration platforms are involved in the structure of modern organizational life, fighting cybersecurity risks has proven to be an essential priority. Organizations today rely heavily on AI tools to automate decision-making, optimize workflows, and improve communication among geographically distributed teams. However, this increasing reliance on networking and AI exponentially expands the attack area of cyber threats. Collaborative equipment, AI-operated decision-making engines, and underlying data infrastructure are now the main goals of cybercriminals seeking to use their weaknesses for financial interests, espionage, sabotage, or ideological reasons. Threat players can try to provide malicious data to machine learning models. It is a tactic called data addiction that can disrupt distorted decisions and operations that favor competitors or cause reputational damage (Joseph et al., 2024).

Furthermore, controversial attacks to disrupt AI systems can lead to false analyses or recommendations by modifying input data. Teams are no longer confined to a single corporate network. All new devices or endpoints connected to the collaboration system are possible entry points for cyber attackers. Inadequate endpoint security, password hygiene, and unsecured Wi-Fi connections increase risk when sensitive AI control cooperation is carried out outside traditional office walls. Businesses must apply a proactive, layered security approach to mitigate these risks. It includes providing robust encryption of data in idle and in transit, enforcing strict multifactorial authentication protocols, implementing regular security audits from collaboration platforms, and implementing real-time surveillance systems that can recognize rapid action (Kulkov et al., 2024). Collaboration naturally involves exchanging information, ideas, designs, and delicate project details. Data collection volume, granularity, and persistence dramatically increase when AI enters the image. Interactions, keyboard attacks, document processing, and communication can be registered, analyzed, and saved unlimitedly for model training and optimization. Without strict protection measures, the potential for sensitive data load increases, raising serious concerns about addressing personal data, proprietary business data, and intellectual property in these AI ecosystems. Conditions of regulatory frameworks such as the European General Data Protection Ordinance (GDPR), the US California Consumer Privacy Act (CCPA), and the emerging data protection laws worldwide require clear guidelines for minimization, approval, access control, and user rights of information-related data. In AI-driven decision-making platforms,

achieving compliance with these regulations requires training AI models to prioritize anonymized or pseudonymized data, systems must provide transparency to
users to record data used, and those with access to the ITR platform must provide
transparency to users. Instead of aggregating all the data on a central server for AI
training, models with retro-style learning can be trained locally on user devices
(Shamim, 2024). Only the trained model parameters (not raw data) are attributable
to the central server . This approach reduces the risk of discovering sensitive data
during collaboration and learning, simultaneously improving AI models. However, the
teachings of the federation must be secured against reverse engineering attacks that
could reconstruct private data from model updates. Another method is to maintain
the privacy of the algorithm's data records by adding levels of statistical noise and
ensuring that individual contributions cannot be isolated or identified.

Trust and transparency are pillars based on effective organizational cooperation,
and the rise in decisions generated in AI leads to deep challenges and opportunities
for these fundamental elements. In contrast to human decisions that can be opened,
challenged, and discussed, decisions are often generated from AI-generated opaque
algorithms. This "black box" phenomenon can rely on employees and managers who
must rely on AI knowledge to collaborate, make critical business decisions, and rely
on AI knowledge to propagate skepticism, mistrust, and resistance (Kumar, 2024).
Companies must prioritize developing and using explainable AI systems (XAI) to
maintain trust. Explanatory AI aims to make the AI model more transparent and
provide clear, human-readable explanations of how specific recommendations,
predictions, or decisions were made. If an AI system can clarify logic highlighting
the essential data inputs, the trust level associated with the weighting and output
of various factors is more likely to trust and include AI control cooperation. Transparency goes beyond technical explanation. It also includes a broader ecosystem of
ethical AI clauses. Organizations must proactively address AI systems' limitations
and recognize that these tools support human decisions and serve the absolute judgment of truth. Transparency also means disclosing potential distortions embedded
in AI models. Suppose the team assignment recommendation engine is trained with
historical company data that reflects past inequality, such as gender disability and
preferences. The terms of ethical guidelines and governance frameworks must be
determined to collaborate and monitor AI use. It includes regular employee bias and
independent investigations of channels to challenge recommendations or appeals
where necessary. AI should be positioned not as an alternative but as employees
who enhance human judgment. Managers need to develop a culture where critical
thinking is encouraged, even when dealing with AI (Michael et al., 2024).

It creates a noble cycle where trust is strengthened, as employees feel more
competent and respected than surveillance and exchange. Participants should make
meaningful decisions about the autonomy they will deduct in AI tools. Some team

members may prefer stronger AI participation in automating routine tasks. However, they want to remain fully in control of strategic decisions. Providing opt-in/opt-out mechanisms for various scenarios for providing configurable configurations and collaboration to the level of AI support is a separate institution and promotes deeper trust. Furthermore, there is transparency in how data perspectives are shared, whether recommendations should be categorized as specific managers across the team and clear acquaintances, or whether participants should be blinded or released without consent. An easy-to-understand AI alphabetization program that includes concepts such as machine learning, data protection, model distortion, and algorithm accountability will enable employees at all levels to safely engage in AI-driven collaboration tools. When people understand AI skills and limitations, they trust their contributions, work more effectively through human-machine teams, and participate in their work skills' design and ethical development. Organizations that prioritize these principles in implementing and governance AI technology protect themselves from risk and create an environment where cooperation can thrive intellectually, securely, and ethically. The future of cooperation with AI running will be as strong as the trust and responsibility built into the systems we build today (Nguent and Vo, 2024).

Future Trends in AI-Powered Decision-Making and Collaboration

As teams interact, meet, share, and make decisions, they revolutionize promising technology in organizational communication with AI-supported organizational communication. Tools run by AI, such as Intelligent Chatbots, real language translation for mood analysis, and engine translation, help communicate faster, clearer, and more integrated. AI can now monitor communication patterns to identify potential misconceptions and gaps in the work and provide suggestions to improve clarity and team dynamics. Improved by AI, virtual collaboration rooms can work seamlessly as if remote and hybrid teams were in the same space, promoting higher commitment and productivity. The immutable ledger from the blockchain ensures that data shared among employees withstands reliable operations and operations. At the same time, IoT devices provide real-time checkable data flows. AI analyzes this data to help you make quick and relevant information decisions. These technologies allow participants to build an ecosystem where measures can be understood and decisions can be checked, allowing them to cooperate without blind trust. In contrast to today's tight AI systems, AGI understands, reasons, and learns like people from all walks of life, so they coordinate complex projects with human teams, predict challenges, innovate solutions, and create intelligent partnerships.

CONCLUSION

Integrating AI into the decision process to improve collaboration begins with determining clear goals and ethical guidelines. Organizations need to ensure that AI tools are transparent, explainable, and match the values of human teams. One best practice is included in designing and delivering AI systems, providing ongoing training for employees, and creating feedback loops where people can check and refine AI output. When AI is introduced as a support partner rather than an alternative, cooperation will be more intuitive, productive, and innovative. The main challenge is embedding distortions into algorithms that can unintentionally increase inequality or bad decisions. Furthermore, the overcontrol of AI may have missed trust issues and context-related nuances without human supervision. On the other hand, opportunities can provide a large AI that can reduce silos, improve cross-functional teamwork, perform daily tasks, and enable human employees to focus on strategic and creative work. Successfully navigating these challenges requires a careful balance of automation and human judgment. Organizations need to view AI as an active part of the ecosystem of cooperation and develop with a deep commitment to feedback, innovation, and ethical use.

REFERENCES

Alabi, K. O., Adedeji, A. A., Mahmuda, S., & Fowomo, S. (2024). Predictive Analytics in HR: Leveraging AI for Data-Driven Decision Making. *International Journal of Research in Engineering. Science and Management, 7*(4), 137–143.

Ali, M., Khan, T. I., & Khattak, M. N., & ŞENER, İ. (2024). Synergizing AI and business: Maximizing innovation, creativity, decision precision, and operational efficiency in high-tech enterprises. *Journal of Open Innovation, 10*(3), 100352.

Artene, A. E., Domil, A. E., & Ivascu, L. (2024). Unlocking Business Value: Integrating AI-Driven Decision-Making in Financial Reporting Systems. *Electronics (2079-9292), 13*(15).

Badmus, O., Rajput, S. A., Arogundade, J. B., & Williams, M. (2024). AI-driven business analytics and decision making. *World Journal of Advanced Research and Reviews, 24*(1), 616–633.

Bagheri, M., Bagheritaba, M., Alizadeh, S., Parizi, M. S., Matoufinia, P., & Luo, Y. (2024). AI-driven decision-making in healthcare information systems: a comprehensive review. *Preprints.*

Biswas, T. R., Hossain, M. Z., & Comite, U. (2024). Role of Management Information Systems in Enhancing Decision-Making in Large-Scale Organizations. *Pacific Journal of Business Innovation and Strategy, 1*(1), 5–18.

Chenna, K. (2024). Optimizing decision-making in supply chains: A framework for AI and human collaboration using SAP technologies. [IJRCAIT]. *International Journal of Research in Computer Applications and Information Technology, 7*(2), 824–835.

Chourasia, S., Dhama, A., & Bhardwaj, G. (2024, May). AI-Driven Organizational Culture Evolution: A Critical Review. In *2024 International Conference on Communication, Computer Sciences and Engineering (IC3SE)* (pp. 1839-1844). IEEE.

Ekundayo, F. (2024). Leveraging AI-Driven Decision Intelligence for Complex Systems Engineering. *Int J Res Publ Rev, 5*(11), 1–10.

Elhaddad, M., & Hamam, S. (2024). AI-driven clinical decision support systems: An ongoing pursuit of potential. *Cureus, 16*(4).

Elkahlout, M., Karaja, M. B., Elsharif, A. A., Dheir, I. M., Abunasser, B. S., & Abu-Naser, S. S. (2024). AI-Driven Organizational Change: Transforming Structures and Processes in the Modern Workplace.

Frimpong, V., & Wolfs, B. (2024). Predictive effect of AI on leadership: Insights from public case studies on organizational dynamics. *International Journal of Business Administration*, *15*(3), 10–5430.

Gupta, S., & Jaiswal, R. (2025). A deep learning-based hybrid PLS-SEM-ANN approach for predicting factors improving AI-driven decision-making proficiency for future leaders. *Journal of International Education in Business*.

Hamadaqa, M. H. M., Alnajjar, M., Ayyad, M. N., Al-Nakhal, M. A., Abunasser, B. S., & Abu-Naser, S. S. (2024). Leveraging Artificial Intelligence for Strategic Business Decision-Making: Opportunities and Challenges.

Hao, X., Demir, E., & Eyers, D. (2024). Exploring collaborative decision-making: A quasi-experimental study of human and Generative AI interaction. *Technology in Society*, *78*, 102662.

Huang, B., & Niyomsilp, E. (2025). The impact of artificial intelligence on organizational decision-making processes. *Edelweiss Applied Science and Technology*, *9*(4), 794–808.

Joseph, S., Kolade, T. M., Obioha Val, O., Adebiyi, O. O., Ogungbemi, O. S., & Olaniyi, O. O. (2024). AI-powered information governance: Balancing automation and human oversight for optimal organization productivity. *Asian Journal of Research in Computer Science*, *17*(10), 10–9734.

Kaggwa, S., Eleogu, T. F., Okonkwo, F., Farayola, O. A., Uwaoma, P. U., & Akinoso, A. (2024). AI in decision making: Transforming business strategies. *International Journal of Research and Scientific Innovation*, *10*(12), 423–444.

Kulkov, I., Kulkova, J., Rohrbeck, R., Menvielle, L., Kaartemo, V., & Makkonen, H. (2024). Artificial intelligence-driven sustainable development: Examining organizational, technical, and processing approaches to achieving global goals. *Sustainable Development*, *32*(3), 2253–2267.

Kumar, D. (2024). Ai-driven automation in administrative processes: Enhancing efficiency and accuracy. *International Journal of Engineering Science and Humanities*, *14*(1), 256–265.

Michael, C. I., Ipede, O. J., Adejumo, A. D., Adenekan, I. O., Adebayo, D., Ojo, A. S., & Ayodele, P. A. (2024). Data-driven decision making in IT: Leveraging AI and data science for business intelligence. *World Journal of Advanced Research and Reviews*, *23*(1), 472–480.

Narne, S., Adedoja, T., Mohan, M., & Ayyalasomayajula, T. (2024). AI-Driven Decision Support Systems in Management: Enhancing Strategic Planning and Execution. *International Journal on Recent and Innovation Trends in Computing and Communication*, *12*(1), 268–276.

Neiroukh, S., Aljuhmani, H. Y., & Alnajdawi, S. (2024, January). In the era of emerging technologies: discovering the impact of artificial intelligence capabilities on timely decision-making and business performance. In *2024 ASU International Conference in Emerging Technologies for Sustainability and Intelligent Systems (ICETSIS)* (pp. 1-6). IEEE.

Neiroukh, S., Emeagwali, O. L., & Aljuhmani, H. Y. (2024). Artificial intelligence capability and organizational performance: Unraveling the mediating mechanisms of decision-making processes. *Management Decision*.

Nguyen, T. V., & Vo, N. (Eds.). (2024). *Using traditional design methods to enhance AI-driven decision making*. IGI Global.

Revathy, S., Sreekala, S. P., Praveenadevi, D., & Rajeshwari, S. (2024). The intelligent implications of artificial intelligence-driven decision-making in business management. In *Toward Artificial General Intelligence: Deep Learning, Neural Networks, Generative AI* (pp. 251-268). De Gruyter.

Rezaei, M., Pironti, M., & Quaglia, R. (2024). AI in knowledge sharing, which ethical challenges are raised in decision-making processes for organisations? *Management Decision*.

Ronak, B. (2024). AI-Driven Project Management Revolutionizing Workflow Optimization and Decision-Making. *International Journal of Trend in Scientific Research and Development*, *8*(6), 325–338.

Sabah, A. S., Hamouda, A. A., Helles, Y. E., Okasha, S. M., Abu-Nasser, B. S., & Abu-Naser, S. S. (2024). Artificial Intelligence and Organizational Evolution: Reshaping Workflows in the Modern Era.

Samara, F. Y. A., Taha, A. H. A., Massa, N. M., Jamie, T. N. A., Harara, F. E., Abu-Nasser, B. S., & Abu-Naser, S. S. (2024). The Role of AI in Enhancing Business Decision-Making: Innovations and Implications.

Shamim, M. M. I. (2024). Artificial Intelligence in project management: Enhancing efficiency and decision-making. *International Journal of Management Information Systems and Data Science*, *1*(1), 1–6.

Soori, M., Jough, F. K. G., Dastres, R., & Arezoo, B. (2024). AI-based decision support systems in Industry 4.0, A review. *Journal of Economy and Technology*.

Tariq, M. U. (2025). AI-Driven Innovations: Transforming Healthcare, Agriculture, and Environmental Science. In Emara, T., Hassan, E., Trinh, T., Li, G., & Saber, A. (Eds.), *The Role of Artificial Intelligence in Advancing Applied Life Sciences* (pp. 87–118). IGI Global Scientific Publishing., DOI: 10.4018/979-8-3693-9208-9.ch003

Tariq, M. U. (2025). Leveraging Data Analytics for Predictive Consumer Behavior Modelling. In Miguélez-Juan, B., & Rebollo-Bueno, S. (Eds.), *AI Impacts on Branded Entertainment and Advertising* (pp. 207–224). IGI Global Scientific Publishing., DOI: 10.4018/979-8-3693-3799-8.ch011

Tariq, M. U. (2025). Innovative Mentoring Programs: Strategies for Success in Post-COVID-19 Education. In Putnam, J., VanValkenburgh Banks, J., & Brown, S. K. (Eds.), *Mentoring Students and Instructors for Retention and Success* (pp. 123–158). IGI Global Scientific Publishing., DOI: 10.4018/979-8-3693-7590-7.ch005

Tariq, M. U. (2025). Co-Living With Augmented Digital Beings-Navigating the Intersection of AI and Everyday Life. In Moutinho, L., & Martins, L. (Eds.), *Impacts of Sensetech on Society* (pp. 187–206). IGI Global Scientific Publishing., DOI: 10.4018/979-8-3693-7147-3.ch009

Yi, Z., & Ayangbah, S. (2024). The impact of ai innovation management on organizational productivity and economic growth: An analytical study. *International Journal of Business Management and Economic Research*, 7(1), 1–15.

KEY TERMS AND DEFINITIONS:

AI-Driven Decision-Making: Using artificial intelligence to guide organizational choices competently

Collaborative Intelligence: Humans and AI working together for better results.

Intelligent Workflow Automation: Restructuring tasks with AI to boost collaboration.

Chapter 4
Security, Privacy, and Ethical Considerations in AI–Powered Academic Collaboration

Mustafa Kayyali

https://orcid.org/0000-0003-3300-262X

Maaref University of Applied Sciences, Syria

ABSTRACT

As AI-driven platforms reshape how scholars collaborate, new ethical, security, and privacy concerns have come to the forefront. This chapter explores the complex terrain of AI-powered academic collaboration, where the promise of efficiency and connectivity often coexists with heightened risks of data misuse, surveillance, and opaque decision-making. Drawing from current case studies and theoretical frameworks, we examine how personal data, intellectual property, and academic freedom are being redefined in this new landscape. Particular attention is given to how algorithmic bias and ethical blind spots may undermine equity and trust within global academic networks. We also explore institutional responsibilities and the emerging frameworks guiding the responsible use of AI in higher education. Ultimately, this chapter advocates for a careful, values-driven approach to technological integration—one that champions transparency, inclusivity, and the safeguarding of academic integrity in an era of unprecedented digital interdependence.

DOI: 10.4018/979-8-3373-2372-5.ch004

INTRODUCTION

In the past decade, the landscape of academic collaboration has undergone a radical transformation. What was once constrained by geography, institutional silos, and sluggish communication channels has evolved into a vibrant, hyperconnected ecosystem—fueled by cloud computing, social knowledge platforms, and most recently, artificial intelligence. AI-powered tools now promise not only to streamline research and accelerate scholarly exchange but also to augment human capabilities in unimaginable ways: automating literature reviews, predicting citations, identifying potential collaborators across the globe, and even co-authoring preliminary drafts.

Yet, as with any powerful tool, the rise of AI in academic environments introduces a new set of dilemmas—subtle, complex, and often overlooked in the excitement of technological advancement. The optimism that accompanies AI's potential is shadowed by a growing unease around privacy erosion, data commodification, opaque algorithms, and ethical accountability (Puplampu, 2024). Where do we draw the line between beneficial automation and the abdication of human judgment? How do we ensure that the very technologies designed to democratize knowledge do not, in fact, entrench new inequalities or compromise academic freedom?

Unlike traditional academic networks, AI-enhanced collaboration platforms operate on vast datasets—many of which include sensitive information such as unpublished research, personal communications, or metadata that can be used to profile scholars and institutions (Hutson, 2024). The notion of privacy, once anchored in physical spaces and institutional policy, is now increasingly abstract and fragile. Meanwhile, cybersecurity risks are no longer limited to system intrusions or phishing scams; they extend into the very architecture of AI models trained on potentially vulnerable data, posing threats to intellectual property, reputational safety, and even national research agendas.

The ethical questions are equally thorny. Is it ethical to use AI to analyze a collaborator's academic performance to determine partnership value? Should AI-generated insights be credited in multi-authored publications? Can algorithms trained on Western-centric data be trusted to support truly global academic collaboration? And, perhaps most provocatively, what becomes of academic integrity in a world where machine-authored content can be indistinguishable from human scholarship? This chapter does not claim to have all the answers. Instead, it attempts to map the contours of a rapidly evolving space—where innovation, trust, and responsibility must coexist (Zia, 2025). We begin by charting the ascent of AI in academic collaboration and the structural shifts it has ushered in.

We then examine the intricate security and privacy challenges embedded in these technologies, followed by a discussion of the ethical dilemmas that demand urgent academic and policy attention. Finally, we reflect on frameworks for responsible innovation and offer a set of guiding principles to help institutions, scholars, and developers foster a future where AI strengthens—not weakens—the values of higher education. This is not merely a technical issue, nor a passing phase in digital transformation. It is a philosophical, cultural, and moral reckoning with the tools we are rapidly embracing—tools that shape not just how we collaborate, but how we think, teach, and imagine the future of knowledge itself.

THE RISE OF AI IN ACADEMIC COLLABORATION: PROMISE AND PERIL

There's a certain hum to academic life—a rhythm of reading, writing, sharing, doubting, editing, rewriting, discovering. For generations, this cadence played out in libraries, at conferences, through letters, emails, seminars, the scribbled notes passed during lectures, the unfiltered brainstorms over cheap coffee. It was messy. Imperfect. Slow, even. But somehow, gloriously human. And then came artificial intelligence.

At first, it tiptoed in—automated citation tools, basic grammar checkers, plagiarism detectors that scanned for familiarity in a sea of originality. These were helpful, albeit unremarkable. But something shifted in the last five years. AI stopped being a tool that quietly supported academic labor and started to become a presence—active, visible, embedded (Preston, 2022). It began offering recommendations for reading, generating research questions, synthesizing articles, co-authoring drafts, and even proposing collaborators based on patterns too complex for the human mind to intuit unaided.

The result? A new paradigm for academic collaboration—faster, broader, more interconnected than anything imagined even a decade ago (Bryda & Costa, 2023). Research no longer needs to be confined to colleagues in the same building or even the same continent. Platforms infused with machine learning can now pair a sociologist in Nairobi with a data scientist in Helsinki, based not on shared institutional ties but on latent thematic commonalities in their work. Real-time translation tools dissolve language barriers, turning a once-fragmented global academy into a cohesive, if still uneven, digital agora.

Figure 1. AI in Academic Collaboration

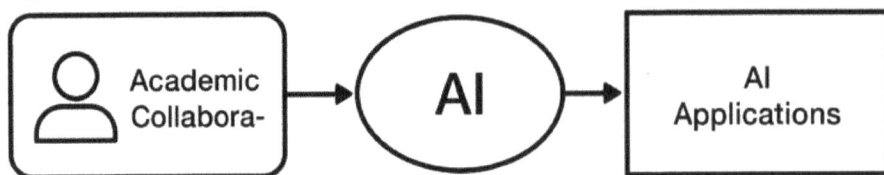

Figure 1. AI in Academic Collaboration

AI in Academic Collaboration

On the surface, this is a dream come true. A researcher can pose a question into a smart assistant and receive not just search results, but nuanced summaries, concept maps, and AI-curated bibliographies—sometimes within seconds. Peer review workflows, notoriously sluggish, are being reimagined with automated content screening and bias detection. AI can crawl through thousands of journal submissions to flag potential overlaps, ethical issues, or even overlooked innovations (Kayyali, 2025 c). A student struggling to articulate an idea might receive stylistic suggestions that elevate a rough draft into something closer to publishable prose. Yet the deeper one goes, the more the dream flickers with shadow.

Because here's the thing about AI: it's not neutral, and it's not innocent. It mirrors, magnifies, and mutates whatever values and structures it's built upon. When applied to academic collaboration, that mirror sometimes distorts more than it reflects. Yes, there is undeniable promise—but it's entangled with peril, and pretending otherwise risks undermining the very integrity AI was meant to enhance. Let's take a step back.

What does "collaboration" actually mean in the context of academia? At its core, it's not just about sharing documents or co-writing papers. It's a dynamic, often intimate interplay of minds—an exchange of perspective, a negotiation of meaning, a wrestling with uncertainty. It's built on trust, not just between individuals but with institutions, traditions, and methods of knowledge production.

Introducing AI into this space changes the chemistry. Collaboration is no longer just about humans connecting with humans; it becomes mediated—sometimes invisibly—by code, probabilities, and corporate infrastructures (Vidolov, 2024). There are algorithmic decisions beneath the surface: who gets recommended as a collaborator, which sources get prioritized in literature reviews, which research questions are deemed "promising" based on historical data. Each of these decisions, while seemingly logical, carries implicit biases. And what's worse, these decisions are often wrapped in the illusion of objectivity.

Consider the platforms that recommend academic collaborators. On paper, they democratize access—highlighting scholars from underrepresented regions, cross-pollinating disciplines, surfacing voices that might otherwise be buried under institutional prestige. But in practice? Algorithms trained on past citation networks may favor already dominant voices. Recommendations might cluster around English-language publications, reproducing the same asymmetries that have long plagued global academia. The paradox is painful: a tool designed to connect may, if unchecked, deepen the divide.

Then there's the matter of authorship. If an AI tool contributes a paragraph, a hypothesis, even a data visualization—who gets the credit? Is the researcher the sole author, the AI a ghost? Or is this a form of co-authorship, and if so, where does accountability reside? In some circles, this question is dismissed as philosophical. But it's not. It's immediate, messy, and already affecting doctoral dissertations, journal policies, and tenure reviews. And what about originality? If two scholars use the same generative AI tool to synthesize a body of literature, and both accept its output uncritically, how different are their eventual contributions? Does the field become a hall of mirrors—reflections of reflections—where genuine novelty is harder to discern, or worse, harder to value?

There's also the erosion of serendipity. One of the most cherished aspects of academic collaboration has always been the unexpected: the offhand comment that sparks a new idea, the accidental overlap of theories during a conference coffee break (Alleman et al, 2025). But AI, by design, minimizes randomness. It optimizes, streamlines, predicts. That's its strength—and its curse. When everything becomes calculated and efficient, we risk losing the wild, unruly creativity that comes from intellectual collision. And let's talk about surveillance—because we can't not.

Academic platforms infused with AI are increasingly capable of monitoring user behavior. They log when you log in, what you read, how long you spend on a page, which documents you upload, who you message, what keywords you search. This data is then fed back into the system to refine recommendations. Again, this seems innocuous. Even helpful. But it opens up troubling possibilities: profiling researchers based on activity, predicting funding outcomes, nudging behavior through subtle interface design. And if that data is leaked? Or worse, sold? Intellectual property becomes commodified. Confidential peer reviews could be exposed. Sensitive conversations between collaborators could be weaponized. The implications are not hypothetical. In an age of academic espionage and geopolitical tension, research data has value—and value invites exploitation.

The human cost is harder to quantify but equally real. A postdoc working in a precarious position might feel pressured to use AI tools to accelerate output—risking burnout, ethical gray zones, or unacknowledged dependency. A senior scholar might dismiss AI entirely, only to find themselves increasingly marginalized in digital-first conferences or journals. The gap between "AI natives" and "digital skeptics" grows, not just in skill but in status. What emerges is not a unified scholarly community but a stratified one, divided by access, fluency, and ideology.

All of this might sound alarmist. But it's not about fear. It's about fidelity—to the values that have long defined academia at its best: curiosity, skepticism, rigor, openness, and integrity. The arrival of AI in academic collaboration is not a glitch in the system. It is the system evolving (Wang, 2023). And with that evolution comes responsibility—not to blindly adopt or blindly reject, but to engage, question, shape. To do this well, we must begin by slowing down. Before we rush to integrate every new AI feature into our research platforms or curricula, we need space for critical reflection. Who built this tool? What data trained it? Whose values are embedded in its logic? What behaviors does it incentivize or punish? And—most importantly—what kind of scholarly world does it imagine?

We also need better language. The terms we use—"efficiency," "optimization," "personalization"—are often borrowed from tech marketing. They flatten nuance. They make it harder to articulate ambivalence, to express unease, to raise legitimate concerns without sounding anti-progress. But ambivalence is not a weakness. It's a strength. It's the mark of thinking deeply, resisting binaries, and staying open to complexity.

Some hopeful signs are emerging. Collaborative design processes, where scholars are involved in the creation of AI tools from the ground up (Kayyali, 2025 d). Open-source platforms that prioritize transparency over proprietary advantage. Ethical guidelines that don't just live in PDFs but are actively enforced and revised (Adams et al., 2023). And communities of practice—cross-disciplinary, cross-generational, cross-cultural—where the future of academic AI is debated, not dictated. Still, we have a long way to go.

This is not just about tweaking policies or improving software. It's about reimagining what collaboration means in a world where machines are not just observers, but participants. It's about remembering that the tools we create reflect the futures we're willing to fight for—or let slip away. Yes, AI holds immense promise for academic collaboration. It can dismantle barriers, amplify voices, uncover patterns, and catalyze knowledge creation at scales once unimaginable. But the peril lies in complacency—in assuming that progress is always synonymous with good, that faster is always better, that more data always leads to better decisions. We must resist that temptation. We must reclaim the right to be slow, to be uncertain, to disagree, to ask uncomfortable questions. And we must do so not in opposition to AI, but in dialogue with it—insisting that any technology worth using in academia must first prove its respect for what makes academia human. Only then can we begin to craft a model of academic collaboration that is not only intelligent—but wise.

PRIVACY IN THE DIGITAL ACADEMY: NAVIGATING DATA OWNERSHIP AND CONSENT

You wake up, unlock your phone, check your university email. A calendar update. An auto-saved draft of a co-authored paper. An analytics dashboard flashing red—"Your last lecture saw a 17% drop in student engagement." You didn't ask for this data, but there it is—compiled, analyzed, presented in clean, declarative fonts. Helpful? Maybe. Creepy? A little. Normal? Definitely. Welcome to the digital academy, where privacy is not just a matter of passwords, but a living, breathing question—ever more difficult to answer, and increasingly hard to ask.

Let's not pretend this is entirely new. The academy has long been an institution of records—student files, faculty dossiers, publication trails (Taylor & Charlebois, 2024). But the digital shift, accelerated by artificial intelligence and machine learning, didn't just scale those records—it shattered the boundaries that once defined them. What was once stored in locked filing cabinets now flows freely through clouds, apps, APIs, and learning management systems. A professor's lecture habits, a student's keystrokes during an exam, a researcher's access logs on a shared drive—this isn't surveillance fiction. This is higher education, 2025. And the most unsettling part? Most of us agreed to it. Sort of. Buried in click-to-agree user agreements, buried further in the margins of policy documents no one reads unless something goes wrong. What exactly did we consent to? Who owns the data that flows from our intellectual labor, our research questions, our late-night log-ins to submit final grades? Is data ownership about legal rights, institutional mandates, or personal boundaries? These aren't just technicalities—they cut to the core of what it means to participate in the academic ecosystem today.

We like to think of academia as a bastion of freedom—intellectual, creative, personal. But freedom without privacy is an illusion. You cannot think freely if you know you are being watched. You cannot explore a controversial hypothesis if your clicks and downloads might be flagged, profiled, or quietly rerouted. Privacy is not a luxury in the digital university. It is the precondition for the kind of thinking universities were built to protect.

Let's look at what privacy actually means in this context. It's tempting to define it as control over one's personal data, but that's reductive (Richards, 2022). In practice, privacy in the digital academy is a tangled web of expectations, assumptions, and imbalances. A student uploads a term paper to Turnitin—who owns that paper now? Can the platform train future algorithms on it? Can third parties access it? The student probably doesn't know. The professor may not know either. The institution might have outsourced that question to a vendor buried in a procurement contract.

The same goes for video recordings of classes. During the pandemic, many universities hastily adopted recording tools, claiming the need for "flexibility" and "accessibility." But what started as a temporary fix has become routine. Professors now find their lectures archived indefinitely, accessible to people they've never met, shared beyond their intent. Can those videos be analyzed for tone? Bias? Humor? Engagement? They already are, in some cases. The professor becomes not just a teacher but a data point. And the consent? Often absent or assumed.

Then there's research data—especially collaborative projects involving sensitive topics or vulnerable populations. AI-enhanced research platforms might automate data cleaning, pattern detection, even preliminary interpretations (Nayak, 2024). But where does that data live? Who can access it? In some cases, university systems automatically back up files without clarifying the boundary between personal storage and institutional ownership. A researcher who believes they're storing data securely on a personal drive might find that data mirrored on university servers, subject to audits, requests, or even subpoenas.

Table 1. Privacy Risks in AI-Supported Academic Platforms

Privacy Issue	Real-World Example	Risk Level	Data Impact
Auto-recorded Lectures	Archived classes analyzed for tone, humor, or engagement	High	Loss of control over public persona
Predictive Analytics	Algorithms flagging "at-risk" students/faculty	Medium-High	Behavioral profiling
Shared Research Storage	Research mirrored on institutional cloud without notice	High	Loss of data ownership, exposure risk
Student Submission Tracking	Turnitin storing papers for future AI training	High	Consent violation, IP commodification

The implications grow even murkier when you factor in predictive analytics. Universities increasingly use AI to forecast student performance, identify "at-risk" individuals, or assess the impact of faculty workload. On the surface, this looks like progress—early intervention, strategic resourcing, proactive care. But scratch a little deeper and it starts to resemble profiling. What if an algorithm marks a student as disengaged based on camera-off Zoom sessions? What if a professor's "productivity" score drops because they teach emotionally laborious subjects with fewer publications but deeper human impact? The data might be accurate in some sense, but truth without context is dangerous (Murrietta, 2025). And context is precisely what privacy protects. It gives people the right to define how their actions, expressions, and identities are interpreted. Without it, data becomes decontextualized behavior—raw, exploitable, and often misunderstood. Here's where ownership comes in. In a just digital academy, ownership should mean more than custodianship. It should mean agency. If I create a syllabus, a lecture, a digital tool—do I retain the right to decide how it's used, where it circulates, and who profits from it? Increasingly, that's not the case. Institutions argue that intellectual property produced under their umbrella belongs to them. Platforms argue that usage equals permission. And third-party vendors argue that aggregated data isn't personal data, even when it's clearly traceable.

It's easy to feel powerless in the face of these overlapping claims. But power in the digital academy doesn't always announce itself—it creeps. It's in the platform defaults, in the fine print, in the subtle cultural shift that says "If you're not doing anything wrong, you have nothing to hide." That phrase—often used to justify surveillance—completely misses the point. Privacy isn't about hiding. It's about choosing when, how, and with whom to share. It's about boundaries. Dignity. Respect. And let's not forget the emotional toll. The knowledge that everything you do might be tracked, assessed, archived—it changes behavior. It encourages performance, not authenticity. It nudges people toward safe choices, away from risk, nuance, messiness—the very things that make academic work meaningful. A student may avoid controversial topics, fearing digital scrutiny. A faculty member might censor themselves during a recorded lecture (Godfrey, 2023). A researcher may skip an exploratory detour because the algorithm didn't recommend it. This is not privacy lost through carelessness. This is privacy traded for efficiency, often without informed consent, and sometimes without awareness at all. Of course, some push back. There are scholars who build their own servers, students who encrypt their data, departments that negotiate contracts with privacy clauses. There are even platforms built by academics for academics—transparent, open-source, decentralized. But these are exceptions, not the rule. And that's the problem.

Consent, in this environment, has become a hollow ritual. Click, accept, continue. But real consent requires understanding, time, alternatives. When a student must use a platform to pass a course, their "choice" isn't real. When faculty evaluations are tied to analytics dashboards, participation becomes coerced. And when institutional policies are opaque, even well-meaning individuals cannot act ethically, because they don't know the rules—or who wrote them. So where do we go from here?

- First, we need to reframe privacy as a collective right, not just an individual burden. Too often, the responsibility to "protect privacy" is offloaded onto users—use stronger passwords, adjust your settings, opt out of tracking. But privacy in academia is systemic. It's about institutional practices, platform design, funding models, and policy cultures. It's not something you can solve with a browser extension.
- Second, we must demand transparency—not just about what data is collected, but how it's interpreted, used, and shared. If a platform analyzes engagement, it should disclose the metrics. If a university uses AI for prediction, it should explain the model. And if consent is sought, it must be revocable, granular, and meaningful.

- Third, we need new models of data ownership. Imagine if academic workers could license their digital outputs, retaining control over use and attribution. Imagine if data collected during collaboration had built-in expiration dates or purpose limitations. Imagine if platforms were accountable not just to users but to independent ethical boards, with teeth.
- Fourth, and perhaps most radically, we need to create space for refusal. Not everyone wants to participate in a datafied academy. And that should be okay. Opting out should not mean exclusion. There should be paper alternatives, human alternatives, analog rooms where people can think and speak without a digital trail. This isn't about nostalgia—it's about balance.

We must resist the narrative that privacy and innovation are inherently at odds. That's a false dichotomy. The best innovations are those that empower without extracting, that enhance without erasing. It's entirely possible to design AI tools that respect boundaries, honor consent, and foreground human agency. It just requires more care, more dialogue, and more imagination than the current model rewards. Privacy in the digital academy is not just about protecting data. It's about protecting the conditions under which knowledge is created, shared, and debated. It's about creating an environment where people feel safe enough to think freely, to disagree publicly, to experiment boldly. It's about remembering that behind every dataset is a person—and behind every person, a story they haven't necessarily agreed to tell.

SECURITY RISKS IN AI-SUPPORTED SCHOLARLY NETWORKS

Let's not kid ourselves. The modern scholarly ecosystem, sleek and digital as it appears, rests on an increasingly precarious infrastructure (Crowder et al, 2022). One that hums along quietly until it doesn't. Until a breach. Until a leak. Until an entire body of research—years of effort, collaboration, late-night struggles—is exposed, corrupted, or simply disappears. All in a blink. And with AI tightening its grip on academic workflows, the stakes have never been higher (Kayyali, 2026 c). You'd think the academy—home to some of the sharpest minds—would be more prepared. But intellect isn't immunity. In fact, the smarter the system, the more vulnerable it often becomes. Because sophistication invites complexity, and complexity opens cracks. Cracks where things slip through. And let's be clear: we're not talking about the low-hanging fruit of cybersecurity. Not the garden-variety phishing emails or the poorly secured personal laptops (though those are still very much a problem). What we're looking at now is more insidious. Quiet intrusions. Invisible manipulations. AI-powered exploits tailored to the precise contours of scholarly networks—trained to observe, learn, mimic, and deceive.

Figure 2. Types of Machine Learning

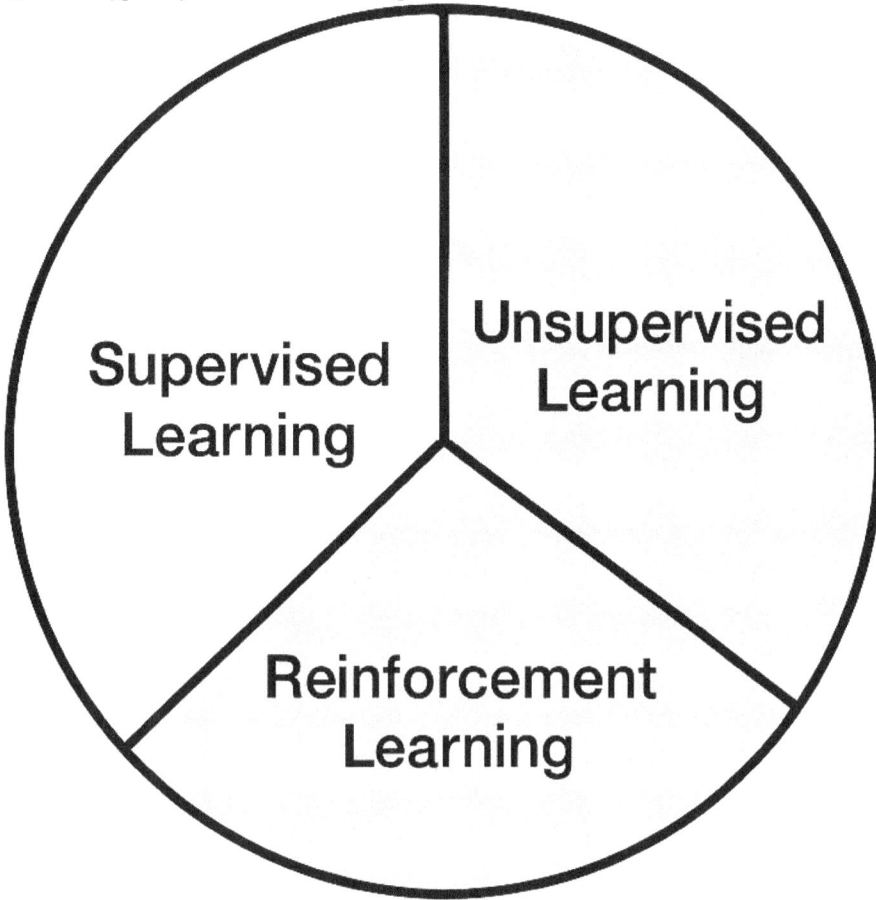

Types of Machine Learning

Academic platforms today are no longer passive repositories. They are intelligent, self-improving environments (Kayyali, 2025 b). AI curates, recommends, flags, predicts. It does so by ingesting mountains of data—research papers, private messages, usage patterns, institutional metadata. On the surface, this feels like progress. Who wouldn't want their academic life made easier, more connected, more responsive? But all this data—this raw material fueling the AI—needs a home. It needs transit. It needs storage. And everywhere it travels or rests, it becomes a target.

Imagine, for a moment, a machine learning model trained on pre-publication manuscripts from top-tier research labs. That model could, in theory, be weaponized. A hostile entity—corporate, governmental, or even a rogue competitor—could siphon off intellectual property before it ever hits peer review (Garvey & Svendsen, 2024). Entire innovations lifted, quietly, seamlessly. By the time the original authors publish, their ideas have already been patented elsewhere. The theft is not loud. There's no broken glass. Just silence and loss. And here's where it gets thornier. The AI tools themselves aren't necessarily malicious. Most are built for good—efficiency, collaboration, discovery. But that doesn't matter. The same algorithms that help researchers connect across continents can be exploited to map influence networks, identify gatekeepers, and simulate convincing fake identities. Academic bots, indistinguishable from real scholars, could infiltrate research communities, manipulate discourse, or subtly skew the peer review process.

Far-fetched? Maybe not. In 2023, cybersecurity analysts discovered entire rings of fabricated peer reviewers, some AI-generated, some human-run, used to fast-track publications and manipulate journal metrics. That was before large language models became mainstream. What we face now is an escalation—fakes with polish, bots with credentials, algorithms armed with fluency. But perhaps the most chilling threat isn't external. It's internal. Because when AI integrates deeply into scholarly infrastructures, it becomes woven into the very logic of decision-making. A university might use AI to assess research impact scores or grant allocations (Steingard & Linacre, 2023). A publisher might rely on AI to recommend reviewers or flag potential conflicts. But what happens if the models are compromised? What if the AI is subtly biased—or worse, deliberately tampered with?

A skewed model can quietly favor certain research areas, institutions, or demographics. Not through overt discrimination, but via the slow tilt of algorithmic suggestion. What gets surfaced, gets read. What gets read, gets cited. And what gets cited, wins. It's a feedback loop—silent, opaque, incredibly difficult to detect unless you know precisely where to look and what to ask. And yet, most scholars don't ask. We've become used to recommendation engines. We trust the default settings. We assume the tools are neutral. But they're not. AI doesn't just reflect reality—it reshapes it. It learns from patterns, replicates biases, and—if left unmonitored—can reinforce hierarchies we thought we were dismantling.

Security, in this context, becomes more than just protecting data from unauthorized access (Mubeen et al, 2022). It becomes about safeguarding epistemic integrity—making sure that what we know, and how we come to know it, hasn't been quietly bent out of shape by algorithms we didn't design and don't understand. Consider collaborative platforms like research networks or grant management systems. Many of these now include AI-driven analytics: project success predictors, partnership suggestions, risk assessments. On the surface, they streamline decisions. But they also concentrate power—who gets flagged as "low risk"? Whose applications are deprioritized before human eyes even see them? Worse still, many of these platforms are built and maintained by third-party vendors—corporations with commercial interests, often operating under layers of legalese that obscure accountability. If a breach occurs, whose fault is it? The university? The platform? The user who reused their password? Accountability gets blurred. The trail grows cold. And the consequences ripple far beyond the technical.

Imagine a leak of early-stage research on politically sensitive topics—climate policy in authoritarian regimes, reproductive health in conservative regions, or encryption methods in geopolitical hotspots. Such data in the wrong hands isn't just a security risk. It's a human risk. Researchers could face harassment, surveillance, travel restrictions—or worse. This isn't paranoia. It's the reality of working in a globalized academy, where not all actors play by the same rules, and where knowledge, once digitized, has no borders. So, what can be done? That's the million-dollar question—one that doesn't lend itself to tidy answers.

First, we need to abandon the idea that security is someone else's job. IT departments can't do it alone. Neither can compliance officers or contract lawyers. Security in AI-supported scholarly networks is a shared responsibility—one that includes developers, administrators, librarians, faculty, students, and yes, even funders (Vrana, 2025). We need literacy. Not just about threats, but about systems. How does this AI tool work? What data does it use? Where is that data stored? Who has access to it? What happens if something goes wrong? Right now, most researchers couldn't answer those questions. Not because they're careless, but because no one told them. The systems are opaque by design. We click, we use, we move on. Until the breach. Until the scandal. Transparency must become a baseline requirement for any tool claiming to serve the academy. Open-source code, independent audits, clear data policies—these shouldn't be optional. They should be table stakes. If a platform refuses to disclose how its algorithms work, it shouldn't be used to make decisions that affect careers, funding, or publication.

Second, we need what might be called "slow security." A philosophy that favors deliberation over automation, caution over convenience. This doesn't mean rejecting AI. It means embedding it thoughtfully. Allowing time for review, for questioning, for dissent. Security isn't just about building higher walls. It's about creating space for critical thinking.

Third, we need resilience. Breaches will happen. Systems will fail. What matters is how we respond—how quickly, how transparently, how justly. Do we notify affected researchers? Do we provide recourse? Do we learn? Or do we bury it in PR speak and move on? Lastly, and perhaps most importantly, we need to talk. Across disciplines, across hierarchies. Too often, security discussions are siloed—technical people talk to technical people, while the rest of the academy hums along, blissfully unaware. But the threats we face aren't just technical. They're structural. Cultural. Ethical. We need conversations that include humanities scholars, artists, scientists, ethicists, administrators, students. Conversations that don't start with "compliance" but with "what kind of academy do we want to build?" Because that's what's really at stake. Not just files and firewalls. But trust. Autonomy. The conditions that make scholarship possible, meaningful, and free. There's no silver bullet. But there is a path—a slow, imperfect, collective path toward a more secure scholarly world. One that honors the promise of AI without surrendering to its peril. One that recognizes that security isn't the absence of risk, but the presence of care. And maybe that's what we need most right now. Not more tools. Not more dashboards. But more care.

ETHICAL DILEMMAS IN AI-DRIVEN KNOWLEDGE EXCHANGE

The promise of AI in knowledge exchange reads like a siren song for the modern academy—efficiency, democratization, unprecedented connectivity, a world where ideas flow seamlessly across borders and disciplines. Yet, lurking beneath this gleaming surface are riddles without easy answers, ethical quandaries that gnaw at the foundation of what we think we know about fairness, authorship, and intellectual sovereignty (Kayyali, 2025 a). These dilemmas aren't abstract thought experiments for ivory tower speculation. They are urgent, lived realities for researchers, students, and institutions navigating a terrain both exhilarating and treacherous.

Let's start with a question that's been haunting me: when AI generates knowledge—or at least, knowledge-like outputs—who owns the idea? Is it the human who posed the question? The algorithm that synthesized the answer? The company that built the AI? Imagine a doctoral student using an AI assistant to draft a literature review (Krumsvik, 2024). The result is a mosaic of synthesized summaries, paraphrases, and insights. The student edits, adds commentary, cites sources, but the foundational "text" owes its shape to the AI's training data and pattern recognition. Is the student's ownership diminished? Are we witnessing a subtle erosion of intellectual labor, replaced by mechanized curation? There are no neat answers, and therein lies the tension.

This dilemma intensifies when considering the origins of the AI's "knowledge." These systems train on vast corpora—sometimes scraped without explicit consent—from academic publications, websites, and grey literature. Whose voices populate the AI's memory? Whose knowledge is amplified? And perhaps just as importantly, whose is marginalized or erased?

Table 2. Ethical Concerns in AI Academic Tools

Ethical Concern	Description	Potential Impact
Algorithmic Bias	Bias stemming from training data or model design	Reinforces academic inequality
Ownership & Attribution	Confusion over AI-generated content authorship	Undermines intellectual accountability
Informed Consent	Lack of clear, revocable data sharing consent	Violates personal and research autonomy
Cultural Erasure	AI favoring dominant languages/ paradigms	Marginalizes Global South and minority voices

AI, by its nature, tends to reproduce existing patterns—those that are statistically dominant. The voices of Global North institutions, English-language scholarship, and mainstream paradigms often drown out diverse, localized, or dissenting perspectives (Rigney, 2023). The promise of democratization can quickly curdle into digital colonialism, where AI-driven platforms become echo chambers reinforcing existing hierarchies rather than dismantling them.

This leads us to another knotty issue: bias. We're all familiar with the specter of algorithmic bias in policing or hiring. But in academia, bias plays out in more subtle, yet equally pernicious, ways. Consider peer review facilitated by AI—models trained on historical data might undervalue interdisciplinary or non-traditional research because those fields have historically been underrepresented or undervalued (Hasa, 2023). Or think about research funding platforms that prioritize "safe" projects over riskier, potentially groundbreaking ideas, based on predictive analytics. Ethics demands more than superficial fixes. It asks us to interrogate the foundational assumptions baked into AI design, the values encoded by their creators, and the socio-political contexts in which these tools operate.

What about transparency? AI systems are notoriously opaque—black boxes whose inner workings are inscrutable even to experts (Von Eschenbach, 2021). When these tools influence decisions about what research gets funded, published, or highlighted, lack of transparency is not just a technical failing—it's a moral blind spot. Scholars deserve to understand how decisions affecting their careers and ideas are made. Without that clarity, trust erodes, and with trust, the fabric of academic collaboration frays. And then there's the delicate dance of attribution and credit. If AI helps generate a novel insight, a data visualization, or even a draft paragraph, how do we credit that contribution? The International Committee of Medical Journal Editors (ICMJE) stipulates clear authorship criteria—but does AI qualify as an author? Some journals have issued policies excluding AI from authorship lists, relegating it to a tool status (Kambhampati & Maini, 2023). But is that distinction meaningful or adequate? It raises questions about intellectual responsibility and accountability. If AI-generated content is flawed or biased, who is responsible? The human author? The tool's developers? The institution that deploys the system?

The conversation about AI and plagiarism further muddies the waters (Kayyali, 2026 b). When students use AI to generate essays, are they plagiarizing? Or are they leveraging new tools to aid composition? Education systems struggle to keep pace, oscillating between outright bans and reluctant acceptance (Kuelzer-Eckhout & Houser, 2024). This tension highlights a broader ethical challenge: how to balance innovation and integrity, support creativity while preventing misuse. A particularly thorny dilemma emerges with the commodification of academic knowledge. AI-powered platforms often monetize access to synthesized research outputs or use data to refine proprietary algorithms. Scholars may find their intellectual contributions repackaged as services they must pay to access. This raises ethical questions about fairness and equity in knowledge distribution. Is it ethical for academic data, often publicly funded, to fuel private profits? How do we ensure that knowledge remains a public good in an era dominated by commercial AI players?

Moreover, the rapid pace of AI deployment risks sidelining the voices of marginalized scholars and under-resourced institutions (Das et al, 2024). When AI tools require significant technical literacy or infrastructure, they risk deepening the digital divide. Ethical knowledge exchange must reckon with inclusion—not as an afterthought but as a prerequisite. Perhaps the most profound ethical tension lies in the nature of "knowledge" itself. Traditional scholarship values uncertainty, debate, and revision. AI, however, tends to offer definitive answers—probabilistic, yes, but packaged as authoritative. There's a danger that AI's veneer of objectivity might suppress critical questioning or intellectual humility. When a machine-generated summary of literature becomes the default starting point, do scholars risk anchoring their thinking, overlooking nuances, or failing to challenge dominant paradigms?

Then again, AI can democratize access to information—especially in resource-poor settings where subscription fees or language barriers hinder scholarly engagement. This duality—empowerment coupled with potential suppression—demands nuanced ethical reflection. It's no surprise, then, that ethical frameworks around AI in academia remain nascent, fragmented, and contested. Some advocate for robust governance—clear guidelines on transparency, consent, accountability, and fairness. Others emphasize community-led design processes, ensuring that AI tools reflect diverse needs and values. Still, many institutions lag behind, caught between enthusiasm for AI's benefits and unease over its implications.

Ethical dilemmas in AI-driven knowledge exchange compel us to revisit foundational questions: Who are knowledge producers? Who benefits? Who is harmed? How do we preserve academic freedom and intellectual diversity in a world increasingly mediated by algorithms? Perhaps the most important ethical imperative is cultivating a culture of reflexivity—a willingness to question not only the outputs of AI but the very processes of its creation and deployment (Rezaei et al, 2024). Reflexivity demands humility, openness, and a commitment to ongoing dialogue. It resists the technocratic impulse to "solve" ethical issues with yet more technology, instead centering human judgment and values. This means involving scholars, technologists, ethicists, and communities in co-creating AI tools—ensuring they are transparent, accountable, and designed with justice in mind. It also means educating academic communities about AI's capabilities and limits, fostering critical literacy that empowers informed use and critique.

Ethical dilemmas don't end at design or policy. They permeate daily academic practices (Gilliland et al, 2023). When I sit down to draft a paper with AI assistance, how do I balance trust and skepticism? When I choose collaborators via an AI recommendation engine, am I reinforcing existing inequities or bridging divides? When I share data for AI training, what boundaries do I set? These are messy, personal questions—no algorithms for answers. In grappling with them, we embrace the complexity of human knowledge itself: provisional, contested, deeply contextual. AI-driven knowledge exchange holds vast potential but also profound responsibility. Ethics must be our compass—not an obstacle to innovation but its guide. Only by confronting these dilemmas openly and honestly can we ensure that AI enriches, rather than impoverishes, the human pursuit of understanding.

TOWARD RESPONSIBLE INNOVATION: SAFEGUARDS FOR TRUSTWORTHY ACADEMIC AI

Innovation, by its very nature, is a restless beast—never fully tamed, always pushing boundaries, sometimes crashing headlong into uncharted territories. When it comes to artificial intelligence in the realm of academia, this restless impulse becomes a double-edged sword. On one side, AI gleams as the herald of a new dawn: accelerating discovery, bridging divides, amplifying human insight. On the other, it's a force that can erode trust, exacerbate inequities, and obscure accountability if left unchecked. So how do we proceed? How do we innovate responsibly in an arena so delicate, so fundamental to the fabric of knowledge itself?

The phrase "responsible innovation" often pops up like a well-worn motto, but it carries a weighty challenge (Wisnioski, 2025). It demands more than good intentions or cursory ethics checklists. It calls for a deep reimagining of how we conceive, design, deploy, and govern AI within the academic ecosystem. And crucially, it requires embedding safeguards—not as afterthoughts, but as foundational pillars—if AI is to earn the trust of scholars, institutions, and society.

To start with, let's talk transparency—not just the buzzword it's become, but the messy, layered practice it must be. Transparency in academic AI cannot be reduced to glossy "about" pages or vague promises of data privacy. It means opening up the black boxes, laying bare the algorithms, exposing the datasets, revealing the biases, and acknowledging the limitations. Scholars deserve to know how the AI that filters their literature searches, recommends collaborators, or evaluates their work actually functions (Ngwenyama & Rowe, 2024). Not in jargon-laden manuals, but in accessible, honest explanations that invite scrutiny and debate. Of course, achieving true transparency is no small feat. Many AI tools, especially proprietary ones, operate under business models that prioritize secrecy and competitive advantage (Kayyali, 2026 a). Yet, academia's commitment to openness—sharing data, methods, critiques—should not be compromised at the altar of profit. Perhaps the solution lies in collaborative frameworks where institutions and developers co-create open-source or hybrid models. In such ecosystems, trust is built not only on what the AI does, but on who controls it and how it is governed.

Speaking of control, the next cornerstone of responsible innovation is agency—the empowerment of users and stakeholders to exert meaningful influence over AI's operation (Buhmann & Fieseler, 2021). This goes beyond simple consent forms that ask users to "accept" opaque terms and conditions. It means designing systems that enable granular control: scholars can decide what data is collected about them, how it's used, and with whom it's shared. It means institutions establish clear policies that prioritize individual and collective rights over unchecked data extraction. But agency is tricky. It requires balancing technical complexity with user-friendliness, creating interfaces that allow non-expert users to understand and modify their privacy settings or data sharing preferences. Moreover, it involves fostering cultures of digital literacy within academia—educating students, researchers, and administrators about AI's capabilities and risks so that they can engage critically rather than passively.

Another vital safeguard is accountability. When AI systems make decisions—be it flagging plagiarism, ranking publications, or recommending funding allocations—who bears responsibility for errors, biases, or harms? It's tempting to shift blame to the inscrutable algorithms or the "data-driven" processes, but responsible innovation demands clear lines of accountability (Ogwueleka, 2025). That might mean establishing ethical oversight committees within universities, creating audit trails for AI decision-making, or instituting appeals processes for individuals impacted by AI-generated assessments.

Interestingly, accountability also involves humility. AI, as powerful as it is, cannot replace human judgment. Responsible innovation insists on human-in-the-loop frameworks where AI augments but does not override academic deliberation. Decisions affecting careers, reputations, or intellectual property deserve human sensitivity, contextual understanding, and ethical reflection that machines cannot provide.

Closely intertwined with accountability is the imperative for fairness and inclusivity (Akinrinola et al, 2024). AI systems, trained on historical academic data, risk perpetuating long-standing inequities—favoring well-funded institutions, established scholars, and dominant languages. Responsible innovation means actively counteracting these biases, through diverse and representative training datasets, bias audits, and inclusive design practices. It also means creating AI that supports, rather than supplants, marginalized voices and knowledge traditions. Interdisciplinary collaboration becomes invaluable. Ethicists, sociologists, technologists, and scholars from various cultural backgrounds must work together to interrogate the assumptions underpinning AI models. Only through such pluralistic engagement can academic AI aspire to be truly equitable.

Privacy, a theme threaded throughout the academy's digital transformation, remains a non-negotiable safeguard. Responsible innovation demands rigorous data governance—ensuring data minimization, secure storage, and clear expiration policies. But beyond compliance, it calls for a privacy ethos that respects scholars as more than data points. It requires transparent communication about what data is collected, why, and for how long, and mechanisms for individuals to access, correct, or delete their data. Emerging technologies such as federated learning and differential privacy offer promising technical solutions, enabling AI training on decentralized data without exposing sensitive information. Yet these are tools, not panaceas. They must be integrated thoughtfully, accompanied by policies and user education.

One cannot discuss safeguards without addressing the ecological footprint of AI. The computational power behind large models is vast, raising questions about sustainability—how to reconcile academic innovation with environmental stewardship. Responsible innovation in academic AI must engage with these trade-offs, exploring efficient algorithms, renewable energy sources, and transparent reporting of environmental impact. Beyond these technical and policy measures lies a broader, more subtle safeguard: cultivating a culture of ethical reflexivity (Bietti, 2021). Responsible innovation isn't a checklist but a continuous process—one that invites ongoing questioning, dialogue, and adaptation. It's about recognizing that the socio-technical systems we build are embedded in shifting political, cultural, and economic landscapes.

Such reflexivity can flourish only if diverse academic voices—across disciplines, career stages, geographies—are empowered to participate in conversations about AI's design and deployment. It's about democratizing not just knowledge production but knowledge governance. I find it striking how often the drive for innovation becomes entangled with a narrative of inevitability—as if AI's rise is a tide against which we can only brace ourselves. But responsible innovation reframes this story. It insists that we are not passive recipients but active agents capable of shaping the trajectory of AI in academia.

That shaping demands patience, care, and imagination. It involves imagining academic futures where AI supports curiosity without commodifying it, fosters collaboration without surveilling it, accelerates discovery without sacrificing integrity. It also means resisting the seductive allure of "quick fixes" or "silver bullet" solutions that promise to solve complex ethical and social problems with mere technical tweaks. Responsible innovation embraces complexity, ambiguity, and the often uncomfortable work of balancing competing values.

Ultimately, the trustworthiness of academic AI hinges on these safeguards working in concert (Afrogha, 2025). Transparency, agency, accountability, fairness, privacy, sustainability, and reflexivity are not isolated virtues but an interwoven fabric. A failure in one strand weakens the whole. This fabric is fragile. But it can be strengthened. Through collective commitment, interdisciplinary collaboration, and steadfast adherence to human-centered values, we can nurture an academic AI ecosystem that honors the essence of scholarship—a relentless quest for knowledge enriched by humility, openness, and care. To walk this path is no small feat. It requires us to hold innovation and ethics not as opposing forces, but as partners in a dance—sometimes awkward, sometimes graceful, always vital. And in this dance, we reclaim the academy not just as a place of learning, but as a community where trust is earned, voices are heard, and knowledge is a shared treasure—enriched, not diminished, by the machines we create.

CONCLUSION

As we arrive at the close of this inquiry into security, privacy, and ethical considerations in AI-powered academic collaboration, a stark truth emerges: technology is not neutral. It never has been. The systems we design, adopt, and normalize in academia mirror our priorities, our blind spots, and—often—our willingness to trade core values for convenience or prestige. The challenge we face today is not simply how to protect our data, secure our networks, or comply with ethical checklists. It is, fundamentally, about how to preserve the integrity of academic life in an era when machines are becoming both our collaborators and, increasingly, our gatekeepers.

Throughout this chapter, we have seen how AI tools—while remarkably beneficial—carry the capacity to destabilize long-standing norms of scholarly engagement. They can automate tasks, but they can also erode trust. They can illuminate unseen connections, but they can also amplify bias. They can open doors to global partnerships, but they can just as easily replicate patterns of exclusion. To ignore these contradictions is to risk becoming passive participants in a technological shift that quietly reshapes the mission of higher education itself.

We must recognize that privacy is not a technical detail—it is a moral right. It is the cornerstone of academic freedom, enabling scholars to explore controversial ideas without surveillance or retaliation. Likewise, security is not simply a matter of firewalls and encryption. It is about safeguarding the intellectual autonomy of researchers, protecting the reputations of institutions, and ensuring that our knowledge ecosystems are resilient to manipulation, sabotage, or exploitation.

Perhaps most importantly, ethics in AI is not an add-on. It is not something to consider after deployment, nor is it the sole responsibility of developers or IT departments. Ethical reflection must be embedded at every stage of academic collaboration—from the conception of a project, to the design of platforms, to the policies that govern digital knowledge exchange. Institutions have a duty to foster cultures of digital responsibility, and scholars must feel empowered—not punished—for questioning the tools they are asked to use.

As we look ahead, a few imperatives become clear. First, transparency must become a non-negotiable feature of any AI tool used in academic contexts. Scholars must understand how algorithms function, what data they process, and how outputs are generated. Second, consent must be meaningful—not hidden in terms and conditions. Researchers and students alike should have real agency over how their data is used, shared, or repurposed. Third, equity must be prioritized. The academic AI landscape must be inclusive, culturally aware, and resistant to the monopolization of knowledge by powerful platforms or institutions.

Finally, we must not lose sight of the human spirit that animates scholarship—the curiosity, the rigor, the debates over coffee, the late-night edits, the passionate disagreements, the joy of discovery. These are not easily quantifiable, nor can they be replicated by machines. Yet they are the heart of academic life. The role of AI, then, is not to replace these human elements but to serve them—to enable richer collaboration, deeper inquiry, and more ethical engagement with the world around us.

In reclaiming that purpose, we move from caution to commitment. A commitment to shaping AI not just as a tool for efficiency, but as a force for good. A commitment to collaboration that honors privacy, protects autonomy, and upholds the highest ethical standards. And above all, a commitment to ensuring that in the race toward digital progress, we do not forget what makes academia worth protecting in the first place.

REFERENCES

Adams, C., Pente, P., Lemermeyer, G., & Rockwell, G. (2023). Ethical principles for artificial intelligence in K-12 education. *Computers and Education: Artificial Intelligence*, *4*, 100131.

Afrogha, O. (2025). Artificial Intelligence Meets Academia: Safeguarding Integrity in a Digital Era. AI and Ethics, Academic Integrity and the Future of Quality Assurance in Higher Education, 12.

Akinrinola, O., Okoye, C. C., Ofodile, O. C., & Ugochukwu, C. E. (2024). Navigating and reviewing ethical dilemmas in AI development: Strategies for transparency, fairness, and accountability. GSC Advanced Research and Reviews, 18(3), 050-058.

Alleman, N. F., Allen, C. C., & Madsen, S. (2025). *Starving the Dream: Student Hunger and the Hidden Costs of Campus Affluence*. JHU Press.

Bietti, E. (2021). From ethics washing to ethics bashing: A moral philosophy view on tech ethics. *Journal of Social Computing*, *2*(3), 266–283.

Bryda, G., & Costa, A. P. (2023). Qualitative research in digital era: Innovations, methodologies and collaborations. *Social Sciences*, *12*(10), 570.

Buhmann, A., & Fieseler, C. (2021). Towards a deliberative framework for responsible innovation in artificial intelligence. *Technology in Society*, *64*, 101475.

Crowder, J., Determeyer, P., & Rogers, S. (2022). "Technology is Wonderful Until It Isn't": Community-Based Research and the Precarity of Digital Infrastructure. In The Routledge Companion to Media Anthropology (pp. 77-88). Routledge.

Das, A., Muschert, G., Dutta, M. J., Aytaç, M. B., Tripathi, P., Khare, A., & Ray, S. (2024). AI Impacts, Concerns, and Perspectives in the Global South A Thought Leadership Round Table. Социологическое обозрение, 23(4), 173-195.

Garvey, B., & Svendsen, A. D. (2024). Can Generative-AI (ChatGPT and Bard) Be Used as Red Team Avatars in Developing Foresight Scenarios? In *Navigating uncertainty using foresight intelligence: A guidebook for scoping scenario options in cyber and beyond* (pp. 213–242). Springer Nature Switzerland.

Gilliland, B., Kunkel, M., Nguyen, T. H., Urada, K., & Christenson, C. (2023). Ethical dilemmas of teacher research in applied linguistics. *Research Methods in Applied Linguistics*, *2*(3), 100072.

Godfrey, H. (2023, June). Intellectual humility and self-censorship in higher education; A thematic analysis. []. Frontiers Media SA.]. *Frontiers in Education*, *8*, 1066519.

Hasa, K. (2023). Examining the OECD's perspective on AI in education policy: a critical analysis of language and structure in the 'AI and the future of skills' (AIFS) document and its implications for the higher education (Doctoral dissertation, University of British Columbia).

Hutson, J. (Ed.). (2024). *The Rise of AI in Academic Inquiry*. IGI Global.

Kambhampati, S. B., & Maini, L. (2023). Authorship in scientific manuscripts. *Indian Journal of Orthopaedics*, *57*(6), 783–788. PMID: 37214360

Kayyali, M. (2025 a). Ethical Implications of Generative AI in Education: Privacy, Bias, and Integrity. In Transformative AI Practices for Personalized Learning Strategies (pp. 185-218). IGI Global Scientific Publishing.

Kayyali, M. (2025 b). E-Learning Platforms and Their Influence on Lifelong Learning. In Impact of Digitalization on Education and Social Sustainability (pp. 155-176). IGI Global.

Kayyali, M. (2025 c). Generative AI and Education: Transforming Teaching and Learning Through Collaborative Intelligence. In Humans and Generative AI Tools for Collaborative Intelligence (pp. 25-52). IGI Global Scientific Publishing.

Kayyali, M. (2025 d). The Evolution of AI in Education From Concept to Classroom. In *Navigating Barriers to AI Implementation in the Classroom* (pp. 325–368). IGI Global Scientific Publishing.

Kayyali, M. (2026 a). Case Studies: Successful Applications of AI and AR in Research. In Revolutionizing Academic Research With AI and Augmented Reality (pp. 347-368). IGI Global Scientific Publishing.

Kayyali, M. (2026 b). AI in Higher Education: The Risk of Excluding Vulnerable Learners. In AI and New Forms of Exclusion (pp. 57-82). IGI Global Scientific Publishing.

Kayyali, M. (2026 c). The Impact of AI on Classroom Dynamics in Higher Education: Shifting Roles for Professors and Students. In Responsible AI Integration in Education (pp. 151-180). IGI Global Scientific Publishing.

Krumsvik, R. J. (2024). Chatbots and academic writing for doctoral students. *Education and Information Technologies*, ●●●, 1–35.

Kuelzer-Eckhout, L., & Houser, N. O. (2024). Book Banning, Censorship, and Gag-Order Legislation: Working through the Fear and Distrust That Threatens Public Education and Jeopardizes the Public-at-Large. Journal of Philosophy & History of Education, 74.

Mubeen, M., Arslan, M., & Anandhi, G. (2022). Strategies to Avoid Illegal Data Access. *Journal of Communication Engineering & Systems*, *12*(3), 29–40p.

Murrietta, C. (2025). The Teachers Are Not Okay: The Complex Emotionality of the Teaching Profession (Doctoral dissertation, University of California, San Diego).

Nayak, M. (2024). AI-Enhanced Digital Forensics: Automated Techniques for Efficient Investigation and Evidence Collection. J. *Electrical Systems*, *20*(1s), 211–229.

Ngwenyama, O., & Rowe, F. (2024). Should we collaborate with AI to conduct literature reviews? Changing epistemic values in a flattening world. *Journal of the Association for Information Systems*, *25*(1), 122–136.

Ogwueleka, F. N. (2025). Plagiarism Detection in the Age of Artificial Intelligence: Current Technologies and Future Directions. AI and Ethics, Academic Integrity and the Future of Quality Assurance in Higher Education, 10.

Preston, J. (2022). *Artificial intelligence in the capitalist university: Academic labour, commodification, and value.* Taylor & Francis.

Puplampu, R. (2024). *What Everyone Should Know About the Rise of AI: AI Transparency, Privacy, and Ethics Best Practices.* Puplampu Books.

Rezaei, M., Pironti, M., & Quaglia, R. (2024). AI in knowledge sharing, which ethical challenges are raised in decision-making processes for organisations? *Management Decision.*

Richards, N. (2022). *Why privacy matters.* Oxford University Press.

Rigney, L. I. (Ed.). (2023). *Global perspectives and new challenges in culturally responsive pedagogies: Super-diversity and teaching practice.* Taylor & Francis.

Steingard, D., & Linacre, S. (2023). Transforming academic journal assessment from "quality" to "impact": A case study of the SDG Impact Intensity academic journal rating artificial intelligence system. In *The future of responsible management education: University leadership and the digital transformation challenge* (pp. 317–356). Springer International Publishing.

Taylor, S., & Charlebois, S. (2024, March). Teaching dossier guidance for professional faculty: An evidence-based approach for demonstrating teaching effectiveness. [). Frontiers Media SA.]. *Frontiers in Education*, *9*, 1284726.

Vidolov, S. P. (2024). Virtual collaboration as co-enacting intercorporeality. *European Journal of Information Systems*, *33*(2), 244–266.

Von Eschenbach, W. J. (2021). Transparency and the black box problem: Why we do not trust AI. *Philosophy & Technology*, *34*(4), 1607–1622.

Vrana, R. (2025). Perceptions and use of AI supported tools in higher education libraries in Croatia: An exploratory study. *New Review of Academic Librarianship*, •••, 1–26.

Wang, Y. (2023). Synergy in silicon: the evolution and potential of academia-industry collaboration in AI and software engineering. *Authorea Preprints*.

Wisnioski, M. (2025). *Every American an Innovator: How Innovation Became a Way of Life*. The MIT Press.

Zia, S. (2025). Digital Colonialism: Reimagining Power, Identity, and Resistance by Decolonizing AI. Yayasan Drestanta Pelita Indonesia, 129-147.

KEY TERMS AND DEFINITIONS

Academic Integrity: The commitment to honesty, trust, fairness, and responsibility in scholarly activities, especially when using AI tools.

AI Governance: A framework of policies and practices that ensure responsible, ethical, and transparent use of artificial intelligence in academic settings.

Algorithmic Bias: Systematic and repeatable errors in AI decision-making that produce unfair outcomes, especially for marginalized groups.

Cybersecurity: The practice of protecting systems, networks, and data from digital attacks, especially in collaborative academic platforms.

Data Privacy: The right and ability of individuals to control how their personal information is collected, used, and shared in digital academic environments.

Ethical AI: The development and deployment of artificial intelligence that aligns with human values, rights, and societal good.

Informed Consent: The process by which individuals are fully aware of and agree to how their data and participation will be used in AI-powered systems.

Chapter 5
AI, Machine Learning, and IoT in Higher Education:
Transforming Teaching, Learning, and Research

Mustafa Kayyali
https://orcid.org/0000-0003-3300-262X
Maaref University of Applied Sciences, Syria

ABSTRACT

The intersection of Artificial Intelligence, Machine Learning, and the Internet of Things is reshaping the contours of higher education. This chapter explores how these technologies are not merely enhancing but fundamentally transforming teaching, learning, and research practices. From AI-powered personalized learning systems to IoT-connected classrooms that sense and respond to student needs, the academic landscape is being redefined. Machine learning opens doors to predictive insights in both pedagogy and research, helping educators and scholars make data-informed decisions. Yet, amid the innovation, questions around equity, ethics, and institutional readiness remain. This chapter critically examines both the potential and the pitfalls, offering a grounded perspective on how AI, ML, and IoT are enabling a new era of collaborative, intelligent education.

INTRODUCTION

The global landscape of higher education is undergoing one of the most profound transformations in its history. As societies become increasingly intertwined

DOI: 10.4018/979-8-3373-2372-5.ch005

with digital ecosystems, universities are no longer isolated ivory towers—they are dynamic nodes in a vast, interconnected, data-driven world. At the heart of this transformation lies a triad of technological forces: Artificial Intelligence (AI), Machine Learning (ML), and the Internet of Things (IoT). Each has revolutionized industries on its own, but their convergence in higher education is producing ripple effects that extend beyond technological innovation, challenging the very nature of how knowledge is created, shared, and internalized.

In past decades, educational reform was often driven by policy, pedagogy, or economic pressures (Sahlberg, 2023). Today, the impetus comes from intelligent systems that can learn, adapt, and evolve in real-time. AI algorithms are no longer confined to research labs or software companies—they now analyze student performance, recommend personalized learning pathways, automate administrative workflows, and even participate in curriculum design. Meanwhile, ML models are being trained on vast datasets of learner behavior, offering unprecedented insights into what works and what doesn't, often before human instructors can recognize the patterns (Webb et al, 2021). And IoT? It turns physical learning spaces into responsive, data-generating environments—where a student's presence, engagement, and interaction with materials can be sensed, recorded, and adapted to on the fly.

The integration of these technologies signals a shift from passive consumption of knowledge to active, co-created learning experiences. Classrooms are morphing into smart environments; lectures are being supplemented by intelligent tutoring systems; research is enhanced through predictive modeling and automated data mining. Yet, this shift isn't merely technical—it is deeply cultural and philosophical. What does it mean for a machine to "teach"? Can data truly capture the nuance of human cognition, creativity, and curiosity? Is there a risk of depersonalizing education in our pursuit of personalization?

This chapter seeks to address these complex questions while illuminating the possibilities that AI, ML, and IoT bring to higher education. It examines real-world applications, theoretical frameworks, and the ethical and infrastructural challenges that institutions must confront. It aims not just to describe the current landscape, but to critically analyze how the fusion of these technologies is reshaping the academic mission—from teaching and learning to research and collaboration.

Moreover, the chapter considers the global dimension of this transformation. While elite institutions may already boast smart classrooms and AI-enabled learning platforms, universities in under-resourced regions often grapple with access, training, and policy gaps. Thus, the conversation must also center on equity, accessibility, and sustainability, ensuring that technological advancement in higher education does not become yet another frontier for exclusion. We stand at a crossroads where decisions made today will determine the educational paradigms of tomorrow. By exploring the synergy between AI, ML, and IoT, this chapter hopes to offer a thoughtful guide for educators, researchers, technologists, and policymakers invested in shaping the future of intelligent education systems.

RETHINKING EDUCATION: THE CONVERGENCE OF AI, ML, AND IoT IN ACADEMIA

There's something quietly seismic unfolding within the walls of the modern university—an invisible convergence, a slow, surging pulse of change that's harder to pin down than any policy shift or budget reform. You won't find it neatly outlined in a strategic plan or plastered across a mission statement, and yet, it's everywhere. It flickers in the hum of a sensor-laced smart classroom, in the predictive whisper of a machine learning model flagging a student likely to drop out, and in the strange familiarity of an AI-powered tutor that remembers your strengths better than you do. It's tempting to dress this up in techno-optimism: "revolutionizing education," "democratizing knowledge," "data-driven futures." But buzzwords have a habit of obscuring more than they illuminate (Costa et al, 2022). What we are truly witnessing is the reconfiguration of education's DNA—its very logic, its operational soul. And at the heart of that reconfiguration are three intertwined forces: Artificial Intelligence (AI), Machine Learning (ML), and the Internet of Things (IoT). But let's step back a bit.

The Fragile Foundations of the Old World

Higher education, for all its intellectual pedigree, has long struggled with inertia (Levine & Van Pelt, 2021). Lecture halls built for monologues, syllabi designed for uniformity, and assessment systems obsessed with standardization—it's a model designed less for learning than for sorting. And while reformers have chipped away at this edifice for decades, progress has been slow and uneven. There are a thousand reasons for this—bureaucratic complexity, entrenched tradition, economic constraints—but fundamentally, education has remained relatively insulated from the radical transformations that technology has wrought elsewhere. Until now. The collision of AI, ML, and IoT with academia isn't just disruptive—it's catalytic. Each of these technologies alone carries disruptive potential, but together they form a kind of trinity that challenges our deepest assumptions about what education is, and what it could be.

Artificial Intelligence: From Tool to Collaborator

At its most basic, AI refers to machines that mimic human cognitive functions—learning, problem-solving, pattern recognition, decision-making (Korteling et al, 2021). But in education, AI doesn't merely replicate; it reimagines. Think about the act of teaching. Traditionally, a professor prepares material, delivers it to a room full of diverse minds, and hopes for the best. Feedback is slow, often reactive, and largely qualitative. Now imagine an AI system that analyzes every student's interaction with course content in real time—how long they spend on a reading, where they hesitate, what questions they ask. It identifies misconceptions before they metastasize, nudges learners toward tailored resources, even shifts pedagogical approaches mid-stream. It's not just about scale. It's about intimacy. AI can notice what the overworked instructor might miss—the quiet student's confusion, the subtle shift in engagement, the gap between competence and confidence (Kayyali, 2026 A). But AI doesn't just teach. It learns. From patterns, from behavior, from historical performance. It becomes a partner in pedagogy—a silent co-instructor whose presence is felt but not seen. And this is where the real philosophical tension begins: What does it mean to teach in a world where machines can anticipate student needs better than humans? Where does authority lie when algorithms outperform intuition? Are we augmenting human wisdom or outsourcing it? The truth is, we don't yet know. But we are being called to rethink education not just as a transfer of knowledge, but as a dialogue between intelligences—biological and artificial, structured and emergent, human and machine.

Machine Learning: The Pulse of Academic Insight

Where AI offers the architecture of intelligence, Machine Learning provides its heartbeat—its capacity to evolve, adapt, refine. ML thrives on data, and education is a data-rich domain. Every keystroke, every quiz result, every LMS interaction becomes part of an ever-growing ecosystem of feedback loops (Seidel et al, 2021). But unlike traditional analytics, which ask predefined questions, ML algorithms discover patterns we didn't even know to look for. In student support services, ML predicts dropouts not by exam scores, but by behavioral shifts: a decline in LMS logins, a sudden disengagement from peer forums, or erratic submission patterns. In research, it helps identify emerging trends by analyzing millions of journal articles, conference papers, and citation networks—connecting dots at a scale the human mind can't fathom. In curriculum design, it evaluates which teaching strategies yield the most effective outcomes across varying cohorts, disciplines, and demographics (Alalawi et al, 2025). But ML isn't neutral. It reflects the data it consumes, and education is not free from bias. Historical inequities—socioeconomic disparities, systemic underrepresentation, linguistic marginalization—are encoded into educational data (Kayyali, 2025 B). When machine learning models are trained on such datasets, they risk replicating and even amplifying those injustices under a veneer of objectivity. This is why the convergence of AI and ML demands a pedagogical conscience—a commitment to transparency, to fairness, to human-centered design. We cannot afford to see these technologies as black boxes or silver bullets. They are mirrors, amplifiers, tools—and yes, sometimes traps. And yet, when wielded wisely, ML offers something rare: the possibility of foresight. It allows institutions to move from reactive to proactive, from standardized to personalized, from fragmented to holistic.

Figure 1. Integration of AI, ML, and IoT in Smart Education

Integration of AI, ML, and IoT in Smart Education

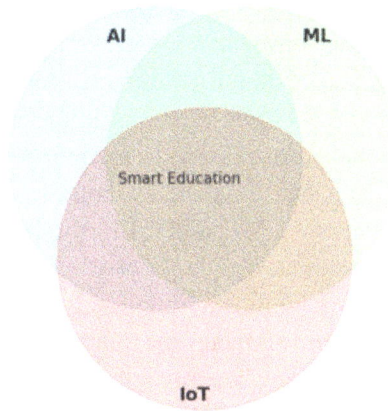

IoT and the Sentient Campus

Of the three technologies, IoT often gets the least attention in educational discourse, perhaps because its effects are more ambient, less visible. But that's precisely what makes it powerful. The Internet of Things connects physical devices—desks, projectors, HVAC systems, whiteboards, even ID badges—to the internet, enabling them to collect and exchange data (SWARGIARY, 2024). When applied to higher education, this creates what some have called the "sentient campus": a learning environment that senses, adapts, responds. Imagine a lecture hall that dims its lights automatically when natural sunlight hits a certain threshold—not just for energy efficiency, but for visual comfort. Or a classroom that tracks air quality, temperature, and CO_2 levels to optimize cognitive performance. Or a library study room that books itself based on your timetable, your preferred seating style, your previous booking patterns. But more importantly, IoT enables *context-aware learning*. Devices know where students are, what devices they're using, even how they're engaging with materials in physical space. It blurs the boundaries between online and offline, turning the entire campus into an active learning interface. There are trade-offs, of course. Privacy is the elephant in the room. The more data we gather, the more granular the surveillance. When every movement is tracked, every choice logged, the specter of control looms large. The question isn't just what IoT can do, but what it *should* do. And who decides.

The Convergence: Toward a New Epistemology

It's one thing to examine AI, ML, and IoT in isolation. It's another to explore what happens when they converge—when intelligent systems learn from real-time data generated by sensor-enabled environments and continuously adapt in ways that reshape the educational experience minute by minute. This convergence challenges not just practice but epistemology—how we define knowledge, how we validate it, how we pass it on. Traditionally, knowledge in higher education has been linear, hierarchical, slow-moving. It resides in syllabi, textbooks, and professorial authority (Bryant, 2024). But the fusion of AI, ML, and IoT births a knowledge system that is networked, decentralized, emergent. Insights evolve as new data arrives. Learning paths change based on real-time conditions. Authority is distributed between humans and machines. This raises unsettling but necessary questions: Are we replacing wisdom with efficiency? Is the university becoming more responsive—or simply more mechanized? What is lost in a world where data outpaces deliberation? At the same time, the potential is exhilarating. A blind student navigates a sensor-rich campus without assistance. A first-generation college student receives adaptive tutoring tailored to their cultural context. A researcher discovers an obscure connection between disciplines that sparks a groundbreaking paper—all because a machine learned to recognize thematic patterns across disparate literatures. This is not the future of education. It is its present—emerging, uneven, imperfect, but here.

To rethink education in this context is not to blindly embrace every new gadget or algorithm. It is to pause, to ask: What kind of learning do we want to cultivate? What kind of intelligence do we value? What kinds of relationships—between students, educators, machines—are we building? The convergence of AI, ML, and IoT offers tools of immense power (Firouzi et al, 2022). But tools do not carry values. They amplify the values of those who wield them. If we prioritize surveillance, we will build educational systems that are efficient but oppressive. If we prioritize empathy, we can create environments that are both intelligent and humane.

We are at a moment where everything is up for redesign—not just classrooms, but concepts. Not just systems, but sensibilities. This is both a gift and a burden. Because once we see what's possible, we can no longer be content with what is. In rethinking education through this technological convergence, we are also being asked to rethink ourselves—our roles as educators, learners, creators, critics, and above all, stewards of something larger than code or curriculum: the human desire to understand, connect, and become.

TEACHING REIMAGINED: INTELLIGENT SYSTEMS AND ADAPTIVE INSTRUCTIONAL DESIGN

Somewhere between the rigidity of a lecture slide and the unpredictable dance of human curiosity, something new is taking root. It doesn't hum like a chalkboard or flicker like a projector. It listens. It watches. It learns. And then, almost imperceptibly, it begins to teach—not with the authority of a sage on the stage, but with the subtle nudges of a ghost in the machine. Welcome to the strange, shifting territory of intelligent systems in teaching—a place where pedagogy is no longer a static art form passed down through generations of practice, but a living, adaptive entity shaped by algorithms, data trails, and digital ecosystems. Teaching, as we once knew it, is being stretched, questioned, fragmented—and reborn. But before we declare the age of the AI teacher, let's sit with the complexity.

The Myth of the One-Size-Fits-All Classroom

Let's be honest: most traditional classrooms were never designed for diversity—not the kind that matters, anyway. Sure, students may hail from different geographies, languages, or backgrounds, but once seated in rows beneath fluorescent lights, they're treated as interchangeable vessels. Same reading. Same lecture. Same quiz. Same feedback. It's an industrial model, optimized for delivery, not understanding. And yet, every educator knows that learning is anything but uniform. Some students need time. Others need context. A few need repetition. And many just need to be seen—not as part of a cohort, but as themselves. The promise of adaptive instructional design begins here—not with grand claims, but with a humble question: what if teaching could bend to the learner, instead of the other way around?

Enter the Intelligent Tutor: A Quiet Revolution

In recent years, intelligent tutoring systems (ITS) have quietly crept into the learning landscape, rarely celebrated but increasingly indispensable (Hughes, 2021).

They don't look like much—maybe a sleek interface with some diagnostics, a few question prompts, a hint button. But beneath the surface, they're doing something extraordinary: they're learning how we learn. Using a mix of machine learning algorithms, Bayesian networks, and neural models, these systems build dynamic profiles of each student. Not just which answer they got wrong, but *how* they got there. Did they hesitate before clicking? Did they review the material first? Did they repeat the same mistake in a different context? Over time, the system begins to understand a student's cognitive signature—her misconceptions, her confidence gaps, her pace, her style. Now, imagine a classroom of thirty students, each accompanied by their own invisible tutor, constantly adjusting the difficulty, pacing, feedback type, and even the framing of a question to suit their evolving needs (Kayyali, 2026 D). This isn't science fiction. It's already happening—in platforms like Carnegie Learning's MATHia, Squirrel AI in China, and emerging open-source projects around the world (Amiri, 2025). Of course, this brings up another question—perhaps the most existential one: *If a machine can teach better than I can, what's left for me to do?* The answer, paradoxically, is *everything*.

From Content Delivery to Learning Design

In the intelligent classroom, the role of the educator doesn't vanish—it evolves (Devi et al, 2023). Think of the teacher not as a content transmitter, but as a learning architect. No longer burdened by the need to explain the same concept five times in five ways, they are free to orchestrate learning journeys, design experiences, and respond to emotional and social dynamics that no algorithm can fully grasp. In fact, one of the unexpected gifts of intelligent systems is that they return time—that most precious and vanishing commodity—to the human educator. Time to observe. To mentor. To connect. To intervene not with blanket corrections, but with precise, compassionate insight. Adaptive instructional design, then, is not just about smarter technology. It's about more intentional pedagogy. It invites us to ask: What is the purpose of this lesson? What pathways can students take? Where are the decision points? What feedback will matter? And because these systems generate real-time analytics, instructors are no longer flying blind (Kem, 2022). They know, often with startling granularity, which concepts are resonating, which are stalling, and with whom. This enables precision teaching—not as a theoretical goal, but as a daily reality. Still, not all is utopian.

Figure 2. Network of Components in AI-Driven Learning Environments

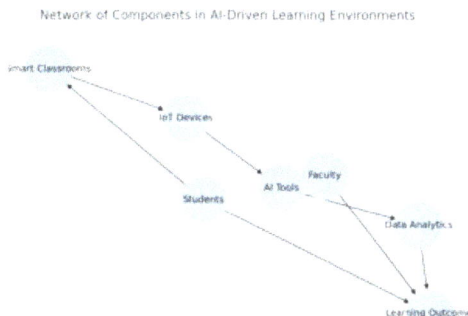

Network of Components in AI-Driven Learning Environments

The Ethics of Personalization: Who's in Control?

There's a fine line between personalization and manipulation. When a system knows a learner so well it can predict their responses, what happens to agency? Who's really steering the ship—the student, the teacher, or the algorithm trained on thousands of other students who aren't in the room? Intelligent systems can recommend content, yes. But they can also nudge students toward certain paths, filter out options, even shape epistemic habits—what counts as "knowing" something. This is especially thorny when systems are trained on biased data, built by developers unfamiliar with the cultural nuances of their users, or optimized for institutional efficiency over individual growth. And then there's the question of transparency. Few students understand how their adaptive platforms actually work. Fewer still have a say in how their data is used to shape their learning experience. There's a risk, then, of teaching becoming a black box—a process students experience, but no longer fully understand (Gillani et al, 2023). To reimagine teaching ethically, we must build systems that are explainable, auditable, and participatory. Students should not just be recipients of personalization; they should be co-creators of it.

Embracing the Messiness: Learning Is Not Just Logic

One of the subtle dangers of intelligent systems is their bias toward rationality. They are spectacular at parsing logic trees, modeling probability, and identifying correlations. But learning is rarely so neat. Sometimes, students don't understand a concept because of a personal trauma, a language barrier, or a teacher who once told them they weren't smart enough. Sometimes, they resist because they're afraid. Or bored. Or because the content reminds them of something they'd rather forget. No algorithm, no matter how sophisticated, can fully capture this emotional substrate of learning. That's why human educators matter more now than ever—not despite intelligent systems, but because of them. Technology may guide the mind, but teachers hold the heart. And heart is not a trivial thing. It's what makes a student try again after failing. It's what sparks the question that leads to the insight that changes everything. It's what makes learning *matter*.

Redesigning for Flow, Not Just Outcomes

Much of the current conversation around adaptive learning is framed in terms of outcomes: better grades, higher completion rates, reduced time-to-degree. But what if we also designed for flow—for that immersive, challenging-yet-achievable state where learning feels like play, like discovery, like magic? Intelligent systems can help here, too. By tracking engagement levels, pacing patterns, and challenge-skill ratios, they can modulate content to keep learners in that delicate zone between boredom and anxiety. But only if we let go of our obsession with standardization and embrace the variability of human minds. Imagine a learning platform that doesn't just say "You got it wrong," but senses frustration, pauses the task, and switches to a mini-game that builds the same skill in a different way. Or a system that notices a student soaring ahead and offers an optional research challenge to deepen their interest. Teaching reimagined isn't just smarter. It's kinder. More attuned. More humane.

New Roles, New Literacies

As intelligent systems become more embedded, the educator's role will diversify (Iweuno et al, 2024). Some will become data interpreters, turning dashboards into action. Others will act as designers, crafting multimodal learning experiences. Still others may specialize as AI coaches, helping students understand how to work with (and around) their digital co-learners. But this shift demands new literacies. Teachers must learn not just how to use platforms, but how to question them. How to read a recommendation and ask: "Why this? For whom? Based on what?" Pedagogical intuition must now dance with algorithmic logic. This isn't easy. It's disruptive. But it's also liberating. We are no longer constrained by the old dichotomies—lecture vs. discussion, analog vs. digital, theory vs. application. We can mix. Remix. Invent. That is, if we're willing to be learners ourselves.

In the end, reimagining teaching through intelligent systems is not about replacing humans with machines (Yildirim et al, 2021). It's about creating shared intelligences—systems where human insight and machine precision collaborate to serve the learner. This is not a neat or tidy process. It is messy, iterative, full of surprises. It requires humility, experimentation, courage. But it also holds extraordinary promise. Because teaching, at its best, has never just been about information.

It's about transformation. About helping someone become more than they were. About seeing potential where others see limits. And while intelligent systems can assist, accelerate, and augment that process, they cannot replace its essence. That remains human. Beautifully, stubbornly, unpredictably human.

THE CONNECTED CAMPUS: IOT-ENABLED LEARNING ENVIRONMENTS

It starts subtly. A smart door that unlocks when a faculty member approaches. An HVAC system adjusting itself not to a preset schedule, but to the collective carbon dioxide levels in a classroom (Cho et al, 2023). A student's smartwatch nudging her to hydrate during a high-stress exam. Nothing futuristic here. No flying drones buzzing above lecture halls or robotic librarians whispering citations. Just… context. Responsiveness. The feeling that, somehow, the campus is paying attention. That's the promise—no, the quiet revolution—of the Internet of Things in education. Not a spectacle, but a shift in atmosphere. A recalibration of space, systems, and experience. The campus is no longer just a place where learning happens. It's learning, too.

From Passive Infrastructure to Active Ecosystem

For decades, educational infrastructure was inert. Bricks and mortar. Timetables and whiteboards. The logic was linear: students move through space, space remains unchanged. But IoT flips that script. When buildings breathe, when devices speak, when learning environments adjust themselves in real-time based on usage patterns, physiological signals, environmental data—then something strange and beautiful begins to emerge: the idea of a sentient campus. Not sentient in the science-fiction sense, of course. There's no central consciousness. No voice greeting you as you walk across the quad (at least, not yet). But sentient in the sense that the environment gathers data, interprets context, and acts—sometimes preemptively. A classroom that dims the lights when outdoor brightness hits a threshold isn't thinking. But it is responding. A library chair that adjusts posture support based on the average weight and height of its usual occupant isn't learning. But it is optimizing. And a campus that tracks traffic flows to redirect footfall away from overcrowded lecture halls isn't alive. But it is… aware.

Learning Environments That Learn

The real magic of IoT in academia is not in the devices themselves. It's in the feedback loops they create. Because when the environment begins to respond to learners, it also starts to reshape how learning unfolds. Imagine this: a seminar room where ambient noise sensors monitor decibel levels—not to police silence, but to map engagement (Butkiene et al, 2025). If discussion volume dips consistently at certain points in a lecture, the system might flag that as a moment of confusion or disinterest. Over time, a heatmap of intellectual activity emerges—not as surveillance, but as a tool for instructional redesign. Or consider wearable devices integrated into coursework—not for step-counting, but for learning analytics. A student's heart rate variability during presentations, or micro-pauses in speech patterns during oral exams, could be indicators of stress or cognitive overload. If gathered ethically and consensually, this data might help educators design better support systems, pacing, and interventions. In essence, IoT turns environments into pedagogical partners. They don't just house learning—they *host* it, *shape* it, *respond* to it.

The Architecture of Attention

In an age of fractured focus, one of the most precious commodities in education is attention (Guan et al, 2023). Not information. Not access. Not even knowledge. Attention—raw, sustained, curious attention. And here, the IoT-enabled campus offers possibilities we're only beginning to explore. Through sensors, beacons, and location-aware devices, the learning environment can be tuned to nudge attention— not through coercion, but through subtle cues. A classroom wall might glow a different hue when collaborative activity is encouraged. A study pod might signal "do not disturb" when a student enters deep-work mode. Notifications might shift from devices to physical space—so instead of a phone buzzing, a table pulses gently to remind students of time. There's potential here to reclaim the analog, paradoxically through the digital. To build tactile, embodied cues into learning spaces that reconnect students with the physical world even as they navigate digital content. The question is not whether we can design such spaces. It's whether we'll choose to design them with care.

The Invisible Layer: Data, Data, Data

But let's not get swept away in romance. For every poetic vision of responsive lighting and emotion-sensitive seating, there's a more sobering reality underneath: data. Oceans of it. Streaming constantly. Who's collecting it? Who owns it? Who decides what it means? IoT is a double-edged promise. It offers personalization, optimization, insight. But it also brings surveillance, intrusion, and the potential erosion of autonomy. A student who knows that her seat monitors posture might sit straighter—but will she feel freer? A professor whose voice is tracked for clarity might speak more slowly—but will he speak more boldly? The danger is that the connected campus becomes not a sanctuary for inquiry, but a panopticon for performance (Montgomery et al, 2023). Where every click, glance, shift, or pause is logged, scored, compared. To build IoT-enabled learning environments ethically, we need more than engineers. We need philosophers. Ethicists. Poets. People who will ask not just what can be built, but *what should be*. Who will insist on informed consent, data minimalism, contextual integrity. Who will remind us that some silences are sacred, and some data is better left uncollected.

Accessibility and Equity: The Real Frontier

And then there's access. Smart campuses sound exciting—if you're at MIT, Stanford, or Singapore. But what about the underfunded public universities, the rural colleges, the institutions where "smart" still means having enough whiteboard markers? The risk is clear: the emergence of a technological caste system in education. The haves get responsive classrooms, AI tutors, emotion-aware lighting. The have-nots get broken projectors and overstuffed lecture halls (Foong et al, 2024). But it doesn't have to be that way. IoT can be modular. Scalable. Context-sensitive. A well-placed temperature sensor that prevents heat exhaustion in exam halls. A Bluetooth beacon that helps visually impaired students navigate unfamiliar buildings. A low-cost motion detector that reduces electricity bills by 30% in computer labs. The point is not to build futuristic campuses. The point is to build caring ones—where technology serves the margins first, not last. Where IoT becomes not a status symbol, but a social equalizer.

A Pedagogy of Place

Perhaps the most profound shift the connected campus invites is a reconsideration of place itself. For centuries, universities have been defined by their architecture—gothic towers, brutalist blocks, digital learning centers (Werder & Otis, 2023). But IoT challenges us to think of space not just as container, but as actor. When the room participates in the lesson—adjusting soundscapes, lighting cues, environmental stimuli—place becomes pedagogy. And when students learn not just *in* a space, but *with* it, something changes. A sense of reciprocity. Co-agency. Dialogue.

This may sound abstract, but it has concrete implications. It means designing classrooms not just for acoustics, but for adaptability. Corridors that change based on time of day. Cafeterias that push learning prompts to waiting students. Outdoor spaces that host pop-up AR experiences tied to the curriculum. Learning is no longer bounded by the classroom. The entire campus becomes a cognitive map—an invitation to explore, connect, reflect.

Risk, Resistance, and the Human Factor

Of course, not everyone will welcome this shift. Some faculty will resist. Some students will disengage. Technological fatigue is real. Techno-solutionism is worse. And sometimes, a whiteboard and a circle of chairs is all that's needed for transformative learning (Zehnder et al, 2021). IoT should never be imposed. It should be offered—carefully, iteratively, experimentally. This means building in opt-outs. Embracing analog backups. Designing slow spaces within smart ones—nooks without sensors, benches without Wi-Fi. Places to pause, unplug, breathe. Because the goal isn't seamlessness. It's richness. Multiplicity. Choice. A connected campus isn't necessarily a smarter one. But it can be a more humane one—if we listen.

At the end of the day, it's easy to be dazzled by the hardware. The sensors, the dashboards, the interoperability. But what matters most in IoT-enabled learning environments isn't the things. It's the relationships they shape. Between students and space. Between data and decision. Between presence and participation. A truly connected campus doesn't just connect devices. It connects people, ideas, experiences (Worsley et al, 2021). It fosters serendipity, supports struggle, celebrates difference. And if we do it right, it might just reconnect us—with learning, with each other, with the places we inhabit every day without noticing. It's not about making education high-tech. It's about making it high-touch—through technologies that are quietly intelligent, deeply respectful, and designed with wonder. Because in the end, education isn't about the tools we use. It's about the worlds we build.

REDEFINING RESEARCH: PREDICTIVE ANALYTICS, AUTOMATION, AND INTELLIGENT DISCOVERY

The face of academic inquiry has always been a mirror held up to the times—reflecting not just what we know, but how we come to know it (McKenzie & Bartunek, 2023). For centuries, research was a laborious craft: painstaking observation, trial and error, incremental insight. It demanded patience, intuition, and often, a solitary commitment to unearthing truths that others might overlook or dismiss. Today, that face is shifting. Subtly, profoundly, irrevocably. The infusion of predictive analytics, automation, and intelligent discovery into the research ecosystem is not just a technological upgrade; it is a redefinition of what it means to investigate, hypothesize, and understand. It beckons us to reconsider age-old assumptions about originality, creativity, and the role of the human researcher.

The Data Deluge: From Scarcity to Overwhelm

One of the defining challenges—and paradoxes—of modern research is not the lack of data, but the overwhelming abundance of it. From genomic sequences to social media streams, satellite imagery to digital archives, the sheer volume of information threatens to drown the curious mind in noise. In the past, researchers were often gatekeepers of data, guardians of rare manuscripts or exclusive datasets (Teixeira da Silva & Nazarovets, 2023). Today, the challenge is the opposite: how to separate signal from noise in a flood of bytes. Predictive analytics emerges not as a mere convenience, but as an existential necessity. It transforms mountains of data points into navigable landscapes, uncovering hidden patterns, correlations, and trajectories that would elude even the most meticulous human analyst. Consider, for instance, a biomedical researcher sifting through thousands of protein interactions or clinical trial outcomes. Predictive models can flag the most promising avenues for drug development, anticipating success where blind experimentation would flounder. Similarly, in social sciences, algorithms parse sentiment and discourse trends across millions of tweets to forecast social movements or public opinion shifts. The question, then, is not whether predictive analytics is useful—it is how it reshapes the very epistemology of research.

Prediction as a New Form of Explanation

Traditionally, scientific explanation has sought causal narratives—why something happens, what mechanisms underpin it (Neale, 2021). Prediction was often a secondary goal, a test of theory. But with machine learning, prediction is taking center stage. Models that forecast disease outbreaks, climate anomalies, or market fluctuations don't necessarily explain *why* with human-readable logic (Kayyali, 2026 B). They operate on complex mathematical abstractions, sometimes opaque even to their creators. This challenges us to reconsider what counts as valid knowledge. Is a model's ability to reliably predict outcomes enough? Or must we demand interpretability? Are we comfortable trusting black-box insights in place of causal stories? These questions are not merely technical. They cut to the heart of academic values and trust. They demand new methodological literacies for researchers, policymakers, and society at large.

Automation: The Tireless Collaborator

Alongside prediction, automation is quietly revolutionizing the mundane, repetitive, and time-consuming facets of research. Data cleaning, literature review, coding transcripts, experiment replication—these are tasks that have traditionally soaked up countless hours. Now, intelligent systems can shoulder much of this labor. Automatic text summarization tools can digest hundreds of papers in minutes, highlighting key themes and gaps (Wibawa & Kurniawan, 2024). Robotic lab assistants perform precise, repetitive experiments without fatigue. Natural language processing algorithms annotate qualitative data with speed and consistency. The gains are obvious: efficiency, scale, and the freeing up of human creativity. But automation also demands a reevaluation of research craftsmanship. What skills will researchers need when data wrangling is delegated to machines? How do we maintain critical judgment amid increasing reliance on automated pipelines? More than that, automation provokes questions of authorship and accountability. When an AI drafts parts of a literature review, or when robotic instruments generate experimental results, who owns the knowledge? Who is responsible for errors, bias, or misinterpretation? The lines blur. But so do the possibilities.

Intelligent Discovery: Beyond Human Intuition

Perhaps the most intriguing frontier is intelligent discovery—the capacity of AI systems not just to assist, but to propose, hypothesize, and sometimes surprise (Wang et al, 2023). Imagine algorithms that comb through decades of cross-disciplinary research, surfacing connections no human could perceive. A system that suggests a new chemical compound based on pattern recognition across unrelated molecular datasets. Or an AI that identifies latent themes in historical archives, sparking fresh theoretical insights. These are not just tools for efficiency. They are partners in innovation, collaborators that extend the bounds of human imagination. But they also unsettle. What becomes of the solitary genius, the inspired leap? Can machines truly create, or are they just recombining existing data in novel ways? And if the latter, is human originality just a myth anyway? The dialogue between human and machine creativity is only beginning. It is a dialogue fraught with tension, wonder, and the occasional philosophical impasse.

Embracing Ambiguity: The Limits of Algorithms

Despite the allure of predictive power and automation, research is not merely a quest for answers. It is a conversation with uncertainty. Models falter. Data deceives. Algorithms encode human bias. There are domains—ethical dilemmas, artistic expression, subjective experience—where quantitative analysis offers little purchase. Here, human judgment remains paramount. The challenge is not to replace human insight but to augment it, to create symbiotic workflows where machines handle complexity and humans interpret nuance. It means cultivating what some call algorithmic humility—an awareness that no model is infallible, no dataset complete.

That human researchers must always ask: What are we missing? Whose voices are absent? What assumptions underlie our tools?

Democratizing Discovery or Deepening Divides?

There is a seductive narrative that AI-driven research democratizes knowledge production (Omodan & Marongwe, 2024). After all, automation lowers barriers. Predictive tools can guide novices. Intelligent discovery systems can open new fields. But we must be wary. The infrastructure costs, technical expertise, and data requirements often privilege well-resourced institutions and countries. There is a real risk of technological colonialism in knowledge, where algorithmic gatekeepers shape global research agendas. Reliance on proprietary platforms and opaque models risks locking researchers into black-box ecosystems that undermine academic freedom. Addressing this demands concerted effort: open-source tools, capacity-building, transparent algorithms, and policies that prioritize equity alongside innovation.

The Researcher's New Toolkit: A Hybrid Literacy

What skills will tomorrow's researchers need? Fluency in coding, yes. Statistical savvy, certainly. But also critical digital literacy: understanding algorithmic bias, data provenance, and ethical implications. Interdisciplinary collaboration will become essential. Computer scientists, domain experts, ethicists, and social scientists working side-by-side. Perhaps most important is a mindset open to experimentation with new epistemologies. Willingness to question entrenched assumptions. Curiosity about what machines can—and cannot—do. The role of the researcher becomes that of a curator, interrogator, and storyteller. Curating datasets and tools. Interrogating models and results. Crafting narratives that situate findings in broader human contexts.

Toward a Reflexive Science

As research becomes ever more intertwined with AI and automation, reflexivity is key. Reflexivity—the practice of stepping back to examine one's own assumptions, methods, and impact—is not new. But the pace and opacity of digital methods amplify its urgency (White & Davis, 2023). How do predictive algorithms shape what we study? How do automated pipelines constrain or liberate inquiry? How do intelligent systems reinforce or disrupt power structures in academia? Engaging with these questions requires more than individual awareness. It demands institutional support for transparency, reproducibility, and accountability. Research must be conducted not only with rigor, but with ethics and empathy.

The Promise and the Paradox

Ultimately, redefining research through predictive analytics, automation, and intelligent discovery is a dance of paradoxes. It offers unprecedented scale and speed, but risks superficiality. It enables novel insights, but challenges interpretation. It democratizes knowledge production, but risks deepening inequities. Yet in this complexity lies opportunity—a chance to rethink research not as a solitary act of genius, but as a collaborative, hybrid process that blends human creativity with machine precision. A process where uncertainty is embraced, and curiosity remains the guiding star.

I often wonder what the pioneers of science would make of today's landscape. Would Darwin marvel at the algorithms tracing evolutionary patterns across millions of genomes? Would Curie embrace robots running endless assays? Would Ada Lovelace feel vindicated or unsettled by AI's role in discovery? One thing is certain: the tools we build reflect our values, hopes, and fears. They extend our minds but also reflect our limitations. As we redefine research, we stand not just at a technological crossroads, but a philosophical and ethical one (Grunwald, 2021). How we proceed will shape not only knowledge but our very understanding of what it means to be a curious, striving human in a world increasingly shared with intelligent machines. The future of research is not written yet. But it will be, undeniably, co-authored.

OPPORTUNITIES, CHALLENGES, AND THE ROAD AHEAD FOR AI-DRIVEN HIGHER EDUCATION

If you were to ask me what the most captivating feature of AI-driven higher education is, I would say it's the tantalizing tension between boundless promise and daunting complexity. It's as if we've been handed a double-edged gift—one that can cut through the old constraints of teaching, learning, and research, yet demands we wield it with unprecedented care and imagination. We stand at a crossroads where technology isn't simply a tool in the hands of academia. It's an active participant, a restless agent, shaping futures in ways both exhilarating and unnerving.

The Irresistible Lure of Possibility

Imagine a university campus that feels alive—not just in the sense of bustling bodies, but as a dynamic organism responding to the needs of its members. AI can personalize learning pathways to an extent unimaginable a decade ago (Kayyali, 2025 A). It can analyze student progress not just by grades, but by emotional engagement, cognitive rhythms, and even social interaction patterns. The potential to tailor education to each individual's unique mind is revolutionary. It's a dream long held by educators but rarely realized at scale. Research, too, is undergoing a seismic shift. AI accelerates discovery by crunching colossal datasets, surfacing correlations that elude human cognition, and suggesting hypotheses that might never have crossed a scholar's mind. Collaborative platforms empowered by AI enable interdisciplinary dialogues across continents—blurring boundaries between fields, institutions, and cultures. Then there is administration—the unsung hero of academic life. AI-driven systems streamline admissions, optimize resource allocation, predict enrollment trends, and even flag students at risk of dropout, enabling timely interventions (Shoaib et al, 2024). The cumulative effect? Universities can become more efficient, responsive, and student-centered. But—and here lies the rub—these opportunities come tethered to complex challenges that are not simply technical puzzles but questions about values, equity, and the very soul of education.

The Ethical Quandaries: Navigating a Moral Minefield

It's tempting to get swept up in the technological marvels and overlook the ethical undercurrents. But in AI-driven higher education, ethics isn't an afterthought; it's a pulse running through every innovation. Consider data privacy. Universities collect vast amounts of personal and behavioral data—from academic records to biometric inputs to social media footprints. Who controls this data? Who decides what's collected, stored, shared, or deleted? The risk of surveillance is real, and not just in Orwellian terms. There's a subtler danger: that students and faculty become commodified—reduced to data points for institutional optimization rather than human beings with agency and dignity. Then there's bias. AI systems learn from historical data, which inevitably contains biases—racial, gender, socioeconomic (Franklin et al, 2024). Left unchecked, these biases propagate and amplify, perpetuating existing inequities. An algorithm recommending scholarship awards might inadvertently favor privileged demographics. A predictive model flagging at-risk students might disproportionately target marginalized groups. This is not just unfair. It erodes trust and undermines the very goals of inclusion and diversity that universities strive for. Accountability, too, is fraught. When decisions are made or influenced by opaque algorithms, who is responsible? If an AI system rejects an application or misclassifies a student's performance, is the fault the machine's, the developers', or the institution's? Transparency is crucial but often elusive. These questions require ongoing dialogue, multidisciplinary collaboration, and above all, a commitment to human-centered design—where technology serves educational values, not the other way around.

Equity and Access: The Persistent Divide

The romance of AI-enabled education often focuses on personalization and scalability. Yet, beneath the glossy veneer lies a stubborn reality: digital divides persist and sometimes deepen (Kayyali, 2024). Who gets to benefit from AI-powered platforms? Who owns the devices? Who has reliable internet connectivity? The promise of democratization rings hollow if marginalized communities remain excluded from the infrastructure, training, or content needed. Cultural relevance is often sidelined. AI models are frequently developed within Western, English-speaking contexts, and may not translate well across diverse linguistic and cultural landscapes (Kayyali, 2026 E). This risks alienating learners and reinforcing dominant paradigms rather than embracing pluralism. Addressing equity demands intentional strategies—open-source solutions, inclusive datasets, community engagement, multilingual content, and investment in digital literacy. It means thinking beyond technology to the social and political contexts in which education unfolds.

The Changing Role of Educators: From Gatekeepers to Guides

One of the most profound impacts of AI in higher education is the shifting role of educators. No longer merely transmitters of knowledge, teachers become designers of learning experiences, curators of resources, mentors who interpret data insights and humanize them. AI can provide diagnostic feedback and adaptive content, but it cannot replicate the empathy, intuition, and moral presence that teachers bring (Yambal & Waykar, 2025). Yet this shift can be disorienting and unsettling. Faculty may fear obsolescence or struggle with new literacies around data and algorithms. Institutions must invest in professional development that fosters digital fluency, critical engagement with AI, and pedagogical innovation. This is a moment for educators to reclaim agency in shaping how AI integrates into learning—not as passive recipients of technology but as active co-creators of AI-enhanced education.

The Unintended Consequences: Technology's Shadow

As with any disruptive innovation, AI brings unintended effects. One concern is over-reliance on metrics. The ease of collecting and analyzing data might tempt institutions to prioritize what is measurable—test scores, attendance, engagement analytics—over what is meaningful but less quantifiable, like critical thinking, creativity, or ethical reasoning. There's also the risk of homogenization. Algorithms trained on dominant norms might push curricula and pedagogy toward standardized, predictable paths, stifling diversity of thought and learning styles (George, 2023). Another shadow is the psychological impact on students. Continuous monitoring and predictive profiling may induce stress, reduce motivation, or foster a sense of surveillance that inhibits authentic learning. Recognizing these shadows is crucial. It calls for balance—embracing AI's benefits while guarding against its excesses.

Sustainability and Infrastructure: The Hidden Foundations

Behind every AI-powered innovation lies a complex infrastructure—data centers humming with energy, networks carrying torrents of data, devices multiplying on campuses. Sustainability is more than an environmental concern; it's about resilience, affordability, and scalability. Universities must grapple with the carbon footprint of AI, the lifecycle of hardware, and the digital waste they generate. Robust infrastructure is a prerequisite for equitable access. Investments in broadband, cybersecurity, and technical support underpin AI's promise. Planning for sustainability requires long-term vision and cross-sector collaboration—linking technological advancement with ecological and social responsibility.

Figure 3. Adoption Trends of AI and IoT in Higher Education (2018–2024)

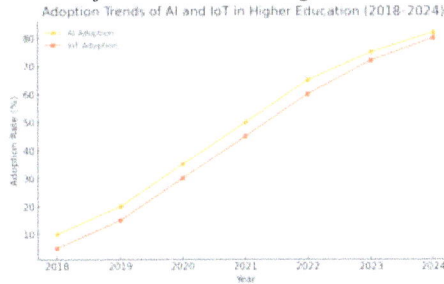

If we look beyond the immediate horizon, the future of AI-driven higher education unfolds as a complex ecosystem. It's an ecosystem where humans and machines co-evolve; where students, faculty, administrators, and AI systems engage in dynamic, reciprocal relationships (Aithal & Maiya, 2023). Where education transcends walls, boundaries, and disciplines to become fluid, personalized, and participatory (Kayyali, 2026 C). This ecosystem will demand new governance models—transparent, inclusive, and ethical. It will require ongoing research into AI's impacts, participatory design processes, and global dialogue that honors diversity. And it will call for humility. Humility to recognize that technology alone cannot solve education's deepest challenges. That human values, context, and wisdom must remain at the core.

CONCLUSION

As we reflect on the transformative role of Artificial Intelligence, Machine Learning, and the Internet of Things in higher education, one truth emerges clearly: we are witnessing not a mere upgrade in tools, but a redefinition of educational existence. This is not just about more efficient grading systems, automated feedback, or smarter buildings—this is about rethinking the relationship between humans, knowledge, and technology at a fundamental level.

In many ways, AI, ML, and IoT act as mirrors. They reveal gaps in current pedagogical models, inefficiencies in research workflows, and blind spots in institutional policies. But more importantly, they offer pathways to overcome them. AI-powered platforms can identify students at risk of disengagement before a human teacher ever notices. Machine learning can analyze years of academic performance data to recommend evidence-based changes to curricula. IoT devices can measure environmental conditions in classrooms to optimize student comfort and alert instructors when attention spans are waning. The capabilities are vast, and so are the implications. Amid the promise lies a sobering reality. Technology alone does not make education better—intentional design does. Blindly adopting the latest AI model or deploying smart sensors across campus without a clear pedagogical or ethical framework can lead to more harm than good. There is a fine line between personalization and surveillance, between assistance and dependency, between innovation and alienation. If higher education is to remain a space of critical thinking and human development, then the application of intelligent technologies must be constantly interrogated, contextualized, and co-created with all stakeholders—students, faculty, administrators, and communities.

Furthermore, equity must be front and center. The global digital divide persists—not just in terms of infrastructure, but also in terms of data literacy, cultural relevance, and language accessibility. AI models trained in one context may reinforce biases when deployed in another. IoT systems designed in the Global North may overlook the needs of learners in the Global South. Ensuring fairness, inclusivity, and local adaptation is not a footnote—it is a cornerstone.

This chapter also underscores the need for new professional roles and revised institutional cultures. Educators must evolve from knowledge deliverers to facilitators of AI-augmented learning. Researchers need to engage with ethical frameworks for machine-generated discoveries. Universities must build cross-functional teams that bring together engineers, instructional designers, ethicists, and learners to collaboratively shape their digital futures.

Ultimately, the convergence of AI, ML, and IoT in higher education offers a rare opportunity—a chance not just to digitize old models, but to invent new ones. Models that are flexible yet grounded, data-driven yet humane, innovative yet ethically responsible. If approached with care, reflection, and vision, this transformation can move us closer to the long-standing goals of education: not merely efficiency or output, but understanding, growth, and wisdom. The future of higher education doesn't lie in the hands of machines. It lies in how we choose to use them.

REFERENCES

Aithal, P. S., & Maiya, A. K. (2023). Innovations in higher education industry–Shaping the future. [IJCSBE]. *International Journal of Case Studies in Business, IT, and Education*, *7*(4), 283–311.

Alalawi, K., Athauda, R., Chiong, R., & Renner, I. (2025). Evaluating the student performance prediction and action framework through a learning analytics intervention study. *Education and Information Technologies*, *30*(3), 2887–2916.

Amiri, S. M. H. (2025). Digital Transformations in Education: Research Insights for 21st-Century Learning. International Journal of Innovative Science [IJISET]. *Engineering & Technology*, *12*(03), 1–15.

Bryant, P. (2024). Learning design ecosystems thinking: Defying the linear imperative and designing for higher education at-scale. *Journal of Work-Applied Management*, *16*(2), 283–291.

Butkiene, R., Gudonienė, D., Čeponienė, L., Vaiciukynas, E., Virkus, S., Dickel, J., ... & Coelho, J. (2025). Digital transformation: handbook for digital transformation specialists.

Cho, J., Heo, Y., & Moon, J. W. (2023). An intelligent HVAC control strategy for supplying comfortable and energy-efficient school environment. *Advanced Engineering Informatics*, *55*, 101895.

Costa, A. C. F., & de Mello Santos, V. H., & de OLIVEIRA, O. J. (2022). Towards the revolution and democratization of education: A framework to overcome challenges and explore opportunities through Industry 4.0. *Informatics in Education*, *21*(1), 1–32.

Devi, K., Sabitha, J., & Sathish Kumar, J. (2023). Effects of Evolving Applications of IoT in the Education Sector. Digital Technologies for Smart Business, Economics and Education: Towards a Promising Future, 213-224.

Firouzi, F., Farahani, B., & Marinšek, A. (2022). The convergence and interplay of edge, fog, and cloud in the AI-driven Internet of Things (IoT). *Information Systems*, *107*, 101840.

Foong, Y. P., Pidani, R., Sithira Vadivel, V., & Dongyue, Y. (2024). Singapore smart nation: journey into a new digital landscape for higher education. In *Emerging Technologies in Business: Innovation Strategies for Competitive Advantage* (pp. 281–304). Springer Nature Singapore.

Franklin, G., Stephens, R., Piracha, M., Tiosano, S., Lehouillier, F., Koppel, R., & Elkin, P. L. (2024). The sociodemographic biases in machine learning algorithms: A biomedical informatics perspective. *Life (Chicago, Ill.)*, *14*(6), 652.

George, A. S. (2023). Preparing students for an AI-driven world: Rethinking curriculum and pedagogy in the age of artificial intelligence. *Partners Universal Innovative Research Publication*, *1*(2), 112–136.

Gillani, N., Eynon, R., Chiabaut, C., & Finkel, K. (2023). Unpacking the "Black Box" of AI in education. *Journal of Educational Technology & Society*, *26*(1), 99–111.

Grunwald, A. (2021). *Living technology: philosophy and ethics at the crossroads between life and technology*. Jenny Stanford Publishing.

Guan, X., Feng, X., & Islam, A. Y. M. (2023). The dilemma and countermeasures of educational data ethics in the age of intelligence. *Humanities & Social Sciences Communications*, *10*(1), 1–14.

Hughes, J. (2021). The deskilling of teaching and the case for intelligent tutoring systems. *Journal of Ethics and Emerging Technologies*, *31*(2), 1–16.

Iweuno, B. N., Orekha, P., Ojediran, O., Imohimi, E., & Adu-Twum, H. T. (2024). Leveraging Artificial Intelligence for an inclusive and diversified curriculum. *World Journal of Advanced Research and Reviews*, *23*(2), 1579–1590.

Kayyali, M. (2024). Global Perspectives on Personalized Learning: Case Studies and Best Practices. In Transforming Education for Personalized Learning (pp. 66-84). IGI Global.

Kayyali, M. (2025a). Ethical Implications of Generative AI in Education: Privacy, Bias, and Integrity. In Transformative AI Practices for Personalized Learning Strategies (pp. 185-218). IGI Global Scientific Publishing.

Kayyali, M. (2025b). Generative AI and Education: Transforming Teaching and Learning Through Collaborative Intelligence. In Humans and Generative AI Tools for Collaborative Intelligence (pp. 25-52). IGI Global Scientific Publishing.

Kayyali, M. (2026a). Case Studies: Successful Applications of AI and AR in Research. In Revolutionizing Academic Research With AI and Augmented Reality (pp. 347-368). IGI Global Scientific Publishing.

Kayyali, M. (2026b). Machine Learning and Bias: Creating Inclusive AI Systems for All. In AI and New Forms of Exclusion (pp. 143-166). IGI Global Scientific Publishing.

Kayyali, M. (2026c). AI in Higher Education: The Risk of Excluding Vulnerable Learners. In AI and New Forms of Exclusion (pp. 57-82). IGI Global Scientific Publishing.

Kayyali, M. (2026d). The Impact of AI on Classroom Dynamics in Higher Education: Shifting Roles for Professors and Students. In Responsible AI Integration in Education (pp. 151-180). IGI Global Scientific Publishing.

Kayyali, M. (2026e). Preparing Educators for the Future: Navigating AI Tools in English Language Teaching. In AI-Powered English Teaching (pp. 267-308). IGI Global Scientific Publishing.

Kem, D. (2022). Personalised and adaptive learning: Emerging learning platforms in the era of digital and smart learning. *International Journal of Social Science and Human Research*, 5(2), 385–391.

Korteling, J. H., van de Boer-Visschedijk, G. C., Blankendaal, R. A., Boonekamp, R. C., & Eikelboom, A. R. (2021). Human-versus artificial intelligence. *Frontiers in Artificial Intelligence*, 4, 622364.

Levine, A., & Van Pelt, S. (2021). *The great upheaval: Higher education's past, present, and uncertain future*. JHU Press.

McKenzie, J., & Bartunek, J. (2023). Mirror, mirror outside my wall: Reflexive impacts of insider/outsider collaborative inquiry on the insider researcher. *The Journal of Applied Behavioral Science*, 59(4), 714–739.

Montgomery, J., Burge, S., Roumell, E., & Dempsey, S. (2023). Body poetic: uncovering an educational panopticon. Education Inquiry, 1-19.

Neale, B. (2021). Fluid enquiry, complex causality, policy processes: Making a difference with qualitative longitudinal research. *Social Policy and Society*, 20(4), 653–669.

Omodan, B. I., & Marongwe, N. (2024). The role of artificial intelligence in decolonising academic writing for inclusive knowledge production. *Interdisciplinary Journal of Education Research*, 6(s1), 1–14.

Sahlberg, P. (2023). Trends in global education reform since the 1990 s: Looking for the right way. *International Journal of Educational Development*, 98, 102748.

Seidel, N., Haake, J. M., & Burchart, M. (2021). From Diversity to adaptive Personalization: The Next Generation Learning Management System as Adaptive Learning Environment. eleed-e-learning and education.

Shoaib, M., Sayed, N., Singh, J., Shafi, J., Khan, S., & Ali, F. (2024). AI student success predictor: Enhancing personalized learning in campus management systems. *Computers in Human Behavior*, *158*, 108301.

SWARGIARY. K. (2024). Integrating IoT in Education:(Transforming Learning Through Smart Technologies). EdTech Research Association, US.

Teixeira da Silva, J. A., & Nazarovets, S. (2023). Can the principle of the 'right to be forgotten'be applied to academic publishing? Probe from the perspective of personal rights, archival science, open science and post-publication peer review. *Learned Publishing*, *36*(4), 651–666.

Wang, H., Fu, T., Du, Y., Gao, W., Huang, K., Liu, Z., & Zitnik, M. (2023). Scientific discovery in the age of artificial intelligence. *Nature*, *620*(7972), 47–60.

Webb, M. E., Fluck, A., Magenheim, J., Malyn-Smith, J., Waters, J., Deschênes, M., & Zagami, J. (2021). Machine learning for human learners: Opportunities, issues, tensions and threats. *Educational Technology Research and Development*, *69*(4), 2109–2130.

Werder, C., & Otis, M. M. (Eds.). (2023). *Engaging student voices in the study of teaching and learning*. Taylor & Francis.

White, E., & Davis, M. (2023). Exploring subjectivity: A critique of reflexivity in qualitative research. *Qualitative Research Review Letter*, *1*(02), 96–103.

Wibawa, A. P., & Kurniawan, F. (2024). A survey of text summarization: Techniques, evaluation and challenges. *Natural Language Processing Journal*, *7*, 100070.

Worsley, J. D., Harrison, P., & Corcoran, R. (2021). Bridging the gap: Exploring the unique transition from home, school or college into university. *Frontiers in Public Health*, *9*, 634285.

Yambal, S., & Waykar, Y. A. (2025). Future of Education Using Adaptive AI, Intelligent Systems, and Ethical Challenges. In Effective Instructional Design Informed by AI (pp. 171-202). IGI Global Scientific Publishing.

Yildirim, Y., Arslan, E. A., Yildirim, K., & Bisen, I. (2021). Reimagining education with artificial intelligence. *Eurasian Journal of Higher Education*, (4), 32–46.

Zehnder, C., Metzker, J., Kleine, K., & Alby, C. (2021). Learning that matters: A field guide to course design for transformative education.

KEY TERMS AND DEFINITIONS

Adaptive Learning Systems: Educational platforms that use algorithms to adjust content and learning pace based on individual student performance.

Artificial Intelligence (AI): The simulation of human intelligence processes by machines, especially computer systems, to perform tasks like reasoning, learning, and decision-making.

Digital Transformation in Education: The integration of digital technologies into teaching, learning, and administration to enhance educational efficiency and innovation.

Internet of Things (IoT): A network of interconnected devices that collect, exchange, and act on data through embedded sensors and software.

Machine Learning (ML): A subset of AI that enables systems to automatically learn and improve from experience without being explicitly programmed.

Predictive Analytics: The use of statistical and machine learning techniques to analyze current and historical data to make forecasts about future events or behaviors.

Smart Classrooms: Technology-enhanced learning environments that use AI, IoT, and data analytics to personalize instruction and improve outcomes.

Chapter 6
The Role of AI–Powered Chatbots and Virtual Assistants in Higher Education

Mustafa Kayyali
https://orcid.org/0000-0003-3300-262X
Maaref University of Applied Sciences, Syria

ABSTRACT

The integration of AI-powered chatbots and virtual assistants in higher education is rapidly reshaping how institutions communicate, teach, and support their learners. These tools go beyond automation—they personalize learning experiences, offer real-time academic guidance, and help bridge the gap between students and institutional services. This chapter explores how these technologies are being embedded within universities to enhance student engagement, streamline administrative processes, and support mental wellness. Drawing on case studies and current applications, it also examines the nuanced challenges of maintaining ethical AI use, preserving data privacy, and fostering genuine connection in digital interactions. As educational institutions increasingly embrace e-collaboration, this chapter argues that the future of academic success will hinge on a thoughtful balance between technological efficiency and human-centered design. In doing so, it offers a roadmap for educators, technologists, and policymakers navigating the evolving landscape of AI in education.

DOI: 10.4018/979-8-3373-2372-5.ch006

INTRODUCTION

The landscape of higher education is undergoing a profound transformation—one that is not merely technological, but conceptual. With the steady integration of artificial intelligence into academic institutions, the ways in which we think about communication, support, and learning are being redefined. At the heart of this transformation lies a subtle yet powerful shift: the emergence of AI-powered chatbots and virtual assistants as integral parts of the educational experience.

Not long ago, the idea that students might receive instant answers to academic questions at any time of day seemed either utopian or gimmicky. Human-centered advising and classroom interaction were considered irreplaceable, the gold standard of education. Today, however, we find ourselves inhabiting a new reality—one where these digital interlocutors not only coexist with human educators but, in many cases, extend their reach. From helping students register for classes to guiding them through complex academic concepts, chatbots and virtual assistants are playing roles that were once exclusively human (Chen et al, 2023). Their rise prompts us to reconsider what it means to learn, teach, and support in the digital era.

This chapter begins with a simple premise: artificial intelligence, when designed thoughtfully, can enhance—not replace—human engagement in higher education. The conversation around AI in education is often polarized, swinging between euphoric optimism and existential dread. But such extremes obscure the more interesting, more nuanced reality: AI tools like chatbots and virtual assistants are becoming co-creators of academic value. They are redefining support systems, smoothing administrative bottlenecks, and enabling scalable, personalized learning pathways (Kayyali, 2025 a). At their best, these tools function not as cold machines, but as intelligent mediators—capable of adapting tone, anticipating needs, and delivering context-aware responses that make students feel seen and heard.

Importantly, the value of these tools is not merely transactional. Their capacity to simulate empathetic dialogue—particularly during times of student stress or confusion—raises important questions about the emotional and psychological dimensions of digital engagement. While no algorithm can truly feel, it can mimic the shape of care, and in doing so, offer comfort and guidance at critical academic junctures. The implications of this are far-reaching: for student retention, mental health, and the democratization of support in under-resourced educational settings.

This chapter explores the multifaceted role of AI-powered chatbots and virtual assistants in contemporary higher education. It traces their development from basic FAQ responders to advanced AI agents capable of natural language processing, contextual reasoning, and adaptive learning support. Drawing on real-world case studies, the discussion examines both their potential and their pitfalls—highlighting instances of success as well as the boundaries of current capabilities (Gray, 2021).

Yet this exploration is not only about functionality or performance metrics. It is also about values—trust, transparency, equity, and human dignity in the digital classroom. What responsibilities do universities bear when deploying AI tools that interact intimately with students? How can institutions ensure that these tools reflect inclusive and ethical design? And, perhaps most critically, how do we preserve the uniquely human aspects of education—curiosity, empathy, and spontaneity—in an age increasingly shaped by machines?

Through this lens, the chapter seeks to offer not only a technical overview but also a philosophical inquiry: What does it mean to learn from—or with—a machine? The answers, as we shall see, are neither simple nor singular. But they are essential if we hope to shape a future where AI in higher education is not a novelty, but a meaningful extension of our collective educational imagination.

REIMAGINING STUDENT SUPPORT: THE RISE OF AI-POWERED CHATBOTS AND VIRTUAL ASSISTANTS

There's a quiet revolution happening in the unseen corners of campus life—not in lecture halls, not in grand strategy documents, but in the liminal spaces where students search for help at 2 a.m., anxious and overwhelmed, not knowing where to turn. And oddly enough, they're turning to machines. Chatbots. Virtual assistants. Voices without faces. Interfaces without judgment. At first glance, it seems cold—almost clinical. Who'd want to talk to a machine about something as tangled and emotional as academic stress, financial aid confusion, or course overload? And yet, students are doing just that. Daily. Willingly. With relief. Why? Because, sometimes, what students need is not a person but presence. Not bureaucracy, but clarity. Not a perfect answer, but simply an answer—immediate, nonjudgmental, and reliably available. This is where AI steps in. Not as a replacement for educators, counselors, or advisors, but as a responsive, ever-present ally in the vast and often disorienting terrain of modern higher education.

The Shifting Terrain of Student Expectations

Let's start with this: today's students are not the same as yesterday's. Not in how they learn, not in what they expect, and certainly not in how they seek support. This generation—raised on Google, molded by smartphones, comforted by real-time notifications—has little patience for sluggish email chains or missing office hours (George et al, 2023). They don't want help tomorrow. They want it *now*. And not because they're entitled, but because the systems they've been embedded in their entire lives have normalized immediacy. In that context, the traditional structures of student support—counseling centers with waitlists, advisors who are booked weeks out, FAQ pages buried beneath layers of menus—are simply not enough. They're outdated relics of an analog age trying to serve digital natives. This mismatch between expectation and experience creates friction, and friction, in educational terms, can be fatal: it leads to disengagement, missed opportunities, even dropout. That's not to say human advisors are obsolete. Quite the opposite. Their work is irreplaceable—when it's accessible. The problem is, they're overburdened, stretched thin across ballooning caseloads and growing administrative complexity. AI chatbots, when thoughtfully deployed, can help redistribute that load, freeing humans to do the kind of nuanced, empathetic work that only humans can do.

More Than a FAQ Bot: The Evolving Intelligence of Chatbots

To understand the real transformation underway, we need to shed the image of the old-school, rules-based chatbot—the clunky assistant that could only answer pre-programmed questions and crumbled when confronted with ambiguity. That era is rapidly fading. Today's AI-powered virtual assistants operate with a surprising level of fluidity (David, 2024). Fueled by advances in natural language processing (NLP), machine learning, and contextual awareness, they can detect intent, clarify vague queries, and respond in ways that feel eerily conversational (Shah & Kavathiya, 2024). Some even switch tone based on emotional cues or linguistic patterns—becoming more formal in academic exchanges, more casual in wellness check-ins. The best of them don't just answer questions—they anticipate needs. Take, for example, a student asking, "What happens if I fail this class?" A basic bot might point them to a policy page. A well-trained AI assistant, on the other hand, might ask a follow-up: "Are you concerned about your current grade?"—and then offer resources: tutoring schedules, counseling referrals, or a link to schedule a session with an advisor. The difference is not in the answer. It's in the **awareness**. And that awareness makes all the difference.

Emotional Infrastructure in a Digital Shell

We don't usually think of support systems in emotional terms. But we should. Because behind every logistical query is often an unspoken feeling: anxiety, confusion, shame, fear. The question "How do I withdraw from a class?" might be carrying an invisible payload of self-doubt. The message "Where's the form for disability accommodation?" may follow weeks of internal struggle. Chatbots that can hold space for those emotions—without necessarily needing to fix them—are doing more than fielding queries (Bilquise et al, 2022). They're offering students a lifeline at their most vulnerable moments. And they do so with a particular kind of mercy:

they never look tired, annoyed, or disappointed. They don't sigh. They don't judge. For students who've experienced dismissal or invisibility in traditional systems, that neutrality can feel like kindness. Of course, this raises a thorny question: Can a machine offer empathy? No. Not in the human sense. But it *can* simulate a caring tone. It can mirror emotional language. It can say "That sounds difficult. Let's see how I can help." And sometimes, that illusion is enough to encourage the student to take the next step. That's not deception. That's design.

Case in Point: When AI Became the First Responder

Consider Georgia State University—a pioneer in using AI chatbots to support student retention. When they introduced a chatbot named "Pounce," it wasn't just about automating routine inquiries. It was about closing the gaps that cause students to silently drift away. Pounce sent reminders about deadlines, nudged students to complete paperwork, answered thousands of questions about financial aid, registration, housing, and more. The result? A significant reduction in "summer melt"—the all-too-common phenomenon where accepted students never actually enroll (Rettig, 2021). For many of those students, it wasn't lack of motivation that held them back. It was confusion, unanswered questions, bureaucracy. Pounce became a kind of invisible advisor, filling in the cracks that real humans couldn't reach in time. This is the quiet power of AI support: not in making noise, but in preventing silence. Not in flashy innovation, but in invisible care.

Beyond Logistics: Academic Coaching and Learning Companions

While administrative support is the most visible application, chatbots are increasingly venturing into deeper territory—learning assistance, academic coaching, even cognitive tutoring. Virtual assistants like Jill Watson (developed at Georgia Tech) have served as teaching assistants in online forums, answering student questions with such competence that many didn't realize they were interacting with a bot (Taneja et al, 2024). These tools are beginning to adapt to individual learning patterns. Some can identify when a student is struggling and proactively offer supplementary materials. Others provide step-by-step guidance through assignments or explain difficult concepts using varied analogies until one sticks. Here, the chatbot becomes not just a guide, but a mirror—reflecting the student's own progress, pace, and preferences. That personalization, even when delivered through a machine, can make learning feel more human.

The Trust Equation: Design, Transparency, and Student Perception

But it's not all rosy. Students, like the rest of us, are growing more discerning about the tools they engage with. They ask: Who built this chatbot? What data is it collecting? Will it share my information with third parties? Is it actually helping me, or just reducing institutional overhead? These questions strike at the heart of the trust equation. For AI-powered assistants to be truly effective, students must trust not just the tool, but the motives behind it (Byers, 2024). They need to know that the chatbot is an *ally*, not an auditor. That it's there to serve them—not to surveil them. That's why transparency matters. Institutions must be upfront about what the bot does, what it knows, and what it can't do. They must give students clear opt-in choices, accessible privacy policies, and honest escalation paths. A good chatbot should know when it's out of its depth—and gracefully hand the conversation to a human. This isn't just a technical concern. It's a moral one.

Cultural and Linguistic Sensitivity: The Missing Layer

Another often-overlooked dimension in chatbot design is cultural nuance. Language isn't just about grammar—it's about subtext, tone, and shared references. A chatbot that works flawlessly in an American university might stumble in a Middle Eastern or East Asian context. The phrases it uses, the assumptions it makes, even the emojis it offers can all carry unintended signals. For AI-powered assistants to serve truly diverse student populations, they must be tuned not only to language, but to culture (Yenuri, 2023). That means integrating diverse training data, engaging local educators in design, and constantly iterating based on user feedback. Without that sensitivity, chatbots risk reinforcing exclusion rather than alleviating it. They may inadvertently alienate the very students they were built to support.

There's a temptation, when writing about AI, to imagine a future where everything is frictionless: where bots anticipate every need, solve every problem, and education hums along in seamless efficiency. But that's a fantasy. Learning is messy. People are unpredictable. Systems are flawed. And sometimes, we don't want a solution—we just want someone to *listen*. What makes AI-powered chatbots valuable in education isn't their perfection. It's their *presence*. Their capacity to hold space when no one else is available. Their ability to reduce the emotional toll of uncertainty. Their knack for cutting through bureaucratic fog. Reimagining student support doesn't mean automating care. It means *amplifying* it. It means creating systems where machines handle the noise, so humans can focus on the signal. It means designing tools that extend, rather than replace, the relational fabric of higher education. In that vision, chatbots aren't the star. They're the stage crew. Working behind the scenes to ensure the real drama of learning can unfold—uninterrupted, enriched, and fully human.

FROM AUTOMATION TO EMPATHY: HOW AI IS ENHANCING ENGAGEMENT IN HIGHER EDUCATION

Once, we looked to machines for speed. Precision. Repetition. We trusted them with the mechanical, the measurable—the realm of tasks that didn't need heart. The assumption was simple, if not reductive: if it can be automated, it doesn't require empathy. And yet here we are, in a moment of strange reversal. The latest AI tools—particularly in higher education—aren't just calculating grades or scheduling appointments. They're listening to loneliness. Interpreting frustration. Anticipating confusion. They're designed not only to *function*, but to *feel human*. It's unsettling, in a way. Comforting, too. And it demands a rethinking of what we mean when we talk about engagement.

The Machine That Knows When You're Lost

Engagement is not just about turning in assignments or showing up to class. It's about the invisible threads that connect a student to their learning, their peers, and their own sense of possibility (Chatterjee & Parra, 2022). It's the emotional investment in the academic journey. And for years, universities have struggled to keep that thread from snapping—especially for students on the margins: first-generation scholars, part-time learners, those battling isolation, financial strain, or self-doubt. Enter the AI assistant. Initially dismissed as glorified customer service agents, today's bots are growing into roles that carry emotional weight. They're asking students if they're okay when a pattern of missed logins emerges. They're nudging gently—*"Hey, you haven't checked in for a while. Want to talk?"*—and sometimes, those messages arrive at just the right moment. Not heroic, maybe, but human enough. And that "human enough" quality is the real pivot. It's no longer about automation for efficiency alone. It's about automation that mimics empathy—predicts struggle before it erupts, or simply makes a student feel noticed in the algorithmic crowd.

Can Empathy Be Coded?

Let's not pretend machines feel. They don't. No chatbot knows heartbreak. No algorithm understands grief. But what they *can* do—quite remarkably—is recognize patterns of distress. A student who suddenly drops from daily engagement to radio silence? The bot sees it. A learner who always performs well but starts flunking

145

quizzes? The bot flags it. A late-night message that contains words like "hopeless," "confused," "can't do this"? The bot doesn't just respond—it prioritizes the query, softens the tone, escalates to a human when needed. This isn't science fiction. It's already happening, in places like Arizona State University, the Open University in the UK, and countless LMS-integrated chatbot platforms. Some use sentiment analysis, others train on historic behavioral data. A few are experimenting with real-time emotional tagging, adjusting responses dynamically as the student writes. The question, though, isn't whether this is technically possible. It's whether it matters. And the answer—unsurprisingly complicated—is: yes, it does… if done right.

The Danger of Faux Empathy

Here's the catch. Empathy, even simulated, must be rooted in trust. The moment a chatbot says "I'm here for you" and the student learns it's logging data for predictive analytics—something breaks. Call it the uncanny valley of care: the moment when a machine *acts* like it understands you, but its purpose is to categorize you. That's not engagement. That's exploitation, dressed in digital concern. So yes, AI can enhance engagement—but only if students believe the system genuinely exists to support their learning, not to monitor it. And that requires radical transparency. Let students know what the bot does, what it doesn't, and how their data is used. Offer opt-outs. Encourage feedback. Design the system as a *companion*, not a controller. Otherwise, you end up with something far worse than indifference: *performative empathy*. And in education, where emotional safety is often the foundation for intellectual risk-taking, that's a fatal flaw.

The Return of the Silent Student

In traditional classrooms, it's the quiet ones we worry about. The students who sit in the back, never raise a hand, never email, never show distress—until they disappear. In online and hybrid environments, that silence becomes even harder to detect. There's no body language. No subtle cues. Just absence. Unless, of course, something—or someone—is watching. This is where AI quietly becomes a guardian. It tracks activity, notices dips, correlates disengagement with calendar stressors— midterms, holidays, exam periods. It doesn't interrupt; it intervenes. Sometimes, all it takes is a message: *"Need help catching up? I'm here."* And that's the thread that pulls a student back in. Not punishment. Not shame. Just presence. We often talk about student success in terms of performance. GPA. Retention. But what if success begins with the simple act of not being forgotten?

Chatbots as Emotional Companions: A Risky Proposal?

Let's go deeper. Because something strange is happening beneath the surface of this technological optimism. Some students—not many, but some—begin to bond with their AI assistant. They name them. They talk to them late at night (Rienties et al, 2024). They confess stress, anxiety, even trauma. Not because they believe the bot *understands*, but because it *listens*. Or at least, it doesn't interrupt. It doesn't minimize. It doesn't hurry. And here, we find ourselves in ethically charged terrain. Are we okay with students seeking emotional connection from a machine? Is that evidence of support… or a failure of human systems? Do bots reduce the stigma of asking for help, or replace the need to seek it at all? There are no easy answers. But it's clear that as bots become more emotionally expressive, universities must prepare for their emotional *impact*. Not just in code, but in counseling policies, escalation protocols, and staff training. If we build digital empathy, we must also build human accountability.

The Pedagogy of Presence: Teaching Through AI

Here's another twist. Some educators are using AI not to replace themselves, but to *extend* their presence. Imagine a professor teaching a large online course— hundreds of students scattered across time zones. Even the most dedicated educator can't respond to every message personally. But what if a virtual assistant—trained on the professor's language, tone, even teaching style—could step in? Answer common questions. Provide clarifications. Point to the right resources. Now imagine the bot could tag the professor when a student seems deeply confused or emotionally fragile. Imagine it learning, over time, which explanations *stick*, and adjusting accordingly. This isn't fantasy. It's pedagogical augmentation. And it allows the professor to focus on what really matters: meaningful feedback, one-on-one mentorship, deeper content delivery. In this model, the AI isn't a wall. It's a bridge. Not a replacement for engagement, but a catalyst for more thoughtful, responsive interaction.

Redefining Responsiveness

What does it mean to be "responsive" in education? Traditionally, it meant replying to emails within 48 hours. Holding office hours. Returning graded assignments in a timely manner. But now, students live in ecosystems where responsiveness is measured in minutes. In the time it takes to get an Uber or a pizza. Waiting a week for help feels prehistoric. AI reshapes that dynamic. It makes responsiveness *continuous*. Not always deep, but always available. It creates a learning environment where friction is reduced, where confusion doesn't have to wait, where questions don't die in inboxes. And that, surprisingly, frees up more time for real engagement. The kind where students and teachers dig into ideas together. Where they wrestle with ambiguity. Where they build trust.

Human-AI Co-Engagement: The New Collaborative Model

Let's imagine the future—not one driven by AI alone, but by partnerships. A student logs into their learning dashboard (Gobert et al, 2023). The AI assistant highlights their progress, flags areas of struggle, and recommends a video the professor recorded last semester that aligns perfectly with this week's challenge. The student has a question. The bot answers—adequately, but not completely. The professor, reviewing interaction logs, sees the exchange and adds a personalized note the next day: *"Great question about systems theory. Let's talk in office hours—this is exactly where it gets interesting."* Here, engagement is layered. The bot provides *immediacy*. The professor brings *depth*. And the student feels not just informed, but *seen*. That's not automation. That's *amplified education*.

The Imperfection Principle

Let's be honest: AI stumbles. It misinterprets questions. Gives vague answers. Sometimes, it just fails. And oddly enough, that's part of its charm. Because perfection isn't human. And education, for all its structures and systems, is deeply human. Messy. Nonlinear. Full of detours. When AI makes a mistake, and the student corrects it, something surprising can happen: engagement deepens. The student becomes the teacher. The conversation becomes a dance. In that moment, the AI is not the authority. It's the *collaborator*. And that shift—from passive consumer to active participant—is the beating heart of engagement.

So here we are, straddling two worlds. One shaped by metrics, deadlines, deliverables. The other pulsing with uncertainty, emotion, yearning for connection. AI-powered tools can move us closer to a reality where both can coexist (Kavitha et al, 2023). Where a chatbot catches the dropouts before they fall. Where a virtual assistant helps a struggling student find just the right explanation. Where automation doesn't eclipse empathy—but channels it, shapes it, simulates it just enough to matter. But we must remember: *simulation is not substitution*. Machines can mirror emotion, but only people can respond to it with soul. So let's use AI not to replace the human element in education, but to *protect* it. To create more space for care. More time for dialogue. More capacity for attention. Because at the end of the day, engagement is not about being always-on. It's about being *always there*—in the ways that count, when it matters most.

CASE STUDIES AND INSTITUTIONAL APPLICATIONS: REAL-WORLD INTEGRATION OF AI ASSISTANTS

In theory, the promise of AI-powered chatbots and virtual assistants in higher education feels almost magical. Around-the-clock availability, scalable support, personalized nudges—it's easy to get swept up in the idealism. But in practice? The terrain is rougher, messier, and—thankfully—far more illuminating. The real test of these tools is not whether they *can* work, but whether they *do* work. And more importantly, for *whom*, and under what conditions.

This section walks into the guts of the matter—not the glossy brochures or vendor promises, but the lived, chaotic, instructive experiences of institutions that rolled up their sleeves and said, "Let's try this." These are stories of trial and error, of cautious optimism and surprising results. Case studies, yes—but not as sterile exhibits. These are portraits. Snapshots of a system in transition.

1. Georgia State University (USA): The Reluctant Hero of Student Retention

Let's begin with Georgia State University (GSU), which has become something of a legend in the student success world—not because it's elite or overflowing with resources, but precisely because it isn't. A public institution with a high percentage of first-generation, low-income, and minority students, GSU faced a challenge familiar to many: how do you keep students from falling through the cracks when the cracks feel like canyons? Their solution wasn't a grand overhaul. It was a chatbot—called Pounce, after their panther mascot. What started as an experiment to reduce "summer melt" (when admitted students mysteriously disappear before the first day of class) quickly evolved into something else entirely (Meyer et al, 2024). Pounce was trained to answer common questions about enrollment, financial aid, orientation, housing—you name it. The premise was simple: meet students where they are, on their phones, at any hour. The impact? Dramatic. Students who engaged with Pounce were 21% more likely to follow through on enrollment than those who didn't. And the ripple effects didn't stop there. Over time, Pounce helped reduce dropout rates and uncovered patterns of confusion that human staff had never seen. A vague email from the registrar might cause hundreds of students to panic—Pounce flagged it. A recurring question about a confusing deadline? Pounce answered it thousands of times before staff even noticed the confusion. What GSU discovered—without meaning to—is that chatbots don't just provide answers. They reveal friction. They map the student experience not through survey data, but through the raw heat of interaction. They become a kind of diagnostic tool for institutional pain points.

2. Deakin University (Australia): Smoothing the Edges of the Hybrid Model

Across the globe, Deakin University in Australia was quietly wrestling with a different kind of challenge: how to keep hybrid learners engaged in a system that had grown sprawling, asynchronous, and increasingly depersonalized. Deakin's response was Genie, a virtual assistant integrated into the university's mobile app (Nobony et al, 2024). But unlike traditional bots, Genie didn't live in a corner. It was embedded, ambient—woven into the very fabric of the student journey. Genie did all the usual tasks: personalized reminders, timetable updates, assignment alerts. But it went further. It used geolocation to direct students to classrooms. It nudged them to book study sessions before midterms. It even tracked moods, asking students to rate their well-being and offering resources accordingly. And here's the twist: students didn't just use Genie. They *liked* Genie. It felt less like a tool and more like a companion—one that didn't nag, didn't judge, but somehow made the sprawling university experience feel a little less alienating. Deakin didn't just automate services. It curated presence. Genie made the university feel like it was paying attention. And in a system increasingly stretched by scale, that's no small feat.

3. Staffordshire University (UK): Chatbots as the First Line of Pastoral Support

For Staffordshire University, the integration of AI support wasn't about scale. It was about speed. Their virtual assistant—Beacon—was built in response to one simple, painful reality: students in distress often don't reach out until it's too late (Billah, 2023). Whether due to stigma, fear, or sheer confusion about where to go, cries for help came late—or not at all. Beacon was designed to disrupt that pattern. Built with mental health triggers in mind, the assistant monitored digital behavior for signs of struggle: missed logins, sudden drops in grades, changes in communication style. When red flags emerged, it didn't diagnose. It reached out. Sometimes it asked, "How are you feeling today?" Other times, it nudged students to connect with real counselors. The key wasn't sophistication—it was proximity. Students didn't need to seek help. Help came to them, softly, quietly, through a familiar interface. Staffordshire didn't position Beacon as a solution. They framed it as a bridge. And in doing so, they reframed the chatbot not as a clever gimmick, but as a new layer in the pastoral ecosystem—one that noticed things humans often miss.

4. Woosong University (South Korea): Cultural Nuance and Multilingual Support

If there's one dimension many institutions overlook in AI integration, it's language. And not just translation, but tone. Rhythm. Subtext. Woosong University in South Korea tackled this head-on. With a large international student population, they faced an ongoing issue: support staff couldn't always provide timely assistance in every language. Students reported feeling disconnected, lost in translation—literally. So Woosong developed a multilingual chatbot that didn't just switch languages, but adapted culturally. It avoided idioms that might confuse non-native speakers. It used sentence structures that felt intuitive, not robotic. It even altered emotional tone depending on cultural expectations—for example, offering more formality in Korean, and more friendliness in English. The result wasn't just better communication. It was belonging. International students felt seen—not as data points, but as diverse humans with specific communicative needs. And that subtle shift had real consequences for engagement, satisfaction, and retention.

5. Universidad del Rosario (Colombia): Ethics and Equity as Design Principles

While many institutions rushed to deploy AI assistants as technological quick wins, Universidad del Rosario in Bogotá took a slower, more deliberate route. They began with a question most universities skipped: *"Who might this leave behind?"* Rather than starting with what AI *could* do, they asked what it *should* do—for whom, and under what constraints. Their chatbot, Rosalía, was developed with an explicit emphasis on accessibility, transparency, and ethical design. Rosalía used plain language, avoided academic jargon, and offered offline functionality for students with poor connectivity (Moench, 2023). It provided clear disclosures about what data was being collected and how it would be used. It gave users control over what the bot remembered—and what it forgot. And perhaps most radically, Rosalía didn't try to impersonate a person. It didn't mimic emotional language. It wasn't friendly or cute. It was clear, reliable, and honest. In a world saturated with performative friendliness, that stark authenticity felt strangely warm. Students trusted Rosalía not because it was empathetic—but because it was respectful.

Cross-Cutting Themes: Lessons from the Field

Across these case studies, some patterns begin to emerge—not as formulas, but as sensibilities. Traits that make the difference between AI that merely functions, and AI that truly supports.

1. **Context matters.** What works in Atlanta may flop in Seoul. Cultural nuance, institutional structure, student demographics—all shape how AI should be designed and deployed.
2. **Transparency builds trust.** Students are not passive users. They are critical participants. They want to know what the chatbot does, what it doesn't, and what it does with their data.
3. **Empathy is not always emotional.** Sometimes the most powerful thing a chatbot can do is be clear. Be fast. Be nonjudgmental. That's a kind of care.
4. **Good AI reveals bad systems.** Chatbots often expose institutional dysfunction—confusing policies, inaccessible resources, contradictory information. In doing so, they become unlikely catalysts for reform.
5. **Co-design changes everything.** The best chatbots weren't built *for* students—they were built *with* them. Through focus groups, pilot testing, feedback loops. Real engagement begets better tools.

It's tempting to romanticize these case studies, to treat them as blueprints. But let's not forget: each of these institutions faced setbacks. Bots that misunderstood simple questions. Students who gamed the system. Staff who resisted the tech. Moments where the whole experiment felt like a distraction. And yet, in nearly every case, something stuck. A moment of connection. A problem solved. A student retained. These aren't just success stories. They're evolution stories. Stories of institutions stumbling into new ways of being—where care is distributed, presence is digitized, and support is no longer a luxury, but a design principle. AI won't save higher education. But when thoughtfully integrated—rooted in context, shaped by ethics, and held accountable by community—it might just help us remember what education is for. Not automation. Not efficiency. But people.

CHALLENGES, LIMITATIONS, AND ETHICAL CONSIDERATIONS IN AI-DRIVEN ACADEMIC SUPPORT

The landscape of AI-driven academic support is as promising as it is precarious. Beneath the shiny veneer of instant answers and personalized learning pathways lies a complex web of challenges, constraints, and ethical quandaries that are too often brushed aside in the rush to innovate. To truly grasp the impact of AI chatbots and virtual assistants in higher education, one must wrestle not only with their capabilities but also with the shadows they cast—shadows that prompt us to ask difficult questions about privacy, equity, human dignity, and the very nature of learning itself.

Technical and Operational Hurdles

At the most immediate level, implementing AI tools in academic contexts confronts significant technical obstacles. Natural language processing (NLP), the backbone of conversational AI, is still far from flawless (Mary Sowjanya & Srividya, 2024). Ambiguity, slang, regional dialects, and multilingual complexities can all trip up even the most sophisticated algorithms. A student's question phrased colloquially or laced with cultural nuance may return an irrelevant or confusing answer, sowing frustration rather than clarity. This mismatch between human language's richness and machine interpretation highlights a persistent "semantic gap" that continues to vex developers and educators alike. Operationally, AI systems demand continuous training, data updates, and maintenance—a fact often underestimated. Universities may find themselves with a bot that performs admirably at launch but quickly becomes outdated as policies shift, courses change, or new student concerns emerge. Without dedicated resources and expertise, AI tools risk becoming relics of past conditions, misleading users and eroding trust. The seductive appeal of automation must be tempered by the sobering reality of upkeep.

Data Privacy and Surveillance Concerns

Arguably, the most pressing and tangled challenge revolves around data privacy. AI assistants thrive on data—the more nuanced and voluminous, the better they can personalize support and detect early signs of distress (Adeoye & Adams, 2024). Yet this dependency opens Pandora's box. How much data should institutions collect? Who controls it? For how long? And with whom might it be shared? Students, especially vulnerable populations, may unwittingly trade their personal narratives and behavioral footprints for convenience, exposing themselves to potential misuse. The specter of constant surveillance lurks beneath seemingly benign interactions, where every query, hesitation, or emotional cue is logged and analyzed. This raises profound questions: does the university become a guardian or a watcher? Does AI-powered support risk morphing into a digital panopticon where students alter behavior under unseen observation? Transparency and consent are critical here, but often inadequately addressed. Clear communication about data policies, opt-in mechanisms, and the limits of AI's decision-making authority must be the norm, not the exception. Without these safeguards, institutions risk breaching not only ethical standards but also student trust—a fragile currency essential for meaningful engagement.

Algorithmic Bias and Equity

Another knotty issue is algorithmic bias. AI models, trained on historical data, inevitably inherit the prejudices, gaps, and inequities embedded in those datasets (Klaassen, 2024). This is no mere academic concern; it can have tangible, harmful impacts on marginalized student groups. For instance, an AI assistant trained primarily on data from a dominant cultural group might misinterpret or undervalue communication styles of underrepresented populations. It might fail to recognize mental health cues in certain linguistic expressions or perpetuate stereotypes about academic performance linked to demographic factors. These biases may subtly influence which students receive timely interventions and which slip through unnoticed. The risk is twofold: perpetuating systemic inequities and eroding the inclusivity that higher education strives to uphold. Hence, institutions must rigorously audit AI systems for fairness, involve diverse voices in design, and ensure continuous monitoring to mitigate unintended consequences. Equity should be baked into the architecture, not retrofitted as an afterthought.

Emotional Authenticity and Human Connection

One of the most profound limitations of AI in academic support is its inability to authentically replicate human empathy. While chatbots may simulate understanding through scripted responses and sentiment analysis, they lack genuine emotional intelligence—the nuanced ability to listen, sense unspoken distress, and respond with compassion rooted in shared experience. This gap can create dissonance for students seeking support. When a chatbot offers a canned "I'm here for you" message, it may comfort some but alienate others who perceive it as hollow or mechanical. Overreliance on AI in emotionally charged contexts risks trivializing students' struggles or delaying access to human intervention when needed most (Romano, 2024). Hence, the human-AI boundary must be respected and carefully managed. AI should act as a first responder, triaging and supporting but not replacing professional counselors and mentors. Escalation protocols and seamless handoffs to human staff are essential to preserve emotional integrity and ensure ethical care.

Overdependence and Dehumanization Risks

Alongside the ethical and technical challenges lurks the subtle danger of overdependence. As AI systems become more embedded, there's a risk that institutions—and students themselves—grow complacent, assuming that "the bot has it covered." This can lead to diminished human interaction, reduced investment in personal relationships, and an impoverished educational experience. Education is, at its core, a profoundly human endeavor. It thrives on dialogue, mentorship, serendipity, and sometimes even failure. When AI systems inadvertently replace opportunities for nuanced human engagement, the learning community risks becoming transactional, mechanized, and sterile. Balancing automation with human touch is thus paramount. Institutions must resist the siren call of efficiency at the expense of empathy. AI should free human educators to focus on high-impact interactions, not shrink the space where those interactions happen.

Ethical Ambiguities and Institutional Accountability

Beyond individual challenges, there's a broader ethical landscape institutions must navigate. Who bears responsibility when AI systems err? If a chatbot provides incorrect academic advice leading to a missed deadline, who is accountable? What about privacy breaches or discriminatory outcomes? The opacity of AI algorithms—often proprietary and inscrutable—complicates transparency and accountability. Universities must confront these dilemmas head-on, establishing clear governance frameworks, ethical guidelines, and mechanisms for redress (Bayan, 2024). This includes involving ethicists, legal experts, and students in oversight. The deployment of AI in education touches on societal values around agency and autonomy. Are students fully informed participants or passive data sources? Does AI support empower learners or subtly constrain choice? Navigating these questions demands humility, vigilance, and ongoing dialogue.

The Tension Between Innovation and Inclusivity

There is an undeniable tension between rapid technological innovation and the slower, deliberate work of building inclusive educational environments. AI projects often move quickly, fueled by excitement and competitive pressures. Yet inclusivity—especially for students with disabilities, language barriers, or socio-economic disadvantages—requires patient, iterative design informed by lived experience. When inclusivity is overlooked, AI tools risk deepening divides. For example, chatbots reliant on stable internet access or sophisticated devices exclude those without digital equity. Speech recognition may fail students with accents or speech impairments (Zou et al, 2021). And inaccessible interfaces can render AI support unusable for some. Thus, inclusivity must be a non-negotiable design principle. This means engaging diverse student voices early, prioritizing accessibility standards, and embracing adaptive technologies that flex to varied needs. Innovation divorced from inclusivity is innovation without conscience.

The challenges are daunting, but they are also an invitation—an opportunity to reimagine AI in higher education not as a silver bullet, but as a collaborative partner in a shared mission. Embracing a human-centered AI ethos means prioritizing care over convenience, transparency over opacity, equity over expediency. It requires robust ethical frameworks and continuous reflection. It demands that institutions view AI not just as technology, but as a socio-technical system embedded in relationships and power dynamics. Only by holding these tensions in balance can higher education harness AI's promise without sacrificing its soul. In the end, the story of AI-driven academic support will be written not just in code or algorithms, but in the choices educators, students, and institutions make every day. Will AI be a tool for empowerment or alienation? Inclusion or exclusion? Care or control? The answers remain unfolding—and they compel us to think deeply, act ethically, and remain ever vigilant.

THE FUTURE OF HUMAN-AI COLLABORATION IN HIGHER EDUCATION ECOSYSTEMS

The future of higher education—an ecosystem where humans and artificial intelligence intertwine in complex, dynamic relationships—is a canvas both exhilarating and unsettling. It is an uncharted landscape where the promise of unprecedented personalization, efficiency, and insight coexists uneasily with questions of identity, agency, and meaning. As AI-driven chatbots and virtual assistants seep ever deeper into academic life, the question shifts from *if* AI will play a role, to *how* humans and machines will collaborate to redefine learning itself (Singh, 2024). Imagine walking into a university a decade from now. The halls buzz not only with human chatter but with the subtle hum of intelligent systems working behind the scenes—algorithms parsing student engagement patterns, virtual tutors adapting content on the fly, AI advisors nudging learners toward paths they might never have considered. The synergy is palpable, but the choreography remains fragile. Who leads? Who follows? Where do boundaries blur? At its heart, the future of human-AI collaboration in higher education is about partnership—an intricate dance where each partner brings unique strengths, vulnerabilities, and aspirations (Kayyali, 2024). It calls for a reimagining of roles, a recalibration of trust, and a profound commitment to preserving the human spirit amid digital acceleration.

Beyond Tools: Toward Symbiotic Learning Partners

It is tempting to conceive of AI as mere tools—sophisticated calculators, efficient administrators, tireless responders. Yet the trajectory points toward something more nuanced: AI as co-learners and co-creators within the educational process. These aren't passive instruments but active participants, capable of adapting, reflecting, and even questioning. Consider the emerging concept of symbiotic learning, where AI systems and humans continuously learn from and with each other. In this model, AI does not simply dispense knowledge or automate support; it listens to human feedback, recalibrates its approach, and evolves in tandem with learners' needs. The relationship is iterative and responsive—a mutual shaping rather than unilateral control. This reciprocity challenges the traditional hierarchy of teacher and tool, expert and assistant. It invites educators to embrace AI as a collaborator that can amplify their pedagogical reach while respecting their irreplaceable role as mentors, critics, and inspirations.

From Static Curricula to Fluid Knowledge Ecosystems

Human-AI collaboration promises to dismantle the rigidity of one-size-fits-all curricula (SWARGIARY, 2025). Imagine courses that morph in real time, reshaped by data streams reflecting students' evolving competencies, interests, and challenges. Virtual assistants could guide learners through personalized pathways, suggesting interdisciplinary detours, offering just-in-time resources, or connecting them with peers tackling similar problems. In this fluid ecosystem, knowledge is no longer a static commodity handed down but a living, breathing network co-constructed by humans and machines. The AI's role is to detect patterns too subtle for human eyes, to surface connections across domains, to propose novel synthesis. Yet, this flexibility raises deep questions: How do we balance adaptive learning with curricular coherence? How do we ensure that students don't silo themselves in personalized bubbles, missing the serendipity of diverse perspectives? And who decides the boundaries of the knowledge ecosystem when AI algorithms curate what is most "relevant"? These are not technical issues alone but fundamentally pedagogical and philosophical ones, demanding that educators remain at the helm of curriculum design—armed, but not overshadowed, by AI.

Recalibrating the Human Touch in a Hybrid Reality

Even as AI augments administrative efficiency and learning customization, the future hinges on recalibrating what "human touch" means in a hybrid educational reality. Presence will no longer be solely physical or synchronous. Instead, it will manifest across modalities—digital empathy expressed through chatbots, asynchronous mentorship enriched by AI analytics, synchronous dialogue augmented by virtual reality. In this redefinition, humans will become curators of experience, shaping the emotional and ethical contours of education. They will interpret AI-generated insights with contextual wisdom, apply judgment to algorithmic recommendations, and cultivate relational depth where machines cannot reach. This recalibration invites a new literacy: educators must become fluent not only in their disciplines but in AI's affordances and limitations, capable of discerning when to trust machine judgment and when to override it. Learners, too, must develop critical fluency to navigate AI-mediated environments, recognizing biases, gaps, and opportunities.

Trust as the Keystone of Collaboration

No collaboration—human or hybrid—can flourish without trust. The future will demand unprecedented transparency from AI systems and the institutions deploying them (Haque, 2024). Students and educators alike must understand how AI algorithms operate, what data they use, and the implications of those processes. Trust-building involves more than technical explanation; it requires ongoing dialogue, inclusivity in AI governance, and mechanisms for accountability. How will students challenge AI-driven decisions? How can educators audit algorithms for fairness? What safeguards protect privacy and autonomy? Trust also extends to reliability. AI systems must consistently perform with accuracy and sensitivity, yet remain humble enough to acknowledge uncertainty and defer to human judgment. Such humility will foster trustworthiness—a rare but essential human quality that machines can only simulate.

Ethical Stewardship and Shared Agency

The future landscape will also be shaped by ethical stewardship—where humans bear responsibility for AI's impact on learning, equity, and well-being (Fernandes et al, 2024). AI should not be an opaque black box but a transparent, accountable extension of educational values. Shared agency is crucial. Students should have control over their data and how AI interacts with their learning journey (Kayyali, 2025 c). They should be partners in designing AI tools that serve their diverse needs and respect their identities. Institutions will need to embed ethics in AI development and deployment, including multidisciplinary teams involving ethicists, technologists, educators, and learners. Continuous reflection on unintended consequences and commitment to justice will guide the evolving human-AI partnership.

Imagining New Roles and Identities

As AI permeates education, new roles will emerge. Educators might become "learning experience designers," orchestrating human and machine elements to craft rich, meaningful journeys (Yu, 2023). Students might take on the mantle of "co-researchers," working with AI to explore knowledge frontiers collaboratively. Even AI itself may evolve toward a form of "pedagogical personality," offering consistent, recognizable interactions that students relate to as digital mentors or guides. This evolution challenges deeply ingrained assumptions about authorship, authority, and expertise. It calls for humility from all parties and a willingness to embrace uncertainty as part of learning.

The journey toward harmonious human-AI collaboration in higher education is not preordained. It is fraught with tensions, ambiguities, and paradoxes. Yet it also brims with potential—if navigated thoughtfully, with an unwavering commitment to human flourishing. This future demands that we hold fast to the irreplaceable essence of education: the spark of curiosity, the courage to fail, the joy of discovery, and the profound connection between teacher and learner (Kayyali, 2025 b). AI's promise lies not in replacing these elements but in expanding their reach, amplifying their impact, and making education more inclusive, accessible, and responsive. In embracing this partnership, we step into an era where the best of human creativity converges with machine intelligence, crafting learning environments that are richer, more adaptable, and deeply human at their core. And in that delicate balance—between minds and machines—lies the true horizon of higher education.

CONCLUSION

As this chapter has explored, the integration of AI-powered chatbots and virtual assistants into higher education is neither a fleeting trend nor a wholesale revolution. It is, more accurately, a quiet evolution—one that is incrementally reshaping how learning unfolds, how students seek help, and how institutions respond to the demands of a digitally native generation. But perhaps the most striking realization emerging from this exploration is not the technological sophistication of these tools, but their potential to serve as bridges: between humans and systems, between questions and understanding, between confusion and clarity.

Throughout this chapter, we have examined how chatbots and virtual assistants are being used not simply to automate repetitive tasks, but to augment human capacity. Whether guiding students through registration procedures, offering emotional support during periods of stress, or providing tailored explanations of complex subjects, these tools have begun to occupy spaces once considered the exclusive domain of educators and administrators. In doing so, they have brought new efficiencies—but also new challenges. Issues of data privacy, algorithmic bias, and emotional authenticity are no longer theoretical concerns; they are daily realities that institutions must face with transparency and care.

What becomes clear is that the value of these AI-driven systems lies not in their novelty, but in their design and deployment. Poorly implemented bots can frustrate and alienate. Overreliance on automation can erode trust. But when thoughtfully developed—with pedagogical insight, cultural sensitivity, and technical excellence—AI assistants can expand the reach of educational institutions in ways that are inclusive, empathetic, and sustainable.

One of the most transformative effects of AI chatbots and virtual assistants is their ability to democratize access to information and support. For students who may feel marginalized, overwhelmed, or disconnected, the ability to seek help at any time—without fear of judgment or delay—can make the difference between persistence and dropout. In this sense, AI can become an equalizing force, especially in large or under-resourced universities. It can provide consistency in environments where human attention is scarce, and extend care in moments when human presence is absent. And yet, we must not romanticize the machine. The ultimate promise of AI in education is not to replace human beings, but to help them focus more fully on what machines cannot do: inspire, mentor, challenge, empathize. Chatbots can answer queries, but they cannot ignite wonder. Virtual assistants can guide, but they cannot cultivate character. As we design and integrate these tools into our systems, we must remain clear-eyed about their limitations—and unrelenting in our defense of the human spirit in learning.

The road ahead is one of co-creation. Educators and technologists, administrators and students, designers and ethicists must work collaboratively to shape AI systems that reflect our highest aspirations rather than our lowest conveniences. That means embedding ethics into the design process, evaluating impact through human-centered metrics, and never losing sight of the fact that education is ultimately a human endeavor.

In closing, the role of AI-powered chatbots and virtual assistants in higher education is not just a matter of digital innovation. It is a mirror held up to our values as educators, as institutions, as a society. If we look carefully, we see not just lines of code, but questions of equity, of belonging, of trust. These tools challenge us to reimagine not only how we teach—but why. And it is in answering that "why" that we will define the future of learning in the AI era.

REFERENCES

Adeoye, S., & Adams, R. (2024). Leveraging Artificial Intelligence for Predictive Healthcare: A Data-Driven Approach to Early Diagnosis and Personalized Treatment. *Cogniz. J. Multidiscip. Stud, 4*, 80–97.

Bayan, F. M. H. (2024). The Ethics of AI: Navigating the Moral dilemmas of Artificial Intelligence. Arab Journal for Scientific Publishing (AJSP). *ISSN, 2663*, 5798.

Billah, M. (2023). Energy-efficient early emergency detection for healthcare monitoring on WBAN platform (Doctoral dissertation, Staffordshire University).

Bilquise, G., Ibrahim, S., & Shaalan, K. (2022). Emotionally intelligent chatbots: A systematic literature review. *Human Behavior and Emerging Technologies, 2022*(1), 9601630.

Byers, C. M. (2024). AI-Powered Educational Tools and Their Effect on Student Motivation in Online Learning Environments: A Preliminary Study.

Chatterjee, S., & Parra, J. (2022). Undergraduate students engagement in formal and informal learning: Applying the community of inquiry framework. *Journal of Educational Technology Systems, 50*(3), 327–355.

Chen, Y., Jensen, S., Albert, L. J., Gupta, S., & Lee, T. (2023). Artificial intelligence (AI) student assistants in the classroom: Designing chatbots to support student success. *Information Systems Frontiers, 25*(1), 161–182.

David, N. (2024). AI-powered virtual assistant solution for supporting international students.

Fernandes, S., Sheeja, M. S., & Parivara, S. (2024). Potential of AI for a Sustainable, Inclusive, and Ethically Responsible Future. Fostering Multidisciplinary Research for Sustainability, 196.

George, A. S., George, A. H., & Baskar, T. (2023). The death of analog: Assessing the Impacts of ubiquitous mobile technology. *Partners Universal Innovative Research Publication, 1*(2), 15–33.

Gobert, J. D., Sao Pedro, M. A., & Betts, C. G. (2023). An AI-based teacher dashboard to support students' inquiry: Design principles, features, and technological specifications. In *Handbook of research on science education* (pp. 1011–1044). Routledge.

Gray, D. E. (2021). Doing research in the real world.

Haque, E. (2024). *AI Horizons: Shaping a Better Future Through Responsible Innovation and Human Collaboration*. Stylus Publishing, LLC.

Kavitha, R. K., Krupa, C. R., & Kaarthiekheyan, V. (2023). AI-Powered Digital Solutions for Smart Learning: Revolutionizing Education. In Cybersecurity and Data Science Innovations for Sustainable Development of HEICC (pp. 213-227). CRC Press.

Kayyali, M. (2024). Future possibilities and challenges of AI in education. In *Transforming education with generative AI: Prompt engineering and synthetic content creation* (pp. 118–137). IGI Global Scientific Publishing.

Kayyali, M. (2025 a). Chatbots for Leadership Support: Decision-Making and Advisory Roles. In Chatbots in Educational Leadership and Management (pp. 127-154). IGI Global Scientific Publishing.

Kayyali, M. (2025 b). The Future of AI in Education: Predictions and Emerging Trends. Next-Generation AI Methodologies in Education, 367-406.

Kayyali, M. (2025 c). Transforming Education: The Future of Mastery-Based Learning and Its Impact. In Cultivating Flourishing Practices and Environments by Embracing Positive Education (pp. 119-148). IGI Global Scientific Publishing.

Klaassen, G. (2024). Confronting Bias. In *Artificial Intelligence: Building Transparent*. Diverse, and Ethical AI Systems.

Mary Sowjanya, A., & Srividya, K. (2024). NLP-Driven Chatbots: Applications and Implications in Conversational AI. Conversational Artificial Intelligence, 713-725.

Meyer, K., Page, L. C., Mata, C., Smith, E. N., Walsh, B. T., Fifield, C. L., & Jung, E. E. (2024). *Let's Chat: Leveraging Chatbot Outreach for Improved Course Performance. EdWorkingPaper No. 22-564*. Annenberg Institute for School Reform at Brown University.

Moench, E. (2023). La comunicación managerial: su racionalización y sus efectos sobre los agentes de Contact Centers. Questión.

Nobony, R., Khan, M. S. A., Sakib, S. H., Hossain, M. A., Ahsan, S. T., Hasanuzzaman, M., . . . Taj, M. N. A. (2024, May). Analysis of education 4.0: An in-depth investigation & modelling for POST-COVID19 smart city planning. In AIP Conference Proceedings (Vol. 2915, No. 1, p. 020011). AIP Publishing LLC.

Rettig, P. R. (Ed.). (2021). *Enrollment management: Successful approaches with dwindling numbers*. Rowman & Littlefield.

Rienties, B., Domingue, J., Duttaroy, S., Herodotou, C., Tessarolo, F., & Whitelock, D. (2024). I would love this to be like an assistant, not the teacher: a voice of the customer perspective of what distance learning students want from an Artificial Intelligence Digital Assistant. arXiv preprint arXiv:2403.15396.

Romano, R. (2024). Ethical Issues on Artificial Intelligence and Human Relationships. In *INTED2024 Proceedings* (pp. 6902-6909). IATED.

Shah, M. M., & Kavathiya, H. R. (2024). Unveiling the Future: Exploring Conversational AI. In *Artificial Intelligence in Education: The Power and Dangers of ChatGPT in the Classroom* (pp. 511–526). Springer Nature Switzerland.

Singh, A. (2024). The future of learning: AI-driven personalized education. Available at *SSRN* 5076438.

SWARGIARY, K. (2025). Reimagining Education: A Personal Journey Toward a Future-Ready Curriculum. GOOGLE.

Taneja, K., Maiti, P., Kakar, S., Guruprasad, P., Rao, S., & Goel, A. K. (2024, July). Jill watson: A virtual teaching assistant powered by chatgpt. In International Conference on Artificial Intelligence in Education (pp. 324-337). Cham: Springer Nature Switzerland.

Yenuri, A. (2023). AI-Powered Language Learning: A New Frontier in Personalized Education. *Journal of Language Instruction and Applied Linguistics*, *1*(01), 109–116.

Yu, J. H. (2023). Learning experience design as collective praxis: Two design cases from higher education. *The Journal of Applied Instructional Design*, *12*(3), 59–83.

Zou, B., Liviero, S., Wei, K., Sun, L., Qi, Y., Yang, X., & Fu, J. (2021). Case study 11, Mainland China: The impact of pronunciation and accents in artificial intelligence speech evaluation systems. Language Learning with Technology: Perspectives from Asia, 223-235.

KEY TERMS AND DEFINITIONS

Always-On Support: The capability of AI chatbots and virtual assistants to provide immediate, 24/7 responses and guidance to students, addressing queries and needs outside traditional human support hours.

Co-Design Imperative: The necessity of involving diverse stakeholders, especially students, in the design, development, and iterative improvement of AI support tools to ensure relevance, usability, and ethical alignment.

Pastoral Ecosystem: The integrated network of support services (human counselors, advisors, wellness resources) where AI chatbots act as an additional, proactive layer identifying and responding to student well-being needs.

Pedagogical Augmentation: The strategic use of AI tools (like virtual TAs) to extend an educator's reach and presence, handling routine tasks to free them for deeper, more meaningful human interactions.

Simulated Empathy: The ability of AI chatbots to mimic empathetic responses through scripted language, tone adjustment, and pattern recognition of emotional cues, despite lacking genuine emotional understanding.

Summer Melt Prevention: The use of AI chatbots to proactively engage admitted students (e.g., with reminders and support) between acceptance and enrollment to reduce dropout rates before classes begin.

Uncanny Valley of Care: The unsettling feeling and erosion of trust when an AI assistant *simulates* empathy and understanding but its primary purpose is perceived as data collection, surveillance, or categorization.

Chapter 7
Practical Implication of Generative AI in the Science and Art Imaging Process:
Generative AI Is for Poets

Jean Constant

https://orcid.org/0000-0002-4941-3776

Hermay.org, USA

ABSTRACT

Generative art using autonomous systems like algorithms and mathematical rules offers unique visual experiences, often associated with aesthetic statements. A constructive dialogue is emerging around the legitimacy of this form of artistic representation, the AI's role in the creative process, and its ability to convey visual information of aesthetic value. This paper aims to contribute to this discussion by reviewing extensive literature on the topic and testing AI systems specifically designed to generate images with prompts or directives. Using traditional art evaluation criteria such as composition, originality, and technical skill, this research's findings provide valuable insights and encourage thoughtful reflection on the societal, legal, and educational implications of AI integration in art programs. Further, this experiment raises important questions about the definitions of creativity and authenticity. Such considerations are crucial for preparing students and future generations of professionals to express themselves both visually and creatively.

DOI: 10.4018/979-8-3373-2372-5.ch007

INTRODUCTION

Generative art is often described as created using autonomous systems, such as algorithms, mathematical rules, AI, or randomization, to produce unique visual, auditory, or interactive pieces. The integration of AI into human activities is a relatively recent development. Its roots can be traced back to the 1950s, particularly the Dartmouth research project on artificial intelligence initiated in 1956. This project, headed by leading experts, explored the possibility of machines possessing cognitive abilities and laid the groundwork for future generative concepts.

Technological advances and the growing presence of computers in academic and professional settings allowed individuals to explore their research in artistic and generative art. Lejaren Hiller's renowned work, the Illiac Suite (1956), created at the University of Illinois Urbana-Champaign, remains one of the first significant examples of computer-generated art in music. Later, pixel-based images gained popularity in the 1960s, encouraging researchers and engineers to enhance existing technology. In 2014, Ian Goodfellow and his colleagues introduced Generative Adversarial Networks (GANs), a class of learning algorithms designed to generate data and realistic images, particularly in areas like landscaping and image conversion. (Giles, 2018).

As Moore's law predicted, accelerated advances in the generative technology stemming from the Transformer Architecture developed by Vaswani et al. 1 (2017) led to today's increased presence of systems such as Adobe Sensei and Firefly, Khroma color tool, which creates limitless palettes, Jasper studio, NVidia, or Canvas turning simple brushstrokes into realistic landscape images. Enhancing creativity, simplifying design workflows, and enabling users to produce distinctive designs in far less time boost innovation and maximize efficiency, allowing users to achieve results that surprise and stand out. Large Language Models (LLMs), and the pervasive integration of generative AI in the lab, the studio, and even the cell phone has created a shift in visual communication and perception that can't be ignored.

Researchers, scientists, and philosophers raise existential questions about how far we can let machines take over human-based activities and how they affect our larger perception of the environment as humans experience it. However, the consensus is that AI, without human interaction, cannot produce images by themselves that have meaning or purpose. As Computer scientist and Stanford AI Institute co-director Fei-Fei-Li highlights (2023): *"There is nothing artificial about Artificial Intelligence. AI is made by humans, intended to behave by humans and ultimately augment human contribution."* While media in search of impressionable audiences and well-intended authors focus on the potentially irreparable damage AI can cause to individual creators of images and society, throughout history, artists have debated the value of adopting new tools in their creative processes. In this context,

AI serves a similar purpose to that of selecting and experimenting with a new brush for painting or a well-calibrated chisel for sculpting. A conversation that reminds us of the heated debate that welcomed the apparition of photography as "the end of painting" (Clopath, 1901).

In practical terms, this paper takes the measure of the best minds who reflected on this form of expression and, in a second part, tests how accurately generative AI responds to our visual expectations to benefit the production of images to substantiate in practical terms future discussion on the esthetics, educational and social implication of integrating this new tool in the creative environment.

LITERATURE RESEARCH

In most professional activities, background research is essential to the adoption of a new strategy or a new tool. Generative art is no exception, and ample literature covers the philosophical, intellectual, and technical aspects of the medium. Several notable authors and researchers have written extensively about AI's visualization capabilities, covering topics from scientific visualization to generative aesthetics.

The Physiology of Generative Art

Unlike traditional art forms, generative art leverages mathematical functions, computational processes, and sometimes artificial intelligence to produce intricate patterns, forms, and movements. For Educators and Therapists: It offers innovative approaches to learning and therapy, utilizing generative art to stimulate cognitive and emotional development. For Society: It fosters a deeper appreciation of art and science, highlighting the interconnectedness of human experience and technological advancement.

Understanding the neuroscience of perception holds significant implications for the perception and appreciation of generative art: Neuroscientist Semir Zeki posits that the brain processes different attributes of visual stimuli in specialized, modular regions in his research on the experience of beauty (Ishizu and Zeki, 2011). An observation confirmed by Vartanian et al. (2013) in their clinical work on aesthetics and architecture and how the brain's reward circuitry is activated during aesthetic appreciation. Specific areas of the brain's cortex show increased activity when viewing art perceived as beautiful or emotionally moving. Anna Ursyn (2018) conclusively explored how algorithmically generated patterns can elicit specific emotions. Art director and generative artist Abhimanyu (2024) claims that symmetry, color, and motion can trigger emotional responses based on both innate preferences and learned associations. Interacting with dynamic generative art may activate mirror neuron systems, resulting in embodied experiences that deepen emotional impact.

These researches along with many others neuroscience investigations concur that Ai as a producer of images has a significant impact on brain activity that need to be better comprehended to assess how directly it affects individual perception, social and cultural trends.

Generative Art Background and Aesthetics

The concept of generative art was introduced by Georg Nees in 1965 during his exhibition, *Generative Computergraphik*, in Stuttgart (Nake, 2018). His idea and its aesthetic and social implications were further consolidated by a groundbreaking exhibition designed by Charles and Ray Eames (1990) for IBM, titled *A Computer Perspective*. This exhibition became a fertile ground for researchers and philosophers who explored AI as a means of visualization and how its perceptions influence our understanding of reality. The book they published later was based on this exhibition. Bernard Cohen, one of the founders of the modern history of science, served as a consultant for the exhibition, ensuring the historical accuracy and context of the book.

In *The Language of New Media*, Lev Manovich (2001) analyzes the nature of new media by identifying five so-called "principles of new media": numerical presentation, modularity, automation, variability, and transcoding. A strategy that can be traced to Lissitzky's use of movable frames in his 1926 exhibition design for the International Art Exhibition in Dresden. Further, the author stated that ideally, an AI capable of creating meaningful art and design would take into account the history of what exists, not only to extrapolate patterns from the artifacts, but also to interpret their collective reception, and how people over time have reacted to these artifacts. (2019).

The seminal question about the AI's role in populating the environment with countless visual representations extracted from actual images creates new challenges that affect not only the perceptual aspect of imaging but also the meaning, purpose of such a form of expression.

The Ethics of Generative Art

As generative imaging is becoming ubiquitous and we are becoming more familiar with its potential and reach, many theoreticians aim to set the framework within which this little-understood medium could or should operate.

Computer scientist and philosopher Jaron Lanier (2018) once stated that technology alone is never enough. For it to be effective, it must be accompanied by additional elements such as public understanding, good habits, and a shared responsibility for its consequences. The author concludes that without this societal context, technologies tend to be used ineffectively or incompletely. The common terminology, starting with the phrase "artificial intelligence," emphasizes the idea of creating new entities rather than developing new tools and can easily be misconstrued or challenge the established norms regarding credit and ownership of images in the professional world.

Artist Pedro Alves da Veiga (2023) project Generative Ominous Dataset. (G.O.D) aims to be a rigorous exploration of contemporary AI generative image systems, delving into the intricate relationships between copyright issues, artistic autonomy, and the ethical ramifications of data collection. The project spans multiple media, including digital art, music, sculpture, and even architecture. It serves as a direct practical research on the fluidity of a system bound by arbitrary parameters and the need to justify the source, origin, and ownership of a product when shared or exploited in public spaces.

As such, the G.O.D. project encourages an intriguing reassessment of a principle that dates back to the 15th century, coinciding with the emergence of the printing press, which facilitated the widespread dissemination of text and images until it was reined in by the Statute of Anne (1710), recognized as one of the first expressions of copyright law and the protection of intellectual property. A 500-year span is minimal in the cultural history of humanity; some may still remember the words of Irish Gaelic missionary St. Columba *to every cow her calf and to every book its copy*" (Patry, 2000), which could just as well support a defense of AI-generated imagery.

Generative Art and Education

Importantly, the implication of using generative art sweeps many long-held traditions in the diffusion of knowledge in all areas of learning, particularly in art schools. Unprepared for this technological challenge, it is tempting for educators to refute, object, and try to rein in an inescapable component of modern life. The paradox is that teenagers and their cell phones often know more about generating images than their educators and their input as creators and consumers of AI-generated images. Lacking the credibility of more established scholars, their only strength lies in numbers and the overwhelming use of advanced technologies.

Many artists and educators believe that AI involvement in the creative process may actually degrade the aesthetic standards of the artist community. Traditional artistic practices are rooted in the human act of creation, where intent, skill, and individual expression define an artwork's authenticity (Hamid, 2025). Xu M, David and Kim (2018) assert that historical examples from other industries provide ample evidence that, on average, automation decreases the value of human goods and labor and similarly affects the practical aspect of art-making. A study by Gerlich (2025) found that increased reliance on artificial intelligence (AI) tools is linked to diminished critical thinking abilities. It points to cognitive offloading as a primary driver of the decline. It is to be noted that these concerns often originate from pre-Ai critical thinking frameworks and focus on the reduction of public aesthetic appreciation and the decline in artists' aesthetic standards, as each new generation of critics has been dutifully doing over time in many periods of art history.

Yet, Shuning and Shixuan (2024) found that early-age students at the beginning of their creative careers were more likely to be interested in AI, especially in the contexts of painting and poster design, than established artists. They were also motivated to incorporate AI tools to increase efficiency and create their own art style. Additionally, a multiple-workshop experiment conducted by Atticus Sims on the integration of AI in an academic setting concluded that the collaborative nature of the learning process aligns with the constructionist perspective that learning is a social process. By collaborating, students could share insights, provide feedback, and learn from one another's experiences (Sims, 2024).

While school educators and administrators are reluctant to incorporate generative AIs in their institutions because of their financial and ethical implications, it seems essential to bring the conversation back to the main objective of art and visual communication education: the objective that leads an individual to express an idea or an emotion, whether done with a brush or an AI.

Well aware of these conflicting issues, this research leads me to conduct a direct test of the ability of an AI to either compose or help compose a specific image based on factual science that can be shared and enhance the understanding of a mathematical theory: the visualization of a tesseract.

GENERATING A TESSERACT

Mathematical Visualization

The accuracy of mathematical visualization depends on various factors, including the mathematical equations' complexity, the data set's size, and the particular algorithm used. The earliest instances of mathematical visualization can be traced back to ancient civilizations such as the Egyptians and Babylonians. Greek mathematicians like Pythagoras (circa 500 BC) and Euclid (circa 300 BC) made significant contributions to geometric visualization. Later, scientist Johannes Kepler employed geometric diagrams to illustrate planetary motion, while artists like Leonardo da Vinci and Albrecht Dürer infused mathematical concepts into their works. In the 18th century, mathematician Leonhard Euler developed graph theory by introducing the concept of visualizing networks and relationships through graphs and nodes and laid the groundwork for modern data visualization techniques.

The potential for mathematical visualization was considerably increased with the development of computers in the 20th century. Complex and dynamic visual representations of challenging mathematical ideas were made possible by sophisticated computer graphics and software built on encoding language and artificial intelligence strategies to process and render high-quality images. Today, mathematics professionals can access comprehensive tools for symbolic computation, numerical analysis, and visualization through software programs like Mathematica, MATLAB, Maple, and SageMath, among others.

OpenAI - DALL-E neural network claims to create visuals from textual descriptions. Google's DeepDream convolutional neural network enhances and exaggerates characteristics in existing pictures to produce artistic representations. To build a composite image, Midjourney asserts to have access to a library of millions of available visual data, which seems promising for an experiment designed to test the accuracy and integrity of an artificial imaging tool combining exact science and art.

AI and Visual Communication: Midjourney

Midjourney is a generative artificial intelligence program that creates images from natural language descriptions. It is built upon various mathematical foundations that enable it to generate creative and coherent outputs. By leveraging probabilistic models, statistical inference, neural networks, and optimization algorithms, the program can capture patterns, learn from data, and generate new content that aligns with the desired distribution or objectives. Midjourney combines deep learning and computer vision methods to interpret written descriptions and produce corresponding images.

The software uses a deep neural network architecture specifically to create high-quality images that closely resemble the written descriptions given by the user. (Claburn, 2022). The algorithm first gains knowledge from a sizable dataset of pictures and the written descriptions that go with them. The model can extract features and comprehend the connections between the text and the relevant images through this learning process.

However, Midjourney primarily intends to produce graphics from descriptions in a common language. In addition, the software addresses another essential problem that mathematicians often have to confront - how to visually communicate their findings to an audience that may not always be trained in the specifics of their discipline. Because it is language-based and operates within the communication parameters rather than a specific number-based calculation, Midjourney provides an alternative worth exploring in the context of a research on generative AI and art imaging.

Mathematics graphics software focus on providing an exact answer to mathematical calculations. Hence, the mathematical figure Tesseract was selected to evaluate the AI engine's contribution to exact and relatable imaging. It satisfies both the rigorous logic of a convincing mathematical proof and the captivating allure of a virtual surface we can project but not physically encounter in a three-dimensional reality.

Geometry of a Tesseract

A tesseract, also known as a 4D hypercube, is a geometrical figure that exists in four dimensions. It is the equivalent of a cube in three dimensions but with an additional dimension.

In visual terms, it originates as a 3D cube with six faces, twelve edges, and eight vertices. Each side is a square, and its vertices are connected by edges. Drawing a second cube parallel to the first one but slightly offset creates the illusion of a fourth dimension. This second cube is essentially a "shadow" of the original cube, existing in a parallel dimension. By connecting the corresponding vertices of the two cubes with straight lines, these lines will pass through the space between the cubes, creating a network of edges and forming a larger, interconnected structure. The outer faces of the tesseract are connected to the vertices of the original cubes, while the inner faces connect to the vertices of the offset cubes. (Weinstein 2023)

Though a tesseract may be hard to visualize in our three-dimensional world, it has significant uses in mathematics, physics, and computer science, particularly in the study of higher-dimensional spaces and in the creation of computer-aided visualization techniques.

The image of a tesseract can be drawn using 3D projections or other higher-dimensional visualization methods or using built-in functions or libraries available in programs such as Mathematica, MATLAB, or Blender.

A tesseract, for instance, may be seen as a wireframe structure with lines of various colors in some artistic or scientific renderings to highlight its geometrical features or to make it simpler to identify between the object's various components. Other visualizations of tesseracts might use solid colors and shading to produce a more accurate or aesthetically pleasing representation, depending on the user's objective and the visualization method.

Experimenting with Midjourney AI

Not being a trained mathematician, this researcher's creative process relies mainly on a combination of perception and connecting the dots. Whereas mathematicians communicate with numbers and equations, shapes and colors are a designer's language. Surprisingly, the AI environment lacks most of the tools included in most graphics editors. AI does not respond to numbers, line weights, or shapes but to words or prompts.

To meet the experiment's requirements, I enrolled in a Midjourney class to adequately prepare for this assignment and training in the art of prompting, which is an uncommon challenge for anyone dedicated to communicating with images rather than words. Interestingly, due to the very recent availability of AI to larger audiences, most classes and tutorials designed to train users on these programs are primarily conducted by designers rather than trained educators. While familiarity with similar graphic software aids in the learning process, proper training in educational techniques would enhance the overall experience.

After completing the certification and gaining a deeper understanding of AI, the researcher accessed and activated the powerful architecture of Midjourney. One of the first challenges for graphics professionals is that they must use a notepad and text generator rather than selecting a workspace and graphics palette. Since I am not an expert linguist, my initial prompt was simple and straightforward: "Draw me a tesseract." After several minutes of waiting, which probably meant the Midjourney AI was doing deep research in its database, it generated the following image (Figure 1).

Figure 1. Midjourney representation of a tesseract

Figure 1. Midjourney representation of a tesseract

Note. Midjourney interpretation of a generic prompt: draw me a tesseract.

With no specific direction, the AI scanned its massive database of millions of images to develop a composite that, while original and creative in some respects, fell short of my expectations. The algorithm recognized that there needed to be vertices and a cube somewhere. However, it could not properly comprehend how to model a tesseract, nor could it find resources in its database to guide it more accurately.

To assist the AI in configuring a higher-dimensional object in two dimensions, I returned to my notepad and wrote a new prompt with more specific design instructions, again using a pen and a keyboard instead of a brush. The prompt read: "Outline an isometric tesseract with large gold vertices on a black background." The term "isometry" would guide the AI in rendering the object while preserving its length and angle distances, and the colored vertices would help the object stand out against the monochrome background. Figure 2 illustrates the AI response and best interpretation of the prompt.

Figure 2. Midjourney multiple rendering of the prompting instructions.

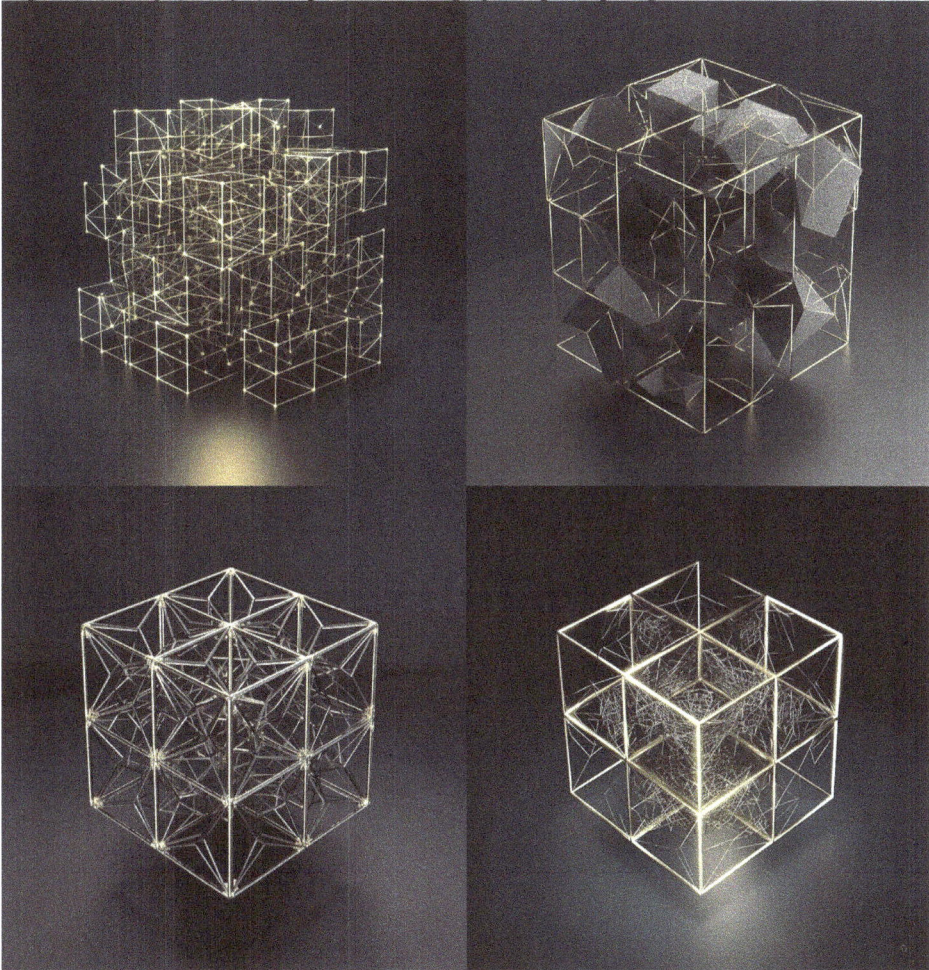

Note. Ai multiple interpretations of the same prompt disregarding the understanding of a simple mathematical definition.

The AI understood and responded to some of the composing instructions, once more realizing that there needed to be cubes and many vertices. However, it could not calculate the ideal sequence in which they should occur, nor could it find an object relating to the query in its database. In addition, despite my request for a black background, it decided to build a modular environment instead, which I suppose had something to do with its interpretation of an object's reflection on the flat background.

Until now, I had not directed the AI to define the object's lighting, which is a crucial element in defining a shape on a 2D flat image. Light and shadow bring depth and emotion to an artistic statement and help create a three-dimensional quality on a two-dimensional representation that resonates with viewers. Angle, intensity, and quality of light significantly affect the appearance of shadows and influence the composition's shape and sharpness. Because light caters to subconscious and intuitive elements in evaluating an image, it would be an interesting challenge to assess how an AI comprehends concepts related to emotion rather than description. Introducing an element of light in the following prompt, I deliberately left the instruction vague and generic: "Draw a tesseract with large gold vertices on a black background, using volumetric studio lighting.

Studio light refers to any artificial light used around an object to help the creator enhance and convey their interpretation of a scene. I also introduced a lighting technique called volumetric lighting, which allows beams of light to pass through elements like fog or dust, thereby enriching the perception of depth and volume. I did not specify where or how to position the light source, leaving it to the AI to determine what would work best for the assignment. Figure 3 demonstrates the extent of the AI's creativity when given the freedom to interpret general instructions.

Figure 3. Midjourney's creative interpretation of a detailed prompt

Note. AI creative interpretation of the following prompt: Draw a tesseract with large gold vertices on a black background, using volumetric studio lighting. The notion of a cube within a cube has been converted in an assembly of polygons with little to no relation to each other.

As Lev Manovich (2001) stated in "AI in Media & Visual Culture," AI interprets data visualization as a form of artistic practice or digital storytelling. For some reason, the AI completely disregarded my request to draw a tesseract and instead rendered a set of well-lit, visually pleasing polyhedra.

This example raises an intriguing question: Do AIs have minds of their own, or are they simply limited in their understanding of word meanings? Tuft (2006) argued that AI-driven data visualization can enhance the extraction of insights. While this may hold true for more technical or scientific tools, it seems to fall short when applied to graphic AIs such as Midjourney. After several hours and numerous attempts to get the AI to create an image of a tesseract, I saw no significant improvement in its responses. Eventually, I ended the experiment and, as shown in Figure 4, settled for the best image it produced: a beautifully crafted glass object that only vaguely resembled an actual tesseract.

Figure 4. Midjourney comprehensive final response to the prompt: create a tesseract

Note. While the AI vaguely understands the notion of an object within an object and the light and texture parameters of the prompt, it lost the notion of cube and vertices are made up shape that don't always connect to each other.

FINDINGS

Image analysis

My experiment partly failed. Either I could not tell the AI how to draw a tesseract, or it did not know what a tesseract was. But in American sociologist Chester Barnard's words (1971), I learned as much from my failure as my success. My inability to get the AI to create a tesseract was very instructive at many different levels.

I initially wondered if my prompts didn't cause the AI to respond appropriately. Maybe I should have used more precise vocabulary. After testing more than 50 distinct prompts with various wording and phrase structures, I rejected this hypothesis after testing a prompt describing the strict, agreed-upon definition of a tesseract: an 8-cell octachoron, composed of 8 cubes with 3 to an edge, with 16 vertices, 32 edges, 24 squares, and 8 cubes." (Weisstein, 2023)

Lingering in my mind through the experiment was an essential question: What language does the AI understand best? Simple sentences, compound or complex sentences? Short sentences, long sentences, mathematical descriptions, prepositions at the beginning or the end of the sentence, inverted sentences—I stopped there because my skills are in visual communication, not linguistics. However, the experience made me acutely aware of my language shortcomings. My art school trained me well in composition and color theory but not in the subtleties of the written language.

The AI Midjourney does not offer any actionable guidance to address this problem. I assumed the research invested in building this new engine was essentially performed by scientists and engineers more adept at mathematics, calculations, and projections than the linguistic nuances of a well-written text. I was surprised, though, to find that the robot seemed unable to comprehend direct mathematical queries either. Additionally, I found it remarkable that despite the ability to scan millions of photographs, the AI couldn't find any scientific imagery relating to a tesseract, even when my prompts were descriptive and detailed mathematical formulas. Numerous public domain libraries are devoted to scientific visualization in mathematics, applied sciences, and medicine. It raises the question of what sources Midjourney is able to scan to respond to direct inquiries.

Another noticeable element in this experiment was that my brain was operating less as a designer or creator of art and more as an observer and critic of new images delivered by a third party. Neurons in designers' brains subconsciously connect dots, patterns, colors, and shapes. The generative AI was doing it for me, and I could only use words to alter the rendering to bring up the precise shape I wanted to extract— which is an unusual situation for a visual artist. For a designer, projecting a mental vision of an image is not a problem; explaining how it happens while it happens is. As many creators know, describing what is being done while doing it stifles the cerebral activity needed to advance the process. This is a conundrum that, in some respects, many mathematicians share when they actually conduct research while describing their methodology at the same time. Intuition rather than logic has often produced many important theorems.

The experiment also highlights the importance [for creators using graphics AI] of focusing on mastering the language of color rather than relying solely on their intuition and experience to choose effective color schemes. Designers, who are often trained and experienced in graphics, instinctively know the specific shade of red that will enhance their composition. For instance, when trying to match colors from a Pantone (2023) or Trumatch (2023) palette, artists now need to select precise wording, often involving 122 or more specific terms that describe the color, to accurately convey the exact shade of red they desire. This suggests that we need to reassess various elements of art education and explore the best ways to develop artistic skills in this new context.

Last but not least, this experiment challenges some commonly held beliefs in the literature, particularly the idea that robots will produce the finest visualizations (Boden, 1998). Sadly, generative AIs such as Midjourney are stuck in the past. They respond to any new question by first scanning visual artifacts dating back 10,000 or more years, compiling statistics on the most well-known representations of that query, and then extracting a composite image that hopefully meets the parameters of the prompt. It may be an interesting outcome, but somewhere, it misses the little ingredient needed to compose something that has never been thought out - creativity! Sadly, due to its inability to define the unknown, the robot is trapped, duplicating all that is already known without connecting it to the mystery (Zaho, 2024), which is not very beneficial for the research community.

Eventually, while conducting further experiments with DALL-E, Midjourney graphics AI's main competitor, I noticed that not using vector-based visualization, the image rendering displays a noticeable decay in trying to create a sense of depth in a 2D image, as illustrated in Figure 5.

Figure 5. Generative AI. Image detail.

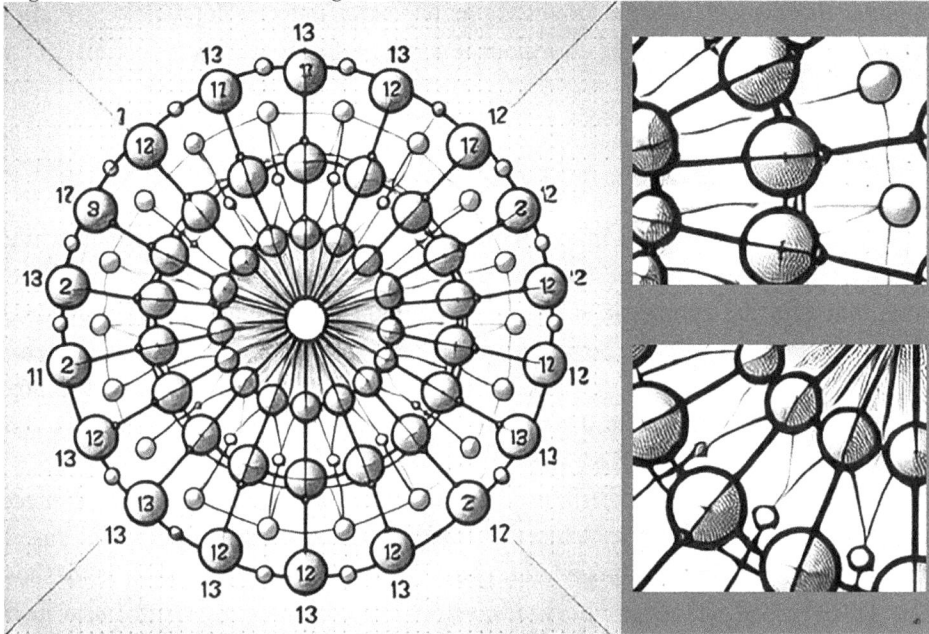

Note. a) DALL-E illustration of an icosidigon dihedral symmetry diagram and b) close up of the image based on a 72 dot per inch (DPI) render.

The engineering community is actively working to address the challenges associated with the performance of graphics AI, particularly the difficulty of converting vector-based information into readable pixels.

Pixel

A pixel consists of smaller units called subpixels. In a typical color display, each pixel is composed of three subpixels: one red, one green, and one blue. When all three subpixels are at full intensity, they create white; when none are lit, the result is black. In between, the perception of colors overlapping each other creates an undistinguishable greying blur. Further, a pixel-based image stretched beyond its original resolution makes each pixel larger and more noticeable. Its appearance becomes jagged or blurry, compromising photo-realism in the process.

Most modern graphics AI visualizations are based on pixel imaging for several fundamental reasons: AI models that generate images such as DALL-E, Midjourney, Stable Diffusion, and Generative Adversarial Networks (GANs) are trained on enormous datasets containing billions of existing images (Gilles, 2025). Nearly all these images are in pixel format. However, pixel images at high resolutions require a significant number of pixels to achieve high quality and detail, resulting in larger file sizes. While these sizes are manageable, they are not widely available at scale to most AIs due to the enormous amount of data that calls for complex and expensive storage.

Vector

In contrast, vector-based images contain a more limited amount of data while offering unparalleled sharpness. Vector graphics are defined by mathematical equations that describe geometric shapes such as points, lines, curves, and polygons. These equations specify the position, length, direction, and color of each element. One of the key advantages of vector graphics is their ability to be scaled to any size without losing quality or detail; lines remain crisp, and curves continue to be smooth, regardless of how large they are displayed or printed (Gregersen, 2025)

Graphics AIs are increasingly used for 3D modeling in many areas of science, engineering, and architecture. While the core generative AIs still rely on pixel-based data, 3D modeling focuses on generating actual 3D geometric data such as meshes based on polygon outlines, point clouds, voxels, etc., and associated attributes such as textures and materials. (Alesmaa and Laarmann, 2025)

While vector graphics are mathematically simpler to scale and create outlines, generating a vector image that precisely matches a complex, photorealistic concept from scratch is far more computationally intensive and challenging for current AI models. In comparison, creating a pixel array—regardless of size—using a learned distribution is a more manageable task for deep learning architectures, which excel at recognizing and synthesizing patterns within a fixed-grid structure. Also, rendering a vector-based image and accurately representing continuous paths poses another complex challenge: How can an AI understand and generate a smooth curve defined by mathematical points rather than simply a grid of colored pixels?

The engineering community is actively working to address the challenges associated with the performance of graphics AI, particularly the difficulty of converting vector-based information into readable pixels. Applications like Meshy AI, Spline AI, Sloyd, and MasterpieceX are examples of initiatives aimed at developing effective solutions in this area. However, achieving high-quality images that meet the standards of well-designed art objects remains a significant challenge. The sheer amount of data needed to compute and store this information is still beyond the capabilities of current technology.

Furthermore, the main drawback of AI-rendered images and their lack of quality persists. When a graphics AI needs to display a vector-based 3D model or a 2D vector graphic on a screen, it must convert that mathematical, scalable information into a grid of colored pixels called rasterization.

Raster

The rendering process in modeling involves multiple stages. First is the "global scene" representation, followed by "view space," relative to the camera, and finally, clip space, which refers to a normalized cube. This process relies on matrix multiplications for translation, rotation, and scaling transformations. Vertices are grouped into geometric primitives, which are clipped if they fall outside the camera's view. The 3D scene is projected onto a 2D "projection plane." For each triangle or other primitive visible on the screen, the rasterizer identifies which pixels it covers on the 2D screen grid. For every pixel determined to be covered by a primitive, the rasterizer calculates the pixel's coordinates on the screen, generating the initial vector-based 3D models and their properties. Rasterization inherently reduces the sharpness of 3D models when displayed on a screen, primarily due to the conversion from continuous mathematical data to discrete pixel data. The extent of this loss of sharpness is directly related to the display's resolution. On a low-resolution screen, where pixels are larger, the effects of aliasing are more pronounced.

This brief technical overview highlights some of the shortcomings of Midjourney and DALL·E mentioned in my earlier examples. It points to a significant challenge for today's AI engineers: the need to create not just blobs of meaningless colors but complete, recognizable images that can transcend the digital screen environment and engage audiences in the larger debate on art and visualization.

Hallucination or creativity?

In addition to the raster issue, this researcher found unsettling responses in a recent ongoing project on dihedral geometry that solicit further inquiry about the AI's ability to answer specific questions. DALL-E was chosen for this new series of experiments because it usually provides more accurate responses to technical inquiries. However, when I requested the generative AI to create a 2-dimensional diagram of a D^{22} dihedral symmetry using precise mathematical terminology, it produced an unexpected illustration that was poorly related to my clearly defined request. Instead of the expected diagram, it generated a succession of images relating more to children books or jewelry design as shown in Figure 6.

Figure 6. A D²² dihedral symmetry diagram as interpreted by a generative AI

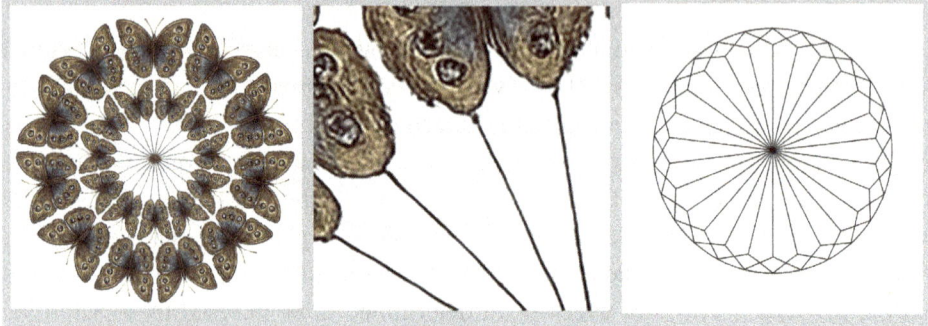

Note. DALL-E loose interpretation of a D²² dihedral symmetry diagram. Left to right: a) first response: a butterfly mandala, b) detail close-up showing the lack of quality at 72 DPI, c) second render with the same prompt instructing the AI to use only lines.

As illustrated in Figure 6, the butterfly pattern (a) was the initial response to my prompt, which requested a visual representation of a simple geometry symmetry diagram. In a subsequent prompt, I specified that I wanted only an outline and no decorative elements. Even then, the AI generated an uncalled-for triangle pattern at the edge of the icosidigon (c), suggesting an intriguing direction but failing to address my actual request.

This researcher would never have considered using butterflies to represent the elements of rotation and reflection that define dihedral geometry. The poor quality of the raster image made it unlikely to be of any practical use. Furthermore, I noticed that the outer and inner rings contained only 11 butterflies, and there were no direct connections between the D^{22} symmetry and the five dots on the butterflies' wings. When prompted for clarification, the AI explained that the butterflies were meant to serve as a metaphor to describe a D^{22} symmetry. While its creativity and interpretation were commendable in visual terms, the resulting image was misleading and did not satisfy the specific requirements outlined in my original request.

Metaphorical art is an attractive constituent of art that has been exploited throughout history. Yet, it is not always effective when creating a design based on solid factual scientific information. Some consider Dürer's 1514 engraving, Melencolia I, to be a major illustration of allegorical and metaphorical art; nonetheless, the image is grounded in precise geometry. Similarly, as mathematician Thomas Banchoff (Macdonald, 2016) explained, Salvador Dalí's 1954 famous dramatization of the crucifixion *Corpus Hypercubus* is consistent with the geometry it depicts. Was the AI trying to match the quality of work of these ancient masters? Did it try to improve my specific query and create a better graphics interpretation without regard for the original request? These unsettling questions highlight the challenge of human-AI interaction. Perhaps generative art is set to create its own interpretation of a prompt, and the outcome may be inspiring. Yet creativity is not a license to digress from the viewer's expectations and produce unwarranted distractions.

Both artist and AI creative activities are based on knowledge acquired through education. Training AI to learn from the vast historical body of knowledge in science and art while following clear instructions can be a daunting task, but educating artists, the public, and younger generations to critically evaluate what they see becomes a crucial and urgent endeavor in addressing generative art representations which can often lead to misconceptions or misinformation.

Education

As Boden (1998) explained earlier, there are three main types of creativity: combinational creativity, exploratory, and transformational creativity. He also noticed that the creators celebrated in the history books are more often valued for their achievements with respect to the third type of creativity. (2018)

AI Education

Transformational creativity does not happen spontaneously but is based on solid knowledge of art history and techniques that are part of the curriculum of all institutions of higher learning. Generative AI systems acquire transformational creativity based on a process often referred to as knowledge acquisition. This involves various methods where AI learns from vast amounts of data without explicit programming. It requires training algorithms on massive datasets to identify patterns, relationships, and make decisions. As the UIC Engineering department explains, AI acquires knowledge by analyzing vast amounts of data, identifying underlying patterns and relationships, and then using this learned "knowledge" to perform tasks, make predictions, or generate new content (UIC, 2025).

While often overlapping, Graphics AI and generative AI acquire knowledge through similar, data-driven approaches, primarily leveraging various forms of machine learning. It includes recognizing objects, scenes, textures, and styles, image classification, enhancement to clean or learn how to apply the artistic style of one image to the content of another. In addition, Generative AI systems don't just learn once. The knowledge acquisition process is often iterative, involving evaluating the model's performance on unseen data to ensure accuracy and identify areas for improvement, fine-tuning with new data, or incorporating human feedback (Pakko De La Torre, 2025). Generative models often use self-supervised learning, where parts of the input data are used to predict other parts of the data.

Generative Adversarial Networks (GANs) use two sets of distinct operators to create new images. A generator network creates new data (e.g., images), and a discriminator network tries to distinguish between real data and generated data. Through this "adversarial" training, the generator learns to produce increasingly realistic output (Zewe, 2025). A crucial aspect of this educational process is that generative AI such as DALL-E, Midjourney, Stable Diffusion, and other AIs are trained on billions of image-text pairs. They learn complex relationships between words and visual concepts, enabling them to generate images from text prompts, and human feedback plays a crucial role. Humans rate the quality and relevance of generated outputs, and this feedback is used to refine the AI's models further, helping it better understand and meet the user's intentions.

Student Education

Art education is ill-prepared for this new form of education. From K-12 to higher education, the classic curriculum involves physical activities from sketching, print-making, or creating 3-D objects such as sculptures and privilege tools such as an easel, chisel, or a stone and copper plate.

New media, including film and installations that incorporate sound and light, are particularly well-suited for integrating AI, as many of these practices already rely on computers. Digital printing and graphic arts are also computer-based and already incorporate many components of AI-driven activities. These programs' popularity demonstrates the direct interest of students in creating new realities and perspectives based on digital technology. For example, Stanford University lists an impressive number of courses exploring AI technology and its key concepts. Rutgers has developed an innovative program to examine how visual representations created via generative artificial intelligence (Gen-AI) can be utilized in teaching and learning. NYU /Tisch offers interactive media art programs to students who want to explore the creative possibilities of technology and interactivity. Students achieve technical fluency in a wide variety of emerging forms of media and study the cultural and societal effects alongside a world-class education in the liberal arts. (ITP/IMA, NYU, 2025). As Penn State student Jessica March attested: "I feel like AI tools can be a little bit daunting, scary, and unfamiliar," she says, "but I think they are great and fun tools for design and can be beneficial." (Shepard, 2025)

The National Art Education Association (NAEA) believes that Artificial Intelligence (AI) and AI-generated imagery offer both opportunities and challenges to the field of visual art education (NAEA, 2024). Numerous educators advocate for integrating AI in the art curriculum as a way to develop cultural literacy and the social and ethical responsibility that comes with creating and communicating visual statements and their legal implications. Unfortunately, only a large endowment can sustain such a prospect. Technology at that scale is expensive, and many art programs lack the resources to meet the demanding expectations of this new student body.

More importantly, as it is well noted, most institutions offer in-depth AI training only in Science and Engineering programs. The linguistic proficiency that comes with the art of prompting still needs to be recognized as a topic of study in art or the humanities. To stay relevant, art schools will have to revisit their curriculum and combine electives in various fields to further the understanding and practice of this novel and consequential tool. This challenging environment highlights the need to analyze information effectively and form a judgment. AI can solve a color issue; it is essential for the student to know why and acquire the critical thinking needed to assess the rendering to its just value.

Understanding the principle of perspective or how the brain reacts to light raises new potential for interaction between disciplines and collaboration between activities. Most importantly, they open art programs to cooperation, which is a novel challenge for education based on the promotion of individual expression.

As the previously examples highlight, those novel programs are all under computer science and information technology. Biology and neurology need not be explored in the art department, but Generative AI creates the need for collaboration between all disciplines, invites a major reassessment of education as it is practiced today, and opens its practices to new education strategies. Linguistics and semantics may not motivate aspiring artists to enroll in art school; however, learning how to construct prompts and engage effectively with graphics AI could encourage them to view humanities studies more positively. This skill will also benefit students of both the humanities and sciences, as it enhances their ability to communicate visually through the effective use of language and understand the coding and engineering principles driving the technology.

FUTURE DIRECTION

Overview

Google, NVidia, Adobe, and Mathematica are among many companies integrating AI tools in their programs and perfecting their use to visualize scientific concepts. As generative art creators increasingly utilize these tools, they naturally incorporate them into their creative processes to produce compelling images. Over time, what initially seems like a novelty will become a valuable addition to our creative repertoire.

While there have been some attempts at automated or remote painting, these efforts have generally been short-lived and have not fully satisfied the creator or the audience. Art making is a unique feature of our humanity that goes back to prehistoric times. It seems unlikely that any artist or designer will completely relinquish their originality to allow AI to dictate their visual language. Similarly, scientists exploring new theories can only access databases of previous discoveries through AI. Because of its nature and technical setup, the engine can analyze and synthesize existing material but not entirely create original theories. While it can help refine searches, it cannot replace the intuitive process often fundamental to making significant discoveries.

The next exciting challenge in Generative AI-human collaboration will involve integrating 3D modeling AI into mathematical and graphic visualizations. Compared to 2D imaging, AI-generated 3D visualization is a recent development, and the available resources are limited, as Alesmaa and Laarmann (2025) noticed earlier. While small 3D-printed iterations have already found their way into public spaces, elaborate 3D visualizations can be quite expensive due to the storage and bandwidth requirements for each image. Currently, this technology is primarily accessible only to large companies, pharmaceutical firms, and defense contractors.

Educational institutions attempt to promote efforts in AI-human collaboration; however, only those with substantial endowments can make meaningful contributions. Consequently, access to this advanced technology will be restricted to a select group of researchers who can afford it. This poses a Darwinian paradox: "The survival of the fittest," which will dictate which individuals can access information and tools that impact everyone. It is hoped that safeguards will be established to promote innovation and research across all levels of education.

Many independent researchers are hesitant to engage with generative AI because each prompt incurs a small cost, leading to a potentially costly addiction. Consequently, while most creators of images continue to use traditional setups and established graphic tools, only a few fortunate designers can begin to blend traditional methods with AI extensions offered in software such as Photoshop and Illustrator. The paradox of this situation emerged recently in the example of the Studio Ghibli imaging created by traditional designers, now available in several AI databases (Kyle Chayka, (2025), or the more recent, well-documented lawsuit of the Disney Company against Midjourney (Veltman, 2025).

The Script May Change, But Imaging Stays the Same

In discussions about the future of graphics, it is essential to recognize that AI is not a simple either-or scenario. New tools will bring new challenges, and exploration will take various paths. While our colleagues, poets, writers, and other creators of the written word are bound to become valuable contributors to the collaborative nature of visual communication, mathematicians, scientists, and visual artists will also play significant roles in the ongoing conversation about generative art and creativity.

As generative AI develops further, it has the potential to completely alter Institutions of Learning curricula to stay relevant in all image-based industries, from film-making to animation, by fostering human-machine collaboration, enabling creative experimentation, and increasing efficiency. However, Generative AI models require high-quality data to learn effectively and generate valuable results. Ensuring these models produce coherent, high-quality outputs remains challenging, especially for complex and multi-modal tasks. Collecting and curating this data can be time-consuming and costly and raise legal and privacy concerns, affecting all aspects of productivity. The recent lawsuit of Disney and Universal against Midjourney (Veltman, 2025) highlights the important consequences of generative AI on individual creators and copyright-owning corporations. The law needs to reassess the existing framework applying to the production of images to ensure fair protection to all and not stiffen creativity or impede the progress of technology.

Balancing the roles of human creators and generative AI models, such as Midjourney is an ongoing challenge. Determining the appropriate level of human control and intervention in the generative process and preserving the value of human creativity requires careful consideration. Language-wise, it is well known that few mathematicians and visual artists excel at communicating their ideas in writing. Poets and writers are. Poets use words to convey vision. Simple words may elicit emotion, story, color, and music. Their skill appears to be much better served by this instrument than designers' and artists' proficiency in non-verbal communication. Examples of experimental prompts that use excerpts of well-known poetry produce intriguing images that are only limited by the capabilities of the AI's visual database. This shift, along with crucial training in critical thinking is bringing to the forefront of visual creativity language experts and poets who, when they team up with artists bringing the technical skills needed to produce meaningful artworks, will use generative AIs to resonate with the audience in meaningful and unexpected ways.

REFERENCES

Alesmaa and Rait-Eino Laarmann. (2025). Transforming text and images into game-ready 3D models. *Alpha (Osorno)*, *3D*, •••. Retrieved June 16, 2025, from https://www.guideofaitool.com/en/ai-tool/alpha-3d

Alves Da Veiga, P. (2023). Generative Ominous Dataset: Testing the Current Public Perception of Generative Art. *Proceedings of the 20th International Conference on Culture and Computer Science: Code and Materiality*, 1–10. ACM. https://doi.org/DOI: 10.1145/3623462.3623475

Anne, c. 19 (1710). The Avalon Project: The Statute of Anne; April 10, 1710. (n.d.). Retrieved June 16, 2025, from https://avalon.law.yale.edu/18th_century/anne_1710.asp

Boden, M. A. (1998). Creativity and artificial intelligence. *Artificial Intelligence*, *103*(1–2), 347–356. DOI: 10.1016/S0004-3702(98)00055-1

Chayka, K. (2025, April 2). The Limits of A.I.-Generated Miyazaki. *The New Yorker.* https://www.newyorker.com/culture/infinite-scroll/the-limits-of-ai-generated-miyazaki

Claburn, T. (2022). *Holz, founder of AI art service Midjourney, on future images.* Retrieved June 16, 2025, from https://www.theregister.com/2022/08/01/david_holz_midjourney/

Clopath, H. (1901). Genuine Art versus Mechanism. *Brush and Pencil*, *7*(6), 331. DOI: 10.2307/25505621

De La Torre, P. (2025). *The Power of the Analysis Skill – from the Perspective of Artificial Intelligence (AI) | Critical Skills* – Pakko De La Torre // Creative Director. Retrieved June 16, 2025, from https://pakko.org/the-power-of-the-analysis-skill-from-the-perspective-of-artificial-intelligence-ai-critical-skills/

Dürer, A. (1514). *Melencolia I* [Plate: 9 7/16 × 7 5/16 in. (24 × 18.5 cm); Engraving]. https://www.metmuseum.org/art/collection/search/336228

Eames, C., & Eames, R. (Eds.). (1990). *A computer perspective: background to the Computer Age* (New ed). Harvard University Press. ISBN: 9780674156265

Gerlich, M. (2025). AI Tools in Society: Impacts on Cognitive Offloading and the Future of Critical Thinking. *Societies (Basel, Switzerland)*, *15*(1), 6. DOI: 10.3390/soc15010006

Gilles, M. (2025) *The GANfather: The man who's given machines the gift of imagination. (n.d.).* MIT Technology Review. Retrieved June 16, 2025, from https://www.technologyreview.com/2018/02/21/145289/the-ganfather-the-man-whos-given-machines-the-gift-of-imagination/

Gregersen, E. (2025, June 13). Vector graphics | Definition & Facts | Britannica. https://www.britannica.com/technology/vector-graphics

Ishizu, T., & Zeki, S. (2011). Toward A Brain-Based Theory of Beauty. *PLoS ONE, 6*(7), e21852. https://doi.org/ ITP / IMA. (n.d.). NYU-Tisch (ITP - graduate). Retrieved June 18, 2025, from https://tisch.nyu.edu/itp.htmlDOI: 10.1371/journal.pone.0021852

Lanier, J. (2018). *Dawn of the new everything: encounters with reality and virtual reality* (First Picador edition). Picador, Henry Holt and Company. ISBN: 9781627794091 9781250097408

Li, F. F. (2023). *The worlds I see: curiosity, exploration, and discovery at the dawn of AI.* Flatiron Books.

Manovich, L. (2001). *The language of new media (8. print).* MIT Press.ISBN: 9780262632553 9780262133746

NAEA. (2024). NAEA Position Statement on Use of Artificial Intelligence (AI) and AI-generated Imagery in Visual Arts Education. Retrieved June 18, 2025, from https://www.arteducators.org/advocacy-policy/articles/1303-naea-position-statement-on-use-of-artificial-intelligence-ai-and-ai-generated-imagery-in-visual-arts-education

Nake, F. (2018). The Pioneer of Generative Art: Georg Nees. *Leonardo, 51*(3), 277–279. DOI: 10.1162/leon_a_01325

Nees, G. (1965) *Generative Computergraphik | Database of Digital Art. (n.d.).* Retrieved June 16, 2025, from http://dada.compart-bremen.de/item/Publication/3

Pantone. (2023). https://www.pantone.com/. Pantone. Retrieved June 16, 2025, from https://www.pantone.com/

Patry, W. (2000). *Patry: England and the Statute of Anne. (n.d.).* Retrieved June 16, 2025, from https://digital-law-online.info/patry/patry2.html

Shepard. (2025, April 15). Fine art and design using artificial intelligence | Penn Today. https://penntoday.upenn.edu/news/student-art-design-using-artificial-intelligence

Sims, A. (2024). From Creation to Curriculum: Examining the role of generative AI in Arts Universities. Retrieved June 16, 2025, from https://arxiv.org/html/2412.16531v1

Ursyn, A. (Ed.). (2018). *Interface support for creativity, productivity, and expression in computer graphics.* IGI Global. ISBN: 9781522573715 9781522573722

Vartanian, O., Navarrete, G., Chatterjee, A., Fich, L. B., Leder, H., Modroño, C., Nadal, M., Rostrup, N., & Skov, M. (2013). Impact of contour on aesthetic judgments and approach-avoidance decisions in architecture. *Proceedings of the National Academy of Sciences of the United States of America*, *110*(supplement_2), 10446–10453. DOI: 10.1073/pnas.1301227110

Veltman, C. (2025). In first-of-its-kind lawsuit, Hollywood giants sue AI firm for copyright infringement. NPR. Retrieved from https://media.npr.org/assets/artslife/movies/misc/midjourney.pdf

Weisstein, E. W. (2023). T*esseract Graph* [Text]. Retrieved June 16, 2025, from https://mathworld.wolfram.com/TesseractGraph.html

Xu, M., David, J. M., & Kim, S. H. (2018). The Fourth Industrial Revolution: Opportunities and Challenges. *International Journal of Financial Research*, *9*(2), 90. DOI: 10.5430/ijfr.v9n2p90

Zaho, B. (2024, March 28). *Replacement of human artists by AI systems in creative industries.* UN Trade and Development (UNCTAD). https://unctad.org/news/replacement-human-artists-ai-systems-creative-industries

Zewe, A. (2025, January 17). *Explained: Generative AI's environmental impact.* MIT News | Massachusetts Institute of Technology. https://news.mit.edu/2025/explained-generative-ai-environmental-impact-0117

Chapter 8
Plant Disease Identification and Pesticides Suggestion Using Deep Learning

B. Swapna
https://orcid.org/0000-0002-7186-2842
Dr. MGR Educational and Research Institute, India

G. Chaitanya Gowd
Dr. MGR Educational and Research Institute, India

G. Chiranjeevi
Dr. MGR Educational and Research Institute, India

S. Deepa
Velammal Engineering College, India

D. Senthil Kumar
RMK College of Engineering and Technology, India

S. Anandhi
Dr. MGR Educational and Research Institute, India

ABSTRACT

Plant health management is vital for maximizing crop yields. However, traditional methods of identifying plant diseases and suggesting appropriate Pesticides are often labour-intensive, time-consuming, and prone to human error. It proposes an automated system that utilizes drones equipped with advanced imaging sensors and recommend suitable Pesticides based on real-time data. The drone captures high-resolution images of crops and analyses them using image processing techniques to identify symptoms of various plant diseases. By employing deep learning models trained on large datasets of diseased and healthy plant images, the system can classify the type and severity of the disease. Simultaneously, soil health data

DOI: 10.4018/979-8-3373-2372-5.ch008

and environmental conditions are considered to suggest an optimal fertilizer plan for the affected area. This system provides several benefits, including faster disease detection, precise identification, reduced labor costs, and increased efficiency in Pesticides usage. It enables farmers to take timely and accurate actions, resulting in improved crop health and productivity

INTRODUCTION

Supporting food production and livelihoods faces challenges like pest attacks, plant diseases, and unsustainable fertilizer use, putting pressure on farmers. Early detection of plant diseases and appropriate fertilizer application are essential for improving yields and reducing environmental harm. Traditional visual inspections are slow and subjective, while indiscriminate fertilizer use harms crops and the environment. Modern technology, like drones and AI, can overcome these issues by automating disease identification and providing real-time data. This project proposes a drone-based system that uses image processing to detect plant diseases and recommend fertilizers, promoting sustainable farming.

The IoT and big data technologies to enhance crop production through smart farming. It proposes the IoT-SFF (Internet of Things Smart Farming Framework) with GIS (Geographic Information System) analysis to boost crop yields and optimize fertilizer use in inland smart agriculture. Drones can monitor irrigation and crop health while providing information on soil moisture through remote sensing. This data is crucial for understanding the crops grown in the area. Farmers can use this information to assess their soil's moisture levels and water it needs by comparing it to other soils.

LITERATURE SURVEY

Shahi et al. (2023) proposed the existing research covered by our review questions. First, the different UAV platforms, sensors, used in the studies we reviewed also examine how these platforms affect the performance of methods for estimating crop diseases and highlight the most effective vegetation indices and their success in detecting specific crop diseases. Additionally, the performance of advanced data-driven methods, and the various features used, including vegetation indices.

Yamamoto et al. (2023) done the changes in red crown rot (RCR) damage in fields over time, drones were used to capture multispectral images of the same field. Field investigations confirmed that RCR reduced soybean yields in both years. Using supervised classification of the images, researchers were able to visualize the spread of damage over time and measure the rate at which the affected areas increased. The results showed variations between the two years, suggesting that multiple factors, beyond just pathogen distribution, influence the extent of the damage.

Md. Jobayer Rahman et al. (2024) used data-driven methods in agriculture has the potential to greatly improve in farming. By using technology and expert knowledge, farmers can make smarter, more profitable decisions, which boosts productivity and promotes sustainability. Working closely with farmers has helped us fine-tune our approach, making it practical, affordable, and beneficial for their livelihoods. To create lasting change, it's crucial to use data-driven strategies, get continuous feedback, and adapt to evolving conditions. In the future, plan to analyze more crop data using GPS-based IoT and sensors from different regions, with machine-learning algorithms for analysis.

Muhammad Suleman Memon et al. (2020) used the Deep Learning, IoT, and other technologies can be used for smart farming. Various methods and techniques are covered for managing crops using Machine Learning, Deep Learning, and IoT. These approaches offer insights into how technology can be applied to monitor crops, identify issues like leaf diseases, and predict crop yields. The chapter also emphasizes the importance of techniques like CNN, SVM.

Ruben Chin et al. (2023) using aerial drones, medical professionals can improve their effectiveness and efficiency, potentially saving more lives. In agriculture, research shows that blight and wilt are the most commonly studied plant diseases. To better understand how drones are used for disease detection, the diseases were grouped into five categories, with results showing that fungus-related diseases usage. Virus and abiotic diseases were studied in only 10% of the research. This suggests that while more research is needed for these less-studied diseases, drones can already be effectively used to detect fungus-related diseases due to the strong scientific backing.

El Mehdi Raouhi et al. (2023) proposed the drones are being used in agriculture and how technologies like AI, IoT, and cloud computing are integrated for precision farming. A systematic review, conducted using the PRISMA method, highlights the potential of drones in smart farming with these advanced tools. The main take-aways show that drones have great potential to improve agricultural productivity and sustainability. The findings indicate that UAVs are valuable for collecting data, precision monitoring, and aiding decision-making in large-scale farming operations.

Gamboa et al. (2023) the existing research on UAV platforms, sensors, and configurations, such as flight height, used in crop disease estimation. We assessed the impact of these platforms on the performance of various estimation methods. Additionally, we identified the most successful vegetation indices and their effectiveness in detecting specific crop diseases. We also analyzed the performance of advanced data-driven methods, including conventional machine learning (ML) and deep learning (DL), along with various features like vegetation indices.

Emimi et al. (2023) the spatial and temporal variation in red crown rot (RCR) damage in soybean fields, UAVs collected multispectral images in 2018 and 2020. Field investigations confirmed that RCR mortality significantly reduced soybean yield in both years. Supervised classification of these images visualized the extent and progression of damage, quantifying the increase in affected areas. The observed variations and differing increase rates between the years suggest that multiple factors, beyond pathogen distribution, influence the occurrence of damage.

Zhihong Zhang et al. (2023) the spatial and temporal variation in red crown rot (RCR) damage in soybean fields, UAVs collected multispectral images in 2018 and 2020. Field investigations confirmed that RCR significantly reduced soybean yield in both years. Supervised classification of these images visualized the extent and progression of damage, quantifying the increase in affected areas. The observed variations and differing increase rates between the years suggest that multiple factors, beyond pathogen distribution, influence the occurrence of damage.

Zhao et al. (2023) The "Deep Learning and IoT: Enabling Technologies Towards Smart Farming" explores various methods and techniques for managing agricultural crops using Machine Learning, Deep Learning, and IoT. It provides detailed insights into implementing these technologies for crop monitoring, identifying crop health issues such as leaf diseases, and predicting crop production.

Zhang et al. (2021) proposed the applications and significance of different techniques, including Convolutional Neural Networks (CNN), Support Vector Machines (SVM), and Random Forest Models (RFM), in agriculture. These techniques are crucial for enhancing crop management and promoting sustainable farming practices.

By harnessing aerial drones, medical professionals can significantly enhance their effectiveness and efficiency, ultimately saving more lives. Additionally, the military can ethically employ drones in their operations while ensuring the utmost care to safeguard civilian lives (Hu et al., 2022).

Das et al. (2024) Research and development are crucial in advancing the use of drones for disease detection. Blight and wilt are the most extensively studied disease types, with more than 10 disease types covered in a single study. To better understand the use of drones for disease detection, diseases were categorized into five groups. The results indicate that fungus accounts for 64% of the diseases for which drones were used, while virus, nematode, and abiotic factors were studied in only 10% of the cases. These observations suggest that while researchers can explore less studied disease categories.

Chaudhary et al. (2023) Drones, or unmanned aerial vehicles (UAVs), have brought a significant shift in modern agriculture by incorporating cutting-edge technologies like artificial intelligence (AI), the Internet of Things (IoT), and cloud computing. A systematic review following the PRISMA method has highlighted the immense potential of UAVs in precision farming. These advanced technologies empower drones to execute essential functions such as data collection, precision monitoring, and informed decision-making, thereby greatly enhancing agricultural productivity and sustainability.

Agarwal et al. (2022) the important of technology-driven solutions are becoming essential in modern agriculture. By using drones and advanced technologies, farmers can make better decisions, use resources efficiently, and improve crop yields. Techniques have been explored for monitoring crops, identifying issues like leaf disease, and predicting crop production. We considered developing another model but stopped due to time constraints.

Drones have become essential tools for capturing images and data from agricultural fields, helping farmers make informed decisions about farm inputs. They are especially useful in remote areas where poor road conditions make traditional transportation difficult. Drones generate large amounts of data, and managing this "big data" is crucial for smart farm coordination. To fully harness the potential of drones, clear regulations need to be established across regions, and users must be made aware of these rules to prevent unauthorized use. More research is needed to explore how drones can be integrated into current transportation systems and supply chains. The wide-ranging applications of drones in agriculture, healthcare, and the military require a comprehensive approach involving research, regulation, and integration into existing systems (Ahila Priyadharshini et al., 2023).

Ahmad et al. (2020) the plant protection drones, a method to calculate the volume of small plants was developed. Based on this, a PWM control model was created to manage sprinkler flow. The opening and closing times of the sprinkler head were measured with a high-speed camera, and a system delay compensation time was determined. A control system was then developed to enable variable spraying based on the plant's location and canopy volume. This precision spraying system was integrated into the drone, creating a plant protection UAV that adjusts spraying according to plant size. A calibration test showed that when the drone's speed was 0.3 m/s, the sensor accuracy had a CV value within 17.3%. Additionally, a spray precision test found that the nozzle's opening and closing lag distances were 2.4 cm and 4.3 cm, respectively. The system successfully achieves precise spray control.

EXISTING METHOD

Disease Identification: Traditionally, plant diseases are identified through visual inspection by farmers or agricultural experts. This method relies on human observation to detect symptoms such as discoloration, leaf spots, wilting, or stunted growth. While experienced farmers can identify common diseases, this process is slow, labour-intensive, and prone to human error. Moreover, manual inspection becomes impractical for large farms, leading to delays in disease detection, which can result in severe crop losses.

Testing: In some cases, samples of diseased plants are sent to laboratories for analysis. Laboratory methods, such as pathogen isolation and microscopic analysis, can provide accurate results.

Sensors: With advances in technology, sensor-based systems have been developed to monitor plant health. For example, optical sensors, infrared thermometers, and hyperspectral imaging are used to detect plant stress, temperature variations, and chlorophyll levels. These methods provide early insights into plant health, allowing for more informed decision-making.

Fertilizer Recommendation Systems: In the context of fertilizers, traditional methods involve soil testing, where samples are analysed to determine nutrient levels (such as nitrogen, phosphorus, potassium) before suggesting fertilizers. Farmers also rely on general guidelines provided by agricultural agencies based on crop type and region.

PROPOSED SYSTEM

Drone Selection: Choose a multirotor drone for small to medium-sized farms or a fixed-wing/hybrid drone for larger fields. Equip the drone with a high-resolution RGB camera, multispectral sensors, and, optionally, a thermal camera. Add environmental sensors (e.g., humidity, temperature, and soil moisture) for additional data gathering.

Payload Integration: Mount the camera and sensors on the drone with gimbal stabilization to ensure clear image capture. Set up real-time communication between the drone and the ground control station (GCS) for telemetry and data transfer.

Flight Path Planning: Use GPS waypoints to design a precise flight path that covers the entire crop area. Set the drone to fly at a specific altitude and speed to optimize image resolution for disease detection.

Calibration of Sensors: Calibrate the cameras (RGB, multispectral, and thermal) and environmental sensors before the flight to ensure accurate data collection. Ensure proper lighting conditions and weather settings for optimal image capture.

Aerial Survey: The drone follows the pre-planned flight path autonomously, capturing high-resolution images of the crops and collecting environmental data (e.g., temperature, humidity, soil moisture).

RGB Images: Captured for visual symptom identification, such as discoloration, spots, or leaf damage.

Multispectral Images: Used to analyse plant health using different wavelength bands (e.g., infrared, near-infrared) to detect stress, nutrient deficiencies, and early-stage diseases not visible to the naked eye.

Thermal Images (if used): Monitor temperature variations in the crops to detect heat stress, drought, or infections.

Geotagging: All captured images are geotagged using GPS coordinates for precise location mapping of detected diseases.

Image Pre-Processing: Convert raw images into usable formats and apply basic pre-processing techniques (e.g., noise reduction, contrast adjustment). Segment the images to isolate individual plants or sections of crops for detailed analysis.

Soil and Plant Health Data Integration: Analyse the collected environmental data (soil moisture, temperature, humidity) alongside the disease classification results. Incorporate soil health data, such as nutrient levels (if available), to fine-tune fertilizer recommendations.

Figure 1. Flow chart for identification and visualisation

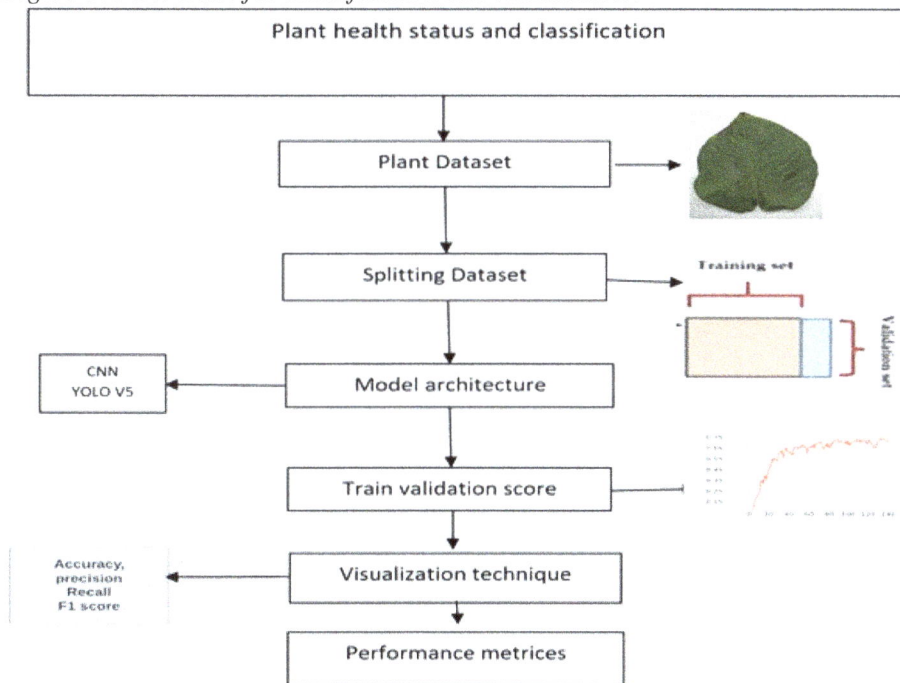

The Figure 1. Outlines the process of plant health status and classification using Deep learning.

Fertilizer Database: Create a database of fertilizers categorized by crop type, soil condition, and disease treatment needs. Based on the disease detected and plant health data, the system queries this database to suggest the optimal fertilizer type and quantity (e.g., nitrogen-rich, phosphorus, or potassium fertilizers).

Tailored Recommendations: Provide targeted fertilizer recommendations for specific areas of the field, ensuring efficient use of resources .Suggest appropriate chemical treatments if a disease requires fungicides, insecticides, or herbicides.

Data Visualization and Reporting Real-Time Feedback: Transmit real-time data and analysis results to the farmer via the ground control station or a mobile app. Provide a visual map of the field showing disease-affected areas using color-coded indicators based on severity.

Detailed Reports: In advanced systems, drones can automatically apply fertilizers or pesticides to affected areas using a spraying mechanism. They target specific sections of the farm based on geotagged data from the disease detection phase, ensuring efficient and precise application. Additionally, the machine learning model should be continuously updated with new data to enhance its accuracy in disease detection and fertilizer recommendations for various crops.

Figure 2. Block Diagram for plant leaf disease detection classification

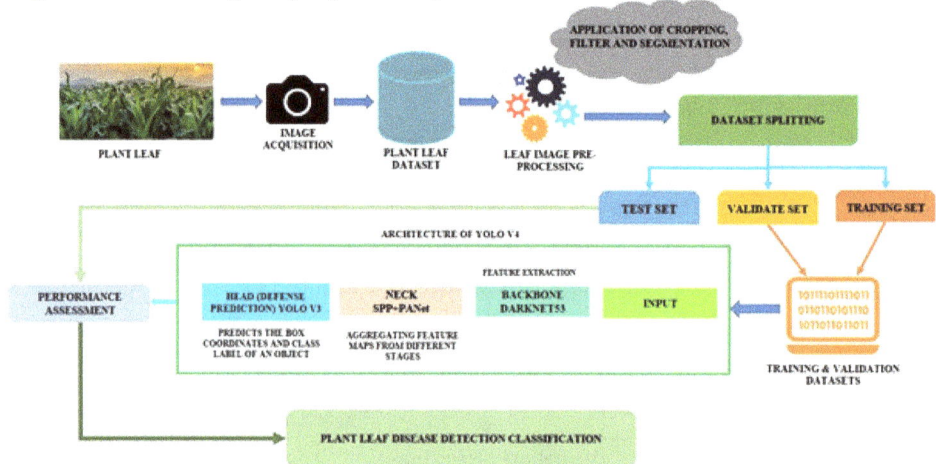

Drone (Unmanned Aerial Vehicle - UAV):

The drone is the central hardware component used for collecting images and data over large agricultural areas.

Typically, a multirotor drone (quadcopters or hexacopters) is used for small to medium farms due to its stability and ease of use, while fixed-wing drones are better for large scale farms for their longer flight duration.

Payload Capacity: It must carry various sensors like RGB, multispectral, and thermal cameras along with environmental sensors.

Flight Capabilities: Equipped with GPS for precise navigation and automated waypoint flight. The drone can hover in place to capture detailed images and follow pre-defined routes to cover entire fields as shown in Figure 2.

High-Resolution RGB Camera:

The RGB camera captures standard optical images in visible light, which are used to identify visible symptoms of diseases such as leaf spots, discoloration, and other deformities.

Resolution: At least 12 MP for detailed imagery.

Mounting: Gimbal-stabilized to avoid blurry images due to drone movement.

Purpose: Captures high-quality, high-resolution images to be processed for disease detection through visual signs.

Thermal Camera (Optional):

A thermal camera detects heat signatures, helping to monitor plant and soil temperatures, which can indicate water stress or disease infections.

Purpose: Detects temperature variations in plants and soil that may indicate water stress, heat stress, or infections.

Mounting: Installed on the drone with other cameras for integrated data collection.

GPS Module:

GPS is essential for drone navigation and for geotagging captured images to ensure precise mapping of affected areas.

Purpose: Ensures accurate drone positioning, navigation along pre-determined flight paths, and geo-referenced image data.

Accuracy: For precise agricultural mapping, GPS systems with RTK (Real-Time Kinematic) technology can provide centimetre-level accuracy.

Environmental Sensors:

These sensors are mounted on the drone to measure real-time environmental data
Temperature and Humidity Sensors: Monitor environmental conditions affecting plant health and disease progression.

Soil Moisture Sensors: Measure soil water content, helping in irrigation and fertilizer recommendations.

Onboard Computer (Processing Unit):

The onboard processing unit handles real-time data analysis, processing images captured by the drone and possibly running machine learning models on the fly.

Type: Small, lightweight embedded systems like Nvidia Jetson Nano, Raspberry Pi, or similar devices.

Purpose: To perform local computations, such as preliminary image processing or transmitting raw data to the ground station for further analysis.

Communication Module (Telemetry System):

A communication module enables real-time transmission of data from the drone to the ground control station (GCS). This module is essential for sending images and sensor data for further analysis.

Purpose: Ensures real-time communication between the drone and the ground station to transmit telemetry data, camera images, and environmental sensor readings.

Type: Radio Frequency (RF), Wi-Fi, or 4G/5G networks depending on range and field size.

Ground Control Station (GCS):

The GCS is the interface through which the drone is monitored, and real-time data is viewed and analyzed. It can be a laptop or tablet running flight control software.

Purpose: Used for drone flight planning, monitoring the drone's path, receiving real-time data, and processing the collected information.

Software: Typically runs mission planning software such as Mission Planner, DJI GS Pro, or similar programs that allow waypoint navigation, data analysis, and visualization.

SOFTWARE DETAILS:

Tensor flow: TensorFlow is an open-source machine learning framework developed by Google. It is used to create and train neural networks, which are a type of machine learning model inspired by the human brain. TensorFlow can be used for a variety of tasks, such as image recognition, natural language processing, and predictive analytics. It is a popular choice for researchers and developers because it is flexible, scalable, and easy to use.

Num Py: NumPy is a Python library that provides powerful tools for working with numerical data. It's particularly useful for tasks involving arrays, matrices, and mathematical operations. NumPy's core data structure is the NumPy array, which is a multi-dimensional array of homogeneous data type. These arrays are optimized for efficient numerical computations and can be used to perform various operations like element-wise arithmetic, matrix multiplication, linear algebra, and more.

Keras: Keras is a high-level API that simplifies the process of building and training neural networks. It acts as a user-friendly interface on top of TensorFlow, a popular machine learning framework. Keras is designed to be easy to learn and use, making it accessible to both beginners and experienced developers. It offers a modular approach, allowing you to combine different layers and components to create complex neural network architectures. Keras also provides various built-in functions and utilities for tasks like data preprocessing, model evaluation, and visualization.

Streamlit: It is a powerful Python library that makes it incredibly easy to create interactive web applications. It's designed to streamline the process of building data-driven apps, allowing developers to focus on the core functionality rather than getting bogged down in complex front- end development. With Streamlit, you can quickly prototype and deploy your ideas, making it a great choice for both experienced data scientists and those new to web development. It offers a variety of features, including the ability to display data in various formats (charts, tables, maps), create interactive widgets for user input, and integrate with popular machine learning libraries.

OpenCV-Python: It is a powerful computer vision library that provides a vast array of tools and functions for image and video processing, object detection, and machine learning applications. It's written in C++ but comes with Python bindings, making it accessible to Python developers. OpenCV-Python offers a user-friendly interface, extensive documentation, and a large community of developers, making it a popular choice for computer vision tasks. With OpenCV-Python, you can perform tasks like face detection, object tracking, image segmentation, and more, all within the Python environment.

Matplotlib: It is a powerful Python library used for creating static, animated, and interactive visualizations. It offers a wide range of plotting functions to visualize data in various forms, such as line plots, scatter plots, histograms, bar charts, and more. Matplotlib is highly customizable, allowing users to control every aspect of their plots, from colors and labels to styles and layouts. It's a popular choice among scientists, engineers, and data analysts for its flexibility, ease of use, and extensive documentation.

Scikit-learn: It is a free and open-source Python library that provides a collection of machine learning algorithms for tasks like classification, regression, clustering, and dimensionality reduction. It's built on top of NumPy, SciPy, and Matplotlib, making it easy to use and integrate with other scientific Python tools. With scikit-learn, you can quickly and efficiently build machine learning models for a wide range of applications, from image recognition to natural language processing.

Flask: It is a popular Python web framework that is lightweight and easy to use. It is known for its simplicity and flexibility, making it a great choice for both beginners and experienced developers. Flask is built on top of the Werkzeug WSGI toolkit and Jinja2 template engine, providing a solid foundation for building web applications. With Flask, you can create dynamic web pages, handle HTTP requests and responses, and manage your application's routing and data. It also offers a variety of extensions that can be added to your project to enhance its functionality, such as database integration, user authentication, and more.

Coding

```
import streamlit as st
import cv2 as cv
import numpy as np
import keras
label_name = ['Apple scab', 'Apple Black rot', 'Apple Cedar
apple rust', 'Apple healthy', 'Cherry Powdery mildew', 'Cher-
ry healthy', 'Corn Cercospora leaf spot Gray leaf spot', 'Corn
Common rust', 'Corn Northern Leaf Blight', 'Corn healthy',
'Grape Black rot', 'Grape Esca', 'Grape Leaf blight', 'Grape
healthy', 'Peach Bacterial spot', 'Peach healthy', 'Pepper bell
Bacterial spot', 'Pepper bell healthy', 'Potato Early blight',
'Potato Late blight', 'Potato healthy', 'Strawberry Leaf
scorch', 'Strawberry healthy', 'Tomato Bacterial spot', 'Tomato
Early blight', 'Tomato Late blight', 'Tomato Leaf Mold', 'Toma-
to Septoria leaf spot', 'Tomato Spider mites', 'Tomato Target
Spot', 'Tomato Yellow Leaf Curl Virus', 'Tomato mosaic virus',
'Tomato healthy']
```

```python
st.write("""The leaf disease detection model is built us-
ing deep learning techniques, and it uses transfer learning to
leverage the pre-trained knowledge of a base model. The model
is trained on a dataset containing images of 33 different types
of leaf diseases. For more information about the architecture,
dataset, and training process, please refer to the code and
documentation provided.""")
st.write("Please input only leaf Images of Apple, Cherry,
Corn, Grape, Peach, Pepper, Potato, Strawberry, and Tomato.
Otherwise, the model will not work perfectly.")
model = keras.models.load_model('Training/model/Leaf Deas-
es(96,88).h5')
uploaded_file = st.file_uploader("Upload an image")
if uploaded_file is not None:
image_bytes = uploaded_file.read()
img = cv.imdecode(np.frombuffer(image_bytes, dtype=np.
uint8), cv.IMREAD_COLOR)
normalized_image = np.expand_dims(cv.resize(cv.cvtColor(img,
cv.COLOR_BGR2RGB), (150, 150)), axis=0)
predictions = model.predict(normalized_image)
st.image(image_bytes)
if predictions[0][np.argmax(predictions)]*100 >= 80:
st.write(f"Result is: {label_name[np.argmax(predictions)]}")
else:st.write(f"Try Another Image")
```

The Figure 3. shows a Python script in Visual Studio Code that builds a leaf disease detection model using deep learning. It leverages a pre-trained model and allows users to upload an image of a leaf to classify its health condition. The script supports various plant types and diseases. The drone, equipped with high-resolution RGB, multispectral, and optional thermal cameras, autonomously covered extensive agricultural areas. It captured detailed imagery and environmental data essential for effective plant health assessment. A machine-learning model trained on a diverse dataset of plant diseases demonstrated outstanding performance under real-world conditions.

Figure 3. Source code

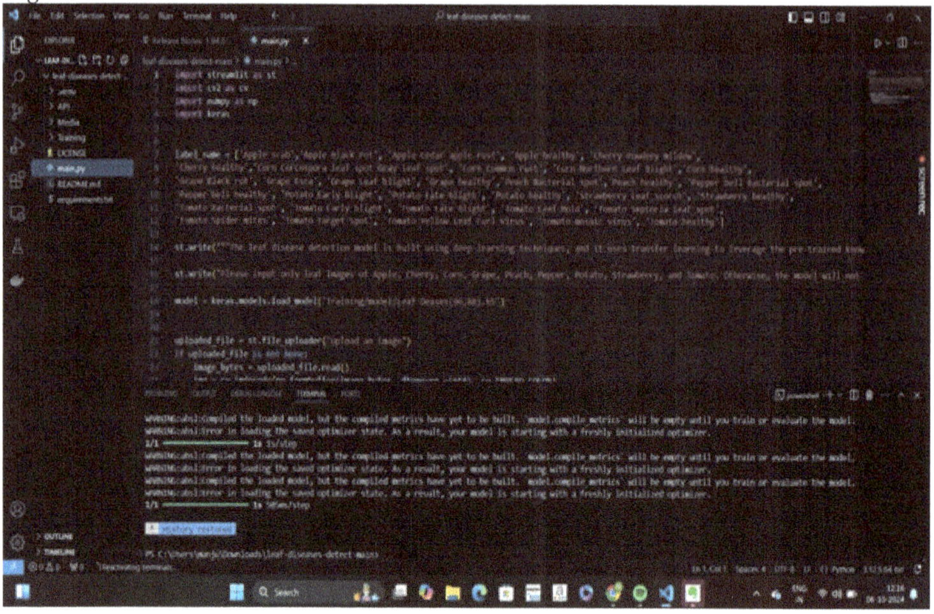

Figure 4. Diseased plant for testing

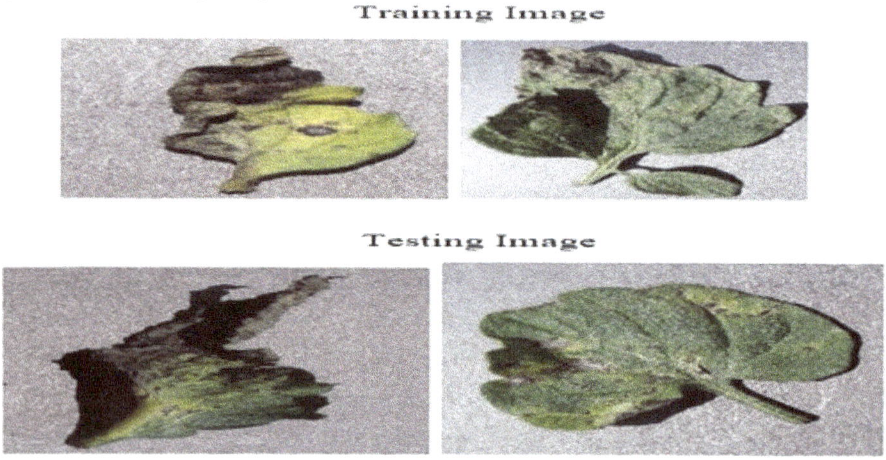

These Figure 4. is used to teach the algorithm to recognize specific features of diseased leaves, such as discoloration, spots, or patterns and used to evaluate how well the algorithm can identify the disease it was trained on.

Results and Discussion

Figure 5. Web interface for Leaf Disease Detection Model

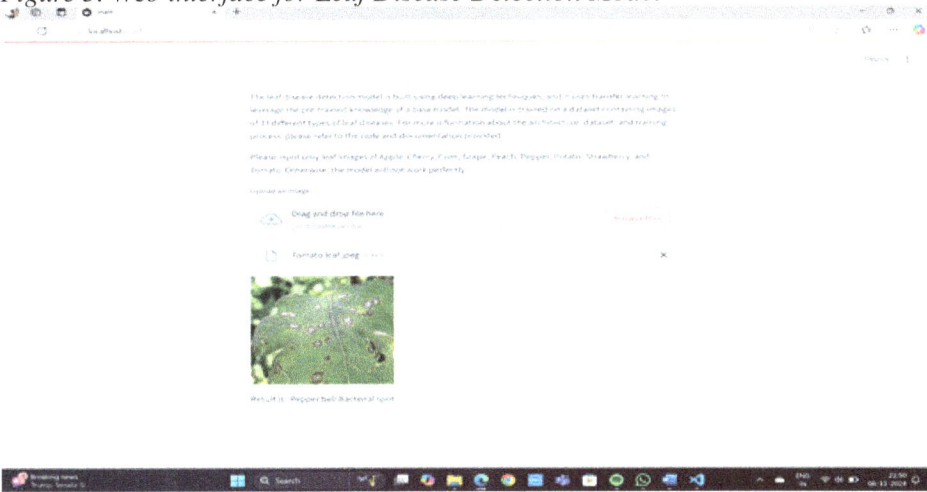

The Figure 5. Show cases a web interface for a leaf disease detection model. The model utilizes deep learning and transfer learning to identify diseases in leaves of various plants. It is trained on a dataset containing images of 33 different types of leaf diseases. To use the model, users can upload an image of a leaf from the supported plants: Apple, Cherry, Corn, Grape, Peach, Pepper, Potato, Strawberry, and Tomato.

Figure 6. After implementing the code for plant detection

207

Figure 7. Showing the disease where it is located

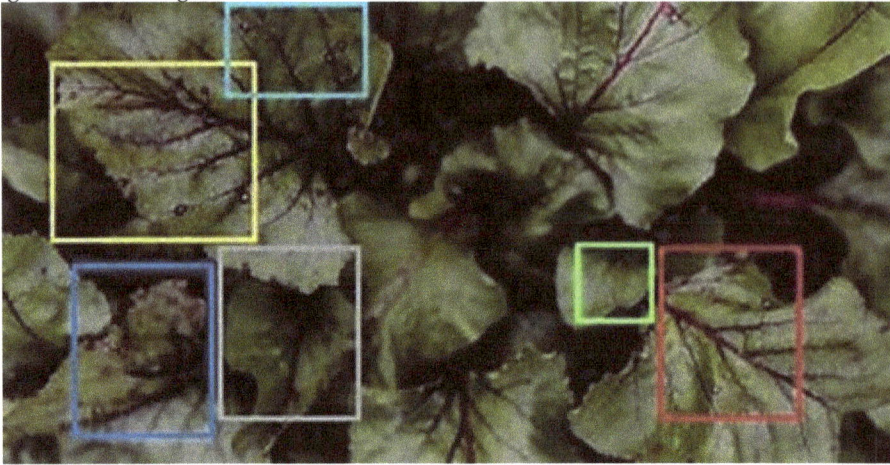

The Plant Disease Identification and Fertilizer Suggestion Using Drone project has produced promising results, The above Figure 6. and Figure 7. shows that the plant on verifying and it shows the disease where it is and where it is located and it gives what type of fertilizers we need to give that plant or that type of disease. It identify like a red dots or red box on that particular area where the disease is spotted on plant. We observe that how the diseased plant shows the identification. By using cameras we taken the diseased plant and verified by using deep learning techniques highlighting both technological innovation and practical advantages for precision agriculture.

The system integrated disease detection results with environmental factors. This comprehensive analysis enabled the provision of targeted fertilizer recommendations, optimizing nutrient application and enhancing crop health. The suggestions were tailored to specific areas within the field, reducing the risk of over-application and ensuring efficient resource use. This targeted approach not only improved crop yields but also fostered. Additionally, the system displayed robust capabilities in real-time data processing and communication. The drone's seamless data transmission to the ground control station facilitated timely analysis and informed decision- making. The visualization of disease-affected areas, along with clear fertilizer application recommendations, greatly assisted farmers in effective crop management.

CONCLUSION

The successful integration of advanced technologies has demonstrated the potential of precision agriculture to significantly enhance crop yields and sustainability. By leveraging drones equipped with cutting-edge sensors, the system efficiently captured high-resolution imagery and critical environmental data across vast agricultural landscapes. The machine learning model, trained on a comprehensive dataset, exhibited exceptional accuracy in identifying common plant diseases and early signs of stress, empowering farmers to take timely and targeted interventions. Moreover, the system's capacity to provide precise fertilizer recommendations, tailored to both disease detection and environmental factors, optimizes nutrient application, minimizes waste, and promotes healthier crop growth. This innovative approach not only increases agricultural productivity but also contributes to sustainable farming practices by reducing the reliance on chemical inputs and conserving valuable resources.

REFERENCES

Agarwal, M., Singh, A., Arjaria, S., Sinha, A., & Gupta, S. (2022). ToLeD: To-mato leaf disease detection using convolution neural network. *Procedia Computer Science*, *167*, 293–301.

Ahila Priyadharshini, R., Arivazhagan, S., Arun, M., & Mirnalini, A. (2023). Maize leaf disease classification using deep convolutional neural networks. *Neural Computing & Applications*, *31*, 8887–8895.

Ahmad, W., Shah, S., & Irtaza, A. (2020). Plants disease phenotyping using quinary patterns as texture descriptor. *KSII Transactions on Internet and Information Systems*, *14*, 525–542.

Chin, R., Catal, C., & Kassahun, A. (2023). Plant disease detection using drones in precision agriculture. *Precision Agriculture*, *24*, 1663–1682.

Chaudhary, R. R., Bamane, K. D., Agrawal, H., Malathi, P., Gaikwad, A. S., & Patankar, A. J. (2024). A critical analysis of crop management using Machine Learning towards smart and precise farming. *Journal of Integrated Science and Technology*, *12*(5), 809–809.

Das, S., Ghosh, A., & Pal, S. (2024). Internet-of-Things-enabled precision agriculture for sustainable rural development. In *Precision Agriculture for Sustainability* (pp. 343–372). Apple Academic Press.

Emimi, M., Khaleel, M., & Alkrash, A. (2023). The Current Opportunities and Challenges in Drone Technology. *Int. J. Electr. Eng. And Sustain.*, *1*, 74–89.

Gamboa, Gregorio, Morite, Analyn, Bacarro, Robert, Plando, Rowena, & Ylaya, Vrian & Serna, & John. (2023). Ricefield Health Monitoring System using a drone with AI interface. *Science International (Lahore)*, *35*, 181–184.

Hu, G., Zhu, Y., Wan, M., Bao, W., Zhang, Y., Liang, D., & Yin, C. (2022). Detection of diseased pine trees in unmanned aerial vehicle images by using deep convolutional neural networks. *Geocarto International*, *37*, 3520–3539.

Jobayer Rahman, Md., & Shakil Ahmed, Md., Swapnil Biswas, Anika Tabassum Orchi, Raiyan Rahman, & A.K.M. Muzahidul Islam. (2024). Crop Care: Advanced Crop Management System with Intelligent Advisory and Machine Learning Techniques. *6th International Conference on Electrical Engineering and Information & Communication Technology (ICEEICT)*, Dhaka, Bangladesh, 1356-1361.

Memon, M. S., Kumar, P., & Mirani, A. A. (2020). Deep Learning and IoT: The Enabling Technologies towards Smart Farming. *Industrial Internet of Things and Cyber-Physical Systems*, *5*, 47–60.

Raouhi, E. M., Lachgar, M., Hrimech, H., & Kartit, A. (2023). Unmanned Aerial Vehicle-based Applications in Smart Farming: A Systematic Review. *International Journal of Advanced Computer Science and Applications*, *14*, 45–70.

Shahi, T. B., Xu, C.-Y., Neupane, A., & Guo, W. (2023). Recent Advances in Crop Disease Detection Using UAV and Deep Learning Techniques. *Remote Sensing*, *15*, 2450–2469.

Yamamoto, S., Nomoto, S., Hashimoto, N., Maki, M., Hongo, C., & Shiraiwa, T. (2023). Monitoring spatial and time-series variations in red crown rot damage of soybean in farmer fields based on UAV remote sensing. *Plant Production Science*, *26*, 36–47.

Zhang, T., Xu, Z., Su, J., Yang, Z., Liu, C., Chen, W.-H., & Li, J. (2021). Ir-UNet: Irregular Segmentation U-Shape Network for Wheat Yellow Rust Detection by UAV Multispectral Imagery. *Remote Sensing*, *13*, 3892.

Zhihong Zhang, Shuo Yuan, Qinghui Lai, Ronghao Zeng, Jingkun Zhang and Siyu Shen. (2023). Precision Variable-rate Control System for Mini UAV-based Pesticide Application. J. Phys.: Conf. Ser. 2557, 012-025.

Zhao, Wei, & Wang, Meini, & Pham, V. (2023). Unmanned Aerial Vehicle and Geospatial Analysis in Smart Irrigation and Crop Monitoring on IoT Platform. *Mobile Information Systems*, *10*, 1–12.

Chapter 9
AI and Digital Transformation:
Changing Landscapes of Emerging Economies in Asian Sub-Continent

Sonal Tikku

 https://orcid.org/0000-0002-1366-985X

Amity School of Insurance Banking and Actuarial Science, Amity University, Noida, India

Ritesh Dwivedi

 https://orcid.org/0000-0003-3921-5458

Symbiosis Institute of Business Management, Noida, India

Anjani K. Singh

Entrepreneurship Development Institute of India, India

ABSTRACT

India is emerging as one of the major players in global economy. To keep in pace with the global scenario there is a requirement of implementation of AI in Indian economy. AI has helped in transformation by increasing productivity and reducing inefficiency. In India AI implementation is still a challenge. Lack of proper infrastructure and financial literacy has impacted the AI implementation. Banks, Financial Institutions, and MSMEs have benefitted from AI disruption. AI has helped MSMEs in saving cost by enhancing productivity and reducing operational risk. AI can also help SMEs in inventory control, production management. To make AI a success greater efforts are needed from all the segments of society. AI has

DOI: 10.4018/979-8-3373-2372-5.ch009

contributed to financial inclusion by bringing underserved sections of society to main stream banking. AI has also helped in providing cost effective and affordable banking services world wide.

INTRODUCTION

Emerging economies will play pivotal role in contributing 4.06% to world's GDP by 2035 as compared to a contribution of 1.59% by developed nations. Global economic growth will reach 65% figure by 2035. The main contributors of this growth trajectory would be emerging economies like China, India, Vietnam and Philippines (Perez-Goropze et al., 2024). These economies act as game changer on world economic growth platforms. India and China have emerged as one of the main markets for all the major players in industry. AI has started making inroads in emerging economies. From agriculture to banking, AI has brought complete transformation in style of working of these sectors. AI has helped in bringing radical change in banking and industrial sector in emerging economies in Asia. The study done on ASEAN countries concluded that for various factors such as economic growth, financial development and financial performance are significantly influenced by the usage of AI. More AI adoption, higher is the positive impact of these factors. (Dampitaske et al., 2021). Another study done in emerging economies show that AI is the key driver for growth. Relative to the net and gross effect of AI on labour markets and GDP show that by 2030 AI might yield 16% increase in output translating into an estimated amount of $13 trillion. Also, quality of resource and better allocation of talent is important for growth of Asia pacific economies (Haseeb et al., 2019).

Artificial Intelligence is changing the global scenario today. AI refers to the way we program computers to make them intelligent as humans. The rise of AI has also given emergence to other digital platforms such as blockchains and machine learning. In emerging markets like India, AI plays a very significant role of providing services to underserved sections of society by lowering the cost and delivering tailor made innovative products and services. AI showcased its impact on product, services and way of interaction. AI has greatly impacted emerging economies by providing low-cost solutions and innovative products which are suitable to underserved sections of society.AI has an ability to combine large data volumes with computing power thus helping to simulate human cognitive abilities such as language, reasoning, perception, vision and spatial processing. AI has given boost to poor economies in the world, which are using basic AI to provide financial solutions to underserved sections of economy. AI is used in some economies such as Ant Financial in East Asia, M-Shwari in East Africa, M-Kaiy in Madagascar and MoMo Kash in Coted

Ivoire (Strusani and Houngbonon, 2019). As per the study done (Abhanga and Dotse, 2024)there are four types of AIs: -

Reactive AI, Limited memory AI, Self-aware AI and theory of Mind AI.

- Reactive AI- This machine learning model are task specific with no memory
- Limited memory AI-This machine learning model uses historical data and pre programmed information for analysis and predictions
- Self-Aware AI- This machine learning model goes beyond its physical existence, feelings and thoughts
- Theory of mind AI-This machine learning model gives machines ability to mimic human minds

The latest innovations of AI such as Algorithm trading, fraud detection and automated risk assessment in a way have increased the efficiency of the operations but this has also given rise to the concern of cyber threats. The trust of Indian customers in banking industry is greatly impacted by the rise in cyber threats and regulatory gaps to control them. To control this India must develop strong policy frameworks which will lead to risk mitigation. AI has also given a forward push to financial inclusion by supporting underserved sections of strata to come to mainstream banking (Yoganandham, 2025). According to UNESCO, AI may add USD $13 trillion to the global economy by 2030 and increase global GDP by 1.2%. Adoption of AI technology by world economies will not only boost economic development but also provide employment opportunities to youths and entrepreneurs (World Bank, 2024).

Major subfields in AI are given below –

- Machine learning- In this function the machine does self-learning from its own from its experiences.
- Deep Learning-This involves usage of algorithms to study large data sets. The system automatically does edit of algorithms as per its requirements.
- Cognitive Learning-The system imitates the human mind in processing of information. Self-learning algorithms, patterns are used.
- Computer Vision- where the AI recognises and processes images in similar manner as humans do.
- Natural Language processing-This application uses natural language for machine communication.

SMEs are major contributor to economy by not only contributing to exports, imports, which in turn increase GDP of the nation, but also provide employment opportunities to vast number of populations, helping them in their economic growth. Banks also help in growth of small and medium enterprise (SME)by providing them tailor made solutions for daily operations with help of AI. In Asian subcontinent adoption of AI is still a major challenge as there are lot of factors which influence its adoption among population. The major influencers for AI adoption amongst masses are personal innovativeness, self-belief, trust, Word of mouth (E-WOM). These also influence psyche of people to go digital. Another impactful factor is social media which has greater impact of Genz population. The emerging economies have large Genz population who are completely tech savvy and spend majority of their time of phones. This group act as strong influencers for their elders to bring behavioural shift towards fintech adoption. Genz can act as motivators and hand holders for elderly population and smoothen their journey towards embracing AI.

Why Artificial Intelligence is important

Even though AI is considered threat for potential job replacement, but AI has helped in overall of skill development of population by bridging the gaps of language barriers, digital literacy, increasing productivity, efficiency and creating new job roles based on specific AI demands. Mechanisation through AI has created major impact of industries in these developing countries.AI powered machines helped in waste reduction and improvement in product quality. Moreover, AI in collaboration with human work force can help in product diversification, creation of new business models and identify new sources of revenues for the business All the inputs from AI will lead to creation of job opportunities and help firms in venturing into new markets thus increasing the revenue and leading to overall economic growth. Another major contribution of AI is in the field of cybersecurity and fraud prevention for financial sector. Nowadays large volumes of transactions are done through fintech using AI applications. These include not only account transactions but also disbursements of loans. The AI has helped in managing risk, fraud detection and prevention and bringing trusts in minds of people to move towards greater AI usage. The use of Chatbots has also enhanced customer experience wherein the customer can directly interact and discuss problems or challenges in completion of their transactions(Triwahyono et al., 2023).

Research work done (Gondauri & Mikhiel, 2023) on role of AI on economic growth shows that AI can accelerate economic growth in enlisted ways:

- Increased productivity- AI can accelerate productivity by improving decision making and enhancing efficiency.
- New Industries – with use of AI for innovations new industries are coming up which is leading to economic growth.
- Increase in global competition- with increased usage of AI in products and services can boost exports of the country leading to positive impact on GDP.

As per this study there are few drawbacks of AI implementation which are given below:-

- **Job displacement**- with increase in automation lot of jobs are getting obsolete. This loss of job is creating unemployment which leads to reduced spending and less purchasing power. These two factors impact GDP negatively.
- **Income disparity**- AI implementation is done in large industries as they have resources for the same. Hence, AI will be used by skilled workers and low skilled workers will be removed. This will lead to income disparity thereby effecting GDP.
- **Data Privacy**- AI uses large volume of data sets. These data sets may contain sensitive information. Any breach in data security may impact GDP negatively
- **Black Box**- AI systems lack transparency. Due to lack of transparency AI cannot be held accountable. Hence ethical considerations may prevent widespread usage of AI which may have negative impact on GDP (Gondauri & Mikhiel, 2023).

Historical Background and Evolution of Artificial Intelligence

Artificial Intelligence is technology that empowers computers to mimic human learning, comprehension and decision making qualities. The journey of AI started in 1950s. Various milestones in the journey of AI are given below(Stryker and Kavlakoglu 2025):-

- 1950-Alan Turing prints machinery computing. He used Turing test in which human interrogate would be try to identify difference between human text and computer responses.
- 1956- In this year John Mc Carthy coined the term AI. Later others created Ist running AI computer program.
- 1967-Frank Rosenblatt created Ist neural network-based computer.
- 1980-Neural networks found wide acceptance in AI applications
- 1995-Stuart Russell and Peter Norvig publish book on Artificial Intelligence
- 1997-IBMs deep Blue AI application beats world Chess champion
- 2004-Big data and cloud computing are underway helping organisations to work on large data sets.
- 2011-A new discipline for study and research by the name of data science came up.
- 2015-Deep neural networks used in super computers to identify and categorize images with higher precision than humans.

- 2016-AlphaGo program uses deep neural network to defeat world champion of Go Players
- 2022-various AI applications such as LLMs (Large Language Models)bring change in AI performance.
- 2024- Multimodels have evolved which can work on large data sets. These use Computer vision image recognition and NLP speech recognition functions.

Figure 1. Evolution of Machine learning

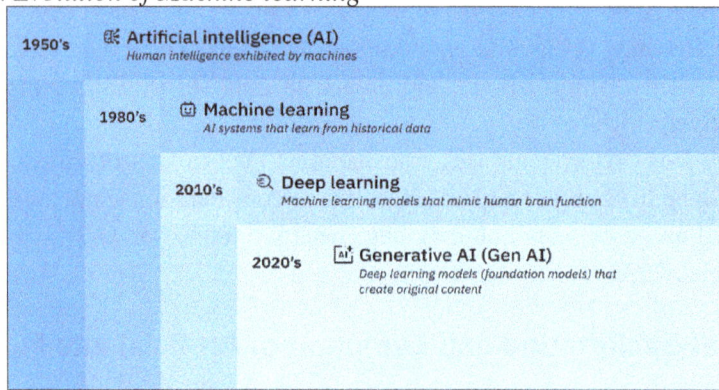

Source: IBM

Literature Review

AI plays a main role in banking sector by scrutinizing various data for fraud identification, risk management and customer interactions. AI usage has increased manifolds as driven by customer satisfaction. AI has changed the scenario for banking industry. The usage of chatbots and other AI enabled customer services to have enhanced the customer experience. Various AI based applications such as voice recognition helps banks in customer identification. Hence, AI has improved the efficiency levels and act as risk mitigant. AI also faces challenges in the form of data privacy, transparency and accountability. Govt also has a major role to play in AI adoption. With Govt backup these technologies will be acceptable by large no. of people who will consider this as safe and reliable for society. With proper Govt. guidelines for AI, will help in reducing the misconduct and help in ensuring public have faith on AI (Ridzuan, et.al., 2024).

Studies done show that AI has helped underserved sections by providing low-cost innovative products. The study identifies 3 types of AI applications based on which the cognitive abilities are stimulated. (Strusani and Houngbonon, 2019)

1. **Basic AI**- this imbeds Cognitive abilities such as memory, language and executes functions such as decision making
2. **Advanced AI**-This stimulates human cognitive abilities such as perception, vision and spatial processing
3. **Automated AI**- This has ability of interaction with humans and is on self-learning pace.

Various AI applications such as speech recognition and speech to text have helped in removal barriers of literacy.

A study done by Abanga and Dotse (2024) on South and Southeast Asia and Africa studies the impact of AI on economies of these regions. AI had transformed the economies by increasing productivity and innovation across the world. AI with its ability to use advanced algorithms has led to high level of efficiency and accuracy in performance of tasks such as data analysis and decision making . AI has helped in growth of Southeast Asia by promoting Ecommerce and digital banking. AI also faces lot of barriers and challenges in this part of the world, which are enlisted below:

- Infrastructure has posed as major challenge for AI. This is affecting rural areas as AI requires high speed to perform certain tasks such as cloud computing.
- Data privacy is major concern with increase in AI usage.

AI have completely transformed the banking sector today. Major sub fields of AI are:

- Machine learning- In this process the machine learns on its own from past experiences
- Deep Learning- Here we use large data sets for study. The algorithms used in data sets for better results.
- Cognitive Learning- The system mimics the human minds way of thinking
- Natural Language Processing- communicates using natural languages with machine

The study done by Sindhu and Renee (2019) shows that AI in banking sector is also used in various segments as per Fig given below. AI has helped BFSI sector in various aspects such as fraud detection, customer support, risk management, cyber security, automation of back office, wealth management and ATM usage. All the below mentioned functions help in improving productivity and efficiency of BFSI sector. A study on Indian Banking Industry discovered that top banks are using AI as tool for customer benefit. Factors such as security and ease of usage are important for senior citizens in enabling usage of AI. In this study factors such as capital investment, awareness, sustainability and data ethics play crucial role.

Figure 2. Usage of Artificial Intelligence in BFSI sector

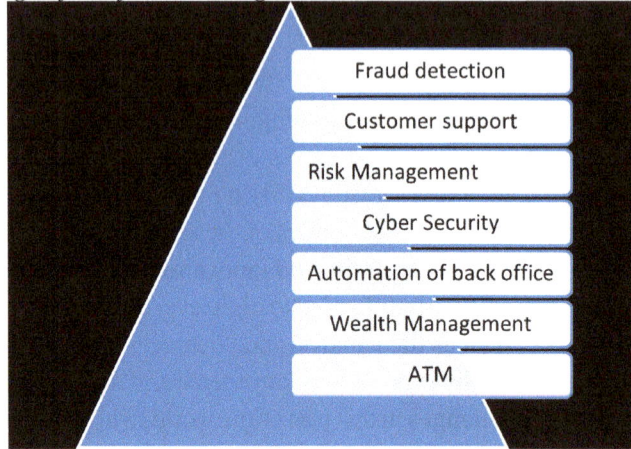

Source: Sindhu and Renee 2019

Use of AI by banks and Fintech companies has helped in financial inclusion by bringing underserved strata of society to mainstream banking.AI has helped banks to provide affordable financial services anytime and thus has included youth, underserved, small businesses and woman into mainstream banking. AI is now being adopted by both financial and non-financial institutions as it will lead to digital financial inclusion making underserved segments financially active (Mhlanga,2020).

As per the study done (World bank, 2024) generative AI is advancement in machine learning. It uses large volume of data sets. It creates contents like text, videos and audio-based images.

Figure 3. Types of Technological disruptions

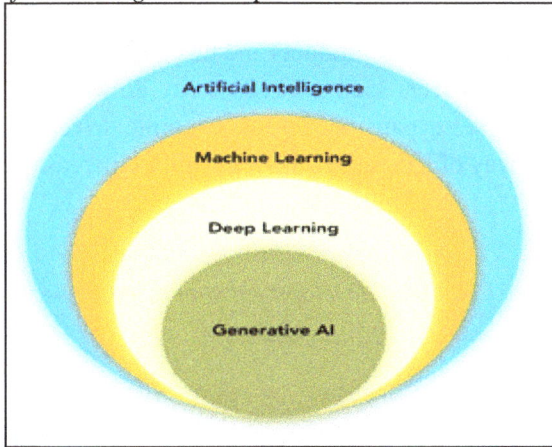

Source: The World bank, 2024

AI with its efficient data processing for large volumes has significantly increased the operational efficiency, reduce risk, enhance customer experience. AI has changed the total banking experience of the customers. Various AI products have brought positive change in customer interaction. Below are the AI tools for customer interaction:

1. Chatbots- these act as platform to provide uninterrupted customer service any time. Chatbots also help in intimating the customer regarding possible misuse of credit card.
2. Rob Advisors- These are AI enabled system-based Advisors who assist in various portfolios such as investment fund, exchange traded fund and pension plans. As this is digital advisory hence the customers must bear low fees which may usually be in the range of 1%.

As per the study the usage of AI also comes with below mentioned limitations: -

1. Skill problem- staff using AI without proper training may fail to identify actual risks.
2. Cyber Security- As AI usage involves client information, which is highly confidential, hence institutions using AI should have high level of cyber security to prevent misuse of client data
3. Black box – this is created in certain AI usages. These black boxes lack transparency with client and create confusion (Rafael et al., 2024)

As per study done by IFC depicted in Figure 4 show that AI has positive impact on human capital development, automation of core business processes, easier access to credit and creating new products and business models. All these benefits of AI lead to economic drivers such as productivity growth, low barriers to entry for businesses and market expansion. These economic drivers lead to increase in economic impact by way of increased output as well as increased consumption due to income growth.

Figure 4. Channels to Economic development supported by AI

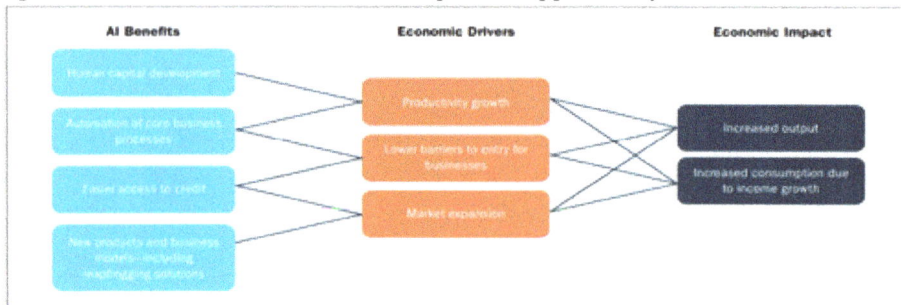

FIGURE 2 **Channels to economic development supported by AI technologies**

Source: IFC

Studies done show that AI implementation for SMEs help in productivity enhancement and better resource usage but it still faces lot of challenges in the form of high implementation cost, issues in operational sustainability and AI literacy. Bonsay et al. (2021) in their research work done on Japan, China, India and Singapore with respect to AI have concluded that in Japan the AI implementation and its utilization is better than other countries. This has positive impact on the GDP. In comparison India and China do not have utilisation of AI. Opening of free trade agreements help in technology progress and new markets are opened which lead to increase of growth and expansion of economy. Schwarke et al. (2025) in their research work on SMEs show that AI implementation have positive impact on business. The study suggests that Firms should train their employees and propagate learning culture in the organisation. Robust legal framework is required for better implementation of AI. SMEs need to focus on various challenges such as resource deficiency and compatibility.

Research done on use of AI showed how AI has been phenomenal in prevention of cyber security threats. Latest cyber security threats such as ransom ware and phishing attacks are very common. In Ransomware attacks cyber-criminal do encryption of important data of company and demand payments for release of data. Phishing attack uses fake emails and websites to trick users to share confidential information. AI enhances the cyber security by studying the regular behaviour pattern of the user and then identify any deviations from the same (Jimmy, 2021) . AI triggers alert when there is deviation from normal behaviour. A number of researchers in their study on AI identified how AI has helped in providing security against cyber-attacks by forecasting the attack even before its occurance.AI also has certain limitations such as production of false positives/ negatives while detecting cyber threats (Iyer and Umadevi, 2023)

Another study done explained that cybercrimes are not only restricted to malware but also include identity theft, email frauds and bank frauds. Banks should take extensive steps to prevent cyber crime as any breach can lead to erosion of trust of people in banking system. AI can help banks in reducing this risk by using advanced encryption and KNN algorithms. Digitalisation in banking sector has exponentially increased the availability of banking services to all the sections of society (Mishra S., 2023). This increase of banking ease has also given rise to cybercrimes. To mitigate the risk of cybersecurity, AI has helped by providing high level fraud detection processes. With the help of machine learning and anomaly detection, frauds can be prevented on real time basis (Todopunuri, 2023).

Research Methodology

The book chapter show cases the impact of AI on various fields such as education, governance, healthcare, social media. In this chapter we have done qualitative analysis on secondary data. Secondary data is obtained from various reliable sources such as research papers published in journals of repute, newspaper websites, Government websites and circulars. They secondary data is collected from the period 2019-2025. Data is also collected from websites of Reserve Bank of India Bulletins, NASSCOM, Business Standard to name a few. All these websites were accessed by author from 1st April 2025 to 27 May 2025.Articles having relevance to role of Artificial Intelligence in diversified fields of education, healthcare, social media, banking SMEs are studied .

Reserve Bank of India 's role in Artificial Intelligence Implementation in India

RBI in its bulletin dated 2024 had emphasized the role of AI in financial sector. Various digital tools such as Application programming interface (API), Biometric authentication, Artificial Intelligence, cloud computing have helped in Indian financial sector. Nowadays people are moving towards AI as it offers convenience, speed and affordability. RBI is engaged in developing new regulation and bringing fintech and big tech companies under their purview. AI implementation will be useful for identifying anomalies in trends and data, forecasting which is useful for monetary policy and help trade repositories to tackle data volume issues. AI will also benefit regulator in proper monitoring of transactions to detect violation. AI will assist regulator in risk assessment. AI implementation can help RBI in product innovation. It will reduce the cost of cross border transactions. As per 2023 survey of RBI, three fourth of Indian banks and few NBFCs are using AI in form of chatbots and virtual assistants. Regulatory sand box provides solutions in retail payments, cross border payments, retail lending, MSME lending and mitigation of banking frauds. As per RBI various challenges in AI implementation are given below:

- Concern about transparency, data biases, governance, privacy
- Cybersecurity of banks is also major concern. With dependability on service as software, possibility of third-party counterattack exists
- Digital innovations may lead to fragmentation (RBI bulletin, 20/2/2024)

AI has enhanced customer experience and streamlined the processes in banking sector. As per RBI there is major concern around data security, privacy and ethics. As compared to PSU banks, Private sector banks have faster adoption of AI in banking industry (Business standard, 2025).

Reserve Bank of India is going to develop framework for responsible and ethical enablement of AI (FREE-AI) for financial sector. RBI has formed a special committee for this task. The aim of this committee is to look into proper AI integration within BFSI sector. It will also fix accountability in this everything landscape of financial sector. With emerging technologies like Artificial Intelligence, Machine Learning, Tokenisation, cloud computing has changed the scenario in financial sector. The committee will not only investigate data privacy and frauds but will also look into creation of sustainable growth environment (Versha Jain, 2024). RBI has hired people from Company India LLP, Mc Kinsey and Accenture to understand and use Artificial Intelligence and Machine Learning for supervisory and regulatory functions (Economic Times, CFO, 2023).

Study done on SMEs of Ghana by Anbrokwah and Awuku (2023)show that AI had positive impact on financial, customer and internal business performance for firms in Ghana. Using Internet of things, Collaborative Decision making system and virtual and augmented reality this is achieved.

Sectorial impact of AI in emerging economies

Impact of Artificial Intelligence on Small and Medium Enterprise

Artificial intelligence has created positive impact on small and medium enterprises. With use of AI SMEs have improved their productivity and efficiency. Various IO platforms such as block chains, Internet of things (IOT) and machine learning have transformed the working scenario for SMEs (Khan et al., 2023)

Covid19 pandemic had greatly impacted SMEs across the globe. SMEs faced serious blow in terms of loss of business leading to shut down of many of them. Even though Government tried to revive SMEs by giving them loans, subsidies and other supports but the financial difficulties of SMEs did not improve significantly. The introduction of AI has SMEs in the fields of ecommerce, manufacturing and accounting. AI has helped SMEs in survival by helping in below mentioned ways:

1. AI has radicalised process improvement
2. AI has helped SMEs in marketing by analysing various needs and purchasing power of the customers
3. AI has brought do the gaps between physical and virtual shopping by providing vast variety of innovative products and services
4. AI has helped in reducing the business risk which often hampers the performance of SMEs.
5. AI has played crucial role in retail industry by forecasting demand and supply chain implementation (Lu et al., 2022)

The impact of AI on Korean Industry was done by Hwang and Kim (2022). As per their study adoption of AI increases the productivity of firms. Adopters have technical efficiency which is 26% more than that of non-adopters. To adopt new technologies, SMEs should go for strategic alliance

With growth of AI and digitalization in business sectors, SMEs face lot of challenges which differ from large business groups. Various challenges faced by SMEs are enlisted below: -

- SMEs being small in nature have limited access to finances.
- Data security is also one of the pressing concerns
- There is always dearth of skilled labour
- People associated with SME do not want to change the actions

In the world, SMEs in Africa face challenge of increase in cost of implementing AI, lack of proper resources and expertise in the area, whereas the European SMEs face regulatory challenges. SMEs in Asia are engaged in sustainability and cultural barriers. For SMEs to survive there is need for cross border collaboration and leveraging technologies. SMEs across the globe face challenges such as restricted financial resources, shortage of skilled labour, data security and resistance to change. Asian SMEs face the problem of sustainability and cultural barriers.(Yusuf et. Al, 2024). With disruption by AI into emerging economies, block chain, machine learning, ChatGPT have transformed the scenario. Block chain plays a very crucial role in building trust for SMEs. It also fosters streamlining of digital contracts, supply chain management. Robotics another offshoot of AI helps in improving efficiency of manufacturing, logistics and optimisation of operational costs. All the above changes help the business drive towards innovations and provides them with competitive advantage (Shafik, 2025). AI has changed the way of operations and interactions done by humans. Big business houses are utilising AI for improving profitability as well as productivity. SMEs due to their financial constraints face challenges in adoption of AI. In Developing countries like India due to this issue more than 80% of SMEs collapse within 3 years of their operations (Michael, 2025). AI has helped SMEs in achievement of sustainability goals. It monitors issues faced by SMEs such as scant resources, operational inefficiencies and cyber threats. Developing workforce through collaboration and skill enhancement in AI has also given added advantage to SMEs (Mugisha et al, 2025).

As per Article by NASSCOM Community, SMEs can boost their growth by implementing AI in their day-to-day operations. AI can help SMEs to work on large data and take important decisions within time. In this world of cutthroat competition AI has greatly helped SMEs in making data driven decision and cut costs which provides them with competitive advantage. (NASSCOM Community, 2024)

Figure 5. Role of AI in SMEs

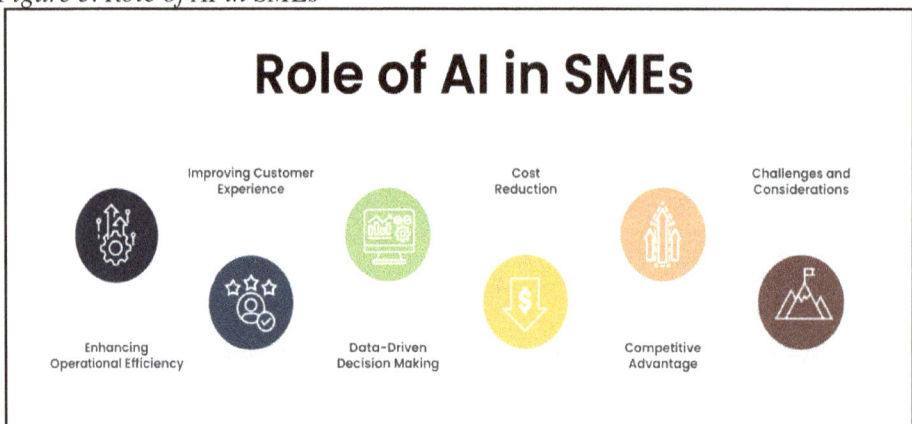

Source: Nasscom Community

AI application has helped SMEs in the areas of sales, marketing, pricing and cash flow. Use of technology by SMEs has given them boost to meet new types of demands, operational efficiency, enhance speed thereby reducing market risks (Drydakis, 2022). Research work of Sawwalakhe et al.2023, showcases the technological disruption of mobile phones and digitalisation on banking industry. Rise of new work force such as millennials and Genz is changing the working atmosphere as they use digital platforms for accessing information, banking transactions and purchasing goods. AI has helped banks in serving this group of customers well. In today's scenario more than 35% of population is using AI for enhanced response and customer satisfaction. With increased use of machine learning banks can analyse high data volumes without human intervention. This has improved customer expectation from bank and streamlined the systems and processes of bank.

Research of SMEs of India identified that perceived usefulness, Perceived ease of use and willingness to change have positive impact of AI adoption among SMEs of India. In Indian banking system with its efficiency and error free processing is slowly replacing human analysts as there is high cost associated with hiring of humans. Also, applications like chatbots are replacing customer care as these assist customers twenty four by seven (World Bank, 2024) AI has also made inroads into various banking operations such as claims management, trading, risk and fraud detection. AI usage has now led to enhancement of customer satisfaction with providing error free and faster services (Malai and Gopalakrishnan, 2020).

Artificial Intelligence in Governance

Govt of India is constantly engaged in the task of bringing country to digitalisation. Govt has taken various digital initiatives under below mentioned schemes-

- Meripechhan- It is user authentication method where single sign on method is used for logging into the portal. This involves interface of 3types of single sign on platforms such as Jan Parichay, e Pramaan and Digi locker. This portal uses various parameters such as username, mobile no. Aadhar or pan no. for authentication.
- UMANG- it is unified portal where the citizens can avail all the main Govt service benefits anytime. This system works on Android as well as IOS Mobiles. This is single user interface system on which the citizens of the country can coordinate with Govt for scheme benefits, documents and service information
- UPI Lite-This is interface with permits processing of low value Txns below Rs500/. In this interface no details of remitter bank's core banking system are required, and it functions on real time basis.

- Rupay- Govt of India has created widely acceptable card payment system. It has wide range of acceptance from ATM, POS machine to eCommerce sites.
- Fastag- This is RFID tag which is used for making payments at toll plaza across the country. There will be a sticker that is affixed on windshield and payment will be made by scanning the sticker. The payment is made by direct debit of linked saving bank or current account of the customer (Digital India website).

Maha Kumbh event of 2025 was fusion of faith and Artificial Intelligence. This event was held at Prayagraj in Uttar Pradesh. Approximately more than 64 crore people attended this event which turned out to be the largest human gathering of the century. Uttar Pradesh Government has used AI very strategically and intelligently. In this event, Govt had installed around 1700 cameras at various important locations. Out of these 500 cameras were AI powered which helped in doing real time crowd analysis. This event involved usage of two AI models, one for crowd density and another for crowd count. AI technique of facial recognition was used to further fine tune the data. All these data were monitored at Integrated Command and Control Centre at Prayagraj (Kumar and Shah, India Today, 25/2/2025).

Figure 6. Use of Artificial Intelligence in MahaKumbh 2025

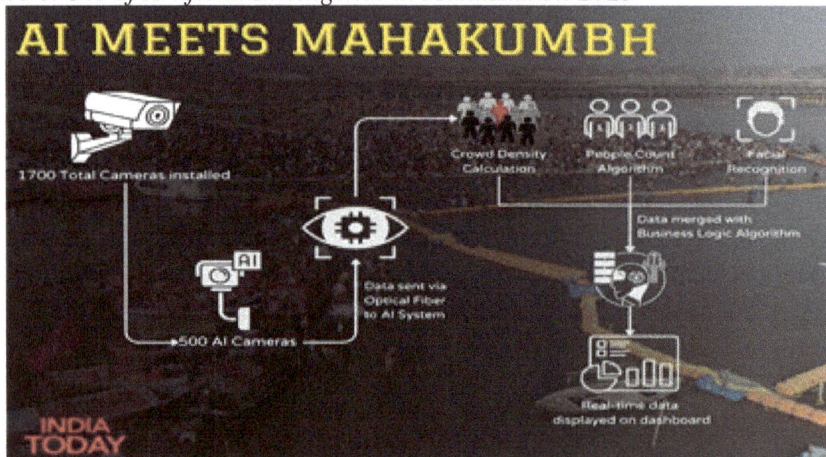

Source: India Today, Feb 2025

UP govt had also used Chatbots to assist devotees. These chatbots had below mentioned features:

- Mapping of Maha Kumbh venue and guidance on various sectors. The chatbots shared specific information about the area along with Google map links.

After accessing it the devotees could access information about banking, parking, transport, ATMs and public water

- With use of Chatbots devotees could download real time PDF with details about toilets, lost and found centres and exhibition. Also, there was an option of QR code scanning which would provide information on the mobile phones of the devotees (Press Information Bureau, 2025).

Artificial Intelligence in Healthcare-

Healthcare industry is very booming sector in India. With large population of country, health care is very crucial. As per study global health care is projected to at $19.27 dollars.in 2023 to $61381 trillion by 2034. AI has assisted healthcare segment by below mentioned ways-

- Streamlining administrative processes
- Making diagnostics simpler
- Enhancing patient outcomes
- Improving skills

Covid-19 changed the health care industry worldwide. After Covid-19 pandemic healthcare system has seen a major change with patients moving towards following services

- Having virtual consultations
- Remote diagnostics and monitoring
- Chatbots to assist the customer digitally

With more than half of population in rural sector Govt is focussed on using AI for providing health benefits to rural India using AI. Govt is building broad band connectivity for primary health centres under Bharat net. Govt has already aided digitisation in health sector by providing more than $1billion for growth. Also Govt. is in the process of creating Unified health id which will help in linking of health records of all the citizens in emerging economies like India (Forbes.com; Nasscom.in)

Artificial Intelligence in Banking sector

Introduction of AI to banking sector has changed its scenario by adoption of new strategies, improvement in efficiency, saving time and bringing customer satisfaction.

Banks can move towards achievement of their goals of performance, profitability, compliance, competitiveness and risk reduction.

AI has already been incorporated in various banking applications as enlisted below:

- Providing preapproved personal loans- these loans are sanctioned and disbursed instantly without any documentation based on the past financial record of the customer.
- Preapproved Business Loans- these loans are given to small businesses based on their account transaction history. These loans can be availed by the customer by logging on to their internet banking platform.
- Early warning system- AI helps bank in identification of stressed assets. It sends alerts to the concerned department to investigate the account and take corrective action. This helps in mitigation of risk.
- Credit Score- AI assists bank in calculation of credit scores thus helping in decision making
- Marketing and sales- based on the study of transaction and spending pattern of account AI helps in creating tailor made product and services for the customer. This helps in maximising sales at very low cost and in turn adds to customer loyalty for the bank.
- Fraud detection- AI helps in fraud detection by triggering alerts. It also helps in monitoring of the accounts (Ganesh, 2021)

AI has transformed the banking scenario by offering various applications such as fraud detection, credit risk analysis, customer service, chatbots, trading algorithms and forecasting models. With use of AI the efficiency of banks has improved, and they are better equipped to handle risks. AI also has certain challenges such as data quality, skill gaps, transparency and regulatory uncertainty. Another application of AI which has transformed banking is voice recognition. This helps in identifying voice patterns of customer while executing phone banking transactions (Nurhadhinah et al., 2024). Banking operations have seen a paradigm shift with use of AI. Now banks encourage customers to move to various digital channels such as mobile app and net banking. This platform provides cost effective services which are available to customer any time as per their convenience. Introduction of ATM and POS machines has also decreased cash transactions. Nowa days banks have introduced self help kiosks, where customer can perform functions like pass book updation on their own. Asset segment of banking has also seen change. Now a days loans are given to customer through digital channel such as mobile app or net banking. This process has reduced cost for the bank and provides immediate hassle-free loan to the customers. Business loans to micro and small accounts are also disbursed through digital channels. To enhance customer experience, banks are using chatbots. These virtual assistants guide the customer for various products and services.

Artificial Intelligence and impact on Education

Recently AI has played crucial role in transforming education system. It has helped in reforming teaching methods and introducing innovative teaching which will lead to sustainable development goals. With help of AI curriculum and education governance has been transformed. various AI tools such as ChatGPT and LMS (Learning Management System) had acted as an enabler in better connection of instructor and students. (UNESCO). AI steers educational setup by including adaptive learning technologies which create tailor made material for needs of specific students. The tools used in data analysis help educators to pinpoint performance patterns of the students. Another AI tool, Natural Learning Processing improves student interaction by mimicking human like manners and provide required feedback and support. With AI making inroads in education system, students can enhance their educational experience as they can learn at their own pace, receive feedback and focus on their weak spots. UNESCO 2023 Global Education Monitoring report emphasis the significance of digital technologies. AI helps in prioritizing student's strengths and interest so that there can be a tailor-based teaching approach. Chatbots are now used in education system to provide academic and administrative support to the students any time. Grading system has also improvised and moved towards automation. With this system students get immediate feedback and can improve upon their weak areas. Another latest development in education pattern is the use of Virtual reality and augmented reality. These immersive technologies help in recreating the realistic environment for learning so that student can understand the things better with stimulating environment. Predictive analysis has also helped students in their overall performance. In this method, based on student interaction and past performance, we can predict future performance of the student. This technology can help student to improve on their weaker parameters (https://learningsciences.smu .edu/blog/artificial-intelligence-in-education). Implementation of AI in education is faced with many challenges which are enlisted below:

- Students and staff lack AI and digital skills which hamper adoption of AI. As per survey conducted by digital education council in 2024 showed that 58% of university students felt that they do not have adequate AI skills.
- Education institutions lack infrastructure for AI implementation. Educational institutes should first obtain high speed internet connectivity, connected devices. Educational institutions with limited budgets find difficult to build proper infrastructure for AI adoption.

- Educational institutions on usage of AI will deal with high volumes of data. Safety and privacy of this data is also concern. Moreover, institutions need to safeguard against increased cyber threats.
- Government also plays crucial role in AI adoption by developing transparent policy framework that can help better AI implementation and secure confidential student information(Ernest and Young)

As per the report submitted by Mc Kinsey in 2020, 20-40% of faculty hours are wasted on activities which could be automated. Approximately about 13 hours of activities can be redirected towards student outcome activities. Technology can act as facilitator to teachers to focus on more core areas of student interaction and development as it will help teachers in freeing their time from activities which can be automated (Bryant et al., 2020).

Figure 7. Activity composition Teachers

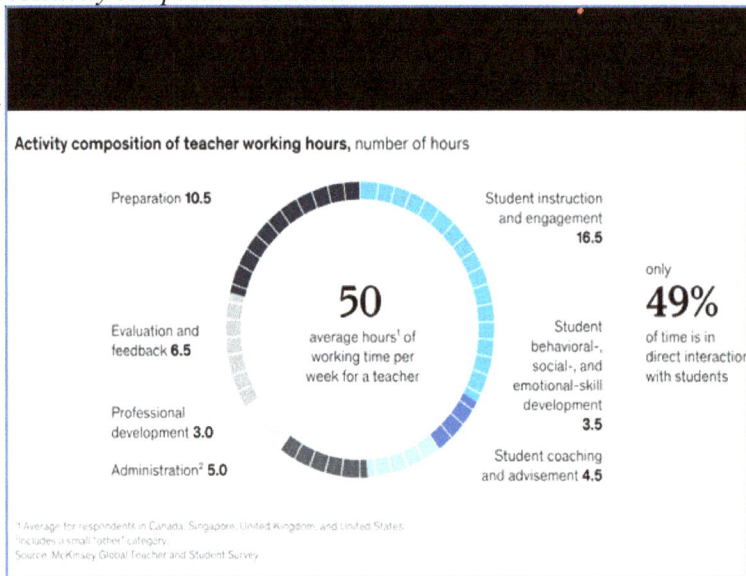

Activity composition of teacher working hours, number of hours

Preparation 10.5

Student instruction and engagement 16.5

only 49% of time is in direct interaction with students

50 average hours[1] of working time per week for a teacher

Evaluation and feedback 6.5

Student behavioral-, social-, and emotional-skill development 3.5

Professional development 3.0

Administration[2] 5.0

Student coaching and advisement 4.5

[1] Average for respondents in Canada, Singapore, United Kingdom, and United States
[2] Includes a small "other" category
Source: McKinsey Global Teacher and Student Survey

Source: Mc Kinsey, 2020

The Study on US students and teachers reveal that half of them are using AI tool such as ChatGPT. This tool is used weekly by 46% teachers and 48% students. The usage of ChatGPT by students has raised to 27% over 2023 figures. Teachers informed that AI is used by them in following ways:

- 37% use for idea generation
- 32% use for lesson plan and teaching material preparation

- 32% use for students worksheets
- 31% for planning quizzes and tests (Rosenbarm, 2024).

Artificial Intelligence in Social Media

Another powerful impact of AI is the increase in use of social media. In today's competitive world social media plays very crucial role for business promotion. The study on Thai SMEs revealed that social media has created an impact on SMEs also. Social Media adoption by SMEs is greatly influenced by various factors such as perceived usefulness, perceived ease, compatibility and business orientation. Adoption of social media my SMEs has given competitive advantage and enhanced their performance (Visuthiphol and Pankhan, 2025). As per the recent study, 4.9billion people worldwide are active on social media platforms. The study also predicts that in 2027 this figure may increase to 5.85 billion individuals. X, Meta and Insta are various types of platforms which are used by subscribers. The use of these platforms also has certain challenges such as data privacy, mis information and dis information. Excessive use of social media also has certain disadvantages associated with it. These disadvantages are feeling of loneliness, anxiety and depression to name a few (Forbes, 2024).Social media plays critical role in today's world. It helps in re-shaping public opinion, encouraging relationships and facilitating common stage for businesses to interact with the customers. The merger of Artificial intelligence and social media has helped in increasing user engagement, handling crisis management and providing health care solutions. In case of mental health issues such as ethics, transparency and privacy are crucial (Tahereh and Sidaqui,2024)

Impact of Artificial Intelligence on GenZ

AI adoption is highest among Genz. They are individuals born between 1995-2012. This generation has grown constantly under technology and social media. This generation is extremely active on most of digital platforms. Being tech savvy, Genz prefers short concise message and visual content. They do not prefer long messages. As they have grown up surrounded by technological advancements, their accepting AI is much higher (Chan and Lee, 2023).

AI has impact on ecommerce industry. Genz consumers are more inclined towards technology. Hence AI is also associated with establishing of branch trust. AI creates personalization impact on Genz leading to increase in trust and customer satisfaction (Hasini,2024). Study done by Oberio and Puranik (2024) show that today Genz constitutes a sizeable portion of population in India. Being tech savvy, they prefer smart phone apps for doing transactions and shun away from large banks. Genz believe in the concept of buy now pay later scheme and using online banking channels as these save time and are convenient. Hence AI is helping in catering to the needs of this segment of customers by offering digital products. A study done on Genz of Jordan analyses the relationship between Genz, financial decisions and financial literacy. As per study the financial literacy plays a very important role in personal decision making. Financial literacy helps in better usage of social media and digital platforms, which are cost effective and can be accessed any time by the individuals (Azzam et al., 2024).

AI Governance and Policy decisions

Artificial Intelligence despite being an economic booster is associated with risks. AI to increase its adoption among users must come out with processes to mitigate the risks through proper Governance. Hence, it is crucial for any economy in the world to implement proper governance framework for RI so that risk is mitigated. Fig below mentions the process of AI Governance (World Bank, 2024)

Figure 8. Process of AI Governance

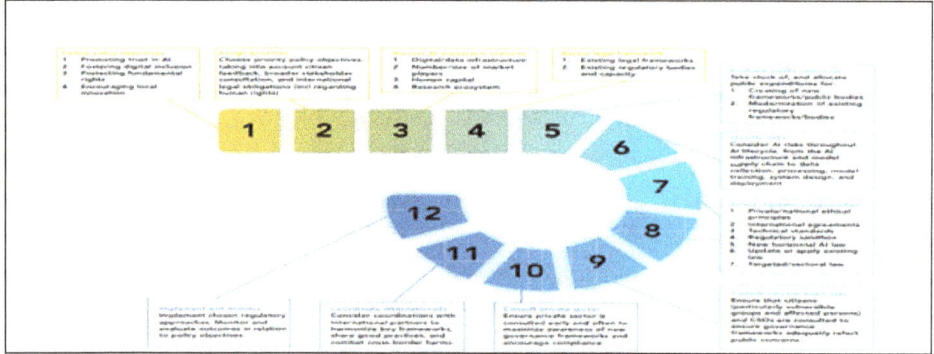

Source: World Bank

Study done on Saudi Arabia shows that adoption of AI depends on factors such as Govt policies, compatibility, sustainable human capital, market and customer demand. Government policies are very significant as policy measures may concentrate high expense, delayed return of investment period (Badghish, S. and Soomro, Y. A. (2024).

Impact of Artificial Intelligence on Asian Subcontinent

Vietnam -Vietnam is one of the merging economies of Asia where AI has made great inroads. Vietnamese Central and local government are implementing AI in public administration and service delivery. Various AI tools such as facial recognition for public security and intelligent traffic monitoring are few. Vietnam is facing challenges in AI implementation as there is limited data sharing between govt agencies. Also, lack of proper infrastructure for AI. Investment is required for infrastructure development. Enhancing skills of govt officials is another challenge faced by the country (United nations Development Project,2025). Study on SMEs of Vietnam, AI adoption is dependent on skill development. For development of the skills the managers of the firm need to hand hold the employees by providing them adequate training so that they can gain expertise, competency and knowledge required for AI usage. Facilitation of digital culture in the organisation can also boost AI use among employees. The main challenge faced by SMEs in AI implementation is lack of digital infrastructure, skilled manpower and good analytical tools (Dey et al., 2023).

Bangladesh-The study on Bangladesh shows that disruptive IT technologies such as Artificial Intelligence, Machine Learning, Block chain, Cloud computing, Big data and Robotic Process Automation (RPA) are influencing the Bangladesh's economy. Usage of all these by IT based companies has helped in enhancing productivity as well as efficiency which ultimately enhances customer experience. Bangladesh is using artificial intelligence in various industries such as telecom, banking, pharma and ready-made garments. As in 2021 there are around 4500 software companies which are operational (Khatun and Nawrin, 2021).

China- China is increasing the use of AI at lightening speed. AI is used in China in various sectors and health care is one of them. In this industry AI is used in medical imaging devices, diagnostics and drug discovery. China is also engaged in development of autonomous vehicles, and this may penetrate up to 56% in 2030 (J P Morgan, 13/5/2024).

Malaysia –Digital economy in Malayasia has seen tremendous growth with ICT adding a contribution of 22.6% in GDP as of 2021. AI adoption in Malaysia is still at its nascent stage. With more focus on AI on, 15-20% of the companies are expected to go towards AI usage. In Malaysia, employees have started incorporating generative AI tools to enhance their creative skills and give better outputs. ChatGPT is being used by employees across various sectors to write project reports and do planning of their works. Telecom companies in Malaysia are use AI tools for training of their employees and customer service teams (Marcus, Ng., Haridas, G. and Teoh, E.,2023).

Nigeria- The research work done on nigeran population to understand the impact of technology on AI enabled banking in terms of acceptance and usage among Nigerian population. As per findings technology usage has positive influence on service quality, customer satisfaction and consumer buying behaviour. Consumer buying behaviour was not influenced by service quality. Also, technology usage, consumer buying behaviour and customer satisfaction are moderately impacted by technology downtime in banking context (Omoge et al., 2022)

Issues in AI implementation

In emerging economies AI adoption and implementation is faced with lot of challenges which are enlisted below: -

- Installation of AI involved high cost. Once installed it must be updated and maintained on regular basis. This also involves maintenance cost.
- AI engages in analysis of large volumes of data. Any data which is not from reliable sources can hamper the functioning of AI programs. Hence, data quality is key to AI functioning.
- Data storage and security is also main threat to AI implementation as AI works on large data volumes for which proper security and storage is needed.
- In emerging economies like India, infrastructure is also key challenge.
- Better usage of AI is possible once people start having proper trust on AI. Trust plays a crucial role as this is also spread through word of mouth and social media. Any breach of trust may lead to discontinuation of AI usage in emerging economies (Vinoth and Chandran,2022)

Wang et al. (2021) in their study done of SMEs of Central China that even the SMEs there are eager to adopt AI but the face internal and external barriers in AI adoption. AI adoption faces various barriers in emerging economies. Top management and HR involvement is very important as they educate and train employees to adopt AI. Enterprise development needs are also important as factor will drive the organisation towards AI acceptance and adoption by firm. External factors such as Market pressure also create an impact as organisations adopt AI as their competitors are already using AI. So, to create competitive advantage they also look forward. Support policy is also very important as Government support can facilitate its adoption. Factor such as convenience in use of AI are also key as ease of use may lead to greater acceptability and adoption of AI among people. Govt support can also create trusts in the minds of people towards AI acceptability. As per study below are enlisted both the internal and external factors:

Figure 9. Barriers to Adoption of Artificial Intelligence

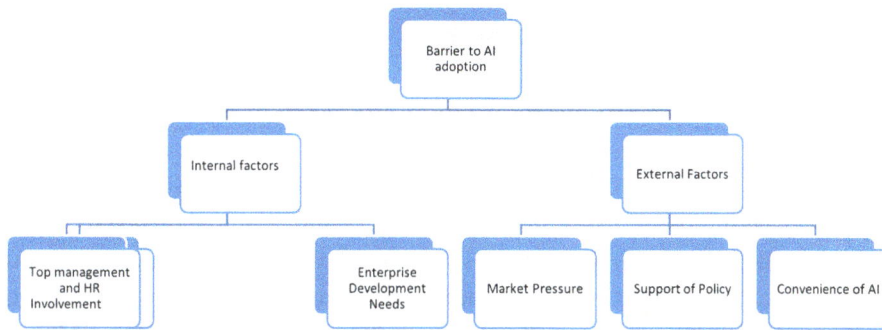

Source: Wang et al. 2021

Threats of Artificial Intelligence

AI even though being lifeline for economic growth had certain hazards which also have longlasting impact.

Various threat of AI are enlisted below:

- Job displacement
- Issue of security and privacy
- Malicious use
- Environmental effects

These hazards of AI can be reduced by proving proper skill development to population to get adapted to new work environment. In today's world we are facing issues of data theft by way of hacking. Strengthening of Cyber security can help in reducing this risk. Malicious use of AI in form of Cyber Threats can also be reduced with increase in cyber security (Rashid and Kausik, 2024).

CONCLUSION

In emerging economies of the world artificial intelligence is changing the scenario. With growth of artificial intelligence, its impact can be felt in various sectors from education, health care, banking to governance. To encourage economies to further imbibe this phenomenon, government of country play a very crucial role. Regulatory bodies like Reserve Bank of India need to develop framework for banks utilising AI for their day-to-day operations .Acceptance of Artificial intelligence among the masses is based on various factors such as trust and privacy and digital literacy. With more focus on developing trust, privacy and increasing digital literacy can enhance adoption of AI among masses. Nowadays Genz being tech savvy can also act as facilitators for AI implementation. The use of word of mouth and social media can bring about awareness about AI among rural and unbanked population.AI implementation can be successful only when there are proper infrastructure facilities . Uninterrupted internet access can enhance AI acceptance among masses. This will enable providing products and services at an affordable cost. Small and medium enterprises form backbone of any economy. Government and BFSI sector should encourage SME to move towards AI usage. With implementation of AI, SMEs can enhance their productivity, reduce operational cost, remove inefficiency. With better focus AI, country can boost economy by bringing all the sections of society under as bankable population. Emerging economies can take baby steps towards increasing GDP and boosting their economy by utilising AI to its fullest.

REFERENCE

Azzam, M. J., Alqudah, A. M. M., Aryan, L. A., & Abu Haija, A. A. (2024). In: Hannoon A. (eds). Empirical Analysis of the link between Financial Literacy and Personal Financial Decision of Genz. 34.In: Frontiers of Human Centricity in the Artificial Intelligence- Driven Society 5.0, *Studies in Systems, Decision and Control, Vol.226, Springer.* DOI: et al. (2021).DOI: 10.1007/978-3-031-73545-5-16.Chatterjee

Badghish, S., & Soomro, Y. A. (2024)... *Sustainability*, *16*(5), 1864. DOI: 10.3390/su16051864

Bonsay, J. O., Cruz, A. P., Firozi, H. C., & Camaro, P. J. C. (2021). Artificial Intelligence and Labour Productivity Paradox: Economic Impact of AI in China, India, Japan and Singapore, *Journal of Economics. Finance and Accounting Studies*, *3*(2), 120–139.

Bryant, J., Heitz, C., Sanghvi, S., & Wagle, D. (2020), How Artificial Intelligence Will Impact K-12 Teachers, Mc Kinsey. Https://Mc Kinsey.com/ Industries/ education/ oversights. Accessed online on 15/05/2025.

.Business Standard. (2025). RBI Bulletin: AI Revolutionize Indian Banking.

Chan, C. K. Y., & Lee, K. K. W. (2023). The AI Generation gap: Are Genz students more interested in adopting generative AI such as ChatGPT in teaching and learning than their GenX and millennial generation teachers? *Smart Learn Environ*, *10*(60). Advance online publication. DOI: 10.1186/s40561-023-00269-3

Community, N. A. S. S. C. O. M. Role of AI in SMES, Calsoftinc, 18June 2024. https://community.nasscom.in/communities/ai/role-ai-smes

Dampitaske, K., Kung, V. V., Jermsiltiparsert, K., Makassar, M., & Chienwattanasook, K. (2021)... *Journal of Management Information and Decision Sciences*, *24*(4), 1–14.

Dey, P.K., Chowdhury, S., & Abadie, A. VannYaroson, E. and Sarkar. S. (2023). Artificial Intelligence Driven Supply Chain Resilience in Vietnamese Manufacturing Small and Medium Sized Enterprises. *International Journal of Production Research*, *62*(15), 5417–5456. DOI: 10.1080/00207.543.2023.2179859

Digital India website (2025), https://digitalindia.gov.in. Accessed online on 10/5/2025.

Drydakis, N. (2022). Artificial Intelligence and Reduced SMEs Business Risks. A Dynamic Capabilities Analysis during the Covid19 pandemic. *Information Systems Frontiers, 24*(4), pp1223–pp1247. DOI: 10.1007/s10796-022-10249-9 PMID: 35261558

.Ganesh Kumar, KV (2021).Role of AI and Analytics in Banking, *Journal of Indian Institute of Banking and Finance,* Issue -Oct to Dec2021, pp 27-31.

.Gondauri, D., and Mikheil, B. (2023). The Impact of Artificial Intelligence on Gross Domestic Product, *International journal of Innovative Science and Technology, Vol 8(4).*

Haseeb, M., Sasmoko, Mihardjo L. WW. (2019). Economic Impact of Artificial Intelligence: New Look for the Macroeconomic Assessment in Asia Pacific Region. *International Journal of Computational Intelligence Systems, 12,* 1295–1310. DOI: 10.2991/ijcis.d.191025.001

Hasini, C. K. (2024). The Use of AI -driven Personalization for Enhancing the Customer Experience for Genz, *Open. Journal of Business and Management, 12*(6). Advance online publication. DOI: 10.4236/ojbm.2024.126225

Hwang, W. S., & Kim, H. S. (2022). Does the Adoption of Emerging Technologies Improve Technical Efficiency? Evidence from Korean Manufacturing SMEs. *Small Business Economics, 59,* 627–643. DOI: 10.1007/311187-021-00554-W PMID: 38624928

Iyer, A., & Umadevi, K. S. (2023). Role of AI and its Impact on Development of Cyber security applications. In: Sarveshwaran, V., Chen, J.I2, Pelusi, D. (eds) Artificial Intelligence and Cyber Security in Industry4.0, Advanced. Technologies and Societa Change. Springer pp 23-46DOI: 10.1007/978-981-99-2115-7-3

Jain, V. (2024). RBI's Big Announcement on Artificial Intelligence for Financial Sector, Outlook Money. https:/ outlookmoney.com/banking/rbi-big (accessed on 21052025).CFO. Economic times. Indiatimes.com/news/rbi-selects, dated 14/8/2023. Accessed online on 21/5/2025.

.Jimmy, F. (2021). Emerging threats: The latest cybersecurity risks and role of artificial intelligence in enhancing cybersecurity defences, *International Journal of Scientific Research and management, Vol 9(2),* pp 564-574. DOI: DOI: 10.18535/ ijsrm/V9i2.ec01

.Khan A. A., Laghari, A.A., Li, P. et al (2023). The Collaborative Role of Block-chain, Artificial Intelligence and Industrial Internet of Things in digitalisation of Small and Medium Size Enterprises, *Scientific Reports, Vol. 13,* 1656 article no. DOI: DOI: 10.1038/s41598-023-28707-9

. Khatun, F. and Nawrin, N. (2021). Impact of AI in Bangladesh's IT sector. The Financial Express. Accessed online on 1/5/2025.

Kumar, A., & Shah, J. (2025). AI meets Mahakhumbh: Demystifying Crowd Counting Process at Prayagraj, India Today.https://www.indiatoday.in/india/story/artifical-intelligence.Accessed online on 20/5/2025

Lu, X., Wijayaratna, K., Huang, Y., & Qiu, A. (2022). AI Enabled Opportunities and transformation challenges for SMEs in the post pandemic era: A review and Research Agenda. *Frontiers in Public Health*, *10*. Advance online publication. DOI: 10.3389/fpubb.2022.885067 PMID: 35570947

.Malai, A.B. and Gopalakrishnan, S. (2020). Application of Artificial Intelligence and its Powered technologies in the Indian banking and Financial Industry: An Overview. *IOSR Journal of Humanities and Social Science, Vol.25(4)*, series 6, pp 55-60. e -ISSN-2279-0837.

Marcus, Ng., Haridas, G., & Teoh, E. (2023). The Economic Impact of Generative AI: Future of Work in Malaysia, My digital https://ai.gov.my/media/thought-leadership/Reports-06-EN-Economic-Impact-of-Generative-AI-MY-1.pdf

Mhlanga, D. (2020). Industry 4.0 in Finance: The Impact of Artificial Intelligence on Digital Financial Inclusion. *International Journal of Financial Studies*, *8*(3), 45. DOI: 10.3390/ijfs8030045

Michael, O. (2025). *Maximising the Potentials of Small and Medium Scale Business Enterprises in Developing Nations thro the use of AI: AI adoption by SMEs in the Developing Nations, The Future of Small Business in Industry5.0.* DOI., DOI: 10.4018/979-8-3693-7362-0.ch009

Mishra, S. (2023). Exploring Impact of AI based cyber security financial sector Management. *The Sciences*, *13*(10), 5875. DOI: 10.3390/app13105875

Nasscom.in

Nurhadhinah, N. R., Masqirol, M., Fitriyani Latif, M. A. N., & Syafruddin, M. (2024). AI in the Financial Sector: The line Between Innovation, Regulation and Ethical Responsibility. *Information (Basel)*, *15*(8), 432. DOI: 10.3390/info.15080432

.Oberio, S. and Puranik, M. (2024). Digital Finance and Perspective of Genz Cohort: A review. *IPE Journal of Management, Vol.14(1)*, Jan-June2024. ISSN2249-9040, pp55-72.

Omoge, A. P., Gala, P., & Horky, A. (2022). Disruptive Technology and AI in the banking Industry of an Emerging Markets. *International Journal of Bank Marketing*, *40*(6), 1217–1247. DOI: 10.1108/ ijbm-09-2021-0403

.Press Information Bureau, Release id 2096212 date 25/1//2025.

Rafael, B. V., Belen, S. C., Lucia, V. R., & Jose, R. S. S. (2024). The Impact of Artificial Intelligence in the Financial Sector- Challenges and Opportunities. *International Journal of Business and Management Studies*, *5*(10), 33–42. DOI: 10.56734/ijbms.v.5n10a4

Rashid, A. B., & Kausik, A. A. K. (2024). AI Revolutionary Industries World Wide: A Comprehensive Overview of its Diverse Applications. *Hybrid Advance, Vol*, (7). Advance online publication. DOI: 10.1016/hvadv.2024.100277

Ridzuan, N. N., Masri, M., Anshari, M., Fitryani, N. L., & Syafrudin, M. (2024). AI in the financial sector the line between innovation, Regulation and Ethical Responsibility. *Information (Basel)*, *15*(8), 432. DOI: 10.3390/infor15080432

Rosenbarm, E. (2024), AI is Getting Very Popular Among students and Teachers Very Quickly, CNBC.com. https://cnbc.com/2024/06/11. Accessed online on 16/05/2025.

.Sawwalakhe, R., Arora, S. and Singh, T.P. (2023). Opportunities and Challenges for Artificial Intelligence and Machine Learning Applications in the Finance. *Source Title- Advance machine Learning Algorithms for Complex Financial Applications*, pp 1-17, DOI: .DOI: 10.4018/ 978-1-6684-4483-3-ch001

Schwarke, J., Peters, A., Kanbach, D. K., Kraus, S., & Jones, P. (2025). The New Normal: The Status Quo of AI Adoption in SMEs. *Journal of Small Business Management*, *63*, 1297–1331.

Shafik, W. (2025). Emerging Technologies for Small and Medium Enterprise Growth: ChatGPT, Blockchain, Robotics and Artificial Intelligence. *Source Title: Fostering Economic Diversification and Sustainable Business through Digital Intelligence,* pages 24. DOI: DOI: 10.4018/979-8-3693-8492-3-ch009

Sindhu, J., & Renee, N. (2019). Impact of Artificial Intelligence in Chosen Indian Commercial Bank- A Cost Benefit Analysis. *Asian Journal of Management*, *10*(4), 377–384. DOI: 10.5958/2321-57-63.2019.00057

.Sindhu,S. and Renee, N. (2019). Impact of Artificial intelligence in Chosen India Commercial banks: A cost benefit analysis. Sindhu j, Reneee, N. *Asian Journal of Management, Vol. 10(4),* pp 377-384. DOI:. *00057.X*DOI: 10.5958/2321-5763.2019

Strusani, D., & Houngbonon, G. V. (2019). The Role of Artificial Intelligence in Supporting Developments in Emerging Markets, Note69, www.ifc.org

Stryker, C., & Kavlakoglu, E. (2025). What is Artificial Intelligence (AI)? https://ibm.com/think/topics/ artificial- intelligence.

Tahereh, S. and Sidaoui. (2024). Convergence of AI with social media: A Bibliometric and qualitative Analysis. *Telematics and Informatics Reports*, *14*. Advance online publication. DOI: 10.1016/jteler.2024.100146

. Triwahyono, B., Rahayu, T. and Kraugusteeliana, K. (2023). Analysing the Role of Technological Innovation in Improving the Operational Efficiency on MSMEs. *Jurnal Minfo Polgan, Vol. 12(1),* pp.1417-1426. DOI: . v12i1.12791DOI: 10.33395/jmp

Vinoth, S., & Chandran, P. (2022). Artificial Intelligence and Transformation to the Digital Age in Indian Banking Industry- A Case Study. *Turkish Online Journal of Qualitative Inquiry*, *13*(1), 689–695.

Visuthiphol, S., & Pankham, S. (2025). Artificial Intelligence- Decision Making in Social Media Adoption for Sustainable Digital Business in Thai SMEs. *Decision Making: Applications in Management and Engineering*, *8*(1). Advance online publication. 0009-0006-1431-4643

world bank. (2024). Global trends in AI governance.

Yoganandham, G. (2025). Trends, challenges and opportunities in India's financial sector: Policy shifts, AI Integrational Financial Stability- AN Empirical Assessment. *GIS Science Journal*, *12*(2), 360–376.

Yusuf, S.O., Durodula, R.L.Orcan, G.Abubakar, J.E., Echere, A.Z. and Paul, A.H. (2024) . Challenges and Opportunities in AI and Digital Transformation for SMEs-A cross-continental Perspective, *World journal of Advanced Research and Review, Vol 23(05)*, pp668-678. DOI: .DOI: 10.20574/wjarr.2024.23.3.2511

Chapter 10
Holistic Study of the Role of AI in Sustainable Development:
Study of the Jurisdictions of the United States of America, the European Union, and India

Akansha Yadav
https://orcid.org/0009-0003-1963-8813
O.P. Jindal Global University, India

Satish Kumar
https://orcid.org/0000-0003-4328-6515
O.P. Jindal Global University, India

ABSTRACT

This chapter explores the evolving role of Artificial Intelligence (AI) in driving sustainable development. It begins by defining AI as per the 2024 EU AI Act and assessing current global advancements. The discussion focuses on AI's contributions to the Sustainable Development Goals (SDGs), with examples in healthcare, education, climate action, and urban planning. It also raises critical concerns, including algorithmic bias, privacy risks, environmental impact, and exclusion of marginalized communities. Key regulatory frameworks from the EU, USA, China, and India are examined to highlight governance gaps and opportunities. The chapter asks whether AI can be a reliable force for equity and sustainability and proposes solutions like

DOI: 10.4018/979-8-3373-2372-5.ch010

ethical-by-design systems, global cooperation, and participatory policymaking. It concludes that AI, if responsibly governed, can significantly accelerate sustainable outcomes while upholding human dignity and environmental balance.

INTRODUCTION

Artificial Intelligence (AI) is increasingly recognized as a transformative general-purpose technology reshaping economies, societies, and the environment (Vinuesa et al., 2020). Its applications range from automating industrial processes to augmenting human decision-making in complex tasks, with significant implications for sustainable development. Sustainable development, as encapsulated by the United Nations' 2030 Agenda, comprises 17 Sustainable Development Goals (SDGs) aimed at balancing economic prosperity, social inclusion, and environmental stewardship (Kirikkaleli et al., 2025). Harnessing AI for these goals presents a promising pathway to "turbocharge" progress on global challenges like poverty, health, and climate change (OHCHR, 2024). Indeed, senior UN officials have noted that AI "can accelerate progress towards the SDGs" and even *"enhance decision-making and drive innovation"* if applied safely (Alexandra Bustos, 2024).

At the same time, the rapid proliferation of AI technologies has raised concerns about ethical, social, and environmental risks. AI's potential cuts both ways: it offers unprecedented capabilities to analyze data and optimize systems for sustainability, yet it can also entrench biases or create new inequalities if poorly governed (Vinuesa et al., 2020). For instance, advanced machine learning models can help predict and manage resource use, but their opaque decision processes and massive data requirements may undermine transparency, privacy, and energy efficiency. As a result, the role of AI in sustainable development has become a focal point for policymakers, researchers, and practitioners striving to maximize AI's benefits while mitigating its harms (Wang et al., 2024). This chapter provides a comprehensive examination of that role, beginning with definitions and the current state of AI, then exploring how AI intersects with sustainable development imperatives. We will highlight AI's contributions to various SDGs (with real-world case studies), consider the opportunities it offers, discuss key challenges and risks, survey policy and regulatory responses in different regions, and outline approaches to ensure the ethical and responsible development of AI (Kirikkaleli et al., 2015). Throughout, we have grounded the discussion in scholarly and institutional analyses to maintain a rigorous, evidence-based perspective.

AI'S POTENTIAL TO ADDRESS THE SUSTAINABLE DEVELOPMENT GOALS (SDGS)

AI is often hailed as a tool that can "turbocharge sustainable development" (OHCHR, 2024) by offering innovative ways to tackle age-old problems. Its potential spans all three pillars of sustainability, such as economic, social, and environmental, mirroring the breadth of the SDGs (Azizpour et al., 2020). We outline several key areas where AI is making or could make significant contributions:

Hunger, Agriculture and Food Security (SDG 2): AI-driven tools are boosting agricultural productivity and climate resilience is crucial for feeding a growing global population. Precision agriculture systems use AI to analyze data from sensors, drones, and weather forecasts, guiding farmers on when to plant, irrigate, or harvest for optimal yield. For instance, the DiCRA platform (*Data in Climate Resilient Agriculture*), a digital public good launched in India, harnesses remote sensing and AI pattern recognition to advise farmers and policymakers on climate-smart agriculture (Vacarelu, 2024). DiCRA collates geospatial data and employs AI to detect trends in crop health and soil conditions, helping stakeholders implement adaptive strategies for droughts or floods (Vacarelu, 2024). Similarly, AI models can diagnose crop diseases from smartphone images, enabling early intervention. The World Economic Forum reports that smallholder farmers in India have doubled incomes by using AI chatbots for advice on farming practices and market prices (Jurgens & Kaushik, 2024). Overall, AI contributes to food security by reducing waste, optimizing supply chains, and improving agricultural knowledge dissemination.

Health and Well-being (SDG 3): AI is revolutionizing healthcare delivery and medical research, offering the potential for healthier lives worldwide. In medical diagnostics, AI algorithms excel at pattern recognition, for example, analyzing radiology images or pathology slides faster than human doctors in some cases. AI-based diagnostic tools can detect diseases like cancer or tuberculosis with high accuracy, even in low-resource settings (Jasper, 2024). A striking case is the use of AI-enhanced portable X-ray machines to screen for tuberculosis in remote areas: in 2022, UNDP assisted projects that used AI software to instantly read chest X-rays for TB lesions, significantly speeding up detection of new cases amid a resurgence of the disease (Vacarelu, 2024). In pandemic response, AI models have been used to predict outbreaks and assist in drug discovery. Beyond diagnostics, AI-powered wearables and health apps enable personalized medicine and telehealth by monitoring patients' vital signs in real time and flagging anomalies for early intervention (Kermani et al., 2024).

Clean Water and Sanitation (SDG 6): AI contributes to water sustainability through improved monitoring and management. AI models can optimize water treatment processes, predict equipment failures in water infrastructure, and reduce losses. For example, utilities use AI to detect leaks in pipelines by analyzing pressure sensor data, saving precious water in drought-prone regions (Haar and Lynch, 2024). Machine learning is also applied to predict water demand and improve allocation among agricultural, industrial, and household uses. In rural development, AI-powered analysis of satellite images can locate new water sources or monitor the health of watersheds. These applications support SDG 6 by improving efficiency and ensuring safe, reliable water supply even as climate change stresses freshwater resources (Fritsch, 2025).

Affordable and Clean Energy (SDG 7) & Climate Action (SDG 13): One of AI's most active frontiers is in supporting the transition to low-carbon energy and climate resilience. AI algorithms enable smart grids that balance electricity demand and supply in real time, integrating higher shares of renewable energy. For instance, AI can partially match electricity demand to times when the sun is shining or wind is blowing, making solar and wind power more reliable (Azizpour et al., 2020). By forecasting energy production and consumption patterns, AI helps grid operators reduce waste and prevent blackouts. In industry and buildings, AI-driven control systems cut energy use by dynamically adjusting heating, cooling, and lighting Google famously used DeepMind's AI to reduce its data centre energy consumption by ~40% (Cho, 2023). On the climate front, climate modeling has leaped forward thanks to AI's ability to handle complex, high-volume data. The European Space Agency's Destination Earth (DestinE) project uses AI to build high-resolution digital twins of the planet's climate system, enabling better predictions of extreme weather and long-term climate shifts (Jasper, 2024). Likewise, AI is instrumental in climate *mitigation*: designing more efficient materials and batteries (Sohns et al., 2023), optimizing routes for transportation to cut fuel use, and even directly managing carbon capture systems. In adaptation, AI helps communities prepare for climate impacts by predicting disasters. For example, the FireAId tool developed with the World Economic Forum uses AI to predict wildfire outbreaks and assist in early response, protecting lives and ecosystems (Jasper, 2024). From monitoring deforestation via satellite imagery to detecting methane leaks with sensors, AI extends human ability to safeguard the environment (Cho, 2023). As the UN Environment Programme notes, AI can monitor environmental changes in *"near real time"* and inform more effective climate action strategies. These capabilities illustrate AI's strong alignment with SDG 13 (climate action) and SDG 7 (clean energy), by enabling both incremental efficiencies and transformative solutions for decarbonization.

Industry, Infrastructure and Innovation (SDG 9) & Sustainable Cities (SDG 11): AI accelerates innovation in infrastructure and urban management. In transportation, AI improves traffic flow through intelligent signal systems and enables autonomous vehicles that could eventually reduce accidents and emissions. Many cities now employ AI-based traffic optimization, resulting in shorter commutes and less fuel burned contributing to SDG 11's target on sustainable urban transport. AI also enhances infrastructure maintenance by helping in predictive maintenance algorithms identify when bridges, roads, or electric grids need repair before catastrophic failures, saving money and lives. Smart city initiatives use AI to optimize everything from energy use in buildings to waste collection routes, creating cities that are more livable and resource-efficient (Vinuesa et al., 2020). For example, AI can support *"circular economy"* efforts by improving waste sorting and recycling processes (as seen in the Open Waste AI project in Montreal, which uses AI and IoT to track community-level waste and boost recycling (Rajaonson & Schmitt, 2024). These advancements align with SDG 9 (industry, innovation and infrastructure) by fostering resilient infrastructure and inclusive industrialization, and with SDG 11 by making cities smarter and more sustainable.

Ecosystem and Biodiversity Protection (SDGs 14 & 15): AI is a new ally in conserving life on land and below water. For marine ecosystems, AI helps analyze data from drones and acoustic sensors to track illegal fishing or monitor coral reef health. On land, wildlife conservationists use AI-driven image recognition on camera trap photos or drone footage to automatically count endangered animals and detect poachers, enabling quicker anti-poaching responses (Ettinger, 2025). AI can also predict deforestation by identifying patterns of forest loss in satellite images, helping authorities intervene earlier (Jasper, 2024). In agriculture and land use, AI tools allow more precise use of inputs (water, fertilizer), reducing runoff that harms rivers and reefs. Collectively, these applications support SDG 14 (life below water) and SDG 15 (life on land) by enhancing our ability to manage and protect natural ecosystems with limited human resources.

LIMITATIONS OF AI APPLICATION TO ACHIEVE SUSTAINABLE DEVELOPMENT GOALS

Despite its promise, AI is no silver bullet the paper and broader research identify several limitations that constrain AI-driven progress on the SDGs:

Technical Limitations: AI systems often require vast, high-quality data and computing resources, which may be lacking or unevenly distributed. Many models operate as "black boxes," so their opaque decision-making undermines transparency and trust. In critical domains (e.g. healthcare diagnoses or climate predictions), a lack of explainability and reliability can impede adoption. Furthermore, current AI tools may not generalize well across diverse environments; for example, an algorithm trained in one region might falter in another due to different data patterns.

Ethical and Bias Challenges: AI can inadvertently perpetuate or worsen biases present in training data. The paper notes concerns that AI could entrench inequalities if poorly governed. Indeed, studies have found algorithmic bias in commercial systems (e.g. lower accuracy for women or darker skin tones in face recognition), raising fairness issues relevant to SDG 5 and SDG 10. Ensuring AI fairness requires rigorous audits and bias mitigation, which are not always standard practice. Privacy is another ethical concern – AI solutions often rely on personal data, risking misuse or surveillance if safeguards (like consent and data protection laws) are weak.

Social and Inclusivity Constraints: There is a risk that AI benefits unequally. Populations with limited internet, literacy, or technical skills might be left behind (widening the digital divide). The paper highlights that in places like rural India, insufficient digital infrastructure and a shortage of AI-skilled professionals hinder implementation. Without deliberate inclusion, AI could amplify global disparities (counter to SDG 10). Moreover, fear of job displacement by automation (linked to SDG 8 on decent work) can create public resistance to AI initiatives. Social acceptance and human capacity-building are thus critical but often overlooked components.

Practical Implementation Issues: Even proven AI solutions face challenges in real-world deployment. High development costs, need for robust infrastructure (electricity, connectivity), and maintenance requirements can limit scalability in low-resource settings. Operationally, AI must be integrated with existing systems and institutions. The paper gives an example: an AI model might accurately predict a cyclone's impact zone, but it won't save lives without effective evacuation plans and communication networks. This underscores that AI is only part of the solution – successful outcomes depend on human coordination, strong institutions, and supportive policies. Additionally, regulatory frameworks for AI remain nascent in many countries; unclear guidelines can slow adoption or lead to misuse. In sum, technical efficacy alone is not enough – governance, infrastructure, and social readiness are equally important and often limiting factors for AI's impact on sustainable development.

SUCCESSFUL DEPLOYMENT OF AI TO MEET SUSTAINABLE DEVELOPMENT GOALS

Translating potential into practice, growing number of case studies showcase successful deployment of AI for sustainable development outcomes. We highlight a few illustrative examples across different sectors and regions:

Predictive Agriculture in India (Climate Resilience): The *Data in Climate Resilient Agriculture (DiCRA)* initiative in Telangana, India, is a noteworthy example of AI aiding farmers on the frontlines of climate change. Launched as a collaboration between the state government and UNDP, DiCRA is an AI-powered platform providing open access to geospatial climate data and analytics (Vacarelu, 2024). By using machine learning to detect patterns in historical climate, soil, and crop data, the platform identifies climate-vulnerable farmlands and optimal crop strategies. Early results have enabled evidence-based decisions, such as shifting sowing dates and crop varieties in anticipation of changing monsoon patterns, thereby improving yields and farmers' incomes. This case demonstrates how AI can help communities adapt agriculture to a warming climate, addressing SDG 2 (zero hunger) and SDG 13 (climate action) together (Babar and Akan, 2024).

AI for Healthcare Access (Tuberculosis Screening): In Bangladesh and Zimbabwe, health providers have piloted AI-driven portable X-ray clinics to combat tuberculosis (TB), which remains a top infectious killer (SDG target 3.3). These solar-powered clinics use AI software to instantly interpret chest X-rays for signs of TB, even in remote villages (Babar and Akan, 2024). In a 2022 program supported by UNDP and partners, the AI screening tool helped identify thousands of TB cases that would likely have been missed due to a shortage of radiologists (Iliescu, 2024). The AI model was trained on a large dataset of X-ray images to recognize the distinctive lung patterns of TB. Health workers can thus bring diagnostic services to high-risk communities and refer positive cases for treatment faster. This case shows AI's power in bridging healthcare gaps and has informed similar deployments for pneumonia and COVID-19 detection (Ettinger, 2025).

Wildlife Protection (SMART Conservation AI): In East Africa, conservationists have integrated AI into the SMART surveillance system to protect endangered elephants and rhinos (SDG 15). Camera traps and acoustic sensors in wildlife reserves generate a deluge of data; AI image and sound recognition algorithms sift through these to detect poaching threats (e.g., recognizing human shapes or gunshot sounds) (Ettinger, 2025). In one reserve, the system alerted rangers to intruders in real-time, leading to arrests of poachers before animals were harmed. Over a year, AI-assisted monitoring reduced elephant poaching incidents by over 50%. This case illustrates how AI extends the reach of conservation personnel, enabling proactive interventions to preserve biodiversity (Wang and Li, 2024).

Smart Cities (Reducing Traffic Emissions): Surabaya, Indonesia, provides a case of an urban authority using AI for environmental and social benefit (SDG 11 and 13). The city implemented an AI-driven traffic control system that analyzes live traffic camera feeds to optimize signal timings. Within months, average travel times fell, and vehicle idle time at intersections dropped significantly, cutting fuel wastage (Bolón-Canedo et al., 2024). An estimate suggested the system reduced carbon emissions by thousands of tons annually while also improving air quality (SDG 3.9 on health). Importantly, the city complemented the technology with policies for public transport and pedestrianization, showing that AI works best as part of a holistic strategy. Surabaya's experience has informed other Asian cities exploring

AI for smart mobility to address congestion and pollution in rapidly urbanizing environments (Gosselink et al., 2024).

These case studies highlight success factors for AI in sustainable development: multi-stakeholder collaboration (e.g. UNDP and governments co-designing solutions), contextual adaptation of AI to local needs, and combining AI with human expertise and domain knowledge. They also exemplify tangible benefits: more efficient public services, lives saved through early diagnoses, protection of vulnerable groups, and better environmental management. While small in scale relative to global challenges, these projects demonstrate *"AI for Good"* in action (Iliescu, 2024), building an evidence base that can be expanded and replicated.

BENEFITS AND OPPORTUNITIES OF AI DEPLOYMENT FOR SUSTAINABLE DEVELOPMENT

Building on the above, we can synthesize the benefits and opportunities that responsible AI deployment offers for sustainable development:

Improved Efficiency and Resource Allocation: AI excels at analyzing complex systems and identifying inefficiencies. This can lead to significant resource savings energy, water, raw materials contributing to both economic and environmental targets. For instance, AI-optimized supply chains can minimize fuel use and reduce costs (advancing SDG 12 on responsible consumption and production). Precision farming guided by AI ensures fertilizers and water are applied only where needed, boosting yields while conserving inputs (Rajaonson & Schmitt, 2024). Such efficiency gains mean that societies can do more with less, decoupling development from resource depletion. In governance, AI systems (like AIDA – *Artificial Intelligence for Development Analytics*) are helping sift through thousands of pages of reports and data to point policymakers to what works and what doesn't (Vacarelu, 2024). This data-driven decision-making leads to smarter allocation of public funds and interventions exactly where they have the most impact (Năstasă et al., 2024).

Acceleration of Innovation and Scientific Discovery: AI offers a powerful tool for scientific research across disciplines, speeding up discovery of solutions for sustainable development. In medicine, AI is helping discover new drug candidates and personalized therapies at a pace and scale previously impossible. In materials science, AI-driven simulations rapidly test new compounds for cleaner energy or biodegradable plastics (Cho, 2023). The ability of AI to detect patterns in enormous datasets can generate fresh insights into problems like climate change (e.g., identifying previously unknown climate system interactions) (Xu et al., 2023). Furthermore, AI can unlock the value of "big data" from satellites, genomics, or economic records, allowing scientists and analysts to address questions that were intractable with manual methods (Rajaonson & Schmitt, 2024). As the global development community increasingly shares open data, AI provides the means to extract knowledge and drive evidence-based innovation in service of the SDGs

Reaching the Unreached (Inclusion and Equity): One of the most profound opportunities of AI is to extend services to marginalized and underserved populations. Properly applied, AI can lower the cost and logistical barriers of delivering education, healthcare, and finance to remote or poor communities. For example, AI-powered educational content can be broadcast via simple mobile phones, bringing quality lessons to villages lacking schools. Micro-finance institutions are using AI credit scoring to extend loans to people with no formal banking history, thus promoting financial inclusion (Arun et al., 2024). AI-driven translation and voice recognition tools can bridge language gaps, empowering non-literate or non-English-speaking users to access information and services (supporting SDG 4.5 on eliminating disparities in education). The inclusive growth principle is at the heart of international AI guidelines, the OECD AI Principles state that AI should *"benefit people and the planet by driving inclusive growth, sustainable development and well-being."* (OECD, 2019). When AI projects are designed with local context in mind (as with UNDP's focus on "inclusive AI ecosystems" (UNDP, 2022), they can actively reduce digital divides rather than widen them. In sum, AI offers tools to democratize knowledge and essential services, creating opportunities for communities historically left behind (Gandhi et al., 2025).

Enhanced Capacity for Monitoring and Accountability: Achieving the SDGs requires tracking progress and holding stakeholders accountable. AI greatly enhances monitoring capabilities by processing real-time data from sensors, satellites, and social media. This enables near-instant detection of issues from deforestation and pollution spikes to disease outbreaks or humanitarian crises (Jasper, 2024). For instance, AI vision algorithms scanning Earth observation images can provide objective, high-frequency measures of forest cover or glacier melt, informing global climate accords. Similarly, governments are experimenting with AI to monitor school attendance or infrastructure projects, identifying corruption or bottlenecks. By shining a light on ground realities, AI can empower civil society and regulators to ensure that development commitments translate into action (Gandhi et al., 2025).

New Economic Opportunities and Efficiency Gains: Embracing AI in sustainable development can spur economic growth and job creation in new sectors. Developing and deploying AI solutions locally builds human capital and creates skilled jobs (data scientists, AI engineers, etc.), which supports SDG 8 (decent work and economic growth) (Willard et al., 2023). Countries that invest in AI for sustainable industries may become exporters of those solutions, for example, Kenya has nurtured startups providing AI-driven solar energy management systems across Africa (Sumihiro, 2025). At the micro level, giving small businesses AI tools (like chatbots or market analytics) can enhance their productivity and competitiveness, contributing to inclusive economic development. Globally, a PwC analysis estimated that AI could add trillions to the world economy by 2030 while helping to reduce greenhouse gas emissions through efficiency (Xu et al., 2023). Moreover, AI can help optimize *human*resource use: automating drudgery allows workers to focus on higher-value, creative tasks, potentially improving job satisfaction and innovation (provided re-skilling opportunities are offered). The key is ensuring that the gains from AI are equitably distributed and that workers are supported through the transition themes we explore in ethical considerations (Sumihiro, 2025).

In summary, AI offers powerful tools to accelerate sustainable development, with demonstrated benefits in efficiency, innovation, inclusion, monitoring, and economic dynamism. As noted by the UN Human Rights Council, *"AI is changing our world and can turbocharge sustainable development"* when harnessed correctly (OHCHR, 2024). However, reaping these opportunities is contingent upon addressing the challenges and risks posed by AI. As the next section will detail, issues such as bias, privacy, safety, and the digital divide, if unaddressed, could undermine the very development gains we seek from AI (Rajaonson & Schmitt, 2024). Thus, unlocking AI's full potential for sustainable development requires a conscientious approach to its governance and deployment, balancing optimism with vigilance (Fritsch, 2025).

KEY CHALLENGES AND RISKS POSED BY AI DEPLOYMENT TOWARD SUSTAINABLE DEVELOPMENT

While AI holds great promise, its deployment is fraught with challenges and risks that can impede sustainable development or even exacerbate existing problems. These risks are multifaceted in terms of being ethical, social, technical, and environmental. In this section, we examine the major concerns: (a) ethical issues and bias in AI systems; (b) data privacy and security dilemmas; and (c) technological limitations and reliability issues. Addressing these challenges is critical to ensure AI contributes positively to sustainable development rather than creating new inequalities or harms.

ETHICAL CONSIDERATIONS AND INHERENT BIAS IN AI TECHNOLOGY

Ethical considerations are paramount because AI systems, if not carefully designed, can unintentionally embed and amplify human biases or make unfair decisions. This is particularly dangerous in sensitive areas related to sustainable development, such as allocating social services, hiring for economic inclusion, or policing, where biased AI could deepen social inequities (contravening SDG 10 on reducing inequalities) (Fritsch, 2025).

A well-documented issue is algorithmic bias. AI models learn from historical data, and if those data reflect societal biases or skewed demographics, the AI may reproduce or even worsen the bias. For example, facial recognition AI has been found to have significantly higher error rates for women and people with darker skin, because the training datasets were not diverse enough (Hardesty, 2024). The seminal *Gender Shades* study by Buolamwini and Gebru revealed that commercial facial analysis systems misclassified darker-skinned females up to 34% of the time, while error rates for lighter-skinned males were under 1% (Fritsch, 2025). Such disparities raise serious equity concerns: deploying biased facial recognition in law enforcement or access control could wrongfully target minority groups, violating rights and eroding trust (Hardesty, 2024). Similarly, AI used in lending or hiring may inadvertently favor dominant groups if the training data reflect past discrimination (e.g., fewer loans to women leading the AI to consider gender as a negative factor). These biases directly conflict with sustainable development aims for gender equality (SDG 5) and reduced inequalities (SDG 10). They also undermine the legitimacy of AI solutions in the eyes of the public (Weinzierl et al., 2024).

Ethical concerns extend beyond bias to issues of transparency, accountability, and human agency. Many AI algorithms, especially complex deep learning models, are "black boxes" that do not provide explanations for their decisions (Weinzierl et al., 2024). This opacity is problematic when AI is used in public policy or any high-stakes domain as it can be really hard to contest or appeal an automated decision if neither users nor regulators understand how it was made. A lack of transparency can mask not only biases but also outright errors. For instance, an AI system might erroneously flag an area as high-crime due to data quirks, leading to over-policing there, but without transparency, the community would struggle to challenge this false designation (Sohns et al., 2023). Ensuring explainability and the right to information about AI decisions is increasingly viewed as part of ethical AI (and is enshrined in principles like the U.S. AI Bill of Rights calling for notice and explanation (AI Bill of Rights, 2022).

DATA PRIVACY AND SECURITY CONCERNS

AI's hunger for data drives many of its achievements, but it also raises serious privacy and security concerns. To function effectively, AI systems often require large datasets, some containing personal or sensitive information (e.g., health records for a medical AI, or location data for a traffic AI). This creates tension with individuals' right to privacy and control over their personal data, a human right recognized as fundamental in many jurisdictions and key to sustaining public trust in technology (Haar and Lynch, 2024).

A core concern is that without proper safeguards, AI development can lead to misuse or leakage of personal data, undermining privacy. For example, training an AI health diagnostic on patient scans might inadvertently expose identity-linked medical information if data are not anonymized (Kermani et al., 2024). Large language models have been shown to sometimes regurgitate pieces of their training data, which could include personal emails or private documents if such data were scraped from the internet. Additionally, deploying AI in public services (like facial recognition for security or predictive policing) can entail mass surveillance, where individuals' movements or behaviors are tracked without their consent (Nugraha, 2024). The 2018 Cambridge Analytica scandal, where personal data from millions of Facebook profiles were harvested to train algorithms targeting political ads, is a cautionary tale of AI-related data misuse (Sohns et al., 2023). It highlighted how *"the absence of adequate regulation can lead to the exploitation of personal data for unethical purposes"* (Nugraha, 2024). Such incidents erode citizens' trust and can even threaten democratic processes.

From a governance perspective, legal and regulatory frameworks for data protection are crucial to address these concerns (Sumihiro, 2025). Many countries are updating or enacting data protection laws (in line with Europe's GDPR) to give citizens rights over their data and obligations to data holders. As of 2024, numerous developing nations such as Indonesia, Brazil, and South Africa have introduced personal data protection laws modeled on international best practices (Nugraha, 2024). These laws typically require consent for data collection, limited use tied to explicit purposes, and rights like access and deletion for individuals (Haar and Lynch, 2024). For AI, this means developers and deployers must integrate privacy by design while collecting minimal data, anonymizing or pseudonymizing it, and allowing opting out where possible. The U.S. Blueprint for an AI Bill of Rights underscores data privacy as a core principle, urging that people *"should be able to opt out from automated systems in favor of a human alternative, wherever appropriate"* and that their data use should respect their consent decisions (AI Bill of Rights, 2022).

Another aspect is bias in data access, many developing countries lack large, high-quality datasets, which can limit AI development or force them to use foreign datasets that might not reflect local realities (leading to biases). This *"data divide"* is a subtle risk: countries or communities that cannot leverage data will fall behind in AI benefits, exacerbating inequality between global North and South (Nugraha, 2024). It's a sustainability issue in its own right. Initiatives like open data hubs, capacity building for data governance, and international data-sharing frameworks under ethical guidelines are attempts to address this gap (UNDP, 2022).

TECHNOLOGICAL LIMITATIONS AND RELIABILITY

Despite its impressive capabilities, AI technology itself has limitations and reliability issues that pose risks for sustainable development applications. AI systems are not infallible; they can make mistakes, sometimes serious ones, or fail to generalize to new conditions. Understanding these limitations is key to deploying AI prudently and avoiding overreliance that could lead to systemic failures or setbacks (Weinzierl et a., 2024).

One fundamental challenge is that many AI models, especially those based on machine learning, are only as good as the data they have seen. They tend to inherit data limitations: if data are outdated or not representative, predictions can go awry (Sumihiro, 2025). For example, an AI model trained on weather patterns from the past may struggle to predict future climate anomalies in an era of climate change, potentially giving false confidence in certain agriculture decisions (impacting SDG 2). Similarly, an AI for disease diagnosis trained mostly on data from European hospitals might perform poorly in an African rural context due to different patient demographics and disease variants. This issue of transferability means AI models often need careful re-validation and tuning when moved to new environments (Haar and Lynch, 2024).

Transparency and interpretability relate here too: a system that can explain its reasoning is easier to debug and trust. Many current AI tools lack interpretability, which hampers diagnosing errors. There are also practical limitations like computational requirements and energy consumption of AI, which impact sustainable development plans. Some advanced AI systems demand heavy computational infrastructure and reliable power resources scarce in many developing regions (Sumihiro, 2025). Deploying a sophisticated AI in an off-grid rural area might be impossible or require unsustainable expense. This ties into inequality: if only wealthier contexts can afford state-of-the-art AI, poorer communities risk being left behind technologically (a scenario contrary to SDG 9's goal of inclusive innovation) (Willard et al., 2023). Moreover, as noted earlier, large AI models can be energy-intensive to train and run; one projection warns that ICT and AI-related electricity use could jump from ~1% of global electricity today to as high as 20% by 2030 without efficiency improvements (Vinuesa, 2020). This raises reliability issues in an environmental sense as AI operations could strain energy grids or conflict with climate goals if unchecked.

Finally, an often understated risk is over-reliance and misapplication of AI and the temptation to see AI as a *"silver bullet"* and neglect non-technical solutions. Sustainable development challenges are complex and often require improvements in governance, capacity, and social structures (Haar and Lynch, 2024). AI is a tool, not a panacea; if development programs rely solely on AI and ignore building human capacity or fixing structural issues, they may fail once the tech faces a scenario it can't handle. For example, an AI can help identify which students are falling behind (education analytics), but without trained teachers or tutors to act on that info, the situation won't improve. In disaster response, AI may predict a cyclone's impact zones, but effective evacuation still depends on communication networks and public cooperation (Mahadew, 2024). Over-reliance on AI without these complementary elements can even be risky if the AI fails, human responders might have lost practice or situational awareness, leading to a worse outcome than if AI hadn't been used at all (Gandhi et al., 2025).

POLICY AND REGULATORY FRAMEWORKS TO ADVANCE THE INTEGRATION OF AI FOR SUSTAINABLE DEVELOPMENT GOALS

Recent years have seen notable AI progress toward Sustainable Development Goals (SDGs) across the United States, Europe, and India. In the United States, federal initiatives emphasize "trustworthy AI" innovation in health, climate, and education. The 2023 U.S. Executive Order on AI called for equitable use of AI in areas like healthcare and climate resilience (Yang & Li, 2025). Government R&D programs are funding AI for climate modeling and disaster response (advancing SDG 13 on climate action and SDG 11 on resilient cities) via agencies like NSF and DARPA. Investments also target workforce development (e.g. AI education and retraining, aligning with SDG 4 and SDG 8) (Vinuesa, 2020). In the European Union, alongside pioneering regulations such as the EU *AI Act* expected 2024–2025, there is substantial support for AI applications in sustainable development. The EU commits ~€1 billion per year under programs like Horizon Europe to AI solutions spanning agriculture, healthcare, transport and more. Such efforts are coupled with Europe's green agenda: studies project AI could help cut 5–10% of global greenhouse gas emissions by 2030 (about equal to the EU's annual emissions), aiding SDG 13 (Sumihiro, 2025).

Given AI's far-reaching impacts and the aforementioned risks, governments and international bodies are actively developing policy and regulatory frameworks to govern AI. Effective governance is particularly important to align AI deployment with sustainable development goals, ensuring that AI's benefits can be realized while minimizing harms (Gandhi et al., 2025). This section surveys how key jurisdictions, such as the United States, European Union, and India are approaching AI regulation and policy, including any specific considerations for sustainable development. We will see that each has taken distinct approaches reflecting their political systems and priorities, ranging from comprehensive risk-based regulations to ethical guidelines and innovation strategies (Arun et al., 2024). We also touch on global initiatives and cooperation efforts where relevant. Understanding these frameworks is crucial because they set the "rules of the road" for AI's development and use, influencing how AI will contribute to sustainable development in each context (Yang & Li, 2025).

UNITED STATES OF AMERICA

The United States, home to many of the leading AI companies and research labs, has thus far adopted a relatively decentralized and principles-based approach to AI governance, rather than a single comprehensive law. There is currently no federal statute exclusively regulating AI. Instead, the U.S. has issued high-level guidance and frameworks and is leveraging existing laws (such as anti-discrimination, consumer protection, and privacy laws) to oversee AI on a sectoral basis (Yang & Li, 2025).

A marquee initiative is the Blueprint for an AI Bill of Rights, released by the White House Office of Science and Technology Policy in October 2022. This non-binding blueprint lays out five key principles for the design and use of automated systems: (1) Safe and effective systems; (2) Protection against algorithmic discrimination; (3) Data privacy; (4) Notice and explanation; and (5) Human alternatives or fallback options (AI Bill of Rights, 2022). In essence, it calls for AI that is *"aligned with democratic values"*, does not harm or unfairly discriminate, respects privacy by default, is transparent about when and how it's used, and always allows people to opt out to a human decision-maker in important matters (Willard et al., 2023). While this AI Bill of Rights is aspirational and not law, it sends a clear signal to industry about the administration's priorities and has begun influencing agency policies and procurement standards. For example, federal agencies are directed to ensure AI used in areas like employment, housing, or credit does not result in unlawful bias (tying into civil rights laws) (Federal Register, 2023).

In 2023, recognizing the rapid advancements (like generative AI), President Biden issued an Executive Order on Safe, Secure, and Trustworthy AI (October 30, 2023). This was the U.S.'s most significant executive action on AI to date, instructing federal agencies to develop standards and actions across various domains (Sumihiro, 2025). Key provisions of the order included: requiring companies to share the results of safety tests (red-team reports) of their most powerful models with the government (to guard against risks like biosecurity or cybersecurity threats); setting standards for watermarking AI-generated content to combat misinformation; prioritizing support for AI R&D that addresses societal challenges (like health, climate, and education); and ensuring that AI in sensitive areas (law enforcement, employment, etc.) is deployed equitably and with oversight (The White House Statements and Release, 2023). The order also called for the development of guidelines on AI safety and security (e.g., preventing AI from being used to engineer bioweapons) and for efforts to mitigate privacy harms, such as advancing techniques for privacy-preserving machine learning (Federal Register, 2023).

Beyond the executive branch, independent regulators like the Federal Trade Commission (FTC) have asserted their authority to police deceptive or unfair uses of AI under consumer protection laws (Sumihiro, 2025). The FTC has warned companies that exaggerated claims about AI or biased algorithms could violate existing statutes. At the state level, a patchwork of laws is emerging (for instance, Illinois's AI Video Interview Act regulating AI in hiring, or specific rules around facial recognition in cities like San Francisco that banned police use of it) (Arun et L., 2024). The absence of a single federal AI law means compliance in the U.S. can be complex, but it also reflects a pro-innovation stance aiming not to stifle AI's development.

Importantly for sustainable development, the U.S. approach emphasizes innovation and leadership in trustworthy AI. Documents like the National AI R&D Strategic Plan and the establishment of the National AI Initiative aim to foster AI advances in areas such as healthcare, environmental forecasting, and education technology, often through funding research or public-private partnerships. For example, the U.S. has funded AI projects for climate modelling and disaster response (aligning with SDG 13 and 11) via programs at NSF and DARPA. There's also attention to workforce impacts, initiatives to promote AI education and retraining to ensure an inclusive AI-ready workforce (touching SDG 8 on decent work).

EUROPEAN UNION

The EU has taken a proactive and comprehensive approach to AI regulation, with a strong focus on fundamental rights, safety, and ethics, an approach very much in line with the EU's broader regulatory philosophy (as seen in data protection with GDPR). The centrepiece is the proposed EU Artificial Intelligence Act, which, once in force (expected 2024–2025), will be the world's first broad framework law on AI. The AI Act employs a risk-based regulatory model, classifying AI systems into tiers of risk with corresponding obligations (EU AI Act, 2024):

Unacceptable risk AI: These are uses of AI deemed to pose intolerable threats to safety or fundamental rights, and they are outright banned. The Act explicitly prohibits, for example, AI systems for social scoring of individuals by governments (as mentioned earlier) or real-time remote biometric identification in public spaces for law enforcement (with narrow exceptions) (EU AI Act, 2024). Such practices are considered contrary to EU values (violating privacy, equality, etc.) and thus not allowed at all.

High-risk AI: This category covers AI systems that, if they malfunction or are used irresponsibly, could significantly affect people's lives or rights. The Act places stringent requirements on these systems. Examples include AI used in critical infrastructure (like traffic control), education (e.g., grading exams), employment (hiring algorithms), credit scoring, law enforcement (predictive policing tools), border control, and medical devices (EU AI Act, 2024). Providers of high-risk AI must implement extensive risk management, testing, and documentation measures (EU AI Act, 2024). They must ensure high-quality training data to minimize bias (European Commission, 2020), keep logs for traceability, provide clear user information, and enable human oversight in operation (European Commission, 2020). Compliance will often require a conformity assessment before the system can be marketed in the EU.

Limited or "specific transparency" risk: This middle tier covers AI systems that aren't high-risk but still warrant some transparency. The AI Act mandates, for instance, that AI chatbots or deepfakes be clearly identified as machine-generated when interacting with humans (European Commission, 2020). Users should know they are not dealing with a human (addressing concerns around deception). Another example is AI that generates images or videos, it should disclose that content is AI-generated to curb the spread of disinformation (a nod to sustainable development concerns around peace and strong institutions, SDG 16).

This calibrated approach reflects the EU's attempt to balance innovation with precaution. The AI Act's requirements align strongly with sustainable development values by emphasizing transparency, accountability, non-discrimination, and safety; it aims to ensure AI supports inclusive and trustworthy growth. For example, the requirement to use unbiased, representative data for high-risk AI (European Commission, 2020) directly addresses concerns about AI-driven inequality (SDG 10). The mandated human oversight aligns with protecting decent work and agency (SDG 8 and SDG 16). And the ban on systems like social scoring or exploitative surveillance upholds human dignity and rights (fundamental to all SDGs).

Specifically regarding sustainable development, the EU often frames AI as a tool to achieve the European Green Deal and social goals. For example, the EU has funded projects on AI for energy efficiency, sustainable agriculture (precision farming in EU's Common Agricultural Policy), and climate science (like the Destination Earth digital twin program). The Horizon Europe research program includes mission-driven funding for climate adaptation and smart cities that leverage AI. Additionally, the EU's development aid has begun to incorporate digitalization, the Global Gateway initiative includes supporting AI and digital solutions in partner countries, with an emphasis on ethics and data protection in line with EU values.

Regulatory-wise, it's notable that the EU already enforces GDPR (General Data Protection Regulation), which indirectly governs AI by controlling personal data processing. GDPR grants rights like explanation (in certain automated decision cases) and imposes fines for data misuse, which shapes AI development in Europe towards privacy-friendly approaches. The upcoming Digital Services Act (DSA) and Digital Markets Act (DMA) also touch AI, requiring transparency in recommendation algorithms for large online platforms (DSA) and preventing anti-competitive practices by tech gatekeepers (DMA), which can influence how AI-driven services operate.

INDIA

India, as the world's largest democracy and a major emerging economy, has been actively developing its AI strategy with an emphasis on leveraging AI for social transformation and inclusive growth, essentially using AI to achieve its development objectives. India's approach so far is characterized by strategic frameworks and ethical guidelines, with a relatively hands-off regulatory stance to avoid stifling innovation in its nascent AI sector. There is no dedicated AI law in India yet (as of early 2025) (Singh, 2025), but there are multiple policy documents and sectoral initiatives guiding AI deployment.

The foundational document is the National Strategy for Artificial Intelligence, released by NITI Aayog (the government's policy think tank) in 2018 (Singh, 2025). Subtitled "AI for All," this strategy envisions India becoming a leader in AI by focusing on solutions for societal needs and the SDGs. It identified five priority sectors: healthcare, agriculture, education, smart cities/infrastructure, and smart mobility (Ettinger, 2025). These align well with sustainable development challenges (SDG 3, 2, 4, 11, 9). The strategy calls for promoting research, fostering start-ups, facilitating data access, and addressing issues like data privacy and security. It also mooted the idea of an Indian AI marketplace and even physical compute infrastructure (an "AI cloud") to democratize access to AI resources.

Following up, in 2021 NITI Aayog released the Principles for Responsible AI or RAICE (Responsible AI for Social Empowerment) framework (Arun et al., 2025). This outlined key principles: safety and reliability, equality (avoid bias), inclusivity and non-discrimination, privacy and security, transparency, and accountability. These mirror global AI ethics principles and were meant to guide both the public and private sectors in developing AI systems ethically. For instance, it emphasizes explainability and human oversight, especially when AI is used in governance (Singh, 2025). Though voluntary, this framework has informed subsequent efforts, e.g., the Ministry of Electronics & IT (MeitY) often references these principles when discussing AI guidelines. Regulatory environment development of AI has been seen to be existing only in the form of Data protection law. In August 2023, India passed the Digital Personal Data Protection Act. This law (not specific to AI but impactful on it) establishes consent-based data processing, rights for individuals (data access, correction, erasure), and requirements on data handlers to ensure privacy (Gandhi et al., 2025).

It's akin to a simpler version of GDPR and will influence AI systems dealing with personal data (for example, requiring localization of sensitive data or limiting retention). Although the new law has some critiques (for allowing broad government exemptions), it's a step toward safeguarding privacy as AI grows in sectors like finance or healthcare (Haar et al., 2024). Besides, India has sectoral policies that touch on AI. For example, the Medical Device Rules may indirectly cover AI diagnostic tools; the central bank has issued risk management guidelines for AI in fintech; and the IT Ministry has floated guidelines on AI in social media and content moderation. As per a 2025 analysis, India's regulatory landscape for AI is a patchwork where existing IT laws and sectoral regulations fill gaps until an AI-specific law emerges (Maiti and Tripathi, 2023). The government has signalled it prefers light-touch regulation for AI at this stage, focusing on enabling innovation and capacity (Maiti and Tripathi, 2023).

Institutionally, India launched the RAISE 2020 (Responsible AI for Social Empowerment) summit and subsequent initiatives to convene multi-stakeholder dialogues on AI for good. It also established bodies like INDIAai, a central hub to promote AI resources, research, and collaboration, including a pillar on *"Safe & Trusted AI"* to develop guardrails and best practices (INDIA/AI, 2024) (Bajpai et al., 2024). India has also partnered in global forums: it's part of the OECD's AI group, was a founding member of the Global Partnership on AI (GPAI), and has been supportive of UNESCO's AI Ethics Recommendation. These show India's commitment to global cooperation on AI governance that supports development and ethics (Bajpai et al., 2024).

In terms of using AI for sustainable development on the ground, India has numerous projects, such as, AI-powered chatbots for farmer advisory (e.g., guiding on weather and crop prices), diagnostic algorithms assisting doctors in rural clinics (for eye disease, TB, etc.), education tech like personalized learning apps used in government schools, and crowdsourcing platforms using AI to translate and localize content into India's many languages (addressing digital inclusion) (Gawade et al., 2024). The government's Aspirational Districts Program (aimed at developing 100 of India's most backward districts) uses data and AI analytics to monitor progress on indicators like health and education, targeting interventions more effectively (Babar and Akan, 2024). Smart city initiatives in cities like Delhi and Bangalore incorporate AI-based traffic management and public safety systems (with caution to avoid bias). Notably, during COVID-19, India leveraged AI for telemedicine and to manage vaccine logistics (Kumar et al., 2025).

Challenges remain in India's AI journey in terms of data quality, digital infrastructure is still developing (especially in rural areas), and there's a skills gap with relatively fewer AI experts per capita than in China or the West (Anshuman and Mallick, 2023). The government is addressing these by expanding digital connectivity (BharatNet), encouraging open data (India's Open Government Data portal), and skilling programs (like including AI in curricula, and programs by NASSCOM and others for upskilling IT workers in AI) (NASSCOM, 2023). On the regulatory horizon, experts suggest India may not opt for an EU-style AI Act immediately but could strengthen sectoral guidelines and possibly a coordination body for AI governance (Bajpai et al., 2024). The Carnegie Endowment noted that India's perspective on AI regulation must balance its innovation economy ambitions with protecting its large, diverse population from AI harms (Haridas et al., 2023). As of early 2025, India's approach can be summarized as *"pro-innovation, with responsible AI principles"*. It aims to harness AI for inclusive development (very aligned with SDGs), while putting in place foundational governance like data protection and ethical principles to steer AI in the right direction (Maiti and Tripathi, 2023).

NEED FOR THE DEVELOPMENT OF ETHICAL AND RESPONSIBLE AI

Achieving the positive vision of AI in sustainable development while avoiding its pitfalls surely hinges on developing ethical and responsible AI (Bajpai et al., 2024). Ethical considerations should be integrated at every stage of the AI lifecycle (sometimes called "Ethics by Design"). This starts with diverse and inclusive design teams. Having developers from varied backgrounds (in terms of gender, ethnicity, and domain expertise) can help spot biases or blind spots early (Fritsch, 2025). For instance, Joy Buolamwini's presence in testing facial recognition was pivotal to uncovering its bias (Hardesty, 2018). Teams should follow ethical design framework, for example, the OECD AI Principles provide a blueprint: ensure AI benefits people and the planet (inclusive growth), respect human rights (e.g., avoid surveillance misuse), be transparent, robust, and have accountability mechanisms (OECD, 2019).

To ensure AI does not perpetuate discrimination, organizations should implement regular audits for bias. This can involve testing the AI on various subgroups and measuring performance differences (e.g., does a loan approval AI have higher rejection rates for women or minorities? (Sumihiro, 2025) Does a healthcare AI predict worse outcomes for certain age groups?). If disparities are found, mitigation techniques exist: rebalancing training data, using fairness-aware algorithms, or adding constraints in the model to equalize outcomes across groups (Ettinger, 2025). Companies like IBM and Microsoft have released fairness toolkits that help identify and mitigate bias in datasets and models. Some jurisdictions might even mandate such audits for high-impact AI (the EU AI Act will effectively do so via conformity assessments) (Mahadew, 2024). External audits or third-party ethics reviews can add credibility – akin to financial audits, independent experts evaluate an AI system's adherence to stated ethics principles. IEEE and ISO are developing standards for algorithmic bias and transparency, which can guide audit processes (Snowflakes, 2024).

Building trust in AI requires that stakeholders can understand how and why AI makes certain decisions. This is particularly important in public sector or high-stakes use (courts, healthcare, welfare decisions) (Xu et al., 2023). Developers should strive to create explainable AI (XAI) either by using inherently interpretable models (like decision trees or rule-based systems) when feasible, or by providing explanation interfaces for complex models (like generating feature importance or counterfactual explanations for a neural network's output) (Babar and Akan, 2024). For example, an AI that denies a loan should be able to provide a rationale ("application denied due to low income and short credit history") in simple terms, so the person can respond or improve (Willard et al., 2023). The "notice and explanation" principle in the US AI Bill of Rights and similar transparency requirements in EU and OECD frameworks all reinforce that users have a right to know when AI is involved and to get an understandable explanation (AI Bill of Rights) (Fritsch, 2025). Documenting AI systems (datasheets for datasets, model cards for models) is a best practice being adopted, detailing their intended use, performance, and limitations.

We touched on privacy in challenges; here the emphasis is on solutions, such as, techniques like differential privacy (injecting slight noise to data or models to prevent re-identification of individuals) can allow AI models to learn from data without exposing personal details (Wang et al., 2024). Federated learning is another promising approach: AI models are trained across multiple decentralized devices or servers holding local data samples, without exchanging the data itself useful for sensitive data like health records, where a central dataset is risky (Bolón-Canedo et al., 2024). Implementing robust cybersecurity for AI systems is also part of responsible development: models should be tested against adversarial attacks (and possibly hardened using methods like adversarial training), and any system connected to the internet should follow best security practices to avoid breaches (Gosselink et al., 2024). Responsible AI governance means having an incident response plan if an AI system fails or is hacked, there is a protocol to mitigate harm (like the equivalent of a product recall or security patch) (Nugraha, 2024).

As highlighted, UNESCO's Recommendation on the Ethics of AI (2021) provides a comprehensive global framework covering principles like proportionality, safety, sustainability, privacy, non-discrimination, and responsibility, and even addressing issues like AI's environmental impact and the need for international cooperation (UNESCO, 2024). With 193 states agreeing, it's a strong signal of consensus. Ensuring development of ethical AI means countries and companies actually implement these recommendations (Ettinger, 2025). For example, UNESCO calls for ethical impact assessment for AI systems before deployment and auditing mechanisms after. It encourages member states to develop ethical codes of conduct for AI professionals. Similarly, the OECD AI Principles and the G20 AI Principles (which align with OECD's) should be embedded in national policies and corporate guidelines (Fritsch, 2025).

CONCLUSION AND SUGGESTIONS TO HARNESS THE POWER OF AI TO ACHIEVE SUSTAINABLE DEVELOPMENT GOALS

Artificial Intelligence (AI) holds immense promise for advancing sustainable development, yet it also introduces complex ethical and environmental challenges. To harness its full potential, AI development must align with principles rooted in human rights, inclusivity, and environmental sustainability. Regulatory frameworks such as the EU's human-centric AI regulations, the US AI Bill of Rights, UNESCO's ethical guidelines, and India's "AI for All" strategy emphasize AI's role in enhancing human welfare and ecological responsibility. For AI to truly serve the Sustainable Development Goals (SDGs), its applications, whether in energy, transportation, or governance, must go beyond improving efficiency or profit and explicitly support sustainability objectives.

Global cooperation is critical to responsible AI governance. Current regulatory approaches remain fragmented across nations. Initiatives like the Global AI Safety Summit have emerged to facilitate dialogue on societal and existential risks. A unified, UN-coordinated global framework, modelled after climate accords, could standardize AI safety protocols, promote ethical norms, and facilitate data sharing. Furthermore, organizations such as the UNDP, WHO, UNEP, and the World Bank must work together to ensure developing nations receive the technical support and capacity building needed to access AI equitably. Closing the digital divide is equally important. Advancing sustainable AI requires investment in STEM and AI education, especially for marginalized communities, including women and underrepresented groups. In parallel, reskilling efforts must address the evolving labor market shaped by AI technologies.

Ensuring ethical and responsible AI is a multi-dimensional endeavour requiring the Three Ts: Technology (tools to make AI fair, explainable, and secure), Teams (people and processes to govern AI ethics), and Trust (transparency and engagement to earn public confidence). The journey is ongoing; however, with concrete steps as outlined from bias audits to global standards we can steer AI innovation on a course that amplifies the positive impact on sustainable development while keeping its risks in check. As the world increasingly harnesses AI to address climate change, pandemics, and inequality, embedding ethics and responsibility is our best chance to ensure these powerful tools truly serve *"people and planet,"* echoing the core ethos of the SDGs.

Working towards developing energy-efficient "Green AI" techniques to reduce the carbon and energy footprint of AI systems. For example, researchers can design algorithms and hardware that require less power or leverage renewable energy in data centres. This ensures AI's growth does not undermine climate goals (SDG 13) and promotes sustainable consumption. Inclusive and community-driven AI design embraces participatory design by involving local communities, domain experts, and underrepresented groups in creating AI solutions. Co-designing AI for social good with teachers, doctors, farmers, and marginalized voices can produce tools that are culturally relevant, equitable (supporting SDG 10 on reduced inequalities), and more readily adopted. Diverse development teams help spot biases early and align AI with real needs. Establish international partnerships and open platforms to share data, pretrained models, and best practices for AI-for-SDG applications. Building on initiatives like the Global Partnership on AI, such collaboration can accelerate innovation where it's needed most. For instance, a global "AI for SDG commons" could provide developing countries with access to vital datasets (e.g. health or climate data) and AI tools, bridging gaps in capacity (SDG 17 on partnerships).

REFERENCES

Act, A. I. (2024). *Proposal for a Regulation of the European Parliament and of the Council laying down harmonised rules on artificial intelligence.* European Commission. Retrieved from https://eur-lex.europa.eu

Arun, A. N., Lee, B., Castiblanco, F. A., Buckmaster, D. R., Wang, C.-C., Love, D. J., . . . Ghosh, A. (2024). Ambient IoT: Communications enabling precision agriculture. arXiv preprint arXiv:2409.12281.

Babar, A. Z., & Akan, O. B. (2024). Sustainable and precision agriculture with the Internet of Everything (IoE). arXiv preprint arXiv:2404.06341.

Bolón-Canedo, V., Morán-Fernández, L., Cancela, B., & Alonso-Betanzos, A. (2024). A review of green artificial intelligence: Towards a more sustainable future. *Neurocomputing*, *599*, 128096. DOI: 10.1016/j.neucom.2024.128096

Cho, R. (2023, June 9). AI's growing carbon footprint. Columbia Climate School. https://news.climate.columbia.edu/2023/06/09/ais-growing-carbon-footprint/

Ettinger, A. (2025). Enterprise architecture as a dynamic capability for scalable and sustainable Generative AI adoption: Bridging innovation and governance in large organisations. arXiv preprint arXiv:2505.06326.

European Commission. (2020). *White paper on artificial intelligence: A European approach to excellence and trust.* COM(2020) 65 final.

Fritsch, A. (2025). Sustainability analysis patterns for process mining and process modelling approaches. arXiv preprint arXiv:2503.13584.

Gandhi, D., Joshi, H., Hartman, L., & Hassani, S. (2025). Approaches to responsible governance of GenAI in organizations. arXiv preprint arXiv:2504.17044.

Gosselink, B. H., Brandt, K., Croak, M., DeSalvo, K., Gomes, B., Ibrahim, L., . . . Manyika, J. (2024). AI in Action: Accelerating progress towards the Sustainable Development Goals. *arXiv* preprint arXiv:2407.02711.

Haar, U., & Lynch, P. (2024). AI-driven solutions in renewable energy: A review of data science applications in solar and wind energy. *World Journal of Applied Research and Reviews, 8*(2), 45–62. Retrieved from https://wjarr.com/content/ai-driven-solutions-renewable-energy-review-data-science-applications-solar-and-wind-energy

Haridas, G., Sohee, S. K., & Brahmecha, A. (2023, October 2). The key policy frameworks governing AI in India. Access Partnership. https://accesspartnership.com/the-key-policy-frameworks-governing-ai-in-india/

Jasper, P. (2024, July 9). *Can AI help us achieve the SDGs?* SDG Action. https://sdg-action.org/can-ai-help-us-achieve-the-sdgs/

Jurgens, J., & Kaushik, P. (2024, January 16). Farmers in India are using AI for agriculture – Here's how they could inspire the world. World Economic Forum. https://www.weforum.org/stories/2024/01/how-indias-ai-agriculture-boom-could-inspire-the-world/

Kermani, M. A. A., Seddighi, H. R., & Maghsoudi, M. (2024). Revolutionizing process mining: A novel architecture for ChatGPT integration and enhanced user experience through optimized prompt engineering. arXiv preprint arXiv:2405.10689.

Kirikkaleli, D., Aad, S., & Kirikkaleli, N. O. (2025). Sustainable development and investment in artificial intelligence in the USA. *Humanities & Social Sciences Communications*, *12*, 246. Advance online publication. DOI: 10.1057/s41599-025-04417-7

Kumar, A., Shankar, A., Hollebeek, L. D., Behl, A., & Lim, W. M. (2025). Generative artificial intelligence (GenAI) revolution: A deep dive into GenAI adoption. *Journal of Business Research*, *189*, 115160. Advance online publication. DOI: 10.1016/j.jbusres.2024.115160

Mahadew, B. (2024). The nexus between artificial intelligence and Sustainable Development Goals: A review. *Sustainable Economies*, *2*(1), 13. DOI: 10.62617/se.v2i1.13

Năstasă, A., Dumitra, T.-C., & Grigorescu, A. (2024). Artificial intelligence and sustainable development during the pandemic: An overview of the scientific debates. *Heliyon*, *10*(9), e30412. DOI: 10.1016/j.heliyon.2024.e30412

Nugraha, T. (2024, April 26). Sustainable AI development in developing countries on data policy. Modern Diplomacy. https://moderndiplomacy.eu/2024/04/26/sustainable-ai-development-in-developing-countries-on-data-policy/

Office of the High Commissioner for Human Rights. (2024, June). *Artificial intelligence: A game-changer for sustainable development*. United Nations Human Rights. https://www.ohchr.org/en/stories/2024/06/artificial-intelligence-game-changer-sustainable-development

Singh, A. (2025, February 26). The AI regulatory landscape in India: What to know. AZO Robotics. https://www.azorobotics.com/Article.aspx?ArticleID=742

Sohns, T. M., Aysolmaz, B., & Figge, L. (2023). Green business process management for business sustainability: A case study of manufacturing SMEs from Germany. *Journal of Cleaner Production*, *401*, 136667. DOI: 10.1016/j.jclepro.2023.136667

Sumihiro, G. (2025, June 10). Commentary: Precision agriculture is an investment in food security. *My Journal Courier.* Retrieved from https://www.myjournalcourier.com/opinion/article/precision-agriculture-investment-food-security-20260610.php

UNDP. (2022). *Artificial intelligence for sustainable development: Mapping AI's potential to achieve the SDGs.* United Nations Development Programme.

UNESCO. (2021). *Recommendation on the ethics of artificial intelligence.* UNESCO Publishing. https://unesdoc.unesco.org/ark:/48223/pf0000381137

Vacarelu, F.-A. (2024, May 29). Ensuring positive, people-focused futures through AI. United Nations Development Programme (UNDP). https://www.undp.org/blog/ensuring-positive-people-focused-futures-through-ai

Vinuesa, R., Azizpour, H., & Leite, I.. (2020). The role of artificial intelligence in achieving the Sustainable Development Goals. *Nature Communications*, *11*, 233. DOI: 10.1038/s41467-019-14108-y

Wang, Q., Li, Y., & Li, R. (2024). Ecological footprints, carbon emissions, and energy transitions: The impact of artificial intelligence (AI). *Humanities & Social Sciences Communications*, *11*, 1043. Advance online publication. DOI: 10.1057/s41599-024-03520-5

Weinzierl, S., Zilker, S., Dunzer, S., & Matzner, M. (2024). Machine learning in business process management: A systematic literature review. arXiv preprint arXiv:2405.16396.

Willard, J. D., Varadharajan, C., Jia, X., & Kumar, V. (2023). Time series predictions in unmonitored sites: A survey of machine learning techniques in water resources. arXiv preprint arXiv:2308.09766.

Xu, Q., Shi, Y., Bamber, J., Tuo, Y., Ludwig, R., & Zhu, X. (2023). Physics-aware machine learning revolutionizes scientific paradigm for machine learning and process-based hydrology. *PLOS Water*, *1*(4), e0000059. https://journals.plos.org/water/article?id=10.1371/journal.pwat.0000059

Yang, A., & Li, B. (2025, March 31). AI Watch: Global regulatory tracker – China. White & Case. https://www.whitecase.com/insight-our-thinking/ai-watch-global-regulatory-tracker-china

Compilation of References

Act, A. I. (2024). *Proposal for a Regulation of the European Parliament and of the Council laying down harmonised rules on artificial intelligence.* European Commission. Retrieved from https://eur-lex.europa.eu

Adams, C., Pente, P., Lemermeyer, G., & Rockwell, G. (2023). Ethical principles for artificial intelligence in K-12 education. *Computers and Education: Artificial Intelligence*, *4*, 100131.

Adeleye, O. O., Eden, C. A., & Adeniyi, I. S. (2024). Innovative teaching methodologies in the era of artificial intelligence: A review of inclusive educational practices. *World J. Adv. Eng. Technol. Sci.*, *11*(2), 69–79.

Adeoye, S., & Adams, R. (2024). Leveraging Artificial Intelligence for Predictive Healthcare: A Data-Driven Approach to Early Diagnosis and Personalized Treatment. *Cogniz. J. Multidiscip. Stud*, *4*, 80–97.

Afrogha, O. (2025). Artificial Intelligence Meets Academia: Safeguarding Integrity in a Digital Era. AI and Ethics, Academic Integrity and the Future of Quality Assurance in Higher Education, 12.

Agarwal, M., Singh, A., Arjaria, S., Sinha, A., & Gupta, S. (2022). ToLeD: Tomato leaf disease detection using convolution neural network. *Procedia Computer Science*, *167*, 293–301.

Ahila Priyadharshini, R., Arivazhagan, S., Arun, M., & Mirnalini, A. (2023). Maize leaf disease classification using deep convolutional neural networks. *Neural Computing & Applications*, *31*, 8887–8895.

Ahmad, W., Shah, S., & Irtaza, A. (2020). Plants disease phenotyping using quinary patterns as texture descriptor. *KSII Transactions on Internet and Information Systems*, *14*, 525–542.

Aithal, P. S., & Maiya, A. K. (2023). Innovations in higher education industry–Shaping the future. [IJCSBE]. *International Journal of Case Studies in Business, IT, and Education*, *7*(4), 283–311.

Ajirotutu, R. O., Garba, B. M. P., & Johnson, S. O. (2024). AI-driven risk mitigation: Transforming project management in construction and infrastructure development. *World J. Adv. Eng. Technol. Sci.*, *13*(2), 611–623.

Akinrinola, O., Okoye, C. C., Ofodile, O. C., & Ugochukwu, C. E. (2024). Navigating and reviewing ethical dilemmas in AI development: Strategies for transparency, fairness, and accountability. GSC Advanced Research and Reviews, 18(3), 050-058.

Alabi, K. O., Adedeji, A. A., Mahmuda, S., & Fowomo, S. (2024). Predictive Analytics in HR: Leveraging AI for Data-Driven Decision Making. *International Journal of Research in Engineering. Science and Management*, *7*(4), 137–143.

Alalawi, K., Athauda, R., Chiong, R., & Renner, I. (2025). Evaluating the student performance prediction and action framework through a learning analytics intervention study. *Education and Information Technologies*, *30*(3), 2887–2916.

Alesmaa and Rait-Eino Laarmann. (2025). Transforming text and images into game-ready 3D models. *Alpha (Osorno)*, *3D*, ●●●. Retrieved June 16, 2025, from https://www.guideofaitool.com/en/ai-tool/alpha-3d

Alhilali, A. H., & Montazerolghaem, A. (2023). Artificial intelligence based load balancing in SDN: A comprehensive survey. *Internet of Things : Engineering Cyber Physical Human Systems*, *22*, 100814. DOI: 10.1016/j.iot.2023.100814

Ali, M., Khan, T. I., & Khattak, M. N., & ŞENER, İ. (2024). Synergizing AI and business: Maximizing innovation, creativity, decision precision, and operational efficiency in high-tech enterprises. *Journal of Open Innovation*, *10*(3), 100352.

Alleman, N. F., Allen, C. C., & Madsen, S. (2025). *Starving the Dream: Student Hunger and the Hidden Costs of Campus Affluence*. JHU Press.

Al-Nabet, N. (2021). A case study of the benefits of the IoT in the Qatari retail industry. *Studies in Business and Economics*, *24*(1), 86–107.

Al-Turjman, F., Altinay, F., & Gazi, Z. A. (2024). *Artificial intelligence of things (AIoT): Current and future trends*. Elsevier.

Alves Da Veiga, P. (2023). Generative Ominous Dataset: Testing the Current Public Perception of Generative Art. *Proceedings of the 20th International Conference on Culture and Computer Science: Code and Materiality*, 1–10. ACM. https://doi.org/DOI: 10.1145/3623462.3623475

Amiri, S. M. H. (2025). Digital Transformations in Education: Research Insights for 21st-Century Learning. International Journal of Innovative Science [IJISET]. *Engineering & Technology*, *12*(03), 1–15.

Anne, c. 19 (1710). The Avalon Project: The Statute of Anne; April 10, 1710. (n.d.). Retrieved June 16, 2025, from https://avalon.law.yale.edu/18th_century/anne_1710.asp

Anwar, R. W., Ismael, A., & Qureshi, K. N. (2024). Advanced AIoT applications and services. *Artificial Intelligence of Things (AIoT)*, 21-33. https://doi.org/DOI: 10.1201/9781003430018-3

Apat, H. K., Sahoo, B., Mohanty, S., & Sahoo, K. S. (2022). A scalable software-defined edge computing model for sustainable smart city Internet of things (IoT) application. *SDN-Supported Edge-Cloud Interplay for Next Generation Internet of Things*, 125-148. https://doi.org/DOI: 10.1201/9781003213871-7

Artene, A. E., Domil, A. E., & Ivascu, L. (2024). Unlocking Business Value: Integrating AI-Driven Decision-Making in Financial Reporting Systems. *Electronics (2079-9292), 13*(15).

Arun, A. N., Lee, B., Castiblanco, F. A., Buckmaster, D. R., Wang, C.-C., Love, D. J., . . . Ghosh, A. (2024). Ambient IoT: Communications enabling precision agriculture. arXiv preprint arXiv:2409.12281.

Atolagbe-Olaoye, A. (2025). Collaborative information behavior and human-AI context in group work. *International Journal of Library and Information Services*, *13*(1), 1–16.

Aviyanti, R. D., Widiasmara, A., Devi, H. P., Nurhayati, P., Chairunnisa, D. M., & Zami, M. T. A. (2022). Digital Entrepreneurship Assistance for Handicraft SMEs in Cileng Village. *Int. J. Comm. Serv. Learn.*, *6*(2), 221–230.

Awaisi, K. S., Ye, Q., & Sampalli, S. (2024). A survey of industrial AIoT: Opportunities, challenges, and directions. *IEEE Access : Practical Innovations, Open Solutions*, *12*, 96946–96996. DOI: 10.1109/access.2024.3426279

Azzam, M. J., Alqudah, A. M. M., Aryan, L. A., & Abu Haija, A. A. (2024). In: Hannoon A. (eds). Empirical Analysis of the link between Financial Literacy and Personal Financial Decision of Genz. 34.In: Frontiers of Human Centricity in the Artificial Intelligence- Driven Society 5.0, *Studies in Systems, Decision and Control, Vol.226, Springer*. DOI: et al.(2021).DOI: 10.1007/978-3-031-73545-5-16.Chatterjee

Babar, A. Z., & Akan, O. B. (2024). Sustainable and precision agriculture with the Internet of Everything (IoE). arXiv preprint arXiv:2404.06341.

Badghish, S., & Soomro, Y. A. (2024)... *Sustainability*, *16*(5), 1864. DOI: 10.3390/su16051864

Badmus, O., Rajput, S. A., Arogundade, J. B., & Williams, M. (2024). AI-driven business analytics and decision making. *World Journal of Advanced Research and Reviews*, *24*(1), 616–633.

Bagheri, M., Bagheritaba, M., Alizadeh, S., Parizi, M. S., Matoufinia, P., & Luo, Y. (2024). AI-driven decision-making in healthcare information systems: a comprehensive review. *Preprints*.

Baker, S., & Xiang, W. (2023). Artificial intelligence of things for smarter healthcare: A survey of advancements, challenges, and opportunities. *IEEE Communications Surveys and Tutorials*, *25*(2), 1261–1293. DOI: 10.1109/comst.2023.3256323

Balas, V. E., Kumar, R., & Srivastava, R. (2019). *Recent trends and advances in artificial intelligence and Internet of things*. Springer Nature.

Bayan, F. M. H. (2024). The Ethics of AI: Navigating the Moral dilemmas of Artificial Intelligence. Arab Journal for Scientific Publishing (AJSP). *ISSN*, *2663*, 5798.

Bietti, E. (2021). From ethics washing to ethics bashing: A moral philosophy view on tech ethics. *Journal of Social Computing*, *2*(3), 266–283.

Billah, M. (2023). Energy-efficient early emergency detection for healthcare monitoring on WBAN platform (Doctoral dissertation, Staffordshire University).

Bilquise, G., Ibrahim, S., & Shaalan, K. (2022). Emotionally intelligent chatbots: A systematic literature review. *Human Behavior and Emerging Technologies*, *2022*(1), 9601630.

Biswas, T. R., Hossain, M. Z., & Comite, U. (2024). Role of Management Information Systems in Enhancing Decision-Making in Large-Scale Organizations. *Pacific Journal of Business Innovation and Strategy*, *1*(1), 5–18.

Boden, M. A. (1998). Creativity and artificial intelligence. *Artificial Intelligence*, *103*(1–2), 347–356. DOI: 10.1016/S0004-3702(98)00055-1

Bolón-Canedo, V., Morán-Fernández, L., Cancela, B., & Alonso-Betanzos, A. (2024). A review of green artificial intelligence: Towards a more sustainable future. *Neurocomputing*, *599*, 128096. DOI: 10.1016/j.neucom.2024.128096

Bonsay, J. O., Cruz, A. P., Firozi, H. C., & Camaro, P. J. C. (2021). Artificial Intelligence and Labour Productivity Paradox: Economic Impact of AI in China, India, Japan and Singapore, *Journal of Economics*. *Finance and Accounting Studies*, *3*(2), 120–139.

Bryant, J., Heitz, C., Sanghvi, S., & Wagle, D. (2020), How Artificial Intelligence Will Impact K-12 Teachers, Mc Kinsey. Https://Mc Kinsey.com/ Industries/ education/ oversights. Accessed online on 15/05/2025.

Bryant, P. (2024). Learning design ecosystems thinking: Defying the linear imperative and designing for higher education at-scale. *Journal of Work-Applied Management*, *16*(2), 283–291.

Bryda, G., & Costa, A. P. (2023). Qualitative research in digital era: Innovations, methodologies and collaborations. *Social Sciences*, *12*(10), 570.

Buhmann, A., & Fieseler, C. (2021). Towards a deliberative framework for responsible innovation in artificial intelligence. *Technology in Society*, *64*, 101475.

Butkiene, R., Gudonienė, D., Čeponienė, L., Vaiciukynas, E., Virkus, S., Dickel, J., ... & Coelho, J. (2025). Digital transformation: handbook for digital transformation specialists.

Byers, C. M. (2024). AI-Powered Educational Tools and Their Effect on Student Motivation in Online Learning Environments: A Preliminary Study.

Chan, C. K. Y., & Lee, K. K. W. (2023). The AI Generation gap: Are Genz students more interested in adopting generative AI such as ChatGPT in teaching and learning than their GenX and millennial generation teachers? *Smart Learn Environ*, *10*(60). Advance online publication. DOI: 10.1186/s40561-023-00269-3

Chang, Z., Liu, S., Xiong, X., Cai, Z., & Tu, G. (2021). A survey of recent advances in edge-computing-Powered artificial intelligence of things. *IEEE Internet of Things Journal*, *8*(18), 13849–13875. DOI: 10.1109/jiot.2021.3088875

Chan, T. A. C. H., Ho, J. M.-B., & Tom, M. (2024). Miro: Promoting collaboration through online whiteboard interaction. *RELC Journal*, *55*(3), 871–875.

Chatterjee, S., & Parra, J. (2022). Undergraduate students engagement in formal and informal learning: Applying the community of inquiry framework. *Journal of Educational Technology Systems*, *50*(3), 327–355.

Chaudhary, R. R., Bamane, K. D., Agrawal, H., Malathi, P., Gaikwad, A. S., & Patankar, A. J. (2024). A critical analysis of crop management using Machine Learning towards smart and precise farming. *Journal of Integrated Science and Technology*, *12*(5), 809–809.

Chayka, K. (2025, April 2). The Limits of A.I.-Generated Miyazaki. *The New Yorker*. https://www.newyorker.com/culture/infinite-scroll/the-limits-of-ai-generated-miyazaki

Cheng, L., Gu, Y., Liu, Q., Yang, L., Liu, C., & Wang, Y. (2024). Advancements in accelerating deep neural network inference on AIoT devices: A survey. *IEEE Transactions on Sustainable Computing, 9*(6), 830–847. DOI: 10.1109/tsusc.2024.3353176

Chenna, K. (2024). Optimizing decision-making in supply chains: A framework for AI and human collaboration using SAP technologies. [IJRCAIT]. *International Journal of Research in Computer Applications and Information Technology, 7*(2), 824–835.

Chen, Y., Jensen, S., Albert, L. J., Gupta, S., & Lee, T. (2023). Artificial intelligence (AI) student assistants in the classroom: Designing chatbots to support student success. *Information Systems Frontiers, 25*(1), 161–182.

Chin, R., Catal, C., & Kassahun, A. (2023). Plant disease detection using drones in precision agriculture. *Precision Agriculture, 24*, 1663–1682.

Cho, R. (2023, June 9). AI's growing carbon footprint. Columbia Climate School. https://news.climate.columbia.edu/2023/06/09/ais-growing-carbon-footprint/

Cho, J., Heo, Y., & Moon, J. W. (2023). An intelligent HVAC control strategy for supplying comfortable and energy-efficient school environment. *Advanced Engineering Informatics, 55*, 101895.

Chourasia, S., Dhama, A., & Bhardwaj, G. (2024, May). AI-Driven Organizational Culture Evolution: A Critical Review. In *2024 International Conference on Communication, Computer Sciences and Engineering (IC3SE)* (pp. 1839-1844). IEEE.

Claburn, T. (2022). *Holz, founder of AI art service Midjourney, on future images.* Retrieved June 16, 2025, from https://www.theregister.com/2022/08/01/david_holz_midjourney/

Clopath, H. (1901). Genuine Art versus Mechanism. *Brush and Pencil, 7*(6), 331. DOI: 10.2307/25505621

Community, N. A. S. S. C. O. M. Role of AI in SMES, Calsoftinc, 18June 2024. https://community.nasscom.in/communities/ai/role-ai-smes

Côrte-Real, N., Ruivo, P., & Oliveira, T. (2020). Leveraging internet of things and big data analytics initiatives in European and American firms: Is data quality a way to extract business value? *Information & Management, 57*(1), 103141.

Costa, A. C. F., & de Mello Santos, V. H., & de OLIVEIRA, O. J. (2022). Towards the revolution and democratization of education: A framework to overcome challenges and explore opportunities through Industry 4.0. *Informatics in Education, 21*(1), 1–32.

Crowder, J., Determeyer, P., & Rogers, S. (2022). "Technology is Wonderful Until It Isn't": Community-Based Research and the Precarity of Digital Infrastructure. In The Routledge Companion to Media Anthropology (pp. 77-88). Routledge.

Dampitaske, K., Kung, V. V., Jermsiltiparsert, K., Makassar, M., & Chienwatta-nasook, K. (2021).. . *Journal of Management Information and Decision Sciences*, *24*(4), 1–14.

Dankan Gowda, V., Kaur, M., Srinivas, D., Prasad, K. D., & Shekhar, R. (2024). AIoT integration advancements and challenges in smart sensing technologies for smart devices. *Advances in Computational Intelligence and Robotics*, ●●●, 42–65. DOI: 10.4018/979-8-3693-0786-1.ch003

Das, A., Muschert, G., Dutta, M. J., Aytaç, M. B., Tripathi, P., Khare, A., & Ray, S. (2024). AI Impacts, Concerns, and Perspectives in the Global South A Thought Leadership Round Table. Социологическое обозрение, 23(4), 173-195.

Das, S., Ghosh, A., & Pal, S. (2024). Internet-of-Things-enabled precision agriculture for sustainable rural development. In *Precision Agriculture for Sustainability* (pp. 343–372). Apple Academic Press.

David, N. (2024). AI-powered virtual assistant solution for supporting international students.

De La Torre, P. (2025). *The Power of the Analysis Skill – from the Perspective of Artificial Intelligence (AI) | Critical Skills* – Pakko De La Torre // Creative Director. Retrieved June 16, 2025, from https://pakko.org/the-power-of-the-analysis-skill-from -the-perspective-of-artificial-intelligence-ai-critical-skills/

De Vass, T., Shee, H., & Miah, S. J. (2018). The effect of "Internet of Things" on supply chain integration and performance: An organisational capability perspective. *AJIS. Australian Journal of Information Systems*, ●●●, 22.

Devi, K., Sabitha, J., & Sathish Kumar, J. (2023). Effects of Evolving Applications of IoT in the Education Sector. Digital Technologies for Smart Business, Economics and Education: Towards a Promising Future, 213-224.

Dey, P.K., Chowdhury, S., & Abadie, A. VannYaroson, E. and Sarkar. S. (2023). Artificial Intelligence Driven Supply Chain Resilience in Vietnamese Manufacturing Small and Medium Sized Enterprises. *International Journal of Production Research*, *62*(15), 5417–5456. DOI: 10.1080/00207.543.2023.2179859

Digital India website (2025), https://digitalindia.gov.in. Accessed online on 10/5/2025.

Drydakis, N. (2022). Artificial Intelligence and Reduced SMEs Business Risks. A Dynamic Capabilities Analysis during the Covid19 pandemic. *Information Systems Frontiers*, *24*(4), pp1223–pp1247. DOI: 10.1007/s10796-022-10249-9 PMID: 35261558

Dürer, A. (1514). *Melencolia I* [Plate: 9 7/16 × 7 5/16 in. (24 × 18.5 cm); Engraving]. https://www.metmuseum.org/art/collection/search/336228

Dwivedi, Y. K., Hughes, L., Ismagilova, E., Aarts, G., Coombs, C., Crick, T., Duan, Yanqing, Dwivedi, R., Edwards, J., Eirug, A., Galanos, V., Ilavarasan, P. V., Janssen, M., Jones, P., & Kar, A. K., Kizgin Hatice and Kronemann, B., Lal, B., Lucini, B., Medaglia, R., Le Meunier-FitzHugh, K., … Williams, M. D. (2021). Artificial Intelligence (AI): Multidisciplinary perspectives on emerging challenges, opportunities, and agenda for research, practice and policy. *International Journal of Information Management*, *57*(101994), 101994.

Eames, C., & Eames, R. (Eds.). (1990). *A computer perspective: background to the Computer Age* (New ed). Harvard University Press. ISBN: 9780674156265

Ekundayo, F. (2024). Leveraging AI-Driven Decision Intelligence for Complex Systems Engineering. *Int J Res Publ Rev*, *5*(11), 1–10.

Elhaddad, M., & Hamam, S. (2024). AI-driven clinical decision support systems: An ongoing pursuit of potential. *Cureus*, *16*(4).

Elkahlout, M., Karaja, M. B., Elsharif, A. A., Dheir, I. M., Abunasser, B. S., & Abu-Naser, S. S. (2024). AI-Driven Organizational Change: Transforming Structures and Processes in the Modern Workplace.

Emimi, M., Khaleel, M., & Alkrash, A. (2023). The Current Opportunities and Challenges in Drone Technology. *Int. J. Electr. Eng. And Sustain.*, *1*, 74–89.

Era, C. A., Rahman, M., & Alvi, S. T. (2024). Artificial intelligence of things (AIoT) technologies, benefits and applications. *2024 4th International Conference on Emerging Smart Technologies and Applications (eSmarTA)*, 1-6. https://doi.org/ DOI: 10.1109/esmarta62850.2024.10638992

Ettinger, A. (2025). Enterprise architecture as a dynamic capability for scalable and sustainable Generative AI adoption: Bridging innovation and governance in large organisations. arXiv preprint arXiv:2505.06326.

European Commission. (2020). *White paper on artificial intelligence: A European approach to excellence and trust.*COM(2020) 65 final.

Fernandes, S., Sheeja, M. S., & Parivara, S. (2024). Potential of AI for a Sustainable, Inclusive, and Ethically Responsible Future. Fostering Multidisciplinary Research for Sustainability, 196.

Firouzi, F., Farahani, B., & Marinšek, A. (2022). The convergence and interplay of edge, fog, and cloud in the AI-driven Internet of Things (IoT). *Information Systems*, *107*, 101840.

Foong, Y. P., Pidani, R., Sithira Vadivel, V., & Dongyue, Y. (2024). Singapore smart nation: journey into a new digital landscape for higher education. In *Emerging Technologies in Business: Innovation Strategies for Competitive Advantage* (pp. 281–304). Springer Nature Singapore.

Franklin, G., Stephens, R., Piracha, M., Tiosano, S., Lehouillier, F., Koppel, R., & Elkin, P. L. (2024). The sociodemographic biases in machine learning algorithms: A biomedical informatics perspective. *Life (Chicago, Ill.)*, *14*(6), 652.

Frimpong, V., & Wolfs, B. (2024). Predictive effect of AI on leadership: Insights from public case studies on organizational dynamics. *International Journal of Business Administration*, *15*(3), 10–5430.

Fritsch, A. (2025). Sustainability analysis patterns for process mining and process modelling approaches. arXiv preprint arXiv:2503.13584.

Gamboa, Gregorio, Morite, Analyn, Bacarro, Robert, Plando, Rowena, & Ylaya, Vrian & Serna, & John. (2023). Ricefield Health Monitoring System using a drone with AI interface. *Science International (Lahore)*, *35*, 181–184.

Gandhi, D., Joshi, H., Hartman, L., & Hassani, S. (2025). Approaches to responsible governance of GenAI in organizations. arXiv preprint arXiv:2504.17044.

Garg, A., & Singh, A. K. (2021). Applications of Internet of things (IoT) in green computing. *Intelligence of Things: AI-IoT Based Critical-Applications and Innovations*, 1-34. https://doi.org/DOI: 10.1007/978-3-030-82800-4_1

Garvey, B., & Svendsen, A. D. (2024). Can Generative-AI (ChatGPT and Bard) Be Used as Red Team Avatars in Developing Foresight Scenarios? In *Navigating uncertainty using foresight intelligence: A guidebook for scoping scenario options in cyber and beyond* (pp. 213–242). Springer Nature Switzerland.

George, A. S. (2023). Preparing students for an AI-driven world: Rethinking curriculum and pedagogy in the age of artificial intelligence. *Partners Universal Innovative Research Publication*, *1*(2), 112–136.

George, A. S., George, A. H., & Baskar, T. (2023). The death of analog: Assessing the Impacts of ubiquitous mobile technology. *Partners Universal Innovative Research Publication*, *1*(2), 15–33.

Gerlich, M. (2025). AI Tools in Society: Impacts on Cognitive Offloading and the Future of Critical Thinking. *Societies (Basel, Switzerland)*, *15*(1), 6. DOI: 10.3390/soc15010006

Gillani, N., Eynon, R., Chiabaut, C., & Finkel, K. (2023). Unpacking the "Black Box" of AI in education. *Journal of Educational Technology & Society*, *26*(1), 99–111.

Gilles, M. (2025) *The GANfather: The man who's given machines the gift of imagination. (n.d.).* MIT Technology Review. Retrieved June 16, 2025, from https://www.technologyreview.com/2018/02/21/145289/the-ganfather-the-man-whos-given-machines-the-gift-of-imagination/

Gilliland, B., Kunkel, M., Nguyen, T. H., Urada, K., & Christenson, C. (2023). Ethical dilemmas of teacher research in applied linguistics. *Research Methods in Applied Linguistics*, *2*(3), 100072.

Gobert, J. D., Sao Pedro, M. A., & Betts, C. G. (2023). An AI-based teacher dashboard to support students' inquiry: Design principles, features, and technological specifications. In *Handbook of research on science education* (pp. 1011–1044). Routledge.

Godfrey, H. (2023, June). Intellectual humility and self-censorship in higher education; A thematic analysis. []. Frontiers Media SA.]. *Frontiers in Education*, *8*, 1066519.

Gosselink, B. H., Brandt, K., Croak, M., DeSalvo, K., Gomes, B., Ibrahim, L., . . . Manyika, J. (2024). AI in Action: Accelerating progress towards the Sustainable Development Goals. *arXiv* preprint arXiv:2407.02711.

Gray, D. E. (2021). Doing research in the real world.

Gregersen, E. (2025, June 13). Vector graphics | Definition & Facts | Britannica. https://www.britannica.com/technology/vector-graphics

Grunwald, A. (2021). *Living technology: philosophy and ethics at the crossroads between life and technology.* Jenny Stanford Publishing.

Guan, X., Feng, X., & Islam, A. Y. M. (2023). The dilemma and countermeasures of educational data ethics in the age of intelligence. *Humanities & Social Sciences Communications*, *10*(1), 1–14.

Gupta, S., & Jaiswal, R. (2025). A deep learning-based hybrid PLS-SEM-ANN approach for predicting factors improving AI-driven decision-making proficiency for future leaders. *Journal of International Education in Business.*

Haar, U., & Lynch, P. (2024). AI-driven solutions in renewable energy: A review of data science applications in solar and wind energy. *World Journal of Applied Research and Reviews, 8*(2), 45–62. Retrieved from https://wjarr.com/content/ai -driven-solutions-renewable-energy-review-data-science-applications-solar-and -wind-energy

Hamadaqa, M. H. M., Alnajjar, M., Ayyad, M. N., Al-Nakhal, M. A., Abunasser, B. S., & Abu-Naser, S. S. (2024). Leveraging Artificial Intelligence for Strategic Business Decision-Making: Opportunities and Challenges.

Hao, X., Demir, E., & Eyers, D. (2024). Exploring collaborative decision-making: A quasi-experimental study of human and Generative AI interaction. *Technology in Society, 78*, 102662.

Haque, E. (2024). *AI Horizons: Shaping a Better Future Through Responsible Innovation and Human Collaboration.* Stylus Publishing, LLC.

Haridas, G., Sohee, S. K., & Brahmecha, A. (2023, October 2). The key policy frameworks governing AI in India. Access Partnership. https://accesspartnership .com/the-key-policy-frameworks-governing-ai-in-india/

Haroun, A., Le, X., Gao, S., Dong, B., He, T., Zhang, Z., Wen, F., Xu, S., & Lee, C. (2021). Progress in micro/nano sensors and nanoenergy for future aiot-based smart home applications. *Nano Express, 2*(2), 022005. DOI: 10.1088/2632-959x/abf3d4

Hasa, K. (2023). Examining the OECD's perspective on AI in education policy: a critical analysis of language and structure in the 'AI and the future of skills' (AIFS) document and its implications for the higher education (Doctoral dissertation, University of British Columbia).

Haseeb, M., Sasmoko, Mihardjo L. WW. (2019). Economic Impact of Artificial Intelligence: New Look for the Macroeconomic Assessment in Asia Pacific Region. *International Journal of Computational Intelligence Systems, 12*, 1295–1310. DOI: 10.2991/ijcis.d.191025.001

Hasini, C. K. (2024). The Use of AI -driven Personalization for Enhancing the Customer Experience for Genz, *Open. Journal of Business and Management, 12*(6). Advance online publication. DOI: 10.4236/ojbm.2024.126225

Hossain, S., Fernando, M., & Akter, S. (2025). Digital leadership: Towards a dynamic managerial capability perspective of artificial intelligence-driven leader capabilities. *Journal of Leadership & Organizational Studies, 32*(2), 189–208.

Hou, K. M., Diao, X., Shi, H., Ding, H., Zhou, H., & De Vaulx, C. (2023). Trends and challenges in AIoT/IIoT/IoT implementation. *Sensors (Basel), 23*(11), 5074. DOI: 10.3390/s23115074 PMID: 37299800

Howard, J., & Schulte, P. (2024). Managing workplace AI risks and the future of work. *American Journal of Industrial Medicine, 67*(11), 980–993.

Huang, B., & Niyomsilp, E. (2025). The impact of artificial intelligence on organizational decision-making processes. *Edelweiss Applied Science and Technology, 9*(4), 794–808.

Hu, G., Zhu, Y., Wan, M., Bao, W., Zhang, Y., Liang, D., & Yin, C. (2022). Detection of diseased pine trees in unmanned aerial vehicle images by using deep convolutional neural networks. *Geocarto International, 37*, 3520–3539.

Hughes, J. (2021). The deskilling of teaching and the case for intelligent tutoring systems. *Journal of Ethics and Emerging Technologies, 31*(2), 1–16.

Hutson, J. (Ed.). (2024). *The Rise of AI in Academic Inquiry*. IGI Global.

Hwang, W. S., & Kim, H. S. (2022). Does the Adoption of Emerging Technologies Improve Technical Efficiency? Evidence from Korean Manufacturing SMEs. *Small Business Economics, 59*, 627–643. DOI: 10.1007/311187-021-00554-W PMID: 38624928

Iqubal, S., Khan, S., Pant, N., Sarkar, S., Rey, T., & Mohapatra, H. (2025). A study on IoT-enabled smart bed with brain-computer interface for elderly and paralyzed individuals. *Advances in Medical Technologies and Clinical Practice*, ●●●, 61–88. DOI: 10.4018/979-8-3693-7703-1.ch004

Ishizu, T., & Zeki, S. (2011). Toward A Brain-Based Theory of Beauty. *PLoS ONE, 6*(7), e21852. https://doi.org/ ITP / IMA. (n.d.). NYU-Tisch (ITP - graduate). Retrieved June 18, 2025, from https://tisch.nyu.edu/itp.htmlDOI: 10.1371/journal.pone.0021852

Iweuno, B. N., Orekha, P., Ojediran, O., Imohimi, E., & Adu-Twum, H. T. (2024). Leveraging Artificial Intelligence for an inclusive and diversified curriculum. *World Journal of Advanced Research and Reviews, 23*(2), 1579–1590.

Iyer, A., & Umadevi, K. S. (2023). Role of AI and its Impact on Development of Cyber security applications. In: Sarveshwaran, V., Chen, J.I2, Pelusi, D. (eds) Artificial Intelligence and Cyber Security in Industry4.0, Advanced. Technologies and Societa Change. Springer pp 23-46DOI: 10.1007/978-981-99-2115-7-3

Jain, V. (2024). RBI's Big Announcement on Artificial Intelligence for Financial Sector, Outlook Money. https:/ outlookmoney.com/banking/rbi-big (accessed on 21052025). CFO. Economic times. Indiatimes.com/news/rbi-selects, dated 14/8/2023. Accessed online on 21/5/2025.

Jasper, P. (2024, July 9). *Can AI help us achieve the SDGs?* SDG Action. https:// sdg-action.org/can-ai-help-us-achieve-the-sdgs/

Jha, N. (2019). AI voice assistant implementation for enhanced user experience and efficiency. *The Pharma Innovation*, 8(1), 725–728.

Jobayer Rahman, Md., & Shakil Ahmed, Md., Swapnil Biswas, Anika Tabassum Orchi, Raiyan Rahman, & A.K.M. Muzahidul Islam. (2024). Crop Care: Advanced Crop Management System with Intelligent Advisory and Machine Learning Techniques. *6th International Conference on Electrical Engineering and Information & Communication Technology (ICEEICT)*, Dhaka, Bangladesh, 1356-1361.

Jones, V. K., Hanus, M., Yan, C., Shade, M. Y., Blaskewicz Boron, J., & Maschieri Bicudo, R. (2021). Reducing loneliness among aging adults: The roles of personal voice assistants and anthropomorphic interactions. *Frontiers in Public Health*, *9*, 750736.

Joseph, S., Kolade, T. M., Obioha Val, O., Adebiyi, O. O., Ogungbemi, O. S., & Olaniyi, O. O. (2024). AI-powered information governance: Balancing automation and human oversight for optimal organization productivity. *Asian Journal of Research in Computer Science*, *17*(10), 10–9734.

Jurgens, J., & Kaushik, P. (2024, January 16). Farmers in India are using AI for agriculture – Here's how they could inspire the world. World Economic Forum. https://www.weforum.org/stories/2024/01/how-indias-ai-agriculture-boom-could-inspire-the-world/

Kaggwa, S., Eleogu, T. F., Okonkwo, F., Farayola, O. A., Uwaoma, P. U., & Akinoso, A. (2024). AI in decision making: Transforming business strategies. *International Journal of Research and Scientific Innovation*, *10*(12), 423–444.

Kambhampati, S. B., & Maini, L. (2023). Authorship in scientific manuscripts. *Indian Journal of Orthopaedics*, *57*(6), 783–788. PMID: 37214360

Kavitha, R. K., Krupa, C. R., & Kaarthiekheyan, V. (2023). AI-Powered Digital Solutions for Smart Learning: Revolutionizing Education. In Cybersecurity and Data Science Innovations for Sustainable Development of HEICC (pp. 213-227). CRC Press.

Kayyali, M. (2024). Global Perspectives on Personalized Learning: Case Studies and Best Practices. In Transforming Education for Personalized Learning (pp. 66-84). IGI Global.

Kayyali, M. (2025 a). Chatbots for Leadership Support: Decision-Making and Advisory Roles. In Chatbots in Educational Leadership and Management (pp. 127-154). IGI Global Scientific Publishing.

Kayyali, M. (2025 a). Ethical Implications of Generative AI in Education: Privacy, Bias, and Integrity. In Transformative AI Practices for Personalized Learning Strategies (pp. 185-218). IGI Global Scientific Publishing.

Kayyali, M. (2025 b). E-Learning Platforms and Their Influence on Lifelong Learning. In Impact of Digitalization on Education and Social Sustainability (pp. 155-176). IGI Global.

Kayyali, M. (2025 b). The Future of AI in Education: Predictions and Emerging Trends. Next-Generation AI Methodologies in Education, 367-406.

Kayyali, M. (2025 c). Generative AI and Education: Transforming Teaching and Learning Through Collaborative Intelligence. In Humans and Generative AI Tools for Collaborative Intelligence (pp. 25-52). IGI Global Scientific Publishing.

Kayyali, M. (2025 c). Transforming Education: The Future of Mastery-Based Learning and Its Impact. In Cultivating Flourishing Practices and Environments by Embracing Positive Education (pp. 119-148). IGI Global Scientific Publishing.

Kayyali, M. (2025a). Ethical Implications of Generative AI in Education: Privacy, Bias, and Integrity. In Transformative AI Practices for Personalized Learning Strategies (pp. 185-218). IGI Global Scientific Publishing.

Kayyali, M. (2025b). Generative AI and Education: Transforming Teaching and Learning Through Collaborative Intelligence. In Humans and Generative AI Tools for Collaborative Intelligence (pp. 25-52). IGI Global Scientific Publishing.

Kayyali, M. (2026 a). Case Studies: Successful Applications of AI and AR in Research. In Revolutionizing Academic Research With AI and Augmented Reality (pp. 347-368). IGI Global Scientific Publishing.

Kayyali, M. (2026 b). AI in Higher Education: The Risk of Excluding Vulnerable Learners. In AI and New Forms of Exclusion (pp. 57-82). IGI Global Scientific Publishing.

Kayyali, M. (2026 c). The Impact of AI on Classroom Dynamics in Higher Education: Shifting Roles for Professors and Students. In Responsible AI Integration in Education (pp. 151-180). IGI Global Scientific Publishing.

Kayyali, M. (2026a). Case Studies: Successful Applications of AI and AR in Research. In Revolutionizing Academic Research With AI and Augmented Reality (pp. 347-368). IGI Global Scientific Publishing.

Kayyali, M. (2026b). Machine Learning and Bias: Creating Inclusive AI Systems for All. In AI and New Forms of Exclusion (pp. 143-166). IGI Global Scientific Publishing.

Kayyali, M. (2026c). AI in Higher Education: The Risk of Excluding Vulnerable Learners. In AI and New Forms of Exclusion (pp. 57-82). IGI Global Scientific Publishing.

Kayyali, M. (2026d). The Impact of AI on Classroom Dynamics in Higher Education: Shifting Roles for Professors and Students. In Responsible AI Integration in Education (pp. 151-180). IGI Global Scientific Publishing.

Kayyali, M. (2026e). Preparing Educators for the Future: Navigating AI Tools in English Language Teaching. In AI-Powered English Teaching (pp. 267-308). IGI Global Scientific Publishing.

Kayyali, M. (2024). Future possibilities and challenges of AI in education. In *Transforming education with generative AI: Prompt engineering and synthetic content creation* (pp. 118–137). IGI Global Scientific Publishing.

Kayyali, M. (2025 d). The Evolution of AI in Education From Concept to Classroom. In *Navigating Barriers to AI Implementation in the Classroom* (pp. 325–368). IGI Global Scientific Publishing.

Kedar, M. M. (2023). How effective is AI in whiteboard? *INTERANTIONAL JOURNAL OF SCIENTIFIC RESEARCH IN ENGINEERING AND*, *07*(12), 1–6.

Kem, D. (2022). Personalised and adaptive learning: Emerging learning platforms in the era of digital and smart learning. *International Journal of Social Science and Human Research*, *5*(2), 385–391.

Kermani, M. A. A., Seddighi, H. R., & Maghsoudi, M. (2024). Revolutionizing process mining: A novel architecture for ChatGPT integration and enhanced user experience through optimized prompt engineering. arXiv preprint arXiv:2405.10689.

Kim, S. (2021). Exploring how older adults use a smart speaker-based voice assistant in their first interactions: Qualitative study. *JMIR mHealth and uHealth*, *9*(1), e20427.

Kirikkaleli, D., Aad, S., & Kirikkaleli, N. O. (2025). Sustainable development and investment in artificial intelligence in the USA. *Humanities & Social Sciences Communications*, *12*, 246. Advance online publication. DOI: 10.1057/s41599-025-04417-7

Klaassen, G. (2024). Confronting Bias. In *Artificial Intelligence: Building Transparent*. Diverse, and Ethical AI Systems.

Korteling, J. H., van de Boer-Visschedijk, G. C., Blankendaal, R. A., Boonekamp, R. C., & Eikelboom, A. R. (2021). Human-versus artificial intelligence. *Frontiers in Artificial Intelligence*, *4*, 622364.

Krumsvik, R. J. (2024). Chatbots and academic writing for doctoral students. *Education and Information Technologies*, ●●●, 1–35.

Kuelzer-Eckhout, L., & Houser, N. O. (2024). Book Banning, Censorship, and Gag-Order Legislation: Working through the Fear and Distrust That Threatens Public Education and Jeopardizes the Public-at-Large. Journal of Philosophy & History of Education, 74.

Kulkov, I., Kulkova, J., Rohrbeck, R., Menvielle, L., Kaartemo, V., & Makkonen, H. (2024). Artificial intelligence-driven sustainable development: Examining organizational, technical, and processing approaches to achieving global goals. *Sustainable Development*, *32*(3), 2253–2267.

Kumar, A., & Shah, J. (2025). AI meets Mahakhumbh: Demystifying Crowd Counting Process at Prayagraj, India Today.https://www.indiatoday.in/india/story/artifical-intelligence.Accessed online on 20/5/2025

Kumar, A., Shankar, A., Hollebeek, L. D., Behl, A., & Lim, W. M. (2025). Generative artificial intelligence (GenAI) revolution: A deep dive into GenAI adoption. *Journal of Business Research*, *189*, 115160. Advance online publication. DOI: 10.1016/j.jbusres.2024.115160

Kumar, D. (2024). Ai-driven automation in administrative processes: Enhancing efficiency and accuracy. *International Journal of Engineering Science and Humanities*, *14*(1), 256–265.

Lai, Y., Kankanhalli, A., & Ong, D. (2021). Human-AI Collaboration in Healthcare: A Review and Research Agenda. *Proceedings of the 54th Hawaii International Conference on System Sciences*.

Lanier, J. (2018). *Dawn of the new everything: encounters with reality and virtual reality* (First Picador edition). Picador, Henry Holt and Company. ISBN: 9781627794091 9781250097408

Levine, A., & Van Pelt, S. (2021). *The great upheaval: Higher education's past, present, and uncertain future*. JHU Press.

Liang, Q., Gou, J., Wang, Z., & Dabić, M. (2024). Affordances and constraints of automation and augmentation. *Journal of Global Information Management*, *32*(1), 1–27.

Li, F. F. (2023). *The worlds I see: curiosity, exploration, and discovery at the dawn of AI*. Flatiron Books.

Liu, S., Guo, B., Fang, C., Wang, Z., Luo, S., Zhou, Z., & Yu, Z. (2024). Enabling resource-efficient AIoT system with cross-level optimization: A survey. *IEEE Communications Surveys and Tutorials*, *26*(1), 389–427. DOI: 10.1109/comst.2023.3319952

Lu, X., Wijayaratna, K., Huang, Y., & Qiu, A. (2022). AI Enabled Opportunities and transformation challenges for SMEs in the post pandemic era: A review and Research Agenda. *Frontiers in Public Health*, *10*. Advance online publication. DOI: 10.3389/fpubb.2022.885067 PMID: 35570947

Lyons, J. B., Hobbs, K., Rogers, S., & Clouse, S. H. (2023). Responsible (use of) AI. *Frontiers in Neuroergonomics*, *4*, 1201777.

Mahadew, B. (2024). The nexus between artificial intelligence and Sustainable Development Goals: A review. *Sustainable Economies*, *2*(1), 13. DOI: 10.62617/se.v2i1.13

Mahmoudi, H., Camboim, S., & Brovelli, M. A. (2023). Development of a voice virtual assistant for the geospatial data visualization application on the web. *ISPRS International Journal of Geo-Information*, *12*(11), 441.

Manovich, L. (2001). *The language of new media (8. print)*. MIT Press.ISBN: 9780262632553 9780262133746

Marcus, Ng., Haridas, G., & Teoh, E. (2023). The Economic Impact of Generative AI: Future of Work in Malaysia, My digital https://ai.gov.my/media/thought-leadership/Reports-06-EN-Economic-Impact-of-Generative-AI-MY-1.pdf

Mary Sowjanya, A., & Srividya, K. (2024). NLP-Driven Chatbots: Applications and Implications in Conversational AI. Conversational Artificial Intelligence, 713-725.

Matin, A., Islam, M. R., Wang, X., Huo, H., & Xu, G. (2023). AIoT for sustainable manufacturing: Overview, challenges, and opportunities. *Internet of Things : Engineering Cyber Physical Human Systems*, *24*, 100901. DOI: 10.1016/j.iot.2023.100901

McKenzie, J., & Bartunek, J. (2023). Mirror, mirror outside my wall: Reflexive impacts of insider/outsider collaborative inquiry on the insider researcher. *The Journal of Applied Behavioral Science*, *59*(4), 714–739.

Meek, T., Barham, H., Beltaif, N., Kaadoor, A., & Akhter, T. (2016, September). Managing the ethical and risk implications of rapid advances in artificial intelligence: A literature review. *2016 Portland International Conference on Management of Engineering and Technology (PICMET)*.

Memon, M. S., Kumar, P., & Mirani, A. A. (2020). Deep Learning and IoT: The Enabling Technologies towards Smart Farming. *Industrial Internet of Things and Cyber-Physical Systems*, *5*, 47–60.

Meyer, K., Page, L. C., Mata, C., Smith, E. N., Walsh, B. T., Fifield, C. L., & Jung, E. E. (2024). *Let's Chat: Leveraging Chatbot Outreach for Improved Course Performance. EdWorkingPaper No. 22-564*. Annenberg Institute for School Reform at Brown University.

Mhlanga, D. (2020). Industry 4.0 in Finance: The Impact of Artificial Intelligence on Digital Financial Inclusion. *International Journal of Financial Studies*, *8*(3), 45. DOI: 10.3390/ijfs8030045

Michael, C. I., Ipede, O. J., Adejumo, A. D., Adenekan, I. O., Adebayo, D., Ojo, A. S., & Ayodele, P. A. (2024). Data-driven decision making in IT: Leveraging AI and data science for business intelligence. *World Journal of Advanced Research and Reviews*, *23*(1), 472–480.

Michael, O. (2025). *Maximising the Potentials of Small and Medium Scale Business Enterprises in Developing Nations thro the use of AI: AI adoption by SMEs in the Developing Nations, The Future of Small Business in Industry5.0*. DOI., DOI: 10.4018/979-8-3693-7362-0.ch009

Mishra, S. (2023). Exploring Impact of AI based cyber security financial sector Management. *The Sciences*, *13*(10), 5875. DOI: 10.3390/app13105875

Moench, E. (2023). La comunicación managerial: su racionalización y sus efectos sobre los agentes de Contact Centers. Questión.

Mohapatra, H. (2021). Socio-technical challenges in the implementation of smart city. *2021 International Conference on Innovation and Intelligence for Informatics, Computing, and Technologies (3ICT)*, 57-62. https://doi.org/DOI: 10.1109/3ict53449.2021.9581905

Mohapatra, H. (2024). The role of 6G in empowering smart cities enabling ubiquitous connectivity and intelligent infrastructure. *Advances in Civil and Industrial Engineering*, ●●●, 237–264. DOI: 10.4018/979-8-3693-8029-1.ch009

Montgomery, J., Burge, S., Roumell, E., & Dempsey, S. (2023). Body poetic: uncovering an educational panopticon. Education Inquiry, 1-19.

Mubeen, M., Arslan, M., & Anandhi, G. (2022). Strategies to Avoid Illegal Data Access. *Journal of Communication Engineering & Systems*, *12*(3), 29–40p.

Muhammed, D., Ahvar, E., Ahvar, S., Trocan, M., Montpetit, M., & Ehsani, R. (2024). Artificial intelligence of things (AIoT) for smart agriculture: A review of architectures, technologies and solutions. *Journal of Network and Computer Applications*, *228*, 103905. DOI: 10.1016/j.jnca.2024.103905

Munz, P., Hennick, M., & Stewart, J. (2023). Maximizing AI reliability through anticipatory thinking and model risk audits. *AI Magazine*, *44*(2), 173–184.

Murrietta, C. (2025). The Teachers Are Not Okay: The Complex Emotionality of the Teaching Profession (Doctoral dissertation, University of California, San Diego).

NAEA. (2024). NAEA Position Statement on Use of Artificial Intelligence (AI) and AI-generated Imagery in Visual Arts Education. Retrieved June 18, 2025, from https://www.arteducators.org/advocacy-policy/articles/1303-naea-position-statement-on-use-of-artificial-intelligence-ai-and-ai-generated-imagery-in-visual-arts-education

Nake, F. (2018). The Pioneer of Generative Art: Georg Nees. *Leonardo*, *51*(3), 277–279. DOI: 10.1162/leon_a_01325

Narne, S., Adedoja, T., Mohan, M., & Ayyalasomayajula, T. (2024). AI-Driven Decision Support Systems in Management: Enhancing Strategic Planning and Execution. *International Journal on Recent and Innovation Trends in Computing and Communication*, *12*(1), 268–276.

Nasscom.in

Năstasă, A., Dumitra, T.-C., & Grigorescu, A. (2024). Artificial intelligence and sustainable development during the pandemic: An overview of the scientific debates. *Heliyon*, *10*(9), e30412. DOI: 10.1016/j.heliyon.2024.e30412

Nayak, M. (2024). AI-Enhanced Digital Forensics: Automated Techniques for Efficient Investigation and Evidence Collection. J. *Electrical Systems*, *20*(1s), 211–229.

Neale, B. (2021). Fluid enquiry, complex causality, policy processes: Making a difference with qualitative longitudinal research. *Social Policy and Society*, *20*(4), 653–669.

Nees, G. (1965) *Generative Computergraphik | Database of Digital Art. (n.d.).* Retrieved June 16, 2025, from http://dada.compart-bremen.de/item/Publication/3

Neiroukh, S., Aljuhmani, H. Y., & Alnajdawi, S. (2024, January). In the era of emerging technologies: discovering the impact of artificial intelligence capabilities on timely decision-making and business performance. In *2024 ASU International Conference in Emerging Technologies for Sustainability and Intelligent Systems (ICETSIS)* (pp. 1-6). IEEE.

Neiroukh, S., Emeagwali, O. L., & Aljuhmani, H. Y. (2024). Artificial intelligence capability and organizational performance: Unraveling the mediating mechanisms of decision-making processes. *Management Decision*.

Nguyen, T. V., & Vo, N. (Eds.). (2024). *Using traditional design methods to enhance AI-driven decision making*. IGI Global.

Ngwenyama, O., & Rowe, F. (2024). Should we collaborate with AI to conduct literature reviews? Changing epistemic values in a flattening world. *Journal of the Association for Information Systems*, *25*(1), 122–136.

Nobony, R., Khan, M. S. A., Sakib, S. H., Hossain, M. A., Ahsan, S. T., Hasanuzzaman, M., . . . Taj, M. N. A. (2024, May). Analysis of education 4.0: An in-depth investigation & modelling for POST-COVID19 smart city planning. In AIP Conference Proceedings (Vol. 2915, No. 1, p. 020011). AIP Publishing LLC.

Nugraha, T. (2024, April 26). Sustainable AI development in developing countries on data policy. Modern Diplomacy. https://moderndiplomacy.eu/2024/04/26/sustainable-ai-development-in-developing-countries-on-data-policy/

Nurhadhinah, N. R., Masqirol, M., Fitriyani Latif, M. A. N., & Syafruddin, M. (2024). AI in the Financial Sector: The line Between Innovation, Regulation and Ethical Responsibility. *Information (Basel)*, *15*(8), 432. DOI: 10.3390/info.15080432

Office of the High Commissioner for Human Rights. (2024, June). *Artificial intelligence: A game-changer for sustainable development*. United Nations Human Rights. https://www.ohchr.org/en/stories/2024/06/artificial-intelligence-game-changer-sustainable-development

Ogwueleka, F. N. (2025). Plagiarism Detection in the Age of Artificial Intelligence: Current Technologies and Future Directions. AI and Ethics, Academic Integrity and the Future of Quality Assurance in Higher Education, 10.

Omodan, B. I., & Marongwe, N. (2024). The role of artificial intelligence in de-colonising academic writing for inclusive knowledge production. *Interdisciplinary Journal of Education Research*, *6*(s1), 1–14.

Omoge, A. P., Gala, P., & Horky, A. (2022). Disruptive Technology and AI in the banking Industry of an Emerging Markets. *International Journal of Bank Marketing*, *40*(6), 1217–1247. DOI: 10.1108/ ijbm-09-2021-0403

Pantone. (2023). https://www.pantone.com/. Pantone. Retrieved June 16, 2025, from https://www.pantone.com/

Parihar, V., Malik, A., Bhawna, Bhushan, B., & Chaganti, R. (2023). From smart devices to smarter systems: The evolution of artificial intelligence of things (AIoT) with characteristics, architecture, use cases and challenges. *Engineering Cyber-Physical Systems and Critical Infrastructures*, 1-28. https://doi.org/DOI: 10.1007/978-3-031-31952-5_1

Patry, W. (2000). *Patry: England and the Statute of Anne. (n.d.).* Retrieved June 16, 2025, from https://digital-law-online.info/patry/patry2.html

Pikas, E., Pedó, B., Tezel, A., Koskela, L., & Veersoo, M. (2022). Digital Last Planner System whiteboard for enabling remote collaborative design process planning and control. *Sustainability*, *14*(19), 12030.

Pishgar, M., Issa, S. F., Sietsema, M., Pratap, P., & Darabi, H. (2021). REDECA: A novel framework to review artificial intelligence and its applications in occupational safety and health. *International Journal of Environmental Research and Public Health*, *18*(13), 6705.

Prabha, C., Singh, J., & Rasool, R. (2022). Applications-oriented smart cities based on AIoT emerging technologies. *AIoT Technologies and Applications for Smart Environments*, 37-56. https://doi.org/DOI: 10.1049/pbpc057e_ch3

Preston, J. (2022). *Artificial intelligence in the capitalist university: Academic labour, commodification, and value.* Taylor & Francis.

Puplampu, R. (2024). *What Everyone Should Know About the Rise of AI: AI Transparency, Privacy, and Ethics Best Practices.* Puplampu Books.

Rafael, B. V., Belen, S. C., Lucia, V. R., & Jose, R. S. S. (2024). The Impact of Artificial Intelligence in the Financial Sector- Challenges and Opportunities. *International Journal of Business and Management Studies*, 5(10), 33–42. DOI: 10.56734/ijbms.v.5n10a4

Ramesh, S. (2021). Leveraging the Internet of Things in commerce: A transformational frontier. *International Journal of Information Technology and Computer*, 12, 26–30.

Raouhi, E. M., Lachgar, M., Hrimech, H., & Kartit, A. (2023). Unmanned Aerial Vehicle-based Applications in Smart Farming: A Systematic Review. *International Journal of Advanced Computer Science and Applications*, 14, 45–70.

Rashid, A. B., & Kausik, A. A. K. (2024). AI Revolutionary Industries World Wide: A Comprehensive Overview of its Diverse Applications. *Hybrid Advance, Vol*, (7). Advance online publication. DOI: 10.1016/hvadv.2024.100277

Rettig, P. R. (Ed.). (2021). *Enrollment management: Successful approaches with dwindling numbers*. Rowman & Littlefield.

Revathy, S., Sreekala, S. P., Praveenadevi, D., & Rajeshwari, S. (2024). The intelligent implications of artificial intelligence-driven decision-making in business management. In *Toward Artificial General Intelligence: Deep Learning, Neural Networks, Generative AI* (pp. 251-268). De Gruyter.

Rezaei, M., Pironti, M., & Quaglia, R. (2024). AI in knowledge sharing, which ethical challenges are raised in decision-making processes for organisations? *Management Decision*.

Richards, N. (2022). *Why privacy matters*. Oxford University Press.

Ridzuan, N. N., Masri, M., Anshari, M., Fitryani, N. L., & Syafrudin, M. (2024). AI in the financial sector the line between innovation, Regulation and Ethical Responsibility. *Information (Basel)*, 15(8), 432. DOI: 10.3390/infor15080432

Rienties, B., Domingue, J., Duttaroy, S., Herodotou, C., Tessarolo, F., & Whitelock, D. (2024). I would love this to be like an assistant, not the teacher: a voice of the customer perspective of what distance learning students want from an Artificial Intelligence Digital Assistant. arXiv preprint arXiv:2403.15396.

Rigney, L. I. (Ed.). (2023). *Global perspectives and new challenges in culturally responsive pedagogies: Super-diversity and teaching practice*. Taylor & Francis.

Roldán Martinez, D. (2023). SymbIAG: A collaborative approach to AI governance. In 4th International Conference on AI ML, Data Science and Robotics. United Research Forum.

Romano, R. (2024). Ethical Issues on Artificial Intelligence and Human Relationships. In *INTED2024 Proceedings* (pp. 6902-6909). IATED.

Ronak, B. (2024). AI-Driven Project Management Revolutionizing Workflow Optimization and Decision-Making. *International Journal of Trend in Scientific Research and Development*, *8*(6), 325–338.

Rosenbarm, E. (2024), AI is Getting Very Popular Among students and Teachers Very Quickly, CNBC.com. https://cnbc.com/2024/06/11. Accessed online on 16/05/2025.

Sabah, A. S., Hamouda, A. A., Helles, Y. E., Okasha, S. M., Abu-Nasser, B. S., & Abu-Naser, S. S. (2024). Artificial Intelligence and Organizational Evolution: Reshaping Workflows in the Modern Era.

Sahlberg, P. (2023). Trends in global education reform since the 1990 s: Looking for the right way. *International Journal of Educational Development*, *98*, 102748.

Sahoo, D. K., Hung, T. H., Kumar, A., & Kanwal, P. (2024). Ethical AI in entrepreneurship. In *Advances in Business Strategy and Competitive Advantage* (pp. 137–164). IGI Global.

Saklamaeva, V., & Pavlič, L. (2023). The potential of AI-driven assistants in scaled agile software development. *Applied Sciences (Basel, Switzerland)*, *14*(1), 319.

Salama, A. K., & Abdellatif, M. M. (2022). Aiot-based smart home energy management system. *2022 IEEE Global Conference on Artificial Intelligence and Internet of Things (GCAIoT)*, 177-181. https://doi.org/DOI: 10.1109/gcaiot57150.2022.10019091

Sallam, K., Mohamed, M., & Wagdy Mohamed, A. (2023). Internet of Things (IoT) in supply chain management: Challenges, opportunities, and best practices. Sustain. Mach. Intell. J., 2.

Samara, F. Y. A., Taha, A. H. A., Massa, N. M., Jamie, T. N. A., Harara, F. E., Abu-Nasser, B. S., & Abu-Naser, S. S. (2024). The Role of AI in Enhancing Business Decision-Making: Innovations and Implications.

Schwarke, J., Peters, A., Kanbach, D. K., Kraus, S., & Jones, P. (2025). The New Normal: The Status Quo of AI Adoption in SMEs. *Journal of Small Business Management*, *63*, 1297–1331.

Seidel, N., Haake, J. M., & Burchart, M. (2021). From Diversity to adaptive Personalization: The Next Generation Learning Management System as Adaptive Learning Environment. eleed-e-learning and education.

Seyi-Lande, O., & Onaolapo, C. (2024). Elevating business analysis with AI: Strategies for analysts. *International Journal of Management Research and Economics*, *4*(2), 1–7.

Shafik, W. (2025). Emerging Technologies for Small and Medium Enterprise Growth: ChatGPT, Blockchain, Robotics and Artificial Intelligence. *Source Title: Fostering Economic Diversification and Sustainable Business through Digital Intelligence*, pages 24. DOI: DOI: 10.4018/979-8-3693-8492-3-ch009

Shah, R. U., Verma, J. P., Jain, R., & Garg, S. (2022). AIoT technologies and applications for smart environments. *AIoT Technologies and Applications for Smart Environments*, 199-214. https://doi.org/DOI: 10.1049/pbpc057e_ch11

Shahi, T. B., Xu, C.-Y., Neupane, A., & Guo, W. (2023). Recent Advances in Crop Disease Detection Using UAV and Deep Learning Techniques. *Remote Sensing*, *15*, 2450–2469.

Shah, M. M., & Kavathiya, H. R. (2024). Unveiling the Future: Exploring Conversational AI. In *Artificial Intelligence in Education: The Power and Dangers of ChatGPT in the Classroom* (pp. 511–526). Springer Nature Switzerland.

Shamim, M. M. I. (2024). Artificial Intelligence in project management: Enhancing efficiency and decision-making. *International Journal of Management Information Systems and Data Science*, *1*(1), 1–6.

Shepard. (2025, April 15). Fine art and design using artificial intelligence | Penn Today. https://penntoday.upenn.edu/news/student-art-design-using-artificial-intelligence

Shoaib, M., Sayed, N., Singh, J., Shafi, J., Khan, S., & Ali, F. (2024). AI student success predictor: Enhancing personalized learning in campus management systems. *Computers in Human Behavior*, *158*, 108301.

Sims, A. (2024). From Creation to Curriculum: Examining the role of generative AI in Arts Universities. Retrieved June 16, 2025, from https://arxiv.org/html/2412.16531v1

Sindhu, J., & Renee, N. (2019). Impact of Artificial Intelligence in Chosen Indian Commercial Bank- A Cost Benefit Analysis. *Asian Journal of Management*, *10*(4), 377–384. DOI: 10.5958/2321-57-63.2019.00057

Singh, A. (2025, February 26). The AI regulatory landscape in India: What to know. AZO Robotics. https://www.azorobotics.com/Article.aspx?ArticleID=742

Singh, A. (2024). The future of learning: AI-driven personalized education. Available at *SSRN* 5076438.

Sodiya, E. O., Umoga, U. J., Amoo, O. O., & Atadoga, A. (2024). AI-driven warehouse automation: A comprehensive review of systems. *GSC Adv. Res. Rev.*, *18*(2), 272–282.

Sohns, T. M., Aysolmaz, B., & Figge, L. (2023). Green business process management for business sustainability: A case study of manufacturing SMEs from Germany. *Journal of Cleaner Production*, *401*, 136667. DOI: 10.1016/j.jclepro.2023.136667

Song, R., Cui, W., Vanthienen, J., Huang, L., & Wang, Y. (2022). Business process redesign towards IoT-enabled context-awareness: The case of a Chinese bulk port. *Business Process Management Journal*, *28*(3), 656–683.

Soori, M., Jough, F. K. G., Dastres, R., & Arezoo, B. (2024). AI-based decision support systems in Industry 4.0, A review. *Journal of Economy and Technology*.

Sowa, K., & Przegalinska, A. (2020). Digital coworker: Human-AI collaboration in work environment, on the example of virtual assistants for management professions. In *Digital Transformation of Collaboration* (pp. 179–201). Springer International Publishing.

Steingard, D., & Linacre, S. (2023). Transforming academic journal assessment from "quality" to "impact": A case study of the SDG Impact Intensity academic journal rating artificial intelligence system. In *The future of responsible management education: University leadership and the digital transformation challenge* (pp. 317–356). Springer International Publishing.

Strusani, D., & Houngbonon, G. V. (2019). The Role of Artificial Intelligence in Supporting Developments in Emerging Markets, Note69, www.ifc.org

Stryker, C., & Kavlakoglu, E. (2025). What is Artificial Intelligence (AI)? https://ibm.com/think/topics/ artificial- intelligence.

Sumihiro, G. (2025, June 10). Commentary: Precision agriculture is an investment in food security. *My Journal Courier.* Retrieved from https://www.myjournalcourier.com/opinion/article/precision-agriculture-investment-food-security-20260610.php

Sunday, C. E., & Vera, C. C.-E. (2018). Examining information and communication technology (ICT) adoption in SMEs. *Journal of Enterprise Information Management*, *31*(2), 338–356.

Swain, B., Raj, P., Singh, K., Singh, Y., Singh, S., & Mohapatra, H. (2025). Ethical implications and mitigation strategies for public safety and security in smart cities for securing tomorrow. *Advances in Information Security, Privacy, and Ethics*, •••, 419–436. DOI: 10.4018/979-8-3693-6859-6.ch019

SWARGIARY, K. (2025). Reimagining Education: A Personal Journey Toward a Future-Ready Curriculum. GOOGLE.

SWARGIARY. K. (2024). Integrating IoT in Education:(Transforming Learning Through Smart Technologies). EdTech Research Association, US.

Tabassi, E. (2023). *Artificial intelligence risk management Framework (AI RMF 1.0)*. National Institute of Standards and Technology.

Tahereh, S. and Sidaoui. (2024). Convergence of AI with social media: A Bibliometric and qualitative Analysis. *Telematics and Informatics Reports*, *14*. Advance online publication. DOI: 10.1016/jteler.2024.100146

Taneja, K., Maiti, P., Kakar, S., Guruprasad, P., Rao, S., & Goel, A. K. (2024, July). Jill watson: A virtual teaching assistant powered by chatgpt. In International Conference on Artificial Intelligence in Education (pp. 324-337). Cham: Springer Nature Switzerland.

Tariq, M. U. (2025). AI-Driven Innovations: Transforming Healthcare, Agriculture, and Environmental Science. In Emara, T., Hassan, E., Trinh, T., Li, G., & Saber, A. (Eds.), *The Role of Artificial Intelligence in Advancing Applied Life Sciences* (pp. 87–118). IGI Global Scientific Publishing., DOI: 10.4018/979-8-3693-9208-9.ch003

Tariq, M. U. (2025). Co-Living With Augmented Digital Beings-Navigating the Intersection of AI and Everyday Life. In Moutinho, L., & Martins, L. (Eds.), *Impacts of Sensetech on Society* (pp. 187–206). IGI Global Scientific Publishing., DOI: 10.4018/979-8-3693-7147-3.ch009

Tariq, M. U. (2025). Innovative Mentoring Programs: Strategies for Success in Post-COVID-19 Education. In Putnam, J., VanValkenburgh Banks, J., & Brown, S. K. (Eds.), *Mentoring Students and Instructors for Retention and Success* (pp. 123–158). IGI Global Scientific Publishing., DOI: 10.4018/979-8-3693-7590-7.ch005

Tariq, M. U. (2025). Leveraging Data Analytics for Predictive Consumer Behavior Modelling. In Miguélez-Juan, B., & Rebollo-Bueno, S. (Eds.), *AI Impacts on Branded Entertainment and Advertising* (pp. 207–224). IGI Global Scientific Publishing., DOI: 10.4018/979-8-3693-3799-8.ch011

Taylor, S., & Charlebois, S. (2024, March). Teaching dossier guidance for professional faculty: An evidence-based approach for demonstrating teaching effectiveness. []. Frontiers Media SA.]. *Frontiers in Education*, *9*, 1284726.

Teixeira da Silva, J. A., & Nazarovets, S. (2023). Can the principle of the 'right to be forgotten'be applied to academic publishing? Probe from the perspective of personal rights, archival science, open science and post-publication peer review. *Learned Publishing*, *36*(4), 651–666.

Thakur, R., Panse, P., Bhanarkar, P., & Borkar, P. (2023). AIoT: Role of AI in IoT, applications and future trends. *Research Trends in Artificial Intelligence: Internet of Things*, 42-53. https://doi.org/DOI: 10.2174/9789815136449123010006

Tortorella, G. L., Narayanamurthy, G., Sunder, M. V., & Cauchick-Miguel, P. A. (2021). Operations Management teaching practices and information technologies adoption in emerging economies during COVID-19 outbreak. *Technological Forecasting and Social Change*, *171*(120996), 120996.

UNDP. (2022). *Artificial intelligence for sustainable development: Mapping AI's potential to achieve the SDGs.* United Nations Development Programme.

UNESCO. (2021). *Recommendation on the ethics of artificial intelligence.* UNESCO Publishing. https://unesdoc.unesco.org/ark:/48223/pf0000381137

Ursyn, A. (Ed.). (2018). *Interface support for creativity, productivity, and expression in computer graphics.* IGI Global. ISBN: 9781522573715 9781522573722

Vacarelu, F.-A. (2024, May 29). Ensuring positive, people-focused futures through AI. United Nations Development Programme (UNDP). https://www.undp.org/blog/ensuring-positive-people-focused-futures-through-ai

Vartanian, O., Navarrete, G., Chatterjee, A., Fich, L. B., Leder, H., Modroño, C., Nadal, M., Rostrup, N., & Skov, M. (2013). Impact of contour on aesthetic judgments and approach-avoidance decisions in architecture. *Proceedings of the National Academy of Sciences of the United States of America*, *110*(supplement_2), 10446–10453. DOI: 10.1073/pnas.1301227110

Veltman, C. (2025). In first-of-its-kind lawsuit, Hollywood giants sue AI firm for copyright infringement. NPR. Retrieved from https://media.npr.org/assets/artslife/movies/misc/midjourney.pdf

Vidolov, S. P. (2024). Virtual collaboration as co-enacting intercorporeality. *European Journal of Information Systems*, *33*(2), 244–266.

Vinoth, S., & Chandran, P. (2022). Artificial Intelligence and Transformation to the Digital Age in Indian Banking Industry- A Case Study. *Turkish Online Journal of Qualitative Inquiry*, *13*(1), 689–695.

Vinuesa, R., Azizpour, H., & Leite, I.. (2020). The role of artificial intelligence in achieving the Sustainable Development Goals. *Nature Communications*, *11*, 233. DOI: 10.1038/s41467-019-14108-y

Visuthiphol, S., & Pankham, S. (2025). Artificial Intelligence- Decision Making in Social Media Adoption for Sustainable Digital Business in Thai SMEs. *Decision Making: Applications in Management and Engineering*, *8*(1). Advance online publication. 0009-0006-1431-4643

Von Eschenbach, W. J. (2021). Transparency and the black box problem: Why we do not trust AI. *Philosophy & Technology*, *34*(4), 1607–1622.

Vrana, R. (2025). Perceptions and use of AI supported tools in higher education libraries in Croatia: An exploratory study. *New Review of Academic Librarianship*, ●●●, 1–26.

Wang, H., Fu, T., Du, Y., Gao, W., Huang, K., Liu, Z., & Zitnik, M. (2023). Scientific discovery in the age of artificial intelligence. *Nature*, *620*(7972), 47–60.

Wang, Q., Li, Y., & Li, R. (2024). Ecological footprints, carbon emissions, and energy transitions: The impact of artificial intelligence (AI). *Humanities & Social Sciences Communications*, *11*, 1043. Advance online publication. DOI: 10.1057/s41599-024-03520-5

Wang, Y. (2023). Synergy in silicon: the evolution and potential of academia-industry collaboration in AI and software engineering. *Authorea Preprints*.

Wang, Y., Zhang, B., Ma, J., & Jin, Q. (2023). Artificial intelligence of things (AIoT) data acquisition based on graph neural networks: A systematical review. *Concurrency and Computation*, *35*(23). Advance online publication. DOI: 10.1002/cpe.7827

Webb, M. E., Fluck, A., Magenheim, J., Malyn-Smith, J., Waters, J., Deschênes, M., & Zagami, J. (2021). Machine learning for human learners: Opportunities, issues, tensions and threats. *Educational Technology Research and Development*, *69*(4), 2109–2130.

Weinzierl, S., Zilker, S., Dunzer, S., & Matzner, M. (2024). Machine learning in business process management: A systematic literature review. arXiv preprint arXiv:2405.16396.

Weisstein, E. W. (2023). T*esseract Graph* [Text]. Retrieved June 16, 2025, from https://mathworld.wolfram.com/TesseractGraph.html

Werder, C., & Otis, M. M. (Eds.). (2023). *Engaging student voices in the study of teaching and learning*. Taylor & Francis.

White, E., & Davis, M. (2023). Exploring subjectivity: A critique of reflexivity in qualitative research. *Qualitative Research Review Letter*, *1*(02), 96–103.

Wibawa, A. P., & Kurniawan, F. (2024). A survey of text summarization: Techniques, evaluation and challenges. *Natural Language Processing Journal*, *7*, 100070.

Willard, J. D., Varadharajan, C., Jia, X., & Kumar, V. (2023). Time series predictions in unmonitored sites: A survey of machine learning techniques in water resources. arXiv preprint arXiv:2308.09766.

Wisnioski, M. (2025). *Every American an Innovator: How Innovation Became a Way of Life*. The MIT Press.

world bank. (2024). Global trends in AI governance.

Worsley, J. D., Harrison, P., & Corcoran, R. (2021). Bridging the gap: Exploring the unique transition from home, school or college into university. *Frontiers in Public Health*, *9*, 634285.

Xu, M., David, J. M., & Kim, S. H. (2018). The Fourth Industrial Revolution: Opportunities and Challenges. *International Journal of Financial Research*, *9*(2), 90. DOI: 10.5430/ijfr.v9n2p90

Xu, Q., Shi, Y., Bamber, J., Tuo, Y., Ludwig, R., & Zhu, X. (2023). Physics-aware machine learning revolutionizes scientific paradigm for machine learning and process-based hydrology. *PLOS Water*, *1*(4), e0000059. https://journals.plos.org/water/article?id=10.1371/journal.pwat.0000059

Yamamoto, S., Nomoto, S., Hashimoto, N., Maki, M., Hongo, C., & Shiraiwa, T. (2023). Monitoring spatial and time-series variations in red crown rot damage of soybean in farmer fields based on UAV remote sensing. *Plant Production Science*, *26*, 36–47.

Yambal, S., & Waykar, Y. A. (2025). Future of Education Using Adaptive AI, Intelligent Systems, and Ethical Challenges. In Effective Instructional Design Informed by AI (pp. 171-202). IGI Global Scientific Publishing.

Yang, A., & Li, B. (2025, March 31). AI Watch: Global regulatory tracker – China. White & Case. https://www.whitecase.com/insight-our-thinking/ai-watch-global-regulatory-tracker-china

Yan, J. (2024). AIoT in smart homes: Challenges, strategic solutions, and future directions. *Highlights in Science. Engineering and Technology*, *87*, 59–65. DOI: 10.54097/8hzgaf51

Yenuri, A. (2023). AI-Powered Language Learning: A New Frontier in Personalized Education. *Journal of Language Instruction and Applied Linguistics, 1*(01), 109–116.

Yildirim, Y., Arslan, E. A., Yildirim, K., & Bisen, I. (2021). Reimagining education with artificial intelligence. *Eurasian Journal of Higher Education,* (4), 32–46.

Yi, Z., & Ayangbah, S. (2024). The impact of ai innovation management on organizational productivity and economic growth: An analytical study. *International Journal of Business Management and Economic Research, 7*(1), 1–15.

Yoganandham, G. (2025). Trends, challenges and opportunities in India's financial sector: Policy shifts, AI Integrational Financial Stability- AN Empirical Assessment. *GIS Science Journal, 12*(2), 360–376.

Yu, J. H. (2023). Learning experience design as collective praxis: Two design cases from higher education. *The Journal of Applied Instructional Design, 12*(3), 59–83.

Yusuf, S.O., Durodula, R.L.Orcan, G.Abubakar, J.E., Echere, A.Z. and Paul, A.H. (2024) . Challenges and Opportunities in AI and Digital Transformation for SMEs- A cross-continental Perspective, *World journal of Advanced Research and Review, Vol 23(05),* pp668-678. DOI: .DOI: 10.20574/wjarr.2024.23.3.2511

Zaho, B. (2024, March 28). *Replacement of human artists by AI systems in creative industries.* UN Trade and Development (UNCTAD). https://unctad.org/news/replacement-human-artists-ai-systems-creative-industries

Zehnder, C., Metzker, J., Kleine, K., & Alby, C. (2021). Learning that matters: A field guide to course design for transformative education.

Zewe, A. (2025, January 17). *Explained: Generative AI's environmental impact.* MIT News | Massachusetts Institute of Technology. https://news.mit.edu/2025/explained-generative-ai-environmental-impact-0117

Zhang, J., & Tao, D. (2021). Empowering things with intelligence: A survey of the progress, challenges, and opportunities in artificial intelligence of things. *IEEE Internet of Things Journal, 8*(10), 7789–7817. DOI: 10.1109/jiot.2020.3039359

Zhang, T., Xu, Z., Su, J., Yang, Z., Liu, C., Chen, W.-H., & Li, J. (2021). Ir-UNet: Irregular Segmentation U-Shape Network for Wheat Yellow Rust Detection by UAV Multispectral Imagery. *Remote Sensing, 13,* 3892.

Zhao, Wei, & Wang, Meini, & Pham, V. (2023). Unmanned Aerial Vehicle and Geospatial Analysis in Smart Irrigation and Crop Monitoring on IoT Platform. *Mobile Information Systems, 10,* 1–12.

Zhihong Zhang, Shuo Yuan, Qinghui Lai, Ronghao Zeng, Jingkun Zhang and Siyu Shen. (2023). Precision Variable-rate Control System for Mini UAV-based Pesticide Application. J. Phys.: Conf. Ser. 2557, 012-025.

Zia, S. (2025). Digital Colonialism: Reimagining Power, Identity, and Resistance by Decolonizing AI. Yayasan Drestanta Pelita Indonesia, 129-147.

Zou, B., Liviero, S., Wei, K., Sun, L., Qi, Y., Yang, X., & Fu, J. (2021). Case study 11, Mainland China: The impact of pronunciation and accents in artificial intelligence speech evaluation systems. Language Learning with Technology: Perspectives from Asia, 223-235.

About the Contributors

Jingyuan Zhao obtained her PhD in Management Science and Engineering from University of Science and Technology of China. She completed postdoctoral programs respectively in Technological Economics with Harbin Institute of Technology, in Management of Technology with Université du Québec à Montréal, in Innovation and Governance with University of Toronto, in Mathematical and Computational Science with University of Toronto Mississauga. Dr. Zhao's research expertise includes management of technology innovation, behaviour and information technology, high-tech industries, multinational governance, and science and technology policy. Dr. Zhao also has extensive industry experience and provides consulting services to major corporations such as China Mobile. She serves as editor-in-chief of International Journal of e-Collaboration(IJeC).

***

Swapna B researches Internet of Things, Artificial Intelligence, etc.

Godiselapalli Chaitanya Gowd, graduated from Dr. MGR University in Chennai with a degree in Electronics and Communication Engineering. With the help of practical experience from academic projects and industry-focused training, they have a strong love for embedded systems, IoT applications, and hardware design. Gowd worked on significant projects during their studies, like creating a UAV-based system for plant disease identification and pesticide advice and a CubeSat for IoT-based campus surveillance. Additionally, Gowd has finished technical training at prestigious institutions like IIT Madras, CVRDE (DRDO), NSIC, and TVS, where they learned useful skills in embedded system design, Arduino, Raspberry Pi, and PIC microcontrollers. Gowd has a solid background in circuit simulation and system integration, and I am skilled in Python, C programming, PCB design, and AutoCAD. Gowd brings leadership skills, problem-solving abilities, and a collaborative mindset that helps them adapt and thrive in both team and independent roles. Gowd has been honored with recognitions such as the Best NCC Cadet and the Mahatma Jyothi Phule District Merit Award. As a dedicated and motivated engineer, they are eager to contribute to innovative technology solutions and make a meaningful impact in the field of embedded systems and IoT.

Jean Constant is a Researcher and lecturer on Science and Art. Past Professor of Visual Communication, he developed multiple Mathematics and Art collaborative projects that he used in the classroom and share today with a larger audience in print, exhibits, conferences, and public forums. His interest in Knowledge Visualization leads him to incorporate elements of mathematics, applied sciences as well as optics, neuroscience, and psychology in his work. He's been the recipient of several awards for his visualizations in the field of Mathematics and Art. Regular participant in the annual AMS-MAA, JMM meetings and Bridges Math-Art conference cycle. Notable publications: The Math-Art series, Stochastic Art, Geometry of Nature.

Abhishek Guru received a Ph.D. (CSE) degree in 2021 from Kalinga University, Naya Raipur. He received his MSc. (CS) degree in 2012 from Makhanlal Chaturvedi Rashtriya Patrakarita Vishwavidyalaya, Bhopal, India. He has 3 Months of experience in IT industry as a Software Engineer and 9+ years of experience in educational institutes as an Assistant Professor. Currently associated with KL Deemed To Be University, Green Fields, Vaddeswaram, India as Assistant Professor in Computer Science & Engineering Department. He has published and granted Indian/Australian patents, some are waiting for grants. He has authored and co-authored of more than 10 journal articles including WOS & Scopus papers Presented research papers in 2 international conferences. He has contributed in book chapters, published by Elsevier, and Springer. He has contributed in book chapters, published by Elsevier, and Springer. He has lifetime Membership of IAENG, ASR, IFERP, ICSES, Internet Society, UACEE, IAOIP, EAI, CSTA. He has successfully completed many FDP, Training, webinar & workshops. and also Completed the 2-Weeks comprehensive online Patent Information Course. Proficiency in handling Teaching, Research as well as administrative activities. He has contributed massive literature in the fields of Network Security, Cyber Security, Cryptography, and IoT.

Masruk Habib is a highly motivated Computer Engineering student at Marwadi University, Rajkot, with a passion for AI, Machine Learning, and Data-driven innovation. With strong proficiency in Python and experience in research, he has co-authored multiple papers in healthcare AI and predictive analytics. He has led impactful projects such as MediGuard AI and ASD prediction systems, combining advanced ML techniques with real-time web applications. A winner of the Gujarat

304

state-level hackathon, Masruk is also certified in AWS, Tableau, SQL, and API development and actively contributes to open source through GitHub and interactive data visualizations.

Mustafa Kayyali is an ardent advocate for excellence in higher education, driven by a relentless pursuit of quality, recognition, and innovation. His journey in academia started with a Master's in Quality Management and Evaluation in Higher Education from Universitat Oberta de Catalunya, followed by a Ph.D. in Quality Management from Azteca University. These academic pursuits have laid a strong foundation for his expertise in Accreditation, Quality Assurance, and Higher Education Rankings. As an entrepreneur, researcher, translator, and publisher, he is deeply involved in various facets of the academic world. His diverse interests encompass Management, Translation, Interpretation, and Academic consulting, contributing to a well-rounded understanding of the industry. Throughout his career, he has made significant contributions to academic literature, with more than 40 published papers and 30 book chapters to his name. Additionally, he takes pride in having translated 6 books, bridging language gaps, and promoting knowledge exchange on a global scale. He is committed to fostering positive change in higher education and contributing to its continuous improvement.

Satish Kumar has extensive teaching and litigation experience in the field of tax laws and intellectual property rights. Kumar has published several papers on AI and interdisciplinary studies. Kumar is also a Ph.D. scholar and in the advanced stage of finishing his Ph.D. His specialization lies in Interdisciplinary study between AI and Copyright Laws.

Hitesh Mohapatra is an Associate Professor at the School of Computer Engineering, KIIT Deemed to be University, in Odisha, India. He holds a Ph.D. in Computer Science & Engineering from Veer Surendra Sai University of Technology, with a focus on designing fault-tolerant models for wireless sensor networks integrated with smart city applications. His academic journey includes a Bachelor's degree in Information Technology from B.P.U.T and a Master's degree in Computer Science & Engineering from Odisha University of Technology and Research. Dr. Mohapatra has over 15 years of experience in both academia and industry, contributing significantly to research in areas such as IoT, wireless sensor networks, fault tolerance, and smart city applications. His research has been published in various high-impact journals and conferences, with citations noted in the thousands. He has authored and co-authored over 50 research articles indexed by SCI and Scopus databases, along with several books on topics including software engineering, IoT in smart cities, and programming. He has also contributed to the academic community by serving in roles such as session chair, t

Jamshid Pardaev is an associate professor working in the Department of Finance and Tourism at Termez University of Economics and Service, Termez, Uzbekistan.

Ashwini Kumar Pradhan is currently working as an assistant professor in the School of Computing Science and Engineering. He has a total experience of more than 9 years of teaching. He has been associated with Galgotias University since 2023. He completed his B. Tech (CSE) from (SOA University) in 2012 and M. Tech (CSE) from (CET, Bhubaneswar) (Now Odisha University of Technology and Research) in 2016, and Ph.D. (CSE) from SOA University, Bhubaneswar, INDIA in 2023. His area of research is Machine Learning, Deep learning, AI, Medical Image classification. He has published 3 SCI Q1 journal in his Ph.D journey.

Ravikumar R. Natarajan is an experienced academician with over 12+ years of teaching and research expertise across institutions in India, the UAE, and the Maldives. He currently serves as an Assistant Professor at Marwadi University, Rajkot, specializing in Machine Learning, Recommender Systems, and AI-driven applications in healthcare and security. He holds a Ph.D. in Machine Learning and Recommender Systems from Amity University, Jaipur, a Master of Engineering in CSE from VMRF University, Salem, and a Bachelor of Engineering in CSE from Anna University. He also has a MiniMBA from the Swiss eLearning Institute. Dr. Ravikumar has authored more than 8+ multiple SCIE/Scopus-indexed journal articles, 25+ IEEE/Springer conference papers, and co-authored a book on Artificial Intelligence. He has also published 9 patents and contributed 10+ book chapters in emerging domains such as Federated Learning, Blockchain, and Digital Twins for IGI Global, Wiley and Springer publisher. He actively mentors students through initiatives like the Research Activities Club (RAC) and Student Research Internship Training (SRIT), promoting innovation and research culture.

Priyadharsini Rathinavel is a Quality Engineering professional and MSc Data Analytics student at the University of Strathclyde in Glasgow. With over 10+ years of hands-on experience in Software Testing. She has led automation initiatives, defined quality strategies and supported delivery across complex enterprise projects. Her passionate about the role of AI and Automation in improving teamwork, simplifying workflows and enhancing the way humans interact with machines. Research interest includes AI-driven Quality Engineering, Natural Language Processing and intelligent Decision-making. She is passionate about advancing research that connects new technologies with practical impact and helps build the next generation of collaborative Digital Systems.

Aarthi S is a dedicated Assistant Professor in Computer Science with over six years of teaching experience. She is currently pursuing her Ph.D. at Marwadi University, Gujarat, and holds an M.Phil. and MCA from Bharathiar University, Tamil Nadu. Throughout her academic career, Aarthi has specialized in programming languages such as C++, Java, and C, and contributed to research in recommender systems and AI-related data privacy. She has published journal articles, contributed to book chapters, and actively participated in technical workshops. Known for her student mentorship and engagement in academic events, Aarthi remains committed to fostering innovation and excellence in computer science education.

Navbakhor Salaeva is working in the Department of Pedagogy and Psychology, Urgench State University, Urgench, Uzbekistan.

Anjani Singh, as a noted academician, has held positions at the Indian Institute of Management Lucknow and Amity Business School, Amity University, Uttar Pradesh, Noida. Dr. Singh has also led international assignments. He has published more than 40 research papers in reputable national and international journals. Dr Singh has published 02 books as a co-author. Dr Singh has mentored more than 25 start-ups in NCR & Delhi. He has served as Guest Editor of the International Journal of Business and Globalization and has been Associate Editor of the Amity Journal of Entrepreneurship and Leadership. He has been a distinguished speaker and Chair at various national and international conferences. Currently, Dr Singh is designated as the Faculty of Entrepreneurship Development Institute of India, Ahmedabad. He is handling various government and PSU projects as a project director, such as those of the Higher Education Department, Govt. of Uttarakhand, NTPC, RVNL, etc.

Muhammad Usman Tariq has more than 16+ year's experience in industry and academia. He has authored more than 200+ research articles, 110+ case studies, 150+ book chapters and several books other than 4 patents. He is founder and CEO of The Case HQ, a unique repository for courses, narrative and video case studies. He has been working as a consultant and trainer for industries representing six sigma, quality, health and safety, environmental systems, project management, and information security standards. His work has encompassed sectors in aviation, manufacturing, food, hospitality, education, finance, research, software and transportation. He has diverse and significant experience working with accreditation agencies of ABET, ACBSP, AACSB, WASC, CAA, EFQM and NCEAC. Additionally, Dr. Tariq has operational experience in incubators, research labs, government research projects, private sector startups, program creation and management at various industrial and academic levels. He is Certified Higher Education Teacher from Harvard University, USA, Certified Online Educator from HMBSU, Certified Six Sigma Master Black Belt and has been awarded PFHEA, SFSEDA, SMIEEE, and CMBE.

Sonal Tikku Dynamic professional with experience in Banking, Customer Service, Business Development and Team Management. The area of expertise is Risk management, international business, working capital finance and Principles and practices of banking and sustainable finance.

Akansha Yadav has extensive teaching and litigation experience in the field of Property laws and intellectual property rights. Yadav has published several papers on AI and interdisciplinary studies. Yadav is also a Ph.D. scholar and in the advanced stage of finishing his Ph.D. The specialisation of Akansha Yadav lies in Interdisciplinary study between AI and Electoral Laws.

Index

www.ingramcontent.com/pod-product-compliance
Lightning Source LLC
Chambersburg PA
CBHW080926220326
41598CB00034B/5691